```
YA V-3
940.5318 LEA
Smelser, Ronald M., 1942-
Learning about the
Holocaust : a student's gui
CLO 1066211671
```

WITHDRAWN

WORN, SOILED, OBSOLETE

Provided by

Measure B

which was approved by
the voters in
November, 1998

Learning about the Holocaust
A Student's Guide

Editorial Board

Editor in Chief
Ronald M. Smelser
University of Utah
Salt Lake City, Utah

Advisory Board
Jeff Boyd
West Essex Regional High School
North Caldwell, New Jersey

Paul Fleming
Hume-Fogg Magnet High School
Nashville, Tennessee

Saul David Fript
Latin School of Chicago
Chicago, Illinois

Carl Schulkin
Pembroke Hill School
Kansas City, Missouri

Editorial and Production Staff

Pamela Willwerth Aue
Project Editor

Lisa Clyde Nielsen
Research and Editorial Consultant

Christine Slovey, Lawrence W. Baker
Contributing Project Editors

Nancy K. Humphreys
Indexer

Deanna Raso
Photo Researcher

Evi Seoud
Assistant Manager, Composition
Purchasing and Prepress

Stacy Melson
Buyer

Randy A. Bassett
Image Database Supervisor

Robert Duncan
Senior Imaging Specialist

Kenn Zorn
Product Design Manager

Tracey Rowens
Senior Art Director

Macmillan Reference USA

Elly Dickason, *Publisher*

Jill Lectka, *Associate Publisher*

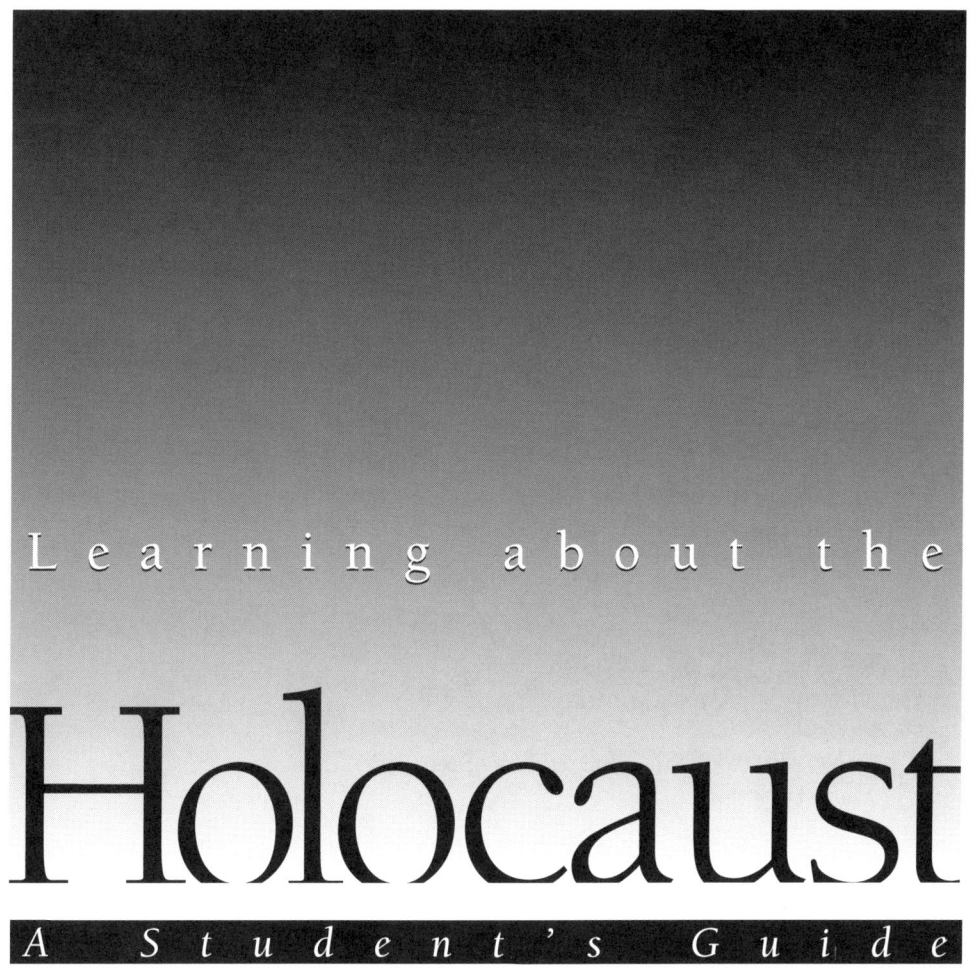

Learning about the Holocaust
A Student's Guide

RONALD M. SMELSER
Editor in Chief

volume 3
L-R

Macmillan Reference USA
an imprint of the Gale Group
New York • Detroit • San Francisco • London • Boston • Woodbridge, CT

Learning About the Holocaust

Copyright (c) 2001 by Macmillan Reference USA

All rights reserved. No part of this book may be reproduced or transmitted in any form or by any means, electronic, or mechanical, including photocopying, recording, or by any information storage and retrieval system, without permission in writing from the Publisher.

Macmillan Reference USA Gale Group
1633 Broadway 27500 Drake Road
New York, NY 10019 Farmington Hills, MI 48331

Library of Congress Catalog Card Number: 00–062517

Printed in the United States of America

Printing Number
1 2 3 4 5 6 7 8 9 10

Library of Congress Cataloging-in-Publication Data
Learning About the Holocaust: a student's guide / Ronald M. Smelser, editor in chief.
    p. cm.
   Includeds bibliographical references (p.) and index.
    ISBN: 0-02-865536-2 (set) – ISBN 0-02-865537-0 (v. 1) –
ISBN 0-02-865538-9 (v. 2) – ISBN 0-02-865539-7 (v. 3) –
ISBN 0-02-865540-0 (v. 4)
    1. Holocaust, Jewish (1939–1945)–Study and teaching (Secondary)
I. Smelser, Ronald M., 1942-

D804.33 .L4 2000
940.53'18—dc21   00-062517

Contents

VOLUME 1

List of Contributors xiii
Preface. xv
Introduction xvii
Recent Publications and Issues xxi
Timeline xxvii

A

Aid to Jews by Poles 1
Aktion (Operation) 1005 4
Aktion (Operation) Reinhard 6
Aliya Bet 9
American Friends Service Committee 13
American Jewish Organizations 14
American Jewry and the Holocaust 16
American Press and the Holocaust 20
Anielewicz, Mordecai 21
Anti-Jewish Legislation 24
Antisemitism. 27
Arrow Cross Party 34
Aryanization 35
Atlas, Yeheskel 38
Auerswald, Heinz 39
Auschwitz 40
Austria. 49

B

Babi Yar. 54
Bach-Zelewski, Erich von dem 56
Badge, Jewish 57
Barbie Trial. 61
Baum Gruppe 62
Belgium. 63
Belorussia 69
Bełżec 73
Benoît, Marie 78
Bergen-Belsen 79
Berlin 83
Best, Werner. 87

CONTENTS

Białystok 88
Biebow, Hans 92
Bielski, Tuvia 93
Blobel, Paul 94
Blum, Abraham 95
Bogaard, Johannes 96
Bohemia and Moravia, Protectorate of 97
Bormann, Martin 100
Bothmann, Hans 101
Boycott, Anti-Jewish 102
Buchenwald 104
Budapest 107
Budzyń 110

C

Central Office for Jewish Emigration 111
Central Union of German Citizens of Jewish Faith 112
Chełmno 114
Choms, Władysława 118
Christian Churches 119
Clauberg, Carl 123
Cohn, Marianne 124
Concentration Camps 124
Crimes Against Humanity 134
Croatia 137
Czerniaków, Adam 141

D

Dachau 143
Dannecker, Theodor 147
Darquier de Pellepoix, Louis 148
Death Marches 149
Deffaugt, Jean 153
Denazification 154
Denmark 157
Deportations 161
Dirlewanger, Oskar 166
Displaced Persons, Jewish 166
Dora-Mittelbau 170
Drancy 172
Dvinsk 174

E

Economic-Administrative Main Office 176
Edelstein, Jacob 177
Eichmann, Adolf 178
Eicke, Theodor 181
Elkes, Elchanan 182
Endre, László 183
Erntefest ("Harvest Festival") 184
Euthanasia Program 186
Evian Conference 189
Extermination Camps 192

Index 193

Contents

VOLUME 2

Timeline xiii

F

Fascism 1
Feiner, Leon 4
Fighting Organization of Pioneer Jewish Youth 5
"Final Solution" 7
Forced Labor 13
France 18
Frank, Anne 26
Frank, Hans 33
French Police 35
Freudiger, Fülöp 36

G

Gas Chambers/Vans 37
Generalgouvernement 39
Generalplan Ost 41
Genocide 43
Gens, Jacob 46
Germany 47
Gestapo 59
Getter, Matylda 63
Glazman, Josef 63
Globocnik, Odilo 65
Goebbels, Joseph 66
Great Britain 67
Grodno 73
Grosman, Haika 75
Gross-Rosen 76
Grüninger, Paul 79
Gurs 79
Gypsies 81

H

Heydrich, Reinhard 87
Himmler, Heinrich 89
Hirsch, Otto 91
Hitler, Adolf 92
Hitler Youth 97
Holocaust 100
Holocaust, Denial of the 100
Homosexuality in the Third Reich 104
Horthy, Miklós 105
Höss, Rudolf 107
Hungarian Labor Service System 108
Hungary 110

I

I. G. Farben 115
Italy 118

J

Jäger, Karl ... 124
Janówska ... 124
Jeckeln, Friedrich ... 126
Jewish Brigade Group ... 127
Jewish Fighting Organization ... 129
Jewish Ghetto Police ... 132
Jewish Law (Statut des Juifs) ... 135
Joint Distribution Committee ... 136
Judenrat ... 139

K

Kaltenbrunner, Ernst ... 144
Kamenets-Podolski ... 145
Kaplan, Josef ... 146
Kapo ... 147
Kasztner, Rezső ... 148
Kharkov ... 149
Kherson ... 150
Kielce ... 151
Kistarcsa ... 154
Koch, Karl Otto ... 155
Kolbe, Maximilian ... 156
Kommissarbefehl (Commissar Order) ... 158
Koppe, Wilhelm ... 159
Korczak, Janusz ... 159
Korherr, Richard ... 162
Kovno ... 163
Kowalski, Władysław ... 166
Kraków ... 167
Kramer, Josef ... 171
Kristallnacht ("Night of the Broken Glass") ... 171
Krüger, Friedrich Wilhelm ... 174
Krumey, Hermann ... 175

Index ... 177

Contents

VOLUME 3

Timeline ... xiii

L

Latvia ... 1
Laval, Pierre ... 4
Le Chambon-sur-Lignon ... 5
Levi, Primo ... 6
Liebehenschel, Arthur ... 8
Liebeskind, Aharon ... 9
Literature on the Holocaust ... 11
Lithuania ... 15
Łódź ... 19

Łódź Ghetto, Chronicles of the ... 25
Lohse, Hinrich ... 28
Lösener, Bernard ... 28
Lublin ... 29
Lutsk ... 33
Lutz, Carl ... 34
Lvov ... 36

M

Madagascar Plan ... 40
Majdanek ... 42
Mauthausen ... 45
Mayer, Saly ... 51
Medical Experiments ... 52
Mein Kampf ... 61
Mengele, Josef ... 62
Minsk ... 63
Mischlinge (Part Jews) ... 66
Mogilev-Podolski ... 68
Morgenthau, Henry, Jr. ... 69
Müller, Heinrich ... 71
Muselmann ... 73
Museums and Memorial Institutes ... 74
Mushkin, Eliyahu ... 78

N

Natzweiler-Struthof ... 79
Nazi Party ... 80
Nebe, Arthur ... 84
Netherlands, The ... 85
Neuengamme ... 91
Nisko and Lublin Plan ... 92
Novak, Franz ... 95
Nuremberg Laws ... 96

O

Oberg, Carl Albrecht ... 97
Office of Special Investigations ... 98
Ohlendorf, Otto ... 100
Operational Squads ... 101
Oradour-sur-Glane ... 108
Organisation Schmelt ... 108

P

Paris ... 111
Partisans ... 113
Pechersky, Aleksandr ... 119
Płaszów ... 120
Plotnicka, Frumka ... 122
Pohl, Oswald ... 123
Poland ... 124
Ponary ... 141
Prisoners of War ... 142
Protocols of the Elders of Zion ... 146
Prützmann, Hans-Adolf ... 148

R

Racism	149
Rasch, Emil Otto	153
Rauff, Walther	154
Ravensbrück	154
Rayman, Marcel	156
Refugees, 1933-1945	157
Reichenau, Walter von	161
Reich Security Main Office	162
Rescue Committee of United States Orthodox Rabbis	164
Rescue of Children	166
Resistance, Jewish	170
Riegner Cable	174
Riga	175
"Righteous among the Nations"	177
Ringelblum, Emanuel	180
Robota, Roza	182
Rosenberg, Alfred	183
Rovno	184
Rumbula	187
Index	189

Contents

VOLUME 4

Timeline	xiii

S

Sachsenhausen	1
Schindler, Oskar	2
SD	4
Sendler, Irena	6
Seyss-Inquart, Arthur	7
Simferopol	9
Skarżysko-Kamienna	9
Slovakia	11
Sobibór	15
Sousa Mendes, Aristides de	19
Soviet Union	20
Special Commando	25
Sporrenberg, Jacob	26
Sprachregelung	27
SS	28
SS Death's-Head Units	31
Stahlecker, Franz Walter	34
Stangl, Franz	34
Starachowice	35
St. Louis	36
Streicher, Julius	37
Stroop, Jürgen	38
Stuckart, Wilhelm	41
Stutthof	42

Sugihara, Sempo ... 44
Survivors, Psychology of ... 45
Szenes, Hannah ... 51

T
Tarnów ... 52
Tenenbaum, Mordechai ... 53
Ternopol ... 55
Theresienstadt ... 56
Transfer Point (Umschlagplatz) ... 61
Trawniki ... 62
Treblinka ... 63
Trials of the War Criminals ... 69

U
Ukraine ... 84
Ukrainian Military Police ... 87
United Partisan Organization ... 88
United States Army and Survivors in Germany and Austria ... 90
United States Department of State ... 92
United States of America ... 93

V
Vallat, Xavier ... 97
Vienna ... 98
Vilna ... 101
Vitebsk ... 105
Volksdeutsche ... 106

W
Wallenberg, Raoul ... 108
Wannsee Conference ... 111
War Refugee Board ... 113
Warsaw ... 115
Warsaw Ghetto Uprising ... 129
Warsaw Polish Uprising ... 133
Westerbork ... 135
Wiesel, Elie ... 137
Wiesenthal, Simon ... 138
Wirth, Christian ... 139
Wise, Stephen Samuel ... 140
Wisliceny, Dieter ... 141
Wolff, Karl ... 142
World Jewish Congress ... 143

Y
Yelin, Haim ... 144
Youth Movements ... 145

Z
Zamość ... 151
Ziman, Henrik ... 152
Zuckerman, Yitzhak ... 153
Zyklon B ... 155

CONTENTS

- Glossary 159
- Primary Source Documents 171
  - Nazi Party Documents 171
  - Official Laws, Orders, and Regulations of the Third Reich 179
  - Secret Nazi Documents 186
  - Nazi Correspondence 190
  - Jewish Resistance 193
  - Life in the Ghettos 197
  - Testimony 199
- Resources for Further Study 201
- Photo Credits 207
- Text Credits 211
- Index 215

Timeline:
The Holocaust in the Context of World Events

1918 November 9: The Weimar Republic is established in Germany.

November 11: The war that would come to be called World War I ends after four years. Germany is defeated.

1919 June 28: The Treaty of Versailles is signed. It establishes the League of Nations and punishes Germany for its aggression in World War I.

September 16: Adolf Hitler joins the German Workers' Party, precursor of the National Socialist German Workers (Nazi) Party.

1920 January 16: The League of Nations convenes for the first time.

August 8: National Socialist German Workers' Party (known as the Nazi party) is founded.

1921 Adolf Hitler takes control of the National Socialist party.

1922 October 27: Benito Mussolini is appointed the premier of Italy.

1923 November 11: Adolf Hitler is arrested for his attempt to overthrow the German government in Bavaria in the Beer Hall Putsch.

1924 April 1: Adolf Hitler is sentenced to five years in prison for the Beer Hall Putsch. While there, he writes *Mein Kampf*.

December 20: Hitler is released from prison after only eight months.

1925 April 26: Paul von Hindenburg is elected president of Weimar Republic (Germany).

November 11: Adolf Hitler's personal guard, the SS (*Schutzstaffel*), is founded.

1926 September 8: Germany joins the League of Nations.

1929 January 6: Heinrich Himmler appointed Reichsführer-SS.

October 24: "Black Tuesday"—the U.S. stock market crash on Wall Street. The Great Depression begins and spreads around the world.

1930 September 14: In Reichstag (Parliament) elections, the Nazi party emerges as a serious new force in German politics, earning 107 seats in the 577-member Reichstag. In the face of massive unemployment, antisemitism in Germany intensifies and spreads throughout Eastern Europe.

TIMELINE

1932 April 10: Paul von Hindenburg is re-elected president of Germany, defeating challenger Adolf Hitler.

July 31: In Reichstag elections, National Socialists (Nazis) become the largest party in Germany, taking 230 of 608 seats.

November 8: Franklin D. Roosevelt is elected president of the United States.

November 9: In Reichstag elections Nazis lose 2,000,000 votes and drop to 196 seats

1933 January 30: Adolf Hitler becomes the chancellor of Germany.

February 28: After a fire in the Reichstag on February 27, the Nazis declare a state of emergency, suspending freedom of speech, restricting freedom of assembly, and ending freedom of the press.

March 4: Franklin D. Roosevelt takes office for his first term as U.S. president. In his inaugural address, he says, "We have nothing to fear but fear itself."

March 23: Political prisoners arrive at Dachau.

March 24: The Reichstag approves the Enabling Act, giving Adolf Hitler dictatorial powers.

April 1: Nazis unleash a nationwide one-day boycott of Jewish businesses.

April 7: Jews are expelled from the German civil service.

April 11: Nazi definitions of "Aryan" and "non-Aryan" are adopted.

April 26: The Gestapo is established.

May 10: Nazis begin staging public book burnings, targeting works by political opponents and Jews. Eventually millions of books will be destroyed.

July 14: The Nazi Party is named the only legal political party in Germany.

July 20: An agreement (concordat) is signed between the Vatican and Nazi Germany.

October 14: Germany leaves the League of Nations.

1934 January 26: Germany and Poland sign a ten-year pact of non-aggression.

June 30–July 2: The Night of the Long Knives—also known as the Röhm Purge. Under Adolf Hitler's orders, the SS purges the SA (Storm Troopers); many SA leaders are killed.

July 20: The SS becomes an independent organization, with Heinrich Himmler as its chief.

August 2: German president Paul von Hindenburg dies.

August 3: Adolf Hitler becomes both president and chancellor. Soon all German officials and soldiers are required to swear allegiance to Hitler personally, not to the people or the country. At the September Nazi Party Congress in Nuremberg, Hitler proclaims his "Third Reich," which he says will last for one thousand years.

1935 January 13: A plebiscite in the Saarland overwhelmingly favors returning to Germany.

March 16: Hitler announces reintroduction of military conscription in violation of the Versailles treaty.

September 15: The Reichstag passes the first two "Nuremberg Laws," the Reich Citizenship Law and the Law for the Protection of German Blood and German Honor, which prohibit marriage and sexual intercourse between Germans and Jews and strip Jews of their remaining civil rights in Germany. These later serve as a model for the Nazis' treatment of Gypsies.

December 31: Jews are dismissed from the civil service in Germany.

1936 March 7: Germany sends troops into Rhineland, breaking the terms of the Treaty of Versailles.

May 9: Italy defeats Ethiopia, which it invaded in October, 1935.

July 18: A civil war erupts in Spain which will last for three years and foreshadows World War II.

August 1: The Summer Olympic Games begin in Berlin. African American runner Jesse Owens wins four gold medals during the games, but Adolf Hitler refuses to recognize the spectacular achievement.

October 25: The Rome-Berlin Axis Pact is signed, cementing an alliance between Adolf Hitler and Italian fascist leader Mussolini.

1937 March 14: In the face of increasing violence toward Jews in Europe, Pope Pius XI condemns racism and extreme nationalism in his encyclical "With Burning Concern."

July 16: Buchenwald concentration camp is opened.

September 7: Hitler declares the end of the Treaty of Versailles.

November 25: Germany and Japan sign a military and political pact.

1938 March 12–13: The *Anschluss*—Germany invades and annexes Austria.

April 26: Jews are required to register their property and financial holdings. It is now illegal for Aryans to pretend to own businesses still run by Jews; the push for "Aryanization" of businesses and property increases.

June 14: Jewish-owned businesses are forced to register with Nazi authorities.

June 15: Fifteen hundred German Jews are put into concentration camps.

July 6–13: Representatives of 32 countries meet at the Evian Conference in France to discuss the Jewish refugee and immigration problem. No solution emerges because virtually every country refuses to increase immigration quotas for Jews.

July 25: Jewish physicians are limited to treatment of Jewish patients.

August 17: Male Jews are required to add "Israel" to their names; female Jews must add "Sarah."

September 27: Jews may no longer work as lawyers.

September 29: At the Munich Conference, the Allies appease Adolf Hitler, granting Sudetenland—part of Czechoslovakia—to Germany.

October 15: Germany occupies Czechoslovakia's Sudetenland.

October 20–21: Jews are first deported to Poland from Vienna, Hamburg, and Prague.

TIMELINE

November 9–10: The massive pogroms known as Kristallnacht explode across Germany and Austria. Synagogues are defaced and destroyed; Jewish homes and businesses are looted and vandalized.

November 15: Jewish children may no longer attend German schools.

December 3: Aryanization of Jewish businesses is mandated by law and carried out by force and intimidation.

1939 March 15–16: Germany invades Czechoslovakia.

April 22: Italy and Germany cement their alliance by signing the Pact of Steel.

May 15: The Ravensbrück concentration camp for women is established.

May 19: The MacDonald White Paper issued by the British government strengthens limits on Jewish emigration to Palestine.

August 23: The Germans and Soviets sign a non-aggression pact.

September 1: Germany invades Poland. Within the month, Poland falls.

September 2: Stutthof camp is established.

September 3: Great Britain and France declare war on Germany.

September 17: The Soviets invade eastern Poland, challenging the Germans.

September 21: SS official Reinhard Heydrich orders the creation of Jewish ghettos and Judenrate (Jewish Councils) in occupied Poland.

October 8: The first ghetto for Jews is established in Poland, in Piotrkow.

October 12: The Germans establish the Generalgouvernement in Poland.

November 23: Jews in occupied Poland are required to wear badges in the shape of the Star of David.

December 5–6: Jewish property in Poland is seized by German authorities.

1940 January 25: Nazis select the town of Auschwitz as the location for a new concentration camp.

February 12: The Nazis begin deporting Jews from Germany to occupied Poland.

April 9: Denmark and Norway are invaded by the Germans.

April 30: Łódź ghetto, established in February, is sealed; more than 200,000 Jews are not able to leave.

May 10: Germany invades the Netherlands, Belgium, Luxembourg, and northern France.

May 10: Winston Churchill becomes the prime minister of Great Britain.

May 20: Auschwitz concentration camp is established.

July 10: The Battle of Britain begins, with a major dogfight over the English Channel, and Germany's blitzkrieg bombing of London.

September 15: Battle of Britain Day—London is heavily blitzed by German bombers and fighter planes. The Luftwaffe meets with stiff resistance in the English Channel, resulting in an important Allied victory and turning point in the war.

September 27: The Tripartite Pact—Japan joins Germany and Italy in the Axis alliance.

October 16: Warsaw ghetto is established; the following month, it is sealed, holding in 400,000 Jews.

1941 March 1: Heinrich Himmler visits Auschwitz and orders an expansion that will increase capacity by at least 100,000 prisoners.

March 3: Krakow ghetto is established.

April 6: Germany invades Yugoslavia and Greece.

May 27: The German warship *Bismarck* is sunk by the British. U.S. president Franklin D. Roosevelt declares a national emergency in May because of events in Europe and Asia.

June 22: Operation Barbarossa—the Germans invade the Soviet Union.

July 8: Jews in the German-occupied Baltic countries are ordered to wear the Star of David badge.

July 21: Hermann Göring appoints Reinhard Heydrich to develop a plan for carrying out the "Final Solution of the Jewish Question"—the extermination of European Jews.

August 14: The Atlantic Charter is signed by Great Britain and the United States; the document outlines basic principles of postwar global rights and responsibilities and forms the beginnings of what will one day be the charter of the United Nations.

September 3: Zyklon B is first used in experiments at Auschwitz.

September 6: The Vilna ghettos are established with 40,000 Jews.

September 29–30: More than 33,000 Jews are massacred at Babi Yar.

October 23: Jewish emigration from Germany is prohibited.

November 24: Theresienstadt ghetto is established in Bohemia-Moravia as the Nazis' "model" Jewish ghetto. Also this month, construction begins on Bełżec extermination camp.

December 7: Japan attacks the United States at Pearl Harbor. Four days later, Germany and Italy declare war on the United States. The United States reciprocates by declaring war on the Axis powers.

December 8: The Chełmno extermination camp opens. Among its first victims are 5,000 Gypsies.

1942 January 20: At the Wannsee Conference, the Nazis coordinate plans for the "Final Solution."

January 21: The United Partisan Organization forms in Vilna.

February 23: The *Struma*, an unsafe cattle boat carrying more than 700 Jewish refugees from a port in Romania, sinks after being refused entry into Palestine.

June 1: Jews in the Netherlands, Belgium, Croatia, Slovakia, and Romania are ordered to wear the yellow Star of David badge.

March: Sobibór and Bełżec camps are established. The first transfer of French Jews to Auschwitz occurs. Marshal Petain approves French collaboration with

TIMELINE

the Nazis. The United States starts supplying the Allies with war materials through the Lend-Lease Bill.

May 27: SS official Richard Heydrich is wounded; he dies early in June. A week later, the Nazis avenge his death by destroying the town of Lidice, in the Protectorate of Bohemia and Moravia (formerly Czechoslovakia).

June 4–6: The Allies win the Battle of Midway. Japan's eastward thrust is decisively thwarted.

June 23: Systematic gassing begins at Auschwitz.

July 19: Heinrich Himmler orders the start of Operation Reinhard.

July 23: Treblinka camp opens. The first victims and prisoners are from the Warsaw Ghetto. The Jewish Fighting Organization (ŻOB) is established in Warsaw.

August 23: The battle for Stalingrad begins. Three months later, the Soviets launch a successful counteroffensive against the Germans.

October 5: All Jews in concentration camps in Germany are to be sent to Auschwitz and Majdanek, on orders of Heinrich Himmler.

November 11: In a crucial turning point victory for Allied forces, the Germans are defeated at El Alamein, Egypt.

1943 January 18–21: A major, armed act of resistance occurs in the Warsaw ghetto.

January 29: All Gypsies in German-occupied territories are ordered arrested and sent to concentration camps.

February 26: The first transport of Gypsies is placed in the "Gypsy Camp" at Auschwitz.

March 5: Allied forces begin bombing Ruhr, a region central to Germany's coal, iron and steel industries.

April 19–30: At the Bermuda Conference, the Allies discuss the rescue of Jews in occupied Europe, but the talks are fruitless. Also this month, the Bergen-Belsen camp is opened.

April 19: The Warsaw ghetto uprising erupts and continues through May 16.

May 19: The Nazis declare Berlin *Judenfrei* (free of Jews).

June 11: Heinrich Himmler orders the liquidation of the Jewish ghettos of Poland and the Soviet Union.

June 22: German U-boats are withdrawn from the North Atlantic; the Allies win the Battle of the Atlantic.

July 5: The Sobibór extermination camp is made a concentration camp.

August 2: Prisoners at the Treblinka camp revolt; 200 escape, but the Nazis hunt them down.

October 2: The Danes rescue more than 7,200 Jews from the Nazis.

October 14: Prisoners at the Sobibór camp revolt; 300 escape. Of these, 50 survive.

November 3: Erntefest ("Harvest Festival") begins, in which 42,000 Jews are killed.

TIMELINE

1944 January 24: War Refugee Board is created in the United States.

March 19: Germany invades Hungary; Hungarian Jews are required to wear the Star of David badge. During the next several months, more than 400,000 Hungarian Jews are deported to Auschwitz.

June 6: D-Day: The Allies land in Normandy, France. Throughout the year, Allied forces penetrate into more and more parts of Europe.

July 20: German officers fail in an assassination attempt against Adolf Hitler.

July 24: Soviet troops liberate the Majdanek camp.

July 28: The first major death march begins: Warsaw to Kutno.

August 4: Anne Frank and her family are arrested in Amsterdam and sent to Auschwitz. Anne and her sister are later sent to Bergen-Belsen.

September 1: Warsaw Polish Uprising begins and lasts until October 2 when the Polish Home Army is defeated by the Nazis.

October 6–7: Prisoners in Special Commandos (*Sonderkommandos*) at Auschwitz stage an uprising.

October 23: The Allies recognize Charles de Gaulle as the head of the provisional French government.

October 30: The last gassings at Auschwitz-Birkenau take place.

December 16–27: The Battle of the Bulge in Luxembourg and Belgium—the Germans are defeated.

1945 January 1: Germans begin full retreat on the Eastern Front.

January 17: Soviet troops enter Warsaw.

January 18: Death March from Auschwitz begins.

January 27: Soviet troops liberate Auschwitz-Birkenau.

February 4–11: Franklin D. Roosevelt, Winston Churchill, and Soviet leader Joseph Stalin meet at Yalta as the Allied forces meet with increasing success worldwide.

April 12: U.S. president Franklin D. Roosevelt dies and is succeeded by Harry S Truman.

April 12: Buchenwald and Bergen-Belsen camps are liberated. As more camps are released from Nazi control, the number of displaced persons (DPs) rises dramatically throughout Europe.

April 28: Benito Mussolini is shot by Italian partisans.

April 29: Dachau camp is liberated by American troops.

April 30: In his Berlin bunker, Adolf Hitler writes his Last Will and Testament, then commits suicide.

April–May: Allied troops liberate Dachau, Ravensbrück, Bergen-Belsen, Buchenwald, Mauthausen, and Theresienstadt camps. With liberation and the end of war in Europe, Displaced Persons (DP) camps are inundated.

May 7: Germany surrenders unconditionally to the Allies.

May 8: V-E Day—Victory in Europe.

TIMELINE

June 5: The victorious Allies divide Germany into four occupation zones.

July 16: The first atomic bomb is tested, at Alamogordo, New Mexico.

July 17–August 2: Allied leaders Winston Churchill, Harry Truman, and Joseph Stalin meet in Potsdam.

August 6: The United States drops an atomic bomb on Hiroshima, and, three days later, on Nagasaki.

August 14: Japan surrenders. World War II is over.

November 20: The Nuremberg War Trials begin in Germany.

1946 January 7: The United Nations holds its first meeting, in London.

January 20: President Charles de Gaulle of France resigns.

October 1: The Nuremberg War Trials conclude.

October 16: The first convicted Nazi War criminals are executed by hanging at Nuremberg.

December 9: Twenty-three former Nazi doctors and scientists are tried at Nuremberg. Sixteen are found guilty; seven are executed by hanging.

1947 June 5: The Marshall Plan is instituted, to help Europe rebuild.

September 15: Twenty-one former SS Operational Squad leaders are tried at Nuremberg. Although fourteen of them are sentenced to death, only four who were group commanders are executed.

1948 May 14: The State of Israel is proclaimed.

June 25: The U.S. Congress creates a Displaced Persons Commission.

October 30: The first boatload of war refugees arrives in the United States.

1949 April 4: The North Atlantic Treaty Organization—NATO—is formed.

May 23: West Germany becomes a separate state, under occupation forces. East Germany becomes a Soviet-bloc state later in the year.

December 9: The United Nations approves the Genocide Convention.

1957 The last Displaced Persons (DP) camp closes.

1960 May 11: Adolf Eichmann is captured in Argentina. He is tried in Jerusalem starting on April 11, 1961. Found guilty, he is executed by hanging on May 31, 1962.

"LANGUAGE REGULATION." SEE SPRACHREGELUNG.

Latvia

Latvia is located on the Baltic Sea, situated between Estonia to the north and Belarus (formerly **BELORUSSIA**) and **LITHUANIA** to the south. Between 1918 and 1940 it was an independent republic. During the course of World War II, Latvia experienced three invasions and subsequent occupations: the **SOVIET UNION** occupied Latvia in June 1940, the Germans invaded in June 1941, and in 1944 the Soviet army expelled the Germans, retaking Latvia. After nearly a half century as part of the Soviet Union, Latvia once again became an independent republic in 1991. Latvia's main regions are Livonia (central Latvia), with the capital, **RIGA**; Kurland in the southwest, with the major city Liepāja; and Latgale in the east, with **DVINSK** (now Daugavpils).

Jews first arrived in Kurland and Livonia in the sixteenth century. At the beginning of the twentieth century about 200,000 Jews lived there, but expulsions, emigration, and the World War I military campaigns cut their numbers to less than half. During the first years of Latvia's post-World War I independence, the Jews, who then constituted about 5 percent of the population, enjoyed equal rights in almost every sphere. Like the other minorities in Latvia, they were granted broad educational and cultural autonomy.

During its period of independence between the two world wars, Latvia had close economic ties with **GERMANY**, fostered by an influential German minority. In 1934 a right-wing revolution brought about a definite deterioration in the Jews' situation.

Soviet Occupation

On October 5, 1939, Latvia was forced to allow the Soviet army to establish bases in its territory. In June 1940 the Soviet army took over Latvia, and a month later the country was declared a Soviet republic. During this occupation, attempts were made to have Latvia conform to the Soviet pattern. National and local civilian administrative bureaus were destroyed, the military and civilian leadership was eliminated, and Latvia's economy was nationalized. All farms over 74 acres (30 hectares) were divided into lots of 25 acres (10 hectares) in preparation for collectivization. On June 14, 1941, about 19,000 Latvians, among them 5,000 Jews, were deported to Siberia.

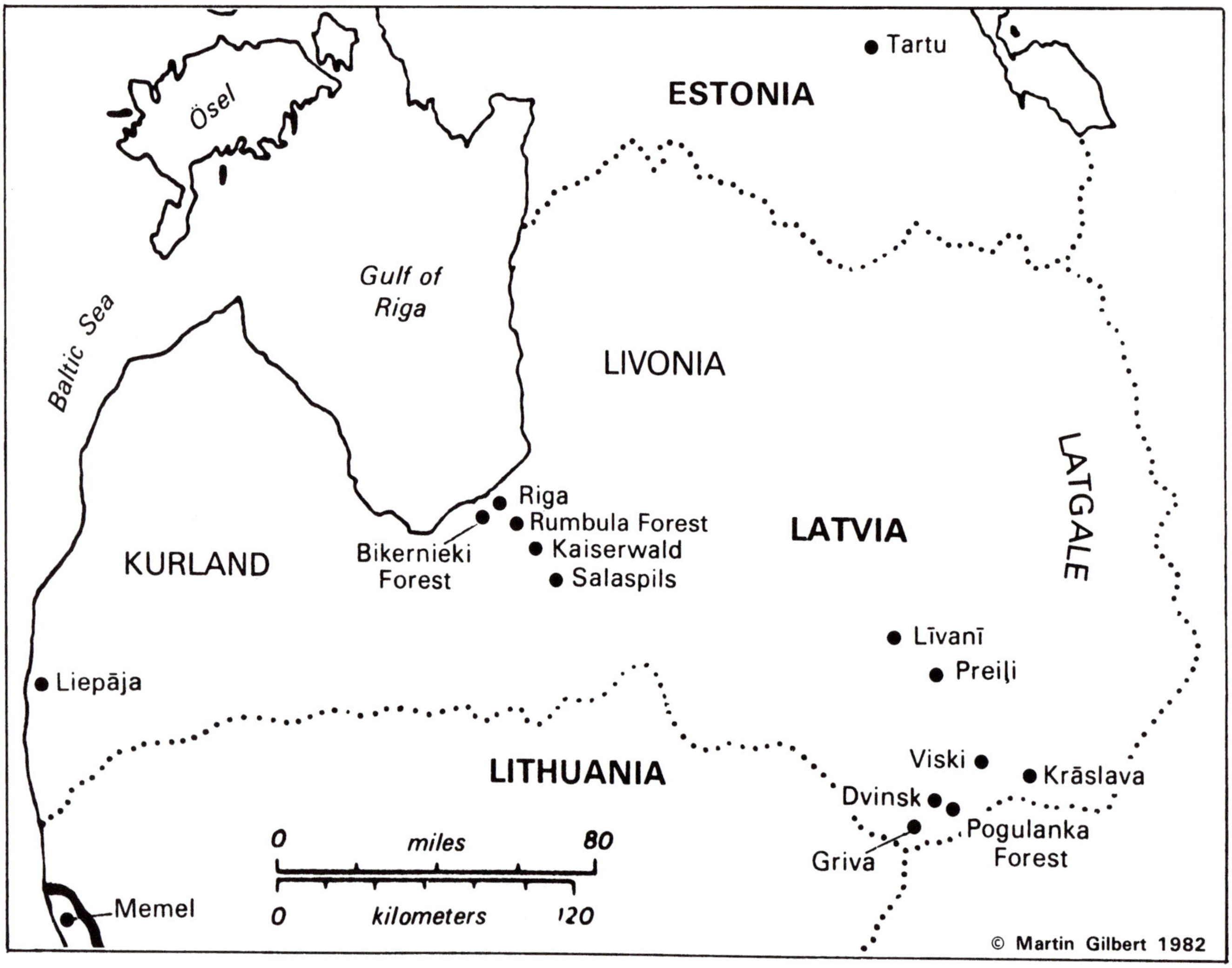

Latvia, September 1944.

While the Soviet occupation was imposed by force, the Soviets did manage to enlist the sympathy, if not the outright support, of about one-tenth of the population. The overwhelming majority of those who served in the Soviet-controlled civil administration and police were Latvian gentiles. Although the number of Jews working in the Soviet administration in the cities was considerable, it was less than their percentage in the general population.

According to a 1935 census, 94,000 Jews lived in Latvia; however, at the time of the German invasion in June 1941, only some 70,000 remained in the country. About 4,000 left Latvia before the Soviet occupation, 5,000 (heads of the Jewish community and members of the cultural and economic elite) were deported to Siberia by the Soviets, and up to 15,000 managed to escape to the Soviet interior ahead of the advancing German army. Of the 70,000 remaining Jews, it is estimated that not more than 3,000 survived the Nazi massacres. In addition to native Latvian Jews, about 20,000 Jews from **Austria**, Czechoslovakia, and Germany were deported to Latvia. Of them, only about 1,000 survived the war.

Nazi Occupation

In their massive invasion of the Soviet Union, June 22, 1941, the German forces swept into Latvia's frontier. Riga was occupied on July 1, and it took the

Wehrmacht (German combined military forces) just ten days to clear Latvia of Soviet troops. Under the command of General Franz Walter STAHLECKER, Einsatzgruppe A entered Latvia along with the *Wehrmacht*. Within hours, Stahlecker's troops began killing Latvia's Jews and other "enemies" of the Nazi regime, specifically Communists and GYPSIES. Latvia became an integral part of Reichskommissariat Ostland and was called General Commissariat Latvia. The general commissioner appointed by the Germans for Latvia was Dr. Heinrich Drechsler. He headed a local administration composed of Latvians.

The German occupation of Latvia was brutal. Although numerous Latvians, especially those who had suffered under the Soviets, greeted the German forces as liberators, the Germans entered Latvia with plans to exploit Latvian economic and labor resources. It is known that as many as 2,000 of Latvia's 4,000 Gypsies, as well as all the patients of mental hospitals, were killed. According to estimates made by a Latvian resistance organization, as many as 20,000 Latvian Communists and members of the national resistance also lost their lives. In addition, tens of thousands of Latvians were put in prison, tortured, or deported to Germany. Throughout the period of German occupation, Latvia's jails were filled to capacity. The Latvian SS Legion numbered 80,000 men, and an additional 30,000 men in the Latvian police corps were deployed against the Soviet army.

> The difficulty of earning a living during the second half of the 1930s drove many young Jews from the villages to the large cities of Riga, Liepāja, and Dvinsk, where two-thirds of the Jews lived on the eve of the first Soviet occupation.

Purging Latvia of Jews

The murder of the Jews in Latvia was carried out in three main stages. The first was from July to October 1941, when about 30,000 Jews from Latvia's provincial towns and about 4,000 more Jews from Riga were killed. The second stage was from November to December 1941, during which most of the Jews living in the ghettos of the larger cities—Riga, Dvinsk, and Liepāja—were annihilated. In October 1941, a change in command of the SD (*Sicherheitsdienst*; Security Service) took place. The main force of Einsatzgruppe A left Latvia for Leningrad, and the police duties for Latvia were taken over by the Higher SS and Police Leader Friedrich JECKELN, who had excelled in the killing operations in the UKRAINE. Jeckeln, like all the Higher SS and Police Leaders, had been given special authority by Heinrich HIMMLER, and he arrived in Riga with a plan to "empty the ghetto." In the so-called Jeckeln Aktion, which took place on November 30 and December 7, 1941, about 25,000 Jews from the Riga ghetto were killed in the RUMBULA Forest. (Jeckeln was convicted and hanged in Riga in 1946 for his part in this operation.)

Initially, Germany hadn't intended to use Latvian troops against the Soviets. Part of Heinrich Himmler's and Reinhard HEYDRICH's plan, however, was to enlist Latvians in the murder of Jews and Communists. Although the commanders of Einsatzgruppe A supervised the killing of Jews, local and national Latvian police units were integrated into the implementation of the "FINAL SOLUTION." These units frequently carried out the killings themselves.

The major Latvian killing unit, which took part in numerous operations in Riga and in the provinces during the war, was led by Viktor Arajs (who was sentenced in 1979 to life imprisonment and died in 1988). His 400-man unit, known as the Arajs Commando, played a major role in the killings in the Bikernieki Forest near Riga, the Latvian provincial areas, the Ukraine, Belorussia, and Russia. Perhaps as many as 30,000 Latvian Jews were slaughtered by the Arajs Commando. The total number of Latvians who actively participated in the killing operations is impossible at present to determine; however, it is clear that more than 2,000 Latvians served the SD in various capacities.

The third stage of planned extermination lasted from January 1942 until July of that year, and during this period as many as 14,000 of the 20,000 Jewish deportees from Austria, Czechoslovakia, and Germany were killed. Most of these Jews were killed in the Bikernieki Forest and at other locations in the vicinity of Riga. At the beginning of 1943 only about 5,000 Jews remained in the ghettos of Riga, Dvinsk, and Liepāja, and in a few labor camps, the largest of which was Kaiserwald. Starting in the fall of 1943, the remaining Jews in the cities were moved to Kaiserwald. Sporadic killings continued until the end of the war. The largest burial grounds of the massacred Jews are in the Rumbula and Bikernieki forests. Altogether, there are perhaps as many as 60 mass grave sites of murdered Jews in Latvia.

During the late summer of 1944, as the Soviet forces were approaching Riga, the remaining Jews in Latvia were transported to Germany, mostly to the **STUTTHOF** camp. Most were marched to work in the German interior under blizzard conditions in early 1945, as the Soviet army closed in on the German forces. Numerous people died on the way from hunger and exposure. Out of the entire Latvian Jewish community only about 150 survived by hiding with the help of Latvian gentiles, and several dozen Jews who had fought with partisan units also survived. No more than 1,000 Latvian Jews returned from camps in Germany.

After the war some 13,000 Jews who had been refugees and exiles in the Soviet interior returned to Latvia. Another 20,000 Jews from other parts of the Soviet Union joined them. In 1970 there were 36,592 Jews in Latvia, and by 1987 about one-third of them had emigrated to Israel.

SUGGESTED RESOURCES

Ezergailis, Andrew. *The Holocaust in Latvia, 1941–1944.* U.S. Holocaust Memorial Museum, 1996. [Online] http://vip.latnet.lv/LPRA/Ezergailis_preface.html (accessed September 1, 2000).

Gitelman, Zvi, ed. *Bitter Legacy: Confronting the Holocaust in the USSR.* Bloomington Indiana University Press, 1997.

Press, Bernhard. *The Murder of the Jews in Latvia, 1941–1945.* Evanston, IL: Northwestern University Press, 1999.

Schneider, Gertrude, ed. *The Unfinished Road: Jewish Survivors of Latvia Look Back.* New York: Praeger, 1991.

Laval, Pierre

(1883–1945)

collaborator:
One who cooperates with the enemy.

Pierre Laval was a French politician and collaborator with the Germans. He was head of the French Vichy government from 1942 to 1944, during the years when the Nazis occupied **FRANCE**. Laval was twice premier (1931–1932 and 1935–1936) before becoming vice-premier of the Vichy government, which operated in the portion of France not occupied by German forces, immediately after its establishment in 1940. Dismissed on December 13 of that year by the premier, Philippe Pétain, Laval was recalled to office in May 1942 with the help of Hitler. He formed a new cabinet and served as chief of government, continuing in that position until the end of the war.

Laval was known as a pragmatist rather than an ideologue, and he championed an agreement with Hitler and the Germans. French fortunes, he argued, were linked with those of a strong **GERMANY**. Consequently, he attempted to comply with Nazi requests on matters he felt were not crucial to French national interests. Among these was the Jewish issue. Believing that he could win the confidence of the occupation authorities by satisfying their demands for foreign Jews, Laval agreed to assist the Germans in rounding up foreign-born Jews and removing them from France in 1942. He coordinated the actions of the **FRENCH POLICE** and government with the Nazis' machinery of destruction. In response to those who said that the Jews were being murdered, Laval adhered rigidly to the propaganda of the **SS**: the Jews were being sent to work camps in the east. In 1943, when the failure of his policies was becoming evident, the outcries against the **DEPORTATIONS** were growing, and the Nazis' most cruel measures increasingly involved native French Jews, Laval's interest in collaboration declined. Although he gradually lost control of events, Laval believed until the end that his program had succeeded.

Laval was tried after the war for plotting against the security of the state and for conducting intelligence with the enemy, and was sentenced to death after a short, poorly run trial. Having failed in a suicide attempt, he was executed in October 1945.

Pierre Laval.

SUGGESTED RESOURCES

Brody, J. Kenneth. *The Avoidable War: Pierre Laval and the Politics of Reality, 1935–1936.* New Brunswick, NJ: Transaction Publishers, 1999.

Chambrun, Rene de. *Pierre Laval: Traitor or Patriot?* New York: Scribner, 1984.

Warner, Geoffrey. *Pierre Laval and the Eclipse of France.* New York: Macmillan, 1969.

Le Chambon-sur-Lignon

Le Chambon-sur-Lignon was a French town in the Haute-Loire department in southern **FRANCE** that became a significant source of shelter and protection for thousands of Jews during the Nazi occupation. The town's overwhelmingly Protestant population responded to the plea of Pastor André Trocmé to extend aid to fleeing Jews and shelter them in private homes and outlying farms, as well as in public institutions in Le Chambon and nearby localities. Pastor Trocmé, who with his wife, Magda, initiated and presided over this vast rescue operation with the help of interdenominational organizations. The pastor has been described as the "charismatic leader" and "living spirit" of Le Chambon, and his wife as the "motor" of the large operation. Trocmé always responded to calls for help to hide Jews in danger of detection by the German police, even when this jeopardized not only his own life but those of his wife and children and members of his community.

Refugee Jews were housed in public institutions and children's homes or with local townsmen and farmers, for various periods of time. With the help of others, such as Pastor Edouard Théis, director of the Collège Cévenol, some were taken on dangerous treks through France and under assumed French names to the Swiss frontier. They were secretly smuggled across the borders and into the waiting hands of other Protestant supporters on the Swiss side; the rescue partners on the Swiss side were extremely important because the Swiss authorities invariably drove back Jews who openly tried to cross into Switzerland.

Daniel Trocmé, a cousin of André Trocmé, directed the children's home Maison des Roches at Le Chambon. He was betrayed, reportedly by a German officer stay-

> "Though they were discreet, as silent and as separate as possible regarding the refugees, the amateurs of Le Chambon had a sense of fellowship with each other in the face of the suffering they were helping to alleviate."
>
> *Philip Hallie,* Lest Innocent Blood Be Shed: The Story of the Village of Le Chambon and How Goodness Happened There *(New York: Harper Torchbooks), 1994, p. 128.*

ing at a military convalescent home in Le Chambon, and was arrested on June 29, 1943, and taken to Moulins for interrogation. He readily admitted his role in the rescue of Jewish children, and was sent to the **BUCHENWALD** concentration camp, where he perished in April 1944. André Trocmé was also arrested by Vichy authorities but he was released, although he refused to sign a statement agreeing to stop giving further help to Jews. It is estimated that some 3,000 to 5,000 Jews found shelter in Le Chambon and its surrounding area at some time between 1941 and 1944.

Asked about his motivations in extending aid to Jews, one Le Chambon resident responded: "We were doing what had to be done. It was the most natural thing in the world to help these people." The rescue operation was remarkable in that an entire community banded together to rescue Jews, seeing this as their Christian obligation.

Pierre Sauvage, born in Le Chambon to Jewish parents who were refugees there, produced a documentary film, *Weapons of the Spirit*, about the rescue operation. André Trocmé, Daniel Trocmé, and Edouard Théis, as well as thirty-two other residents of Le Chambon and its neighboring area, have been recognized by Yad Vashem as **"RIGHTEOUS AMONG THE NATIONS."**

SUGGESTED RESOURCES

Matas, Carol. *Greater Than Angels.* New York: Simon and Schuster Books for Young Readers, 1998.

Rittner, Carol, and Sondra Myers, eds. *The Courage to Care: Rescuers of Jews During the Holocaust.* New York: New York University Press, 1986.

Weapons of the Spirit [videorecording]. First Run/Icarus Films, 1988.

LEMBERG. SEE LVOV.

Levi, Primo

Primo Levi.

(1919–1987)

Primo Levi, born in Turin, **ITALY**, became an Italian Jewish author and chemist. In October 1938, when Levi was a first-year student of chemistry, the leadership of the Italian Fascist party adopted a policy of **RACISM**, and by November, racial laws had been enacted in the country. Until then, being Jewish had been for Levi "a slight and insignificant difference." This was the first time that he felt a wall of separation rising between him and the community in which he was living. In September 1943 he earned a doctorate in chemistry, despite the difficulties he encountered as a Jew. Following Mussolini's downfall and the government's surrender to the Allies, the Germans seized control of the greater part of Italy. Levi fled to the mountains in the north. He had planned to join an anti-Fascist partisan group, but in December 1943, before his partisan unit became consolidated, he was caught by the Fascist militia. Under questioning, Levi admitted that he was Jewish, and was imprisoned in the Fossoli transit camp. In February, 1944 he was deported to **AUSCHWITZ**.

Levi spent ten months as a prisoner in Auschwitz, one of the few Jews from Italy to survive Auschwitz. Fortunately, an Italian civilian working in Auschwitz provided him with some extra food. Also, Levi knew some German and at one point he was taken on to work as a chemist in the Buna Works synthetic-rubber factory, an Auschwitz satellite camp. Due to these unusual circumstances, Levi was spared

Shema

You who live secure
In your warm houses,
Who return at evening to find
Hot food and friendly faces:

    Consider whether this is a man,
    Who labours in the mud
    Who knows no peace
    Who fights for a crust of bread
    Who dies at a yes or a no.
    Consider whether this is a woman,
    Without hair or name
    With no more strength to remember
    Eyes empty and womb cold
    As a frog in winter.

Consider that this has been:
I commend these words to you.
Engrave them on your hearts
When you are in your house, when you walk on your way,
When you go to bed, when you rise.
Repeat them to your children.
Or may your house crumble,
Disease render you powerless,
Your offspring avert their faces from you.

—PRIMO LEVI, 10 JANUARY 1946

Primo Levi, Collected Poems, *translated by Ruth Feldman and Brian Swann (London: Faber and Faber Ltd.), 1984.*

---

many of the difficulties of camp life. In the latter part of January 1945, on the eve of the evacuation of the Auschwitz camp complex, Levi fell ill. He was not put on the death march (*see* **DEATH MARCHES**) and was liberated by the Soviet forces that entered the camp on January 27. When Levi was released from Auschwitz, he did not go back to his home in Italy. Instead, for nine eventful and difficult months, he wandered through **POLAND**, the **UKRAINE**, and **BELORUSSIA**. His account of his experiences in Auschwitz and his observations about life in the camp were published in English as *Survival in Auschwitz: The Nazi Assault on Humanity* (1961). The book's original title was *Se questo è un uomo* (If This Is a Man).

Levi eventually returned to Turin and his profession as a chemist, and worked in an industrial plant. He raised a family and lived in his ancestral home. He was haunted, however, by the experience of Auschwitz; as he described it, Auschwitz "had been, first and foremost, a biological and social experiment of gigantic dimensions." Levi was one of the few survivors of the **CONCENTRATION CAMPS** who was intellectually equipped to observe and analyze the behavior of human beings in the reality of Auschwitz.

Survival in Auschwitz, written in 1947, was Levi's first book on his life in the camp. It was not well received, and a prominent Italian publisher had, in fact, rejected it. It took several years for Levi's talent to be appreciated. Levi had the ability to perceive the inhumane with human eyes, and to present the horror authentically in a style that avoided angry outbursts and generalizations. In 1963 he published *La tregua* (The Lull; published in English as *The Reawakening*, 1965). This is a picaresque story rich in detail, with colorful characters and adventures that the author had gathered in his encounters with people from many countries. The experience of meeting with simple people of various origins was part of a rehabilitation process that enabled him to resume living.

As time went on, Levi's Jewish identity developed more fully and found its expression in *Il sistema periodico* (The Periodic Table; 1984), in which the different chemical elements, which played such an important role in Levi's mind, meet with the world of his forefathers and with his own experience as a man and as a Jew.

Primo Levi came to be widely acknowledged as an outstanding writer. His books have been translated into many languages, and he is regarded as one of the great Italian writers of his time. Sadly, Primo Levi committed suicide in April, 1987 without leaving behind any explanation.

SUGGESTED RESOURCES

Anissimov, Myriam. *Primo Levi: Tragedy of an Optimist.* New York: Overlook Press, 1999.

Levi, Primo. *The Drowned and the Saved.* New York: Summit Books, 1988.

Levi, Primo. *The Reawakening.* New York: Simon and Schuster, 1995.

Levi, Primo. *Survival in Auschwitz: The Nazi Assault on Humanity.* New York: Collier Books, 1986.

Liebehenschel, Arthur

(1901–1948)

Arthur **LIEBEHENSCHEL** was a senior **SS** officer and the commandant of concentration camps. Born in Posen (now Poznań), Liebehenschel studied public administration and economics, and after World War I he served as a sergeant major in the German army, the *Reichswehr*. In February 1932 he joined the **NAZI PARTY** and in August 1934, the SS, where he served in the **SS-DEATH's-HEAD UNITS** (*Totenkopfverbände*).

Liebehenschel served as an assistant in the Columbia Haus (in **BERLIN**) and Lichtenburg (near Prettin) camps. He then held senior administrative posts in the Death's-Head Units headquarters, in the Inspectorate of **CONCENTRATION CAMPS**, and, as a senior director, in the **SS ECONOMIC-ADMINISTRATIVE MAIN OFFICE** (*Wirtschafts-Verwaltungshauptamt*; WVHA). On November 10, 1943, Liebehenschel was appointed commandant of the **AUSCHWITZ** extermination camp, and on May 19, 1944, commandant of **MAJDANEK**. When that camp was evacuated, he was given a senior post in the Manpower Main Office.

After the war, Liebehenschel was arrested by the Americans and extradited to **POLAND**. He was put on trial in Kraków, sentenced to death, and executed on January 24, 1948.

Arthur Liebehenschel at his trial in Kraków.

SUGGESTED RESOURCES

Goldstein, Arthur. *The Shoes of Majdanek.* Lanham, MA: University Press of America, 1992.

Levi, Primo. *Survival in Auschwitz: The Nazi Assault on Humanity.* New York: Collier Books, 1986.

A Teacher's Guide to the Holocaust: Perpetrators. [Online] http://fcit.coedu.usf.edu/holocaust/people/perps.htm (accessed on August 22, 2000).

Liebeskind, Aharon

(1912–1942)

Aharon Liebeskind ("Dolek") was an underground fighter and the leader of the **Fighting Organization of Pioneer Jewish Youth** (*He-Haluts ha-Lohem*) group in **Kraków**, Poland. Born in Zabierzow, a village near Kraków, Liebeskind studied law at Kraków University. In 1938 he became secretary of the *Akiva* movement, a Zionist and Hebrew cultural organization which he had joined at the age of 14. In early 1939 he was appointed national secretary of *Akiva* and went to live in **Warsaw**, although he retained his home in Kraków and continued to lead the movement there. He also managed to complete his doctoral dissertation. His job kept him in Warsaw until the outbreak of the war.

From the onset of the German occupation of **Poland**, Liebeskind was convinced that the Jews would not be able to live under the occupation regime, and he did all he could to get the members of his movement out of Poland. A charismatic figure, much admired by his fellow members and disciples, he did not accept an immigration certificate to Palestine for himself, so as not to abandon his family and followers in time of trouble.

In December 1940 Liebeskind was put in charge of an agricultural and vocational training program in the Kraków area, sponsored by the Jewish Self-Help Society, which had its main offices there. He utilized his position to promote the activities of the Jewish underground in the city, which he had founded and led. Using the society's official stationery, he distributed leaflets and arranged money transfers to the members of the underground. Liebeskind also arranged for the financing of the Kopaliny training farm, headed by Shimshon Draenger, which served as a cover for underground operations. His post enabled him to move around and thereby to maintain and strengthen contact with fellow members in various locations.

The deportation of Jews from the Kraków ghetto in June 1942 convinced Liebeskind that the only course of action left was that of armed struggle, even though there was not much hope of survival. He is credited with saying, "the Jewish fighters are fighting for three lines in history." He initiated the establishment of a broadly based fighting organization in Kraków, forging ties with the other leaders of the *He-Haluts* (pioneer) youth organizations in the city. An especially close tie existed between Liebeskind and Avraham Leibovich ("Laban") of the *Dror* movement, another Zionist organization, and the two became the commanders of the resistance organization, the Fighting Organization of the Pioneering Jewish Youth.

When the authorities began to pursue him, in November 1942, Liebeskind and the organization's headquarters moved to the "Aryan" part of the city. From there he renewed contact with the Polish Communist Workers' party (PPR) and with its Jewish unit. Liebeskind's aim was to launch a large-scale attack on the Germans inside Kraków. On December 22, 1942, The Fighting Organization of the Pioneering Jewish Youth and the Jewish unit of the PPR attacked German targets in Kraków. They inflicted many casualties on the Germans, but following the attack, the headquarters and most of the members of the Fighting Organization fell into German hands. On December 24 Liebeskind was caught in the headquarters bunker and killed in a hand-to-hand fight.

See also **YOUTH MOVEMENTS**.

Aharon Liebeskind.

Zionist
A political movement that promoted the creation of a homeland for Jews in Palestine.

> Since the Nazi presence during World War II polluted neither the American language nor American soil, factors other than first-hand experience of war and mass murder necessarily influence the American encounter with the subject of the Holocaust.

SUGGESTED RESOURCES

Cohen, Asher. *The Halutz Resistance in Hungary 1942–1944.* New York : Institute for Holocaust Studies of the City University of New York : Distributed by Columbia University Press, 1986.

The Ghetto Fighters' House Museum of the Holocaust and Resistance. [Online] http://www.amfriendsgfh.org/Docs/gfh.html (accessed on September 1, 2000).

Rescue and Resistance: Portraits of the Holocaust. New York: Macmillan Library Reference USA, 1999.

Literature on the Holocaust

For the most part, Americans have confronted the **HOLOCAUST** only vicariously, through the experiences and expressions of others, although American soldiers who fought in Europe and the refugees who settled in the **UNITED STATES** certainly have personal memories which influence their perspectives on the topic.

Jewish Culture in American Literature

Emotional responses toward the Jewish catastrophe shifted in the long aftermath of the war. They reflect changing perceptions of the place of the Jew in the Western mind, as well as changing definitions of the American self in relation to its European roots. Of course, distinctions should be made between specifically Jewish literature in America and literature written by Americans who had no direct or indirect connections with the civilization that was destroyed.

American identity was—and continues to be—carved out in juxtaposition with the European past and European culture. However, the specifically Jewish culture of central and eastern Europe began to be an ingredient in American consciousness only from the beginning of the twentieth century, when masses of Jews from Russia and **POLAND** migrated westward. In the decades that followed, an ethnically specific, almost "regional" Jewish literature evolved in America. It was nourished by memories of the European homeland, by the flourishing of Yiddish culture in large urban centers, and by the drama and conflicts of the immigrant experience.

By the mid-1940s, a first generation of native sons and daughters had emerged to claim their literary birth-right. So distinctive was their stake in American culture—and so estranged had many of them become from Jewish communities elsewhere in the world—that in February 1944 the editors of the journal *Contemporary Jewish Record* could conduct a symposium on the centrality of Jewish writing in the United States without making any direct reference to the mass murder that had already reached its final stages in Nazi Europe.

In response to the questions posed by the editors of the symposium, the writer Delmore Schwartz insisted that "the fact of being a Jew became available to me as a central symbol of alienation" and poet Isaac Rosenfeld wrote that the Jew is a "specialist in alienation." The editorial presumption that the children of Jewish immigrants had reached the "front ranks of American literature" and the Jewish writer's assumption of what would become the rather fashionable posture of "alienation" were both a far cry from any identification or even empathy with the actual suffering of Jews in Europe who were, quite literally, *alien* and outcast.

A generic memory rather than an active historical consciousness seems to have fostered a sense of Jewish marginality among these writers. It became more of an

A Cartload of Shoes

The wheels hurry onward, onward.
What do they carry?
They carry a cartload
Of shivering shoes.

The wagon like a canopy
In the evening light;
The shoes—clustered
Like people in a dance.

A wedding, a holiday?
Has something blinded my eyes?
The shoes—I seem
To recognize them.

The heels go tapping
With a clatter and a din.
From our old Vilna streets
They drive us to Berlin.

I should not ask
But something tears at my tongue
Shoes, tell me the truth
Where are they, the feet?

The feet from those boots
With button like dew—
And here, where is the body
And there, where is the bride?

Where is the child
To fill those shoes
Why has the bride
Gone barefoot?

Through the slippers and the boots
I see those my mother used to wear
She kept them for the Sabbath
Her favourite pair.

And the heels go tapping:
With a clatter and a din,
From our old Vilna streets
They drive us to Berlin.

—ABRAHAM SUTZKEVER
TRANSLATED BY DAVID G. ROSKIES

Holocaust Poetry, *compiled and introduced by Hilda Schiff (London: Fount Paperbacks, 1995).*

existential dilemma, a voluntary moral stance, rather than a historically determined condition. The editors of this 1944 symposium noted "ANTISEMITISM" in passing as if it were a kind of social disease. The Jewish fiction that appeared during the immediate postwar years evinces a similar psychosocial approach to racial prejudice as an indwelling but intangible threat. For example, Arthur Miller's *Focus*, Saul Bellow's *The Victim*, and Laura Hobson's *Gentleman's Agreement* all revolve around the Jew who, having been identified (or misidentified) primarily by his appearance, is isolated as a social scapegoat. Two of the themes that dominate this fiction of the 1940s will reemerge later: that of the mistaken (or ambiguous) identity of the Jew based on external traits and that of the social role of the Jew as victim or sacrifice.

Literary Responses to the Holocaust

Specific literary responses to the Holocaust would eventually be shaped by three processes that related only marginally to the events that had taken place in Europe:

1. the return of the American soldiers who had participated in the defeat of **GERMANY** and the liberation of the **EXTERMINATION CAMPS**;

2. the arrival and growing impact of large numbers of survivors; and

3. the trial of Adolf **EICHMANN**, which took place some sixteen years after the war.

> The first specific American encounter with the fate of the Jews of Europe can be found in the stories and poems of American soldiers who encountered traces of starvation, disease, torture, and mass murder when they helped to liberate the concentration camps at the end of the war.

SOLDIER-LITERATURE Examples of "soldier-literature" include William Hoffman's *The Trumpet Unblown* and Stefan Heym's *The Crusaders*. The horrifying sight of piles of mutilated, undifferentiated corpses so exceeded the grasp of the imagination of even the soldier hardened to death and disfiguration on the battlefield that words could barely contain their impressions. For instance, in Randall Jarrell's poem "A Camp in the Prussian Forest" (1948), the very syntax is mutilated in the effort to convey unprecedented reality: "Here men were drunk like water, burnt like wood." In much of this writing, the shock of the encounter is so great that it even precludes the normal compassionate response to tragedy. The soldier-literature did succeed in making Americans more aware of the camps, but it would take many years for the subject to achieve human scale in the imagination.

VICTIM TESTIMONY In the decade or so following the war, while the historical evidence mounted, a certain cultural numbness continued to prevail, resembling in its effect a conspiracy of silence. *The Diary of Anne Frank* helps to illustrate the slowly evolving attitudes toward this subject throughout the 1950s. At first the book was rejected by several editors in the United States who were convinced that there would be no market for it because the "public shie[s] away from such material." Likewise potential producers of the dramatic adaptation claimed that audiences would not "come to the theater to watch on the stage people they know to have ended up in the crematorium; it would be too painful" (Levin, *The Obsession*).

Eventually, both the book and the play reached audiences numbering probably in the millions. But it may be that the published version of the *Diary*—and to an even greater extent the American-written and American-produced play based upon it—enjoyed the popularity they did precisely because they did *not* contain any scenes of horror or computation of loss and because of their comfortable affirmation of the ultimate triumph of the forces of good over evil.

Ten years after the concentration camps were liberated, audiences who should have known better were eagerly applauding Anne's final statement that "it will all come right," and embracing a drama that had largely sanitized the story of its Jewish particularity (see Bruno Bettelheim's "The Ignored Lesson of Anne Frank" in *Surviving*).

A satiric example of how Anne Frank has entered the myths of American culture in the most benign way can be found in Philip Roth's *The Ghostwriter* (1979). The narrator, an aspiring Jewish writer, has fallen in love with a beautiful refugee whom he believes to be Anne Frank (somewhere in the American imagination, that is, she is still alive). He brings his fiancée home to meet his parents, who ask the natural question: "Is she Jewish?" "Yes, she is," he answers sheepishly. "But who is

she?" "Anne Frank." It is in the satirized Hollywood fantasy of such a happy ending that the implications of the refrain "it will all come right" can be appreciated.

EICHMANN TRIAL   The trial of Adolf Eichmann in Jerusalem in 1961 marked a turning point in worldwide Jewish consciousness and had a two-pronged impact on the American imagination. In the first place, as people analyzed Eichmann's psyche and his political function in the Nazi machine, material became available to writers that had previously been cast into the safe realm of a "demonic otherness." Additionally, survivor testimony at the trial demonstrated the poetic potential of the individual's struggle against the collective fate.

Author Hannah Arendt's theory of the banalization of evil (*Eichmann in Jerusalem*), influenced a new literary approach whereby Nazi evil could be tamed and incorporated into the human drama. In the two decades following the Eichmann trial, a kind of "fascination with Nazism" (see Saul Friedländer's *Reflections of Nazism*) came to inform both popular and serious culture in America and in Western Europe. At the level of lowbrow fiction and film, it fed sensationalist, sado-masochistic fantasies (see Alvin Rosenfeld's *Imagining Hitler*); at the level of serious literature and drama, it probed the capacity for evil in Everyman.

Numerous European-produced movies and plays explored the average citizen's collaboration with Nazism as a natural social phenomenon—an indictment of the system rather than of any of the individuals serving it. These were very well received by American audiences (Klaus Mann's *Mephisto*; C. P. Taylor's *Good*). Several American novelists and playwrights expressed variations on that theme through an elaborate confusion of identities. In William Styron's *Sophie's Choice*, the presumption of the banality and universality of the Nazi mentality crystallizes in the person of Nathan, a Jew whose sadistic conduct toward Sophie, the (non-Jewish) concentration camp survivor, cannot be differentiated from that of Hitler's henchmen. In fact, in the same novel, the historical Nazi, Rudolf Höss, commandant of Auschwitz, appears as rather pleasant and eminently human.

Along similar lines, Robert Shaw's *The Man in the Glass Booth*, modeled after the Eichmann trial, confounds and universalizes Nazi identity by presenting the main character as a Jew posing as a Nazi posing as a Jew. This principle of interchangeable identities dissolves the gap between victims and victimizers, between the human and the demonic (see also Arthur Miller's *Incident at Vichy*).

Whereas the sensational appearance of the Nazi has a primarily titillating effect in pornographic literature, the admission of the Nazi bureaucrat into the family of man resonates quite differently in the serious work of the imagination. Consistent with the twentieth-century American tendency to approach behavior on psychological rather than moral grounds, this strategy leaves nothing out of bounds or unapproachable. The most extreme expression of this theme may be Jerzy Kosinski's novel *The Painted Bird*, in which a child—normally represented as the last bastion of innocence, even in a war-torn world—is so utterly corrupted by his environment that, as an act of revenge or gratuitous violence, he derails a trainload of peasants. Whatever humanizing effects it is meant to have on the encounter between the self and its darkest impulses, the leveling of the human tendency for evil also contributes to a blurring of the lines of historical accountability.

Survivor Stories

Parallel and in some respects contrary to these developments has been the emergence (also in the wake of the Eichmann trial) of survivor voices, many of which had fallen silent after they reached American shores.

> The procession of witnesses who testified at the Eichmann trial seemed for the first time to show Holocaust victims as individuals, not anonymous statistics of the Nazi machine. They also highlighted the pathos of the victim's lonely struggle for survival.

Elie WIESEL's was one of the first and most enduring of the survivor voices. Although he writes in French, the impact of his novels and his public presence is most keenly felt in the United States, which he made his home after leaving Europe. Wiesel's first book, *Night*, is both an act of confession and commemoration and a claim for the historical foundation of all the fiction to come. As autobiography, it stretches the genre to its very limits, tracing not the growth but the utter collapse of the integrity of all life-support systems surrounding the young adolescent. In *Night* the American reader encountered the kind of text that Anne Frank might have written had she survived Bergen-Belsen; it is not a story in which it "all comes right."

The narratives of survival, autobiographical and fictional, proliferated and reached wide audiences in America in the decades following the Eichmann trial. The survivor—as writer and as persona—began to emerge as a new kind of hero against a landscape of mass murder. This literature is a far cry from the stories of successful immigrants that make up the melting-pot saga of early twentieth-century America, the Horatio Alger tales of impoverished new Americans who reconstruct their lives in the land of freedom and promise. Nevertheless, they owe much of their impact to the American elevation of the individual in his or her struggle against circumstance.

A few of these narratives were written in English by survivors who had mastered the language of their adopted country (Ilona Karmel's *An Estate of Memory*); the others reached American readers in translation. American-born Jewish writers may have found in these autobiographical fictions a set of literary conventions that would enable them to enter previously uncharted regions (E. L. Wallant's *The Pawnbroker*; Saul Bellow's *Mr. Sammler's Planet*; Susan Fromberg-Schaeffer's *Anya*).

The Pawnbroker (1961) is one of the earliest fictional attempts to reconstruct the postwar life of the survivor in America; the way in which the embittered Sol Nazerman is finally able to confront his repressed memories of torture and loss and to enter a space normally reserved for heroes in American fiction is to become, along with his assistant ("Jesus"), a kind of expiatory Christ figure. The Jew as sufferer and as sacrificial victim thus reemerges schematically in the 1960s and 1970s in the portrait of the survivor or refugee (see also the fiction of Bernard Malamud).

Object Lessons Shaping Cultural and Human Identity

Over the years the events in Europe, which had been, for most American Jews, just beyond the orbit of their own experience and had in fact tested the boundaries of their own identity (see, for example, Philip Roth's early story "Eli the Fanatic"), became a focus of identification with the remnants of Jewish collectives elsewhere. After a generation or two of deliberate disengagement from the European motherland, the idea of "peoplehood" is reaffirmed partly through the imaginative return to ruined communities in Eastern Europe.

But all these processes are disciplined by the larger context in which the minor dramas of an ethnic subculture are being played out. American culture has largely resisted sectarian efforts to mythicize the Holocaust—primarily through monumental acts of commemoration—as a cluster of events somehow central to the American ethos or collective memory. In the Israeli context, the narratives by and about survivors encounter and are included in a powerful national myth of catastrophe and regeneration. In contrast, the survivors and their dead are assimilated into American culture primarily as individuals whose stories are read as object lessons in the power and limits of the human spirit in the face of adversity.

SUGGESTED RESOURCES

Aaron, Frieda W. *Bearing the Unbearable: Yiddish and Polish Poetry in the Ghettos and Concentration Camps.* Albany: State University of New York Press, 1990.

Clendinnen, Inga. *Reading the Holocaust.* New York: Cambridge University Press, 1999.

Kremer, S. Lillian. *Witness Through the Imagination: Jewish-American Holocaust Literature.* Detroit: Wayne State University Press, 1989.

Kremer, S. Lillian. *Women's Holocaust Writing: Memory and Imagination.* Lincoln: University of Nebraska Press, 1999.

Lang, Berel, ed. *Writing and the Holocaust.* New York: Holmes and Meier, 1988.

Meredith, James H. *Understanding the Literature of World War II: A Student Casebook to Issues, Sources, and Historical Documents.* Westport, CT: Greenwood Press, 1999.

Lithuania

Lithuania, southernmost of the Baltic States, was a republic of the SOVIET UNION from 1940, until declaring its independence in 1991, except for the period of German occupation between 1941 and 1945. The country's history can be traced to the thirteenth century when the Lithuanians, who fought the Slavs and the German Teutonic Order, founded a strong state. Between the thirteenth and fifteenth centuries Lithuania became a great power, extending from the Baltic Sea to the Black Sea including within its territories what is today Belarus, most of the areas of the UKRAINE, and broad expanses of western Russia. The majority of the inhabitants of Lithuania were then Slavs. In the late fourteenth century Lithuania became allied with POLAND, and in 1569 the two countries united, with Lithuania as the lesser partner in the united state. In the third partition of Poland, in 1795, Lithuania was annexed to Russia. Between World War I and World War II, however, it was an independent country.

Lithuania was in conflict with Poland (which in 1920 occupied VILNA, the historic capital) and later with GERMANY, because Lithuania controlled Memel (Klaipéda), most of whose inhabitants were Germans and which had special status as an autonomous territory. Independent Lithuania suffered from economic and social problems, had many national minorities (constituting about a fifth of all the inhabitants), and was politically unstable. After a military coup in 1926, Antanas Smetona became president and leader of the fascist Iron Wolf (Gelezinis Vilkas) organization, and Augustinas Voldemaras was prime minister. In 1929 Voldemaras was dismissed, and Smetona became sole ruler.

German Occupation

On March 23, 1939, Germany annexed Memel. The agreements between Germany and the Soviet Union in the wake of the Nazi-Soviet Pact placed Lithuania in the Soviet sphere of influence, and on October 10 of that year, Lithuania was compelled to permit the establishment of Soviet bases on its territory. Vilna, together with a surrounding area of about 3,475 square miles (9,000 square kilometers), was restored to Lithuania (from Poland) on October 30. On June 15, 1940, the Soviet army assumed control of Lithuania, and about seven weeks later the country was officially annexed to the Soviet Union as the Lithuanian SSR.

A number of underground groups formed in reaction to the Soviet occupation of the country. One of these extremist nationalist groups was the Lithuanian

In the first years of Lithuanian independence after World War I, the Jews enjoyed national and cultural autonomy, and a Jewish minister was responsible for their affairs. Even after this autonomy was repealed in 1924, the Jews continued to maintain their own Hebrew and Yiddish educational network. However, the authorities began to systematically exclude the Jews from various sectors of the economy, and there was strong antisemitism in the country. Between the two world wars more than 20,000 Jews left Lithuania, almost half of them emigrating to Palestine.

Activist Front (Lietuviu Aktyvistu Frontas), which strongly supported Nazi Germany. On June 14, 1941, the Soviets exiled tens of thousands of Lithuanians, who were defined as "enemies of the people" and whom the Soviets considered politically or socially unreliable. About a week later, on June 22, the Germans invaded the Soviet Union and occupied all of Lithuania; Lithuanian underground activists followed in the wake of the retreating Soviet army. In the few days it took to occupy Lithuania, most of the leaders and activists of the Soviet rule and of the Lithuanian Communist party fled into the Soviet Union, along with many citizens who did not wish to remain under Nazi occupation.

Most of the gentile Lithuanians welcomed the Germans, and many collaborated with them. Nonetheless, their hope of renewed political independence was disappointed. Lithuania became part of the Reichskommissariat Ostland (Reich Commissariat for Ostland), and its name was changed to General District of Lithuania (Generalbezirk Litauen). It was headed by a German *Generalkommissar* who had a ministerial council (*Generalrat*) consisting of well-known Lithuanian personalities. The Lithuanian national army was not rebuilt, and several of its former officers and soldiers were incorporated into the Lithuanian police battalions. In the wake of the German collapse on the Stalingrad front, the relations of the Lithuanians with the Nazi occupation authorities deteriorated. When the Soviet army returned to Lithuania in the summer and fall of 1944, however, many Lithuanians fled to Germany. With the German expulsion from Memel in January 1945, Nazi rule in all parts of Lithuania came to an end, and Lithuania became once more a Soviet republic.

When Vilna and its vicinity were returned to Lithuania in October 1939, the Jewish population of the country grew by about 100,000. This number included an additional 15,000 refugees from occupied Poland, bringing the total number of Jews to approximately a quarter of a million, about 10 percent of the overall population in Lithuania at that time.

Frustrated by the 1939 Nazi agreement with the Soviet Union, which took away Lithuanian sovereignty, the Lithuanian people greatly increased attacks on Jews and Jewish property. With the entry of the Lithuanian army into Vilna, pogroms were conducted against the Jews with the blessing of the new government, and hundreds of Jews were injured.

Jews in Lithuania

Jews lived in Lithuania beginning in the fourteenth century. From the seventeenth century onward, the country's *yeshivas* (rabbinical academies) attained worldwide fame. In the nineteenth century Lithuania was a center of many Jewish religious and cultural trends. From the end of the nineteenth century onward, it was also a seat of strong **Zionist** thinking and support for Zionist organizations. In the wake of the tsarist-instigated pogroms of 1881 and 1882, many Lithuanian Jews emigrated, principally to the **UNITED STATES** and also to South Africa. Of the masses of Jews who were expelled from Lithuania to Russia during World War I, many never returned. About 150,000 Jews lived in independent Lithuania after World War I.

Zionist
A political movement that promoted the creation of a homeland for Jews in Palestine.

Lithuanian Jewry Under Soviet Rule

The situation of Lithuanian Jewry changed dramatically when the country became a Soviet republic. On the one hand, the Jews were given appropriate representation in the government bodies, the institutions of higher education were opened to them, and they were allowed to join the local and central official establishment, previously closed to them. On the other hand, they were affected significantly by Soviet economic policies. For example, 83 percent of the commercial establishments and 57 percent of the factories that were nationalized belonged to Jews. The Hebrew educational system, encompassing 80 percent of the Jewish pupils, was abolished. The renowned rabbinical academies of Telz, Slobodka, Kelme, and other places were closed down. Jewish workers were compelled to work on the Sabbath and on Jewish holidays, violating their religious beliefs. Political bodies were also closed, apart from the Communist organizations, and almost all the cultural and welfare institutions were shut down with many of their leaders and activists arrested. In the June 14, 1941, mass deportation of "enemies of the people," about 7,000 Jews were exiled to Siberia and other areas of Soviet Asia, 3 percent of all the Jews in Lithuania, as compared to only 1 percent of the rest of the population. Deported heads of families were interned in labor camps and many died as a result of the harsh conditions.

Although the Jews suffered greatly and were severely oppressed under Soviet rule, the Lithuanians regarded them as supporters of the Soviet regime that had enslaved their country. The Lithuanian Activist Front agitated against the Jews. The bulletins it circulated before the anticipated Nazi invasion contained concrete threats against the Jews. Upon the invasion in June 1941, many Lithuanian Jews desperately attempted to flee for their lives in the wake of the retreating Soviet army. However, because of German shelling, difficulties in crossing the old Soviet border, and attacks by Lithuanian underground groups, only about 15,000 Jews succeeded in reaching the Soviet Union. More than a third of these fought the Nazis actively. The overwhelming majority of Lithuanian Jewry, about 220,000 people, remained in their homes. During the Soviet occupation and before the German occupation, the Lithuanians carried out vicious pogroms against the Jews. According to findings based on reliable testimonies from 214 localities, pogroms occurred in at least 40 places, where hundreds if not thousands of Jews were killed and injured. In at least 25 localities, rapes took place, and in 36 areas, rabbis and other community leaders were cruelly abused.

Lithuanian Jews Under German Occupation

The wave of murders and assaults grew with the entry of the German forces, and principally of the **OPERATIONAL SQUADS** (*Einsatzgruppen*). On July 3, 1941, a systematic program of exterminating all of Lithuanian Jewry began. Many of the stages of the extermination, such as confining and guarding the victims, then transporting them to the massacre sites, were carried out by Lithuanian soldiers and policemen. Before being killed, the victims were made to perform physical exercises, to sing and dance, or to strike each other in front of their Lithuanian neighbors, public figures, and heads of the local intelligentsia, who took great delight in this spectacle. In forty-eight localities, individual Jews offered concrete or symbolic resistance. But only in a few instances did any of the victims succeed in escaping from the murder site.

By late 1941 only 40,000 Jews remained in all of Lithuania, and they were concentrated in four ghettos—those of Vilna, **KOVNO**, Šiauliai, and Švenčionys—and in several labor camps. About eight hundred Jews from the towns of western Lithuania were in a labor camp at Heidekrug, in the Memel district. In 1943 the survivors were transferred to **AUSCHWITZ** and from there to **WARSAW**, to work on clearing the ruins of the ghetto. In the summer and fall of that year the ghettos of Vilna and Švenčionys were liquidated, and those of Kovno and Šiauliai became concentration camps, with branches in their vicinities. Approximately 15,000 Jews were transferred

> In July and August 1941 the overwhelming majority of the Jews in the provinces were slaughtered. From September to November, most of the Jews in the large cities, who had been forced into in ghettos, were liquidated in a similar fashion.

Lithuanian militiamen watch the arrival of Jewish women who were brought from the Kovno ghetto.

to labor camps in **LATVIA** and Estonia, where they died. About 5,000 Jews, principally old people, women, and children, were directly sent to extermination camps.

In the second half of 1943 and early in 1944 more than 2,000 Jews escaped from the ghettos and camps. About half of them joined partisan units. The rest, mainly families, found hiding places in monasteries and in the homes of non-Jews in cities and towns. Shortly before withdrawing from Lithuania in the summer of 1944, the Germans transferred about 10,000 of the Jews of Kovno and Šiauliai to concentration camps in Germany. Many who attempted to resist were murdered. Numerous Lithuanian collaborators and killers of Jews accompanied the retreating Nazis.

When Germany surrendered in May 1945, few Lithuanian Jews interned in the concentration camps remained alive. The overall number of Lithuanian Jews who survived in the area under Nazi rule is estimated at 8,000. In places under Soviet rule, about 10 percent of all the Jews living in Lithuania in early 1941 survived, including the fighters in the ranks of the **PARTISANS**.

Soon after the liberation of Lithuania, in the second half of 1944, the Soviet authorities made great efforts to uncover mass-murder sites of **PRISONERS OF WAR** and civilians, and through inquiry commissions to determine circumstances of the slaughter and the number and identity of the victims. At some of the sites monuments were erected with inscriptions in Russian and Lithuanian. The victims were generally commemorated only as Soviet citizens, without mention of their ethnic affiliation. In a few places, after repeated requests to the authorities, Jewish survivors who had raised money were allowed to erect monuments with inscriptions in Yiddish and in Hebrew.

Postwar Years

In the early postwar years and later, many of the Lithuanians who had collaborated with the Nazi occupation authorities were identified, including many of the murderers of the Jews. Some were tried and received sentences ranging from a defined period of imprisonment to execution. The Lithuanians and other killers who had fled to Germany and to countries overseas were tried *in absentia*. Some of them not only found refuge but also integrated successfully into the life of their adopted countries. Only in the 1980s did the American, Canadian, and Australian governments begin to pursue the killers of the Jews, and several were brought to trial. Lithuanian immigrants in these and other countries fiercely opposed exposing the collaborators and perpetrators of the crimes. Financial, political and legal efforts were made to prevent the trials from taking place.

SUGGESTED RESOURCES

Birger, Zev. *No Time for Patience: My Road from Kaunas to Jerusalem.* New York: Newmarket Press, 1999.

Gitelman, Zvi, ed. *Bitter Legacy: Confronting the Holocaust in the USSR.* Bloomington: Indiana University Press, 1997.

Kovno Ghetto: A Buried History [videorecording]. History Channel, 1997.

Łódź

Łódź, a city in **POLAND**, is located about 75 miles (121 kilometers) southwest of **WARSAW**, the capital. In 1827 the population of Łódź was 2,800, of whom 400 were Jews. The city grew rapidly as a result of the development of industry, especially textiles. The Jewish population also grew considerably. Before long Łódź became Poland's second largest city, next only to Warsaw, and the city's Jews came to compose the second largest Jewish community in Poland, after Warsaw. By 1857 the Łódź population was 25,000, including 2,900 Jews. At the end of the nineteenth century it was 300,000, a third being Jews. On the eve of World War II the population had risen to 665,000, of which 34 percent (223,000) were Jews.

The Jews contributed much to the growth of the city. Many of the industrial enterprises were founded by Jews, and more than 50 percent of the Jewish population derived their livelihood from industry. This economic class of industrial workers accounted for much of the Łódź Jewish community's unique character.

Łódź was also an important center of Jewish culture. Its network of Jewish schools included three Hebrew secondary schools, and numerous yeshivas. There were libraries, Jewish theaters, and sports clubs. Outstanding intellectuals, scientists, and artists lived in Łódź, among them poets and writers as well as painters and musicians. Before the outbreak of World War II, the city had two Yiddish and two Polish daily newspapers. There was a great deal of political and social activity among Łódź Jewry.

Early Stage of Nazi Occupation

On September 8, 1939, the Germans occupied Łódź, making it part of the Warthegau (western Poland after its annexation to **GERMANY**). On April 11, 1940,

---

Brutal persecution of the Jews began as soon as Łódź was occupied. The riots, the abduction of people for forced labor, and the harassment of passersby in the streets all soon led to the collapse of the economic and social life of the Jews in the city. Jewish public and cultural institutions were abolished overnight.

yeshivas
Centers for rabbinical studies.

Jewish policeman and a German soldier direct people across the main street which divided the Łódź ghetto.

the occupiers renamed the city Litzmannstadt (after the German general Karl Litzmann, who had conquered it in World War I).

The German authorities began to issue one decree after another designed to make life miserable for the Jews. On September 18, 1939, a number of decrees were put into effect that struck at the heart of the economic life of the Jews. All Jewish-owned bank accounts were blocked, and Jewish cash holdings were restricted. Jews could no longer engage in the textile business, and Jewish enterprises were confiscated and taken over by Germans. Jews could no longer use public transportation, could not leave the city without special permission, and were not allowed to have cars, radios, and various other items in their possession. Synagogue services were outlawed, and Jews had to keep their shops open on Jewish holidays.

On October 13 and 14, 1939, the Germans appointed a **JUDENRAT** (Jewish Council), which was to operate under the strict supervision of the **GESTAPO**. Mordechai Chaim **RUMKOWSKI** was chosen as its chairman.

On November 9, when Łódź was officially annexed to the Reich, the German terrorization of the Jews and Poles intensified. The Germans destroyed all the synagogues in the city, among them the magnificent Reform Synagoga and the Altschule synagogue, dating from 1809. On November 17 Jews were forced to wear yellow badges (*see* **BADGE, JEWISH**) in the form of a Star of David.

From the very beginning of the occupation Jews were subject to expulsions. In the first few weeks hundreds of Jewish apartments were confiscated and their tenants deported. On November 12 a decision was made to launch mass **DEPORTATIONS**, which were to affect 30,000 Jews and an equal number of Poles. By March

1940, 70,000 Jews had left the city, among them those who fled by choice. However, most of the Jews were deported by the Germans, who intended to reduce the Jewish population substantially or even remove it completely.

Establishing the Ghetto

On December 10, 1939, a secret order was issued for the establishment of a ghetto in the northern section of Łódź, where the Jewish Baluty slum quarter was situated. In early February 1940 Jews from the other parts of the city were moved to the ghetto area, a process accompanied by intensified robbery, harassment, and murder.

The ghetto comprised an area of 1.54 square miles (4 square kilometers), of which only .96 square miles (2.5 square kilometers) was built up. Approximately 164,000 Łódź Jews were forced in. In 1941 and 1942 some 38,500 Jews from outside Łódź were moved in. Ultimately, the population in the ghetto totaled 204,800 Jewish men, women, and children. The density of population in the ghetto area was several times as great as it had been before the war.

Nazi Administration

The running of the Łódź ghetto was in the hands of a ghetto administration headed by Hans **Biebow**. The Gestapo section for Jewish affairs in Łódź, Section IV B 4, was also involved in the administration. On May 25, 1940, Biebow issued orders for factories to be set up in the ghetto. Exploiting the Jews of the ghetto as very cheap labor, these factories were to serve the Nazis as a source of easy profits. The Jews in the ghetto, cut off as they were from all other possible sources of livelihood, were prepared to work for no more than a loaf of bread and some soup.

The German authorities allowed the Judenrat, and primarily its chairman, Rumkowski, wide powers in the organization of the ghetto's internal life. The Judenrat's main task was to organize the operation of the factories. It regarded the establishment of factories as the only possible means of saving the ghetto population from unemployment and starvation. The services provided by the Judenrat involved housing and sanitation, as well as the distribution of the small quantities of food permitted by the German authorities. Until October 1941 the Judenrat ran a school system, consisting of 45 elementary schools and two secondary schools, which were attended by 15,000 pupils. Five hospitals were in operation in the ghetto up until the summer of 1942. Internal order in the ghetto was maintained by the Judenrat's **Jewish Ghetto Police** (*Jüdischer Ordnungsdienst*). The Judenrat also administered a prison.

Living Conditions in the Ghetto

The Łódź ghetto had a high mortality rate owing to the extremely poor conditions. The worst affliction of all, however, was starvation. This was the chief problem the ghetto had to contend with throughout its existence. The average daily food ration per person was less than 1,100 calories.

Some 43,500 persons—21 percent of all the inmates—died in the ghetto from starvation, cold, and disease. The mortality rate reached its peak in 1942. The smaller number of deaths from "natural" causes in 1943 was due to the fact that by then most of the children and elderly people had died or been deported. Even so, the 1943 mortality rate was six times that in the prewar period.

> **B**y September 1942 the ghetto had become a single large forced-labor camp: 90 percent of its population was employed in the factories, and only a few children and old people were still to be found.

Deportation

These diary excerpts recall the devastating deportation from the Łódź ghetto of the sick, the elderly, and the children under ten.

Friday, September 4, 1942. The deportation of children and old people is a fact.

This morning the ghetto received a horrifying shock: What seemed improbable and incredible news yesterday has now become a dreadful fact. Children up to the age of ten are to be torn away from their parents, brothers and sisters, and deported. Old people over 65 are being robbed of their last life-saving plank, which they have been clutching with their last bits of strength—their four walls and their beds. They are being sent away like useless ballast....

All hearts are icy, all hands are wrung, all eyes filled with despair. All faces are twisted, all heads bowed to the ground, all blood weeps....

People say: The children are to be taken from their parents as early as today....They are to be sent away—where?...

There are children who do indeed understand. In the ghetto, ten-year-old children are mature adults. They already know and understand what is in

Deportations

Even more devastating than the mass deaths and the hunger from which the ghetto population suffered were the deportations. In the first stage, from December 1940 to June 1942, deportations were to forced-labor camps outside the ghetto, and from there the Jews were sent on to extermination camps. Generally speaking, the Jews imprisoned in the ghetto were not aware of the final destination of the deportations nor of the fate awaiting the deportees.

From January to May 1942, the deportations from the Łódź ghetto went directly to the **Chełmno** extermination camp. Upon their arrival there, all deportees were killed with poison gas (*see* **Gas Chambers/Vans**). The German authorities forced Rumkowski to draw up the lists of candidates for deportation. Rumkowski tried vainly to persuade the Germans to reduce the number of deportees.

Between September 5 and 12 of 1942, a second deportation operation to Chełmno took place. This time the Germans did not require lists from the Judenrat: German forces entered the ghetto, blocked off one section after another, and dragged the Jews out of their homes, using extremely brutal methods in the process. Then, in a heart-breaking episode for the Jews, the Germans chose for deportation those who were less fit for work—children, the elderly, and the infirm. Nearly 20,000 Jews were then deported to Chełmno. Hundreds more were murdered on the spot, while the deportation was in progress. The Germans proclaimed a general

store for them. They may not as yet know why they are being torn away from their parents—they may not as yet have been told. For the moment it's enough for them to know that they are being torn away from their devoted guardians, their fathers and their loving and anxious mothers. It's hard to keep such children in one's arms or to take them by the hand. Such children go out into the streets on their own. Such children weep on their own, with their own tears. Their tears are so sharp and piercing that they fall upon all hearts like poisoned arrows. But hearts in the ghetto have turned to stone. They would rather burst but they can't, and this is probably the greatest, the harshest curse....

Saturday, September 5, 1942. It has begun.

It's only a few minutes after 7 a.m. now. All the people, practically the entire ghetto, are on the street. Whose nerves don't drive them out? Who can sit at home? Who has peace of mind? Who can just sit with his arms folded? No one!...

—JOSEF ZELKOWICZ: DAYS OF NIGHTMARE

A Holocaust Reader, *Lucy S. Dawidowicz, editor (New York: Berhman House), 1976, pp. 298–309.*

curfew in the ghetto, a *Gehsperre* (ban on movement), and that week of bloody murder came to be known as the *Sperre* by the surviving ghetto inhabitants, a term that became deeply imbedded in their memory.

Between September 1942 and May 1944, when the final liquidation of the ghetto was undertaken, there were no more deportations to extermination camps. In effect, the ghetto had become a single large forced-labor camp: 90 percent of its population was employed in the factories, and only a few children and old people were still to be found. The ghetto population at the end of that period, in May 1944, was 77,000.

Ghetto Activities and the Underground

The ghetto as a whole was isolated from the world and had no contacts with any outside organization, either with Jews in other ghettos or with the Polish underground. However, throughout its existence, the ghetto was the scene of animated illegal political, public, and cultural activities.

Public activities in the summer and fall of 1940 concentrated on a search for solutions to the enormous problems of unemployment and lack of food. Mass demonstrations were held to put pressure on the Judenrat to distribute the small amount of food supplied to the ghetto on a more evenhanded basis. These strikes went on as long as the ghetto existed.

The underground organizations in the ghetto were helpless in the face of the deportations to the extermination camps. Although no clear-cut information on the existence of such camps had come to their knowledge, the Jews of the Łódź ghetto sensed the danger faced by the deportees. The underground organizations sharply denounced the Judenrat, and Rumkowski in particular, for having drawn up the lists of candidates for deportation in the first half of 1942. Rumkowski's policy was condemned, but the Łódź ghetto underground was unable to come up with any alternative.

Liquidation

In the spring of 1944 the Nazis decided to liquidate the Łódź ghetto, and they reactivated the Chełmno extermination camp with this purpose in mind. On June 23 the deportations to Chełmno were resumed, on the pretext that they were forced-labor transports to Germany. The method used in early 1942 was revived, and the Judenrat was again forced to organize the transports. By July 15, 7,176 persons had been transferred to Chełmno to be killed there. After August 7, the destination of the deportations was **AUSCHWITZ**. The transports were organized in haste, and the operation took on the form of an evacuation. Section after section of the ghetto was cleared and searched for people in hiding. Each section was then declared out of bounds, and anyone found there was sentenced to death.

The ghetto population resisted only passively, the Jews making desperate efforts to avoid deportation in the hope that the city would soon be liberated by the advancing Soviet army. The last transport left the Łódź ghetto on August 30, 1944. By then, 74,000 persons had been deported to Auschwitz. Six hundred Jews were put into a camp on Jakuba Street, where they were forced to collect the possessions of the Jews who had been deported and prepare them for transmission to Germany. The camp came to be known as the *Aufräumungskommando* ("tidying-up detachment").

The Nazis planned to kill all the prisoners in the Jakuba Street camp before retreating from the area, and they had prepared pits for this purpose in the Jewish cemetery grounds. The prisoners became aware of these plans, and at the appropriate moment they managed to escape and take refuge in the ghetto area. By then numbering about 800, these prisoners were finally liberated by the Soviet army, on January 19, 1945. No precise figures are available for the number of Łódź ghetto inmates who survived the concentration camps, although estimates range from 5,000 to 7,000.

For several years after the war, Łódź contained the largest concentration of Holocaust survivors in Poland. In late 1945 it had a Jewish population of 38,000. In that period, Łódź was also the leading center of the public and cultural activity of Polish Jewry. In the waves of emigration that took place in 1946–1947, 1956–1957, and 1967–1969, however, nearly all the Jews left Łódź, and only a few hundred elderly Jews remained in the city.

SUGGESTED RESOURCES

Ayer, Eleanor H. *In the Ghettos: Teens Who Survived the Ghettos of the Holocaust.* New York: Rosen Pub. Group, 1999.

Grossman, Mendel. *My Secret Camera: Life in the Łódź Ghetto.* San Diego: Gulliver Books, 2000.

Łódź Ghetto [videorecording]. PBS Home Video/Pacific Arts Video, 1992.

Sender, Ruth Minsky. *The Cage.* New York: Alladin, 1997.

Łódź Ghetto, Chronicles of the

This chronological record of events in the ŁÓDŹ ghetto was started and maintained by the archivists of the JUDENRAT (Jewish Council) in order to document the Nazis' unprecedented campaign of hate and terror against the Jews in POLAND. The team consisted of journalists, writers, and scholars. Outstanding among them were a journalist, Julian Zucker (whose pen name was Stanisław Czerski); an engineer, Bernard Ostrowski; an ethnographer, Joseph Zelikowicz; and Dr. Abraham Shalom Kamenetzki, a biblical scholar. The chronicles were initiated in January 1941 and were kept up without interruption until July 30, 1944. The chronicles were written in Polish until September 1942. But the chronicles' contributors, like other ghetto inhabitants, fell victim to starvation and disease, and they were gradually replaced by Jews who had been deported to the Łódź ghetto from other European countries. As a result, Polish was replaced by German, as a new team made up of Jews from Czechoslovakia and AUSTRIA, headed by Dr. Oskar Rosenfeld and Dr. Oskar Singer, inherited the record-keeping tasks.

Entries in the chronicles were based on documents and information provided to the archive by the various departments of the Jewish ghetto administration, on the instructions of Mordechai Chaim RUMKOWSKI, head of the Judenrat. The daily entries usually included a weather report; statistical data on births and deaths; a list

Fragment from an album secretly produced by chroniclers in the Łódź Ghetto: a collage entitled "45,000 deportees from the ghetto vanish without a trace."

Jewish Ghettos in the Third Reich

In the march toward their "Final Solution"—the extermination of European Jewry—the Nazis segregated and exploited the Jews who came under their administration, forcing them to live in controlled areas called ghettos. There were about 400 such "Jewish quarters." In some smaller communities of German-occupied Poland and the conquered Soviet territories, such as Latvia, the Jews were closely monitored by the Nazis, but were able to remain in their homes in so-called open ghettos. The open ghettos seemed at first like a haven from the upheaval of the war, but their residents were among the first to be shipped off to the Nazi concentration and death camps.

In the ghettos surrounded by guarded walls and fences, the Jews were crowded into unbelievably cramped housing. The ghettos were usually located in the poorest, most dilapidated sections of cities, such as in Łódź and Warsaw, Poland. Jews were forced to leave behind their homes and businesses, and most of their belongings, often at a moment's notice. Their property was then looted and seized by the Nazis. Several million Jews were dealt with in this way.

The Germans ordered that Jewish councils be set up to administer daily life in the ghettos. Food was rationed and in most cases was extremely limited; malnutrition and outright starvation were commonplace. In some ghettos the Jews were able to supplement these rations through bartering or smuggling but there was rarely enough food to go around. Unsanitary conditions prevailed, and there was little medicine or fuel for heating and cooking.

of criminal arrests; a food distribution list; data on health conditions; official statements and announcements; and reports on places where Jews were working, on raids, on expulsions, and on executions. From time to time, the chronicles included articles on life in the ghetto and on the mood of the population, vignettes of everyday life, rumors, and even jokes.

The chronicles are an important authentic source, encompassing nearly all aspects of life in the Łódź ghetto. They are not, however, to be regarded as a document that contains the true and full history of the ghetto. The authors and contributors were supervised by Rumkowski's personal staff and lived in the shadow of the Nazi threat. They had to use cautious and restrained language, even when describing assaults and harassment, expulsions, robberies, and murders. The social life of those Jews in the ghetto who did not belong to the official "establishment" was almost completely ignored.

The chronicles that were saved after the liquidation of the ghetto consist of some two thousand typewritten pages. They are now held in part by the Jewish His-

As the Germans hoped, the hideous living conditions took their toll on the Jewish population. People literally froze to death in the winter, and contagious diseases such as typhus and dysentery were rampant. The Jews were progressively and systematically weakened by intolerable conditions and brutal forced labor. They were also isolated not only from the larger surrounding communities but also from Jews in other ghettos.

As much as possible, the residents of the ghetto tried to create a semblance of normal life. Soup kitchens opened, small cultural events were held, and clandestine schools were operated. Underground resistance organizations were also formed as the deadly aim of the Nazis became clear. Significant uprisings eventually occurred in some ghettos, notably in Warsaw, but the efforts of the resistance groups were severely hampered by lack of access to arms and information.

Records of life in the Jewish ghettos, including the Chronicles of the Łódź Ghetto, offer poignant and contemporary perspectives on the daily life-and-death struggles the Jews confronted under Nazi rule. Written archives, supplemented by survivor testimony and records from Nazi sources, reveal that conditions from one ghetto to another were remarkably similar, varying more in degree than in type of discomfort and hardship.

Deportations from the ghettos began as early as December 1941, but the Nazi push to empty the Jewish ghettos began in earnest in the summer of 1942. Within two years, more than two million Jews had been deported from the ghettos to die. The Nazis were well on the way toward achieving their "Final Solution."

torical Institute (Żydowski Instytut Historyczny) in **Warsaw** and in part by the YIVO Institute for Jewish Research in New York. A photostatic copy is kept in the Yad Vashem archives in Jerusalem. Parts of the chronicles were published in Poland in 1965 and 1966, and an extensive selection taken from all parts of the chronicles was published in English translation in the **United States** in 1984.

SUGGESTED RESOURCES

Dobroszycki, L., ed. *The Chronicle of the Łódź Ghetto, 1941–1944.* New Haven: Yale University Press, 1984.

Grossman, Mendel. *My Secret Camera: Life in the Łódź Ghetto.* San Diego: Gulliver Books, 2000.

Łódź Ghetto [videorecording]. PBS Home Video/Pacific Arts Video, 1992.

Sierakowiak, Dawid. *The Diary of Dawid Sierakowiak: Five Notebooks from the Łódź Ghetto.* New York: Oxford University Press, 1996.

Trunk, Isaiah. *Judenrat: The Jewish Councils in Eastern Europe Under Nazi Occupation.* Lincoln: University of Nebraska Press, 1996.

Lohse, Hinrich

(1896–1964)

Hinrich Lohse was a German politician and wartime Reich Commissioner for the Baltic and **Belorussia**n areas. He was born at Mühlenbarbek, in Schleswig-Holstein. Lohse studied commerce and worked as a clerk in a savings bank. He took part in World War I and years later, in 1925, he was appointed *Gauleiter* (district leader) for Schleswig-Holstein. He was elected a member of the Prussian Chamber of Deputies in 1928 and of the **Reichstag** in 1932. In 1933 he was promoted to the Prussian State Council and to the presidency of the province of Schleswig-Holstein. The following year he was made a Lieutenant General in the SA (*Sturmabteilung*; Storm Troopers). Between 1941 and 1944 Lohse functioned as Reich Commissioner for the Ostland, with his headquarters in **Riga**. This was the period when, under his supervision, the **"Final Solution"** was implemented in the Baltic and Belorussian areas.

Lohse instructed his subordinates that Jews, who were now restricted to designated ghettos, were to receive the bare minimum of food rations necessary to sustain life, until the machinery for the "Final Solution" was fully operative. Nonetheless, the mass shootings in the **Vilna** ghetto and elsewhere led him to question whether "all Jews, regardless of age or sex, or their usefulness to the economy (for instance, as skilled workers in the Wehrmacht's ordnance factories), were to be liquidated." When he was informed that this was indeed the case, Lohse acquiesced.

He was arrested in 1945 and sentenced in 1948 to ten years' imprisonment, but was released in 1951 on grounds of ill health.

SUGGESTED RESOURCES

Gitelman, Zvi, ed. *Bitter Legacy: Confronting the Holocaust in the USSR.* Bloomington, Indiana University Press, 1997.

Rice, Earle. *The Final Solution.* San Diego, CA: Lucent Books, 1998.

> **Reichstag**
> The German Parliament.

Lösener, Bernard

(1890–1952)

Bernard Lösener was the *Rassereferent* ("racial expert") of the German Interior Ministry from 1933 to 1943. In this post, Lösener helped draft twenty-seven anti-Jewish decrees. The most important among them were the **Nuremberg Laws** of 1935 and the subsequent legal definitions that made distinctions among those who were only part Jewish ("hybrids," or **Mischlinge**), in effect exempting quarter Jews and secularized half Jews from the full brunt of persecution. After the war, Lösener recalled how he was summoned at the last minute to bring his Interior Ministry files to the 1935 Nazi party rally, where the drafting of the Nuremberg Laws took place over a hectic weekend. His detailed firsthand account of this event has frequently been cited, especially by those historians who emphasize the unplanned and evolutionary nature of Nazi Jewish policy.

Lösener was the son of a minor judicial official. He served as a soldier throughout World War I (1914–1918) and then attended the University of Tübingen. Lösener passed his civil service examinations and became a customs official in 1924.

He joined the NAZI PARTY in December 1930. In April 1933, when experienced officials with party credentials were in short supply, Lösener was summoned from his obscure customs post to the Interior Ministry in BERLIN.

By his own account, Lösener became quickly disillusioned with the Nazis, for two reasons: the inclusion of even one-quarter Jews among those banned from the civil service, and the party's intervention in the internal affairs of the Evangelical church. Like many others, Lösener claimed that he clung to his post to prevent worse from happening and to save those who could still be saved. By his own admission, this meant accepting the impossibility of doing anything for "full Jews," and doing everything possible to prevent quarter and half Jews, as well as the latter's parents living in mixed marriages, from being equated with full Jews. It also meant not allowing himself to show open opposition to these laws and basing his professional behavior on the foundation of Nazi ideology, despite the "internal aversion" and "shame" he felt.

Two factors distinguish Lösener's apologies from those of others. First, he did in fact work consistently, tenaciously, and with considerable success to prevent *Mischlinge* and Jews in mixed marriages from being affected by the regime's anti-Jewish measures. According to his calculations, this saved as many as 100,000 part Jews and 20,000 Jews in mixed marriages from deportation. Second, unlike others who clung to their posts allegedly to prevent worse, but in fact steadily accommodated themselves to the escalating violence, Lösener had a limit beyond which he would not go. When he learned of the December 1941 massacres of the first German Jews deported to RIGA, he requested a transfer from his post as *Rassereferent*. Eventually, in March 1943, he was appointed as a judge.

Lösener was arrested in November 1944 for hiding a couple implicated in the July 1944 attempt to assassinate Hitler. He was expelled from the party for "treason," but survived his Berlin imprisonment until liberation. After two subsequent arrests—first by the Russians and then by the Americans—and submitting to DENAZIFICATION proceedings, he was briefly employed by the German mission of the American Jewish JOINT DISTRIBUTION COMMITTEE in 1949. He then resumed government employment until his death in 1952.

SUGGESTED RESOURCES

Newman, Amy. *The Nuremberg Laws: Institutionalized Anti-semitism.* San Diego: Lucent Books, 1999.

Lublin

Lublin, a center of industry, communications, and culture, is a city in eastern POLAND and the capital of the district bearing that name. Jews lived in Lublin, one of Poland's oldest cities, from the fourteenth century, and in the sixteenth and seventeenth centuries it was the hub of Jewish learning in the country. During the nineteenth and twentieth centuries Lublin was the scene of important Hebrew and Yiddish cultural activities, and Jewish organizations and political parties flourished there. On the eve of World War II, the city had a Jewish population of some 40,000 out of a total of 122,000.

In the first few weeks of the war, thousands of Jews fleeing the German advance found refuge in Lublin. Some of these refugees and several hundred of the town's

Jewish residents moved even farther east, into territory that was annexed to the **Soviet Union** shortly thereafter. The Jewish Community Council helped the refugees. From the beginning of September 1939 until the eighteenth of that month, when the Germans occupied the city, the Jews participated in resistance efforts against the invading German forces. Jewish groups removed the debris caused by German bombing, acted as firefighters, and dug defense trenches.

German Occupation

> As soon as the Germans entered Lublin, they began seizing Jews for forced labor, humiliating them, inflicting bodily harm on them, and confiscating their property.

The Germans lost no time persecuting the Jews of Lublin when they entered the city, beating and robbing them, humiliating them, and discriminating against them in any way possible. By November 1939 the Jews were driven out of the main street, Krakowskie Przedmieście, and their apartments were seized; they were ordered to wear a sign of their Jewishness (*see* **Badge, Jewish**), and their movements in certain areas, both inside and outside the city, were restricted.

Lublin was linked to the Nazis' plan to create the Lublin Reservation, an enclave in which all the Jews of the **Generalgouvernement** and other parts of Poland annexed to the Reich, as well as those from the Reich itself, were to be concentrated (*see* **Nisko and Lublin Plan**). By February 1940, 6,300 deportees had arrived in Lublin under this program, including a group of 1,300 Jews from Stettin. But the plan was implemented in a haphazard fashion, lacking coordination with the various branches of the German administration, and in April 1940 it was dropped. Lublin, however, remained a center where the policy of mass deportation and extermination on Polish soil was carried out. It was the headquarters of Odilo **Globocnik**, the head of **Aktion (Operation) Reinhard**, who was responsible for the operation of death camps in the eastern part of the Generalgouvernement. The **Majdanek** concentration and extermination camp was situated in a Lublin suburb (*See* **Concentration Camps** and **Extermination Camps**).

Following the German occupation, the Jewish Community Council continued to function, with hardly any change from its pre-war composition. It broadened its range of activities in response to German demands and the new needs of the Jewish population. The council had to provide the Germans with daily quotas of **forced labor** and to collect and surrender valuables, furniture, and other items of household equipment. In the Jewish community itself, the council provided aid to the needy and to refugees. On occasion, it intervened with the German authorities for the release of hostages and prisoners, and to reduce fines and ease other economic measures that had been imposed on individuals or on the entire Jewish population.

The Judenrat

On January 25, 1940, the council officially became a **Judenrat** (Jewish Council), consisting of twenty-four members. Few changes in personnel were made; the membership continued to include people who before the war had belonged to a range of political parties. Heading the Judenrat was Henryk Bekker, an engineer, but its outstanding personality was the deputy chairman, Mark Alten. The Judenrat maintained the policy previously pursued by the Jewish Community Council. It built up a broad network of welfare institutions and soup kitchens and made special efforts to provide orphanages and institutions for abandoned children. It also invested much effort in providing health services, setting up two 500-bed general hospitals and a 300-bed hospital for contagious diseases, with outpatient clinics.

An elderly Jew in Lublin being humiliated by a German soldier cutting his beard.

As German policy toward the Jews became harsher, however, the Judenrat found it increasingly difficult to maneuver between compliance with German demands and taking care of the vital needs of the community. In 1940, the Germans stepped up their demands for forced labor, and they seized an increased number of people on the streets for this purpose. Individual Jews and the Judenrat tried to find employment opportunities in factories that were important to the German economy, hoping in this manner to gain immunity from random capture. In this way, many Jews came to be employed in the workshops of the German Armament Works (Deutsche Ausrüstungswerke), located in the prisoner-of-war camp at 7 Lipowa Street. In the summer of 1940, the Germans began rounding up Jews and taking them to work camps outside the city, mainly for labor on the Soviet border. The Judenrat was also ordered to provide laborers for these camps; its compliance led to tension between it and the Jewish population.

Deportations

In preparation for the establishment of a ghetto in the spring of 1941, the Germans ordered part of the Jewish population of Lublin to be deported. From March 10 until the end of that month, 10,000 Jews were expelled from Lublin; 1,250 were deported to Rejowiec, 2,300 to Siedliszcze, 3,200 to Sosnowiec, and the rest to other localities in the area. In these places the deportees faced enormous economic difficulties and suffered from appalling housing conditions.

Although they described the deportation as "voluntary evacuation," the Germans in fact exerted great pressure in order to achieve their goal.

The ghetto was established at the end of March 1941, with a Jewish population of over 34,000. On April 24 the Germans issued a decree forbidding Jews to leave the ghetto, except for those who had special passes or were part of work crews employed outside. In the summer of 1941, a typhus epidemic broke out in the ghetto. Medical teams and a special health service did what they could to control the disease, but they were severely hampered by the prevailing conditions—starvation, overcrowding, and a lack of medicines.

Extermination

Lublin Jews were among the first selected to be the victims of the gas chambers at the BEŁŻEC extermination camp. Their deportation began on March 17, 1942, and proceeded at a rate of 1,400 people per day, the quota fixed by the Germans. Some of the German units and their Ukrainian helpers were positioned on the ghetto perimeter to foil any attempt at escape, while others made house-to-house searches within the ghetto. The *Selektionen* for deportation took place at assembly points. In the initial stage, the passes held by Jewish skilled workers were honored by the Germans, but the workers' families were not exempt. Most of the Jews who had gone into hiding in the ghetto or had crossed over to the "Aryan" sector of the city—some 500 persons—were caught by the Germans; all were murdered on the spot. The *Aktion* came to an end on April 20. Thirty thousand Jews had been deported from Lublin, most of them to their death at Bełżec, and the rest were killed in the forests near the city.

On March 31, while the *Aktion* was in full swing, the Germans reduced the size of the Judenrat by half, from 24 to 12, and named Mark Alten as chairman. Some of those not reappointed were deported to Bełżec. Opinions differ concerning the conduct of members of the Judenrat, especially of Alten. Some informed persons have expressed understanding for the Judenrat's policy and emphasize its efforts on behalf of the community. Others have criticized the members for being out of touch with the people, for personal arrogance, and for capitulating too easily to the Germans. Some of the Jewish police also have been sharply criticized for their behavior.

The "Small Ghetto"

Following the *Aktion* of March and April 1942, the surviving members of the community, now numbering only 4,000, were moved to Majdan Tatarski, a suburb of Lublin. One section of the suburb was emptied of the Poles who lived there and was surrounded by a fence. In this area, dubbed the "small ghetto," the Germans interned the remaining Jews. Conditions were intolerable; some of the prisoners did not even have a roof over their heads. From the first day of the existence of the "small ghetto," the Germans went on a murder rampage. There were lineups and sporadic raids to identify those Jews who did not possess work passes, and many of these "illegals" were killed on the spot.

The population of the "small ghetto" was gradually destroyed. In an *Aktion* on September 2, 1942, 2,000 Jews were sent to their death at the Majdanek camp. The pattern was repeated on October 25, when 1,800 more Jews were sent to their death in Majdanek. In May 1943 several dozen craftsmen who had been employed by the Germans were murdered. In July 1944, shortly before their retreat from Lublin, the Germans killed the last remaining Jewish workers who had been held in Lublin Fortress, where they were employed in small workshops serving the German garrison troops.

After Lublin was liberated on July 24, 1944, the city became an assembly point for survivors from the city and its vicinity, for Jewish **partisans** in the area east of Lublin, and for Jews who had taken refuge in the Soviet Union at the beginning of the war. Until the liberation of **WARSAW** in January 1945, Lublin was the provisional capital of Poland, and it was there that the central institutions of the surviving Jewish community established themselves. A branch of the Jewish Community Cultural Society, a national institution recognized by the Polish government, existed there until 1968. The Jewish community came to an end in the early 1970s, and only a few Jews continue to live in Lublin.

partisans
Underground resistance groups fighting against the Nazis.

SUGGESTED RESOURCES

Bronowski, Alexander. *They Were Few.* New York: Peter Lang, 1992.

Frank, Jacob. *Himmler's Jewish Tailor: The Story of Holocaust Survivor Jacob Frank.* Syracuse, NY: Syracuse University Press, 1999.

LUBLIN RESERVATION. SEE NISKO AND LUBLIN PLAN.

LUCK. SEE LUTSK.

Lutsk

Lutsk (In Polish, Łuck) is a city in the **UKRAINE** and one of the most ancient cities in the former **SOVIET UNION**. Between the two world wars, Lutsk was the capital of the Volhynia district in independent **POLAND**; in September 1939 it was occupied by the Red Army and annexed with all of eastern Poland to the USSR (Soviet Union). Jewish settlement had begun there in the late fourteenth century. On the eve of World War II, 18,000 Jews lived in the city, out of a total of 41,000 residents. During their rule over Lutsk, from September 1939 until June 1941, the Soviets nationalized the economy and liquidated the Jewish institutions and organizations.

Between June 1941 and February 1944, the Germans murdered nearly all of the Jews of Lutsk. By the time the camp was liberated, only 150 Jews remained alive in the city.

Jews under German Occupation

From the first day of their invasion of the Soviet Union, on June 22, 1941, the Germans bombed Lutsk, destroying about 60 percent of its buildings and killing many citizens, including a large number of Jews. On June 25 the Germans entered the city. The following day, Ukrainians conducted a pogrom during which they robbed the Jews, beat them, and killed several of them. Young Jews tried to organize a defense against the rioters. On June 27 special German forces trained to rout out Jews and Communists in newly occupied areas reached Lutsk and found the corpses of many prisoners in the local jail, including numerous Ukrainians who had been killed by the Soviets before their retreat. The German military government and the heads of the nationalist Ukrainian community accused the Jews of murder. In reprisal, they seized 300 Jews, whom they put to death on June 30. On July 2, Jewish men between the ages of 16 and 60 were summoned for work; about 2,000 of them were taken to the ruins of the Lubart fortress and murdered. German soldiers from occupation units stationed in the city participated in the murder. In late July the Germans appointed a twelve-member **JUDENRAT** (Jewish Council), made up mainly

of former communal workers. Valuables, radio receivers, and other items were confiscated, and the Jews had to pay fines in gold, silver, goods, and commodities.

Labor Camp and Mass Murders

On October 19 the **SS** created a labor camp in Lutsk where they imprisoned 500 men. The Jews were moved on December 11 and 12 to a ghetto in the poorest part of the city, where they lived in overcrowded conditions with poor sanitation. On March 18, 1942, several hundred young Jews were sent to Vinnitsa to build Hitler's staff quarters. When the work was completed, all were killed, except for three who escaped to Transnistria and were saved with the help of Jews from Romania.

Between August 20 and 23 of 1942, 17,500 Lutsk Jews were taken outside the city and shot to death alongside pits prepared by a special **SD** (*Sicherheitsdienst*; Security Service) unit. On September 3 another 2,000 or so Jews, who were seized or found in hiding places, were murdered. The only Jews now remaining in Lutsk were those in the labor camp.

Revolt

On December 11, 1942, the Jewish camp elder learned that they were to be put to death the next day. A revolt was quickly organized, led by the prisoner in charge of the carpentry shop and the tinsmith Moshe. In addition to several revolvers and sawed-off shotguns that the Jews possessed, they prepared axes, knives, iron rods, bricks, and acid. On December 12 the Germans surrounded the camp, but when they tried to enter, they encountered a hail of bullets, bricks, and acid. Several of the attackers were wounded, and the face of the German commander was burned by acid. The Germans brought several armored vehicles and opened fire. After several hours, when most of the rebels had fallen, the Germans succeeded in entering the camp and murdered the remaining Jews, except for several who hid and escaped.

Lutsk was liberated on February 5, 1944. Since most of the city had been burned and destroyed, and since the front was not far away, most of the 150 survivors went to **ROVNO**.

SUGGESTED RESOURCES

Retseptor, Yoysef. "Once There Was a Town Named Lutsk and It Was Destroyed," in *Seyfer Lutsk (Memorial Book of Lutsk)*. Former Residents of Lutsk in Israel, 1961. [Online] http://www.jewishgen.org/yizkor/lutsk.html (accessed on September 1, 2000).

Lutz, Carl

(1895–1975)

Carl (Charles) Lutz was a Swiss diplomat who heroically rescued Jews in **HUNGARY** in 1944. Born in Switzerland, Lutz studied in the **UNITED STATES**, and in 1935 served as head of the Swiss consulate in Tel Aviv. At the outbreak of World War II in September 1939, he interceded on behalf of the 2,500 German settlers in Palestine who were being deported as enemy aliens by the British. This act placed him in a good position years later with German authorities in Hungary. On January 2, 1942, he arrived in **BUDAPEST** to represent the interests of the United States, the

United Kingdom, and other countries that had severed relations with Miklós **Horthy**'s Hungary, a member of the Axis nations.

During the fall of 1942, as the representative of British interests, Lutz, in coordination with Moshe (Miklós) Krausz (who represented the Jewish Agency in Budapest), drew up lists of children and gave them certificates of immigration to Palestine. Nearly 200 children and their adult chaperones were able to leave for Palestine before the German occupation of Hungary. When the Germans invaded Hungary on March 19, 1944, Lutz invited Krausz to move into a Swiss office and continue his work from there. Under Lutz's protection, Krausz continued to promote various schemes for immigration to Palestine, and other related rescue projects.

The protection of Hungarian Jews using documents that certified them as foreign nationals had begun before the German occupation. The Geneva representative of the El Salvadoran government had granted papers to thousands of Hungarian Jews certifying them as Salvadoran nationals. Lutz, who also represented Salvadoran interests in Budapest, was responsible for the distribution of these certificates. Also, various diplomats in Budapest and abroad, including Lutz, pressured the Hungarian government to stop the deportations that had begun in mid-May. Early in July, Horthy ordered the deportations stopped, and soon thereafter declared his government's willingness to allow some 7,500 bearers of certificates to leave for Palestine. The stage was now set to bring these Jews under Swiss protection.

Carl Lutz.

With the help of Krausz, a group of fifty Jews was assembled to work with Lutz. Photos were collected from four thousand persons, and Lutz issued four collective passports, each with one thousand names. Each person was then issued a "protective letter" guaranteeing that person's safety until his or her eventual departure for Palestine. To add as many people as possible to these protective letters, Lutz interpreted the permits as representing family units and not individuals. Eventually, protective letters were drawn up for 50,000 Jews.

At the same time, Lutz instructed the recently arrived Swedish diplomat Raoul **Wallenberg** on the best uses of the protective passes, and gave him the names of government contacts with whom to negotiate. This idea served as a model for various types of protective letters issued by other neutral countries and by the International Red Cross. In addition, after the pro-Nazi **Arrow Cross Party** came to power in mid-October of 1944, the Zionist youth underground manufactured and distributed tens of thousands of false documents, perhaps more than 100,000, mostly in the name of Switzerland. Owing to the proliferation of false protective papers, the authorities pressured Lutz and Wallenberg to affirm the validity of the documents they had distributed. Lutz acquiesced to prevent the collapse of the entire rescue project. Late in November, he and his wife sorted out the bearers of legitimate passes from those holding forged.

In the meantime, Lutz and other neutral diplomats interceded to have the new Hungarian government recognize the protective documents, using as bait the recognition of the regime by their governments. With the establishment of two ghettos, one for holders of protective passes and one for the rest of the Jews, Lutz procured 25 high-rise apartment buildings for concentrating the people under his protection. The Glass House, where the document preparation took place, and its annex also became a refuge for about 3,000 Jews.

During the notorious death march (*see* **Death Marches**) of November 10 to 22, 1944, when over 70,000 Jews were forcibly marched toward the **Austria**n border under the most inhumane conditions, Lutz and his fellow diplomats interceded on behalf of many Jews. Lutz made use of Salvadoran certificates still in his possession, following the deportees on their march and filling in many of their names on

the documents. Those saved in this way were allowed to return to Budapest, which was already under siege by the Red Army. Ernst **Kaltenbrunner**, the **Gestapo** head, in a dispatch to the German Foreign Ministry complained about the disappearance of many Jews on this march as a result of intervention by the Swiss diplomats, as well as by the representatives of Sweden, Spain, Portugal, and the Vatican.

With the tightening of the Soviet siege of Budapest in December 1944, all foreign diplomatic representatives were ordered to leave the beleaguered capital. Maximilian Jaeger, the head of the Swiss legation in Budapest, had already departed on November 10. But Lutz, not willing to abandon his protégés, decided to remain behind. Over 30,000 Jews (out of a total of some 100,000) with various protective passes—Swiss, Swedish, Red Cross, and Vatican—were housed in the so-called international ghetto.

Lutz later related that a German diplomat revealed to him that the Arrow Cross had received instructions not to harm the protected houses so long as Lutz remained in Budapest, as a token of **Germany**'s gratitude to him for having looked after the interests of German expatriates in Palestine in 1939 and 1940. For three months thereafter, Lutz, along with his wife and a group of Jewish refugees, lived a precarious existence in the basement of the abandoned, but bombarded, British diplomatic headquarters, almost without food and water. When the Russians stormed the building, Lutz jumped through the window and managed to reach Buda, the section of the city occupied only in February 1945.

In 1965, Lutz was recognized by Yad Vashem as one of the **"Righteous Among the Nations."**

SUGGESTED RESOURCES

Anger, Per. *With Raoul Wallenberg in Budapest: Memories of the War Years in Hungary.* Washington, DC: Holocaust Library, 1981.

"Carl Lutz; Swiss Diplomat Who Saved Jews in WWII." *Simon Wiesenthal Center Museum of Tolerance Online.* [Online] http://motlc.wiesenthal.com/gallery/pg38/pg4/pg38482.html (accessed September 1, 2000).

"'The Righteous Among the Nations' of Swiss Nationality." *Task Force Switzerland.* [Online] http://www.switzerland.taskforce.ch/W/W2/W2c/c6_ei.htm (accessed on September 1, 2000).

Lvov

Lvov (in Polish, Lwów; in German, Lemberg) is a city in Eastern Galicia, now capital of an oblast (district) in the western part of the **Ukraine**, an independent republic that was once part of the **Soviet Union**. An industrial and cultural center, Lvov was founded in the thirteenth century. From 1772 to 1918 it was under Austrian rule, and in the interwar period it was a provincial capital in independent **Poland**. The population was 340,000 in 1939, when its Jewish population of 110,000 made it the third largest Jewish community in the country. Active anti-semitism was widespread, partly because the Poles and the Ukrainians each accused the Jews of helping the other. On the eve of World War II, Jewish Lvov was a center of culture and education and of vigorous political activity by the Jews of many religious, political, and philosophical traditions including Orthodox Jews, Zionists, Bundists, and Communists.

Three weeks after the outbreak of the war, the Soviets entered Lvov and annexed it to the Soviet Union, along with the rest of Eastern Galicia. The Soviet authorities disbanded community institutions, outlawed political parties, nationalized factories, large holdings, and wholesale businesses, restricted retail trade and organized artisans into cooperative societies. Cultural life, however, remained lively. Some 100,000 Jewish refugees from German-occupied western Poland crowded into Lvov. In the summer of 1940 many of them were expelled to the remote regions of the USSR. Following the German invasion of the Soviet Union on June 22, 1941, about 10,000 Jews escaped from Lvov, together with the Red Army, which was retreating from the city.

German Occupation

On June 30, 1941, the Germans occupied Lvov. The killing of Jews began that same day, committed by Einsatzgruppe C (*see* **OPERATIONAL SQUADS**), German soldiers, Ukrainian nationalists, and bystanders caught up in the fervor of violence. As they had in the city of **LUTSK** just days before, the Germans and the Ukrainians spread a rumor that the Jews had taken part in the execution of Ukrainian political prisoners whose bodies had been discovered in the dungeons of the the Soviet political police). In four days of rioting, ending on July 3, 1941, 4000 Jews were murdered. On July 8, Jews aged 14 and older were ordered to wear on their right arm a white badge with a blue Star of David (*see* **BADGE, JEWISH**). From July 25 to 27 the Ukrainians again went on the rampage, murdering 2000 more Jews.

At the end of July 1941, a temporary Jewish committee was established, made up of five prominent community leaders. Within a short time the committee was enlarged and became a **JUDENRAT** (Jewish Council), with Dr. Joseph Parnes as chairman. Throughout the period he was in office, Parnes stood up for the interests of the community. That August, the Jews of Lvov were ordered to pay a ransom of 20 million rubles. The Germans took hostages to ensure payment, and killed them, even though the money was paid at the appointed time.

During the summer of 1941, Jewish property was plundered, the Jews were put on forced labor, synagogues were burned down, and Jewish cemeteries were destroyed. In the fall, the Germans intensifed their demands for Jewish forced labor for road work and for the construction of bridges and military camps. In September a Jewish police force was established, under the Judenrat. Its duties, in the initial period, consisted of keeping order and ensuring cleanliness in the streets inhabited by Jews, confiscating valuables at the Germans' command, and escorting persons who were on their way to forced labor. Parnes, the chairman of the Judenrat, was killed by the Germans at the end of October, when he refused to hand over Jews who were to be moved to the **JANÓWSKA** camp, then being established. Abraham Rotfeld took his place.

The Ghetto

On November 8, 1941, the Germans announced the establishment of a ghetto, giving the Jews until December 15 to move into the area allocated for this purpose. In the course of the move to the ghetto, 5,000 elderly and sick Jews were killed as they were about to cross the bridge on Peltewna Street. The move was not completed by the allotted time, but many thousands of Jews were herded into the Zamarstynów and Kleparów quarters, in which the ghetto was set up. During the winter of 1941–1942, the Germans began sending Jews to labor camps at Laszki Murowane, Hermanów, Vinniki, Jaktorów, Kamionka Strumilowa, and Skole. In

ghetto
A restricted part of a city where Jews were required to live under Nazi supervision.

Soldiers standing over the bodies of Jews in Lvov, July, 1941.

February 1942 Abraham Rotfeld died, and the Germans appointed Henryk Landsberg to take his place as Judenrat chairman.

In March 1942, the Judenrat was ordered to prepare lists of Jews who were to be sent to the east, allegedly to work there. A delegation of rabbis appealed to Landsberg to refuse to cooperate with the Germans in preparing the lists and rounding up the people on them. Landsberg refused, claiming that if the Germans themselves were to carry out the deportation, far more people would be killed. In this *Aktion* (operation), which began on March 19 and continued until the end of the month, 15,000 Jews were taken to the Bełżec extermination camp.

In the spring of that year, the Jews of Lvov tried to find jobs in factories that performed an essential function for the German economy, hoping thereby to be exempt from future deportations. On July 8, 7,000 Jews who could not produce a certificate of employment were seized by the Germans and deported to the Janówska camp, where they were murdered. A month later, on August 10, the "Large *Aktion*" was launched, lasting until August 23. During this time, 50,000 persons were sent to Bełżec. At the beginning of September 1942 Jews who were still living outside the ghetto were herded inside, the ghetto area was greatly reduced, and what remained was sealed off. The Germans hanged Landsberg and a group of Judenrat employees, as well as the Jewish policemen. Eduard Eberson was appointed Judenrat chairman in place of Landsberg.

In November, 5,000 to 7,000 "unproductive" persons were removed from the ghetto, some of them to be sent to the Janówska camp and the rest to Bełżec. Toward the end of 1942, the ghetto came to resemble a labor camp. The inhabitants were assigned lodging in buildings according to their place of employment. Those who possessed no employment card were hunted down systematically and, when caught, were put to death in groups.

Labor Camp

In January 1943 the ghetto officially became a labor camp, a *Julag* (*Judenlager*, or "Jewish camp"). At the beginning of that month, 10,000 Jews were executed, having first been classified as "illegals" because they could show no employment card. On January 30 the Judenrat was disbanded, and most of its members were murdered. An *Oberjude* (chief Jew) was appointed head of the *Julag* to serve as liaison between the surviving inmates of the ghetto-camp and the authorities. On March 17, 1,500 Jews were murdered, most of them in the Piasky area near the city, and at the same time some 800 Jews were deported to **AUSCHWITZ**. In May 1943 the slaughter of the remnant of the community was speeded up. Jews were lined up for evaluation at their workplaces; only those classified as "vitally important" were permitted to stay; the rest were killed.

Liquidation and Resistance

On June 1, 1943, the final *Aktion* was undertaken, to liquidate the ghetto—*Julag*. German and Ukrainian police units surrounded the ghetto and closed every avenue of escape. Additional police units entered the ghetto to round up all the inhabitants. At this point the Germans and their Ukrainian helpers encountered resistance. The Jews threw hand grenades and Molotov cocktails at them and fired on them. Nine persons, Germans and Ukrainians, were killed, and twenty were wounded. The Germans did not dare enter the buildings; instead, they blew them up or set them on fire, in order to kill those who were inside or force them to come out of their hiding places and give themselves up.

In the course of liquidating the ghetto, the Germans seized 7,000 Jews, whom they deported to the Janówska camp, where they were soon put to death. In the ghetto area itself about 3,000 Jews met their death. The liquidation process came to an end on June 2, 1943, but as late as July, searches were still being made for Jews hiding in the ghetto ruins.

As of mid-1942, and especially in the wake of the "Large *Aktion*," efforts were made in the Lvov ghetto to organize an underground. Groups of young people tried to obtain weapons so as to be able to offer armed resistance. Toward the end of 1942, one such group attempted to escape from the ghetto into the nearby forest, where they planned to set up resistance centers against the Germans and their helpers. The attempt failed, and most of the members of the group were killed en route. Nevertheless, more efforts were made to reach the forests situated in the Brody area. In one such attempt, the Germans apprehended the vehicle in which one of the groups was traveling and captured all of its passengers. The driver, a Pole who had undertaken to transport the group to their destination, was suspected of having informed on them to the Germans.

While there was no organized and consolidated resistance movement in the Lvov ghetto, in many instances various forms of action were taken against the Germans and their helpers. One of the Jewish police units attempted to organize resistance to the Germans. An organized resistance group headed by Tadek Drotorski was active in one of the labor camps, on Czwartakow Street, where hundreds of Jews were employed. When the Germans picked up the group's trail, in March 1943, Drotorski shot and killed a German policeman. An underground news sheet was also published in the ghetto.

During March 1943 there were more and more attempts to break out of the *Julag* in order to reach the forest and establish contact with the partisans active in the area. Among those who tried to escape was the Yiddish poet Jacob Schudrych, who managed to reach the forest, only to die there.

In 1939, Lvov was the third largest center of Jewish population in the Ukraine. By June 1943, most of Lvov's Jews had been deported and murdered.

SUGGESTED RESOURCES

Kahana, David. *Lvov Ghetto Diary.* Amherst: University of Massachusetts Press, 1990.

Marshall, Robert. *In the Sewers of Lvov: A Heroic Story of Survival from the Holocaust.* New York: Maxwell Macmillan International, 1991.

Peck, Jean M. *At the Fire's Center: A Story of Love and Holocaust Survival.* Urbana: University of Illinois Press, 1998.

> "I hope completely to erase the concept of Jews through the possibility of a great emigration of all Jews to a colony in Africa or elsewhere."
>
> —Heinrich Himmler, 1940

Madagascar Plan

During the summer of 1940, Nazi policy makers responsible for finding a solution to the "Jewish question" began formulating a plan to expel all European Jews to the island of Madagascar, off the southeast coast of Africa. The ultimate impracticality of the Madagascar Plan led the Nazis to decide that a **"FINAL SOLUTION"** to the Jewish question would have to use means other than expulsion.

Between World War I and World War II, the idea of expelling Jews to Madagascar, then to a French colony, was put forward in Britain by the noted antisemites, Henry Hamilton Beamish and Arnold Leese, and in the **NETHERLANDS** by Egon van Winghene. In 1937 the Poles, who wished to encourage the emigration of a large number of Jews, received permission from the French to send a three-man investigative commission comprised of Major Mieczysław Lepecki, Leon Alter, and Solomon Dyk to Madagascar to explore the possibility of settling Polish Jews there. Lepecki thought that 40,000 to 60,000 Jews could be supported in the cooler highlands, but Alter felt the island could accommodate a maximum of only 2,000 Jews. In addition to the Polish and French governments, the British government and even the **JOINT DISTRIBUTION COMMITTEE** briefly toyed with the notion of resettling Jews in Madagascar. It is not surprising, therefore, that the idea appealed to the Nazis as well.

Resettlement Plans

Anschluss
The annexation of Austria by Germany.

In early 1938, just ten days before the **Anschluss**, Adolf **EICHMANN** was instructed to collect material for a "foreign-policy solution" to the Jewish question (as was being negotiated by **POLAND** with **FRANCE** concerning the possibility of transferring Polish Jews to Madagascar). Various Nazi leaders mentioned the idea during the next few years. However, it did not catch fire until the summer of 1940, when multiple factors made the Madagascar Plan a solution eagerly grasped at by frustrated Nazis.

In the spring of 1940, Heinrich **HIMMLER**'s cherished dream of expelling the Jews and Poles from the incorporated territories of western Poland into the **GENERALGOUVERNEMENT** clashed with the economic arguments of Hermann Göring and the governor general, Hans **FRANK**. They believed that resettlement should be subordinated to the interests of the war economy and the receptive capacity of the Generalgouvernement. The imminent victory over France, however, gave Himmler the opportunity of reviving his plan through a direct appeal to Hitler. Himmler's memorandum "Some Thoughts on the Treatment of the Alien Populations in the East" as discussed with Hitler on May 25, 1940, one week after German troops had reached the English Channel and trapped the units of the Allied armies at Dunkerque. Himmler argued for removing all the "ethnic mush" of Germany to the Generalgouvernement, where citizens would be reduced to a denationalized status i.e., all rights and privileges of citizenship removed.

As for the Jews in particular, Himmler wanted an even more drastic and comprehensive solution: "I hope completely to erase the concept of Jews through the possibility of a great emigration of all Jews to a colony in Africa or elsewhere." Concerning this systematic eradication of the Jews of eastern Europe, Himmler concluded: "However cruel and tragic each individual case may be, this method is still the mildest and best, if one rejects the Bolshevik method of physical extermination of a people out of inner conviction as un-German and impossible." Hitler found Himmler's plans "very good and correct" and permitted Himmler to inform his rivals that the Führer had "recognized and confirmed" them as having official approval.

Himmler's vision of expelling the Jews to an African colony was attractive for a number of reasons. The prospect of imminent victory over France and Britain seemed to place the colonies of France and merchant shipping of Britain at Germany's disposal. Occupation of additional territories in western Europe brought hundreds of thousands of additional Jews into German control; meanwhile, resettlement of even the half-million Jews in the incorporated territories on a **LUBLIN** Reservation had proved impractical (*see* **NISKO AND LUBLIN PLAN**).

The Proposal

In late May 1940, Hitler approved Himmler's general idea of expelling the Jews to some African colony, but it was left to the Jewish expert of the German Foreign Office, Franz Rademacher, to turn the Madagascar Plan into a concrete proposal. Rademacher proposed on July 3, 1940, that Germany exploit the victory over France to send at least some, if not all, Jews out of Europe—"to Madagascar, for example." Hitler almost immediately took up the idea. At a conference on June 18 concerning the fate of the French empire, Hitler and Ribbentrop informed Benito Mussolini and the Italian foreign minister, Count Galeazzo Ciano, of Germany's intention to settle the European Jews in Madagascar. Hitler repeated this intention to Grand Admiral Erich Raeder two days later. Himmler's deputy, Reinhard **HEYDRICH**, quickly asserted his jurisdiction in "a territorial final solution" to the Jewish question. From then on work on the Madagascar Plan was to proceed in both the Foreign Office and the **SS**.

News of the plan rapidly spread to the German occupation authorities in the east. Later that month, Adam **CZERNIAKÓW**, head of the **JUDENRAT** (Jewish Council) in **WARSAW**, recorded in his diary that an SS man had blurted out "that the war would be over in a month and that we would all leave for Madagascar." Governor General Frank was greatly relieved to receive word not only that the impending forced transfer of Jews into his territory was now canceled, but those currently in his area would be removed as well. In the Generalgouvernement, ghetto construction was halted as pointless, in view of the Führer's new plan. Moreover, the expulsion of the **ŁÓDŹ** Jews into the Generalgouvernement, repeatedly postponed and most recently rescheduled for August, was canceled once again, and the German authorities there faced the prospect of having to keep their Jews until the Madagascar Plan could be put into effect.

Meanwhile, work went forward feverishly in **BERLIN** under the auspices of both Rademacher in the Foreign Office and Eichmann, Heydrich's expert for Jewish affairs and evacuations, who had been working since the outbreak of war on expelling Jews and Poles from the Third Reich into the Generalgouvernement. Rademacher consulted various authorities and developed a plan involving numerous German agencies: the Foreign Office would handle negotiations with both France and Britain for the peace treaty, as well as with other European countries for regulating their participation; the Office of the Four-Year Plan would coordinate

> "This ... would prevent the possible establishment in Palestine by the Jews of a Vatican State of their own.... Moreover, the Jews will remain in German hands as a pledge for the future good behavior of the members of their race in America."
>
> **Excerpt from Franz Rademacher's proposed Madagascar Plan, July 3, 1930.**

The failure of the Nisko and Lublin resettlement plan made the idea of exporting Jews to Madagascar very appealing to top Nazi leaders who were seeking a viable answer to the Jewish question in Europe.

the utilization of Jewish property; the Führer Chancellery would coordinate transportation; propaganda would be handled by Goebbels internally and by the Foreign Office abroad; and the SS would be in charge of collecting the Jews in Europe and administering the island "super-ghetto."

Eichmann also conducted extensive research, sending members of his staff to the Tropical Institute in Hamburg and the French colonial archives in **PARIS**. He met with a group of German Jewish leaders in early July 1940 and ordered them to prepare within twenty-four hours a list of considerations that would have to be taken into account for evacuating four million Jews from Europe at the end of the war. Consultation with them came to an abrupt end, however, when they showed enthusiasm only for the destination of Palestine, which Eichmann explicitly ruled out. In contrast to the Foreign Office plan, which provided for broad participation, the SS version that emerged by the end of the summer placed the entire direction of the project—from finance to transport to security and even to diplomatic negotiations—under Heydrich.

The differences between Foreign Office and SS versions of the plan were never reconciled, for work on it came to an abrupt halt with Germany's failure in the Battle of Britain in September 1940. The Madagascar Plan died with Germany's unexpected setback in the skies over **GREAT BRITAIN**. Hitler faced a new strategic dilemma, and Nazi Jewish policy would be caught up in his decision to break out of this dilemma through an attack on the **SOVIET UNION**. The ensuing "war of destruction" against the Soviet Union would unleash a war of destruction against the Jews as well.

The Madagascar Plan has sometimes been dismissed by historians as a misleading reflection of Nazi intentions because of its brief existence and its seeming weakness in contrast to the monumental horrors that followed. But in the summer of 1940, Nazi leaders were not engaged in an elaborate sham; they were making real decisions based on the Madagascar Plan as a reality of Nazi Jewish policy. Though not yet the "Final Solution"—the compulsive and comprehensive program to kill every Jew whom the Nazis could lay their hands on—the Madagascar Plan still implied massive losses among the Jewish population.

SUGGESTED RESOURCES

Browning, Christopher R. *Nazi Policy, Jewish Workers, German Killers.* New York: Cambridge University Press, 2000.

"Madagascar Plan." *The Jewish Student Online Research Center (JSOURCE).* [Online] http://us-israel.org/jsource/Holocaust/Madagascar.html (accessed on September 2, 2000).

Majdanek

Majdanek (sometimes spelled Maidalnek) was first a **CONCENTRATION CAMP** and later an **EXTERMINATION CAMP** run by the Waffen-SS, a military branch of the **SS**. Majdanek was located in a suburb of **LUBLIN**, **POLAND**. It was called the Majdan Tatarski camp, or Majdanek for short. The camp was established on the orders of Heinrich **HIMMLER**, following an agreement with the Wehrmacht—the regular German armed forces—under which some Soviet **PRISONERS OF WAR** would be handed over to the **SS** and put at the disposal of the program for the "Germanization" of the East. Lublin district SS and Police Leader Odilo **GLOBOCNIK** played a decisive role in the establishment of Majdanek.

Until 1943, the camp's designation was Prisoner-of-War Camp of the Waffen-SS Lublin. It was not, however, confined to any particular category of prisoners. Its main function was to destroy enemies of **Germany**. The camp was also meant to take part in the extermination of the Jews, as well as the deportation and "resettlement" of inhabitants of the **Zamość** region. The Majdanek camp covered about 667 acres of uncultivated land on a highway. It had a double barbed-wire fence connected to a high-voltage transmission line, with nineteen watchtowers, each 26.5 feet (8.8 meters) high, equipped with mobile searchlights and 130 lighting fixtures.

The camp was divided into five sections, each serving a different purpose—one, for example, was for women prisoners. In all, there were 227 structures in Majdanek. There were twenty-two prisoner barracks, two of which were used for administration and supplies. Majdanek also had seven gas chambers and two wooden gallows, as well as a small crematorium. Next to the camp were workshops, storehouses, buildings for coal storage, laundries, and so on. A large crematorium, containing five furnaces, was added in September 1943. The section reserved for the SS forces contained their barracks, a casino, and the camp commandant's offices. The plans for the camp provided for the eventual construction of barracks for 250,000 prisoners, the establishment of industrial plants, and the construction of additional gas chambers and a more efficient crematorium. By the time the camp was liberated, only 20 percent of these plans had been put into effect.

The first group of prisoners arrived in Majdanek in October 1941. It was followed by groups from Soviet prisoner of war camps and from other concentration camps. Among the other groups imprisoned in Majdanek were Poles who had been seized in raids or had been held elsewhere. There were also Jews from Poland and other European countries, Polish farmers who had been expelled from the Zamość region, and residents of **Belorussia** (present-day Belarus) and **Ukraine**. In April 1943, several tens of thousands of Jews from **Warsaw** and, later, from **Białystok**, were sent to the camp. Records reveal that prisoner transports to Majdanek carried approximately 250,000 people. Of them, 100,000 were Poles, 80,000 Jews, 50,000 Soviets, and 20,000 of other national origins.

In addition to the murders by lethal gas (*see* **Gas Chambers/Vans**), mainly of Jewish inmates, mass shootings were carried out in the camp and nearby areas. In 1941 and 1942, sick Soviet prisoners of war were shot to death. In April 1942, some 2,800 Jews were murdered this way, as were several thousand other prisoners of different nationalities that spring, 300 Soviet army officers in the summer of 1943, and another 18,000 Jews in November 1943, in the **"Erntefest"** (Harvest Festival) Aktion, or "operation." Majdanek had many satellite camps: these were located at Bliżyn, in the **Kielce** district; at **Budzyń**, near Kraśnik; in Lublin (two labor camps); in Puławy; in Radom; and in Warsaw, on Gesia Street.

The commandants of the Majdanek camp were Karl Otto **Koch** (September 1941 to July 1942), Max Koegel (August to October 1942), Herman Florsted (October 1942 to September 1943), Martin Weiss (September 1943 to May 1944), and Arthur **Liebehenschel** (May to July 22, 1944).

Resistance movements were active in Majdanek at various periods. Several escapes were arranged by individuals and groups. Polish aid organizations, such as the Polish Red Cross, the Central Welfare Council, and the Polish resistance movement, extended help to the Polish prisoners. In July 1944, in the face of the Soviet army's advance, Majdanek was liquidated. About 1,000 prisoners were taken away, half of them reaching **Auschwitz**. Before abandoning the camp, the SS staff destroyed documents and set fire to the buildings and the large crematorium. In

> "At Maidanek no one could be neutral: either you were victim or executioner. Anyone in authority who failed to take advantage of his privilege to beat inmates undermined his status in the camp elite."

Alexander Donat, "Surviving Slave Labor at Maidanek," in The Holocaust: Problems and Perspectives of Interpretation, *Donald L. Niewyck, editor (Lexington, Massachusetts: D. C. Heath and Company) 1992, p. 98.*

Living Conditions

In the following excerpt, a Holocaust survivor describes a particular aspect of life at Majdanek (Maidanek).

What was called a latrine consisted of a wooden box with handles at both ends similar to what hod carriers use to transport cement. Only one such box was assigned to each barrack, which might house two or three hundred inmates, and sometimes as many as five hundred. The overwhelming majority of the camp inmates suffered from diarrhea and almost everyone also had weakness of the bladder, so that the latrine was soon filled and overflowing. The stinking puddles on the floor were nauseating and when men had to wade through them barefoot because they had been thoughtless enough not to put on their wooden shoes, it was worse. But barefoot or shod the inmates trotting to and from the latrine soon tracked the entire barracks up with filth. To add to the dreadful stench the crowd around the latrine was usually noisy, and for our first few nights at Maidanek we found it very hard to bear. Afterward nothing could disturb our sleep.

—ALEXANDER DONAT

Alexander Donat, "Surviving Slave Labor at Maidanek," *in* The Holocaust: Problems and Perspectives of Interpretation, *Donald L. Niewyk, editor (Lexington, Massachusetts: D. C. Heath and Company) 1992, p. 91.*

their rush to withdraw before the Soviet troops arrived, the Germans failed to destroy the gas chambers and the larger part of the prisoners' barracks.

In July 1944, a special Polish-Soviet Nazi Crimes Investigation Commission began to investigate the crimes that had been committed at Majdanek. On September 16 of that year, it published its report in Polish, Russian, English, and French. In November 1944, six SS men who had served at Majdanek were tried in Lublin. Four of them were sentenced to death, and two committed suicide before sentence was passed. This was the first trial of the Majdanek camp staff.

But only a few of the 1,300 staff members of the camp were ever brought to trial. From 1946 to 1948, a trial was held in Lublin of ninety-five SS men who had been at Majdanek, most of them as guards. Seven of the accused were sentenced to death, including the women's camp commandant, Else Ehrich. The rest received long terms in prison. From 1975 to 1980, sixteen former Majdanek staff members, including six women, were tried in Düsseldorf, West Germany. The most important of those accused were Hermann Kackmann, an officer at the camp headquarters; Hermine Braunsteiner, supervisor of the women's camp; Heinrich Schmidt, the camp physician; and an SS staff member, Hildegard Lachert, whom the prisoners had nicknamed "Blutige Brigide" (Bloody Brigide).

Close to 500,000 prisoners, from 28 countries and belonging to 54 different nationalities, passed through Majdanek during its existence. It is believed that of these people, some 360,000 perished. Sixty percent of them died as a result of the brutal conditions in the camp—starvation, exhaustion, disease, and beatings. Forty

Prisoner barracks in Majdanek.

percent were executed or put to death in gas chambers. Some of the prisoners were taken to the gas chambers immediately upon arrival in the camp.

In October 1944 a national museum was established on the site of Majdanek. It maintains the remains of the camp as well as a permanent exhibition, administers an archive, publishes *Zeszyty Majdanka (Majdanek Journal)*, and edits research works on the history of the camp. A Majdanek Preservation Society provides financial support for the museum.

SUGGESTED RESOURCES

Goldstein, Arthur. *The Shoes of Majdanek.* Lanham, MD: University Press of America, 1992.

Kimmelman, Mira Ryczke. *Echoes from the Holocaust: A Memoir.* Knoxville: University of Tennessee Press, 1997.

Rybak, Rywka. *Rywka Rybak: A Survivor of the Holocaust.* Cleveland, OH: Tricycle Press, 1993.

Mauthausen

Mauthausen was a **CONCENTRATION CAMP** near an abandoned stone quarry about 3 miles (5 kilometers) from the town of Mauthausen, in Upper **AUSTRIA**. It was created soon after Nazi **GERMANY** annexed Austria (the Anschluss) in March 1938. The first prisoners were brought to the camp on August 8 of that year. They were put to work in the construction of the camp and at the quarry.

Most of the prisoners brought to Mauthausen in the first year of its existence were criminal offenders. The rest were what the Nazis referred to as "asocial elements"—people the Nazis considered undesirable for one reason or another. Almost all were transferred from the **DACHAU** camp. The first group of prisoners was accompanied by 88 guards from Dachau's **SS-DEATH'S-HEAD UNITS** (*Totenkopfverbände*). In 1938, a total of 1,100 prisoners arrived. The first political prisoners, also from Dachau, arrived in May 1939. Soon afterward, groups of political prisoners were brought from jails in Czechoslovakia. Late in September, the Dachau "Punishment Squad" arrived at the camp. In December 1939, there were 2,666 prisoners, almost all Germans, interned in Mauthausen.

1940–1942

During 1940, about 11,000 new prisoners were recorded in the camp's "book of numbers," along with their camp numbers. There were some German prisoners from the camps of SACHSENHAUSEN (1,032) and BUCHENWALD (300). They were all transferred to Gusen, the first Mauthausen subcamp. Gusen was set up in early 1940 about 3 miles (5 kilometers) from Mauthausen as a branch of the main camp; its prisoners worked at cutting stone in the two Gusen quarries. That year, the number of prisoners in Mauthausen reached 3,833.

Seven shipments of Spanish prisoners arrived in 1941, and their number in the camp reached 7,241. Many Jews were also sent that year, together with groups of Czech prisoners. On May 12, the first Jews from the NETHERLANDS arrived. On October 20, an initial 4,205 Soviet PRISONERS OF WAR arrived. Of them, about 2,000 were transferred to the nearby Gusen subcamp. That year, Mauthausen received a total of 18,000 new prisoners. The death rate was very high.

In 1942, in addition to Czech, Dutch, Soviet (civilians and prisoners of war), and Yugoslav prisoners, inmates also arrived from FRANCE, BELGIUM, Greece, and Luxembourg. A new category of prisoners, those in "protective custody," were transferred from various prisons. A first transport of 218 such prisoners reached Mauthausen on November 26 from the Regensburg jail. Altogether, 13,000 new prisoners came to the camp in 1942.

On August 19 of that year, Nazi official Reinhard HEYDRICH had the concentration camps divided into various categories. Only Mauthausen and Gusen were placed in the most harsh classification. All prisoners in protective custody who were considered incorrigible—who showed negative behavior—were to be sent there.

1943–1945

The stream of prisoners of different nationalities continued throughout 1943. That year, 21,028 new prisoners were recorded. Only a few of them were Jews. Some 8,334 prisoners were entered in the records as having died in Mauthausen and Gusen, along with 147 prisoners of war. In addition, many victims were killed by order of the GESTAPO immediately upon their arrival at the camp. These people did not go through the registration procedures.

In 1944, the number of prisoners reaching Mauthausen increased a great deal. Many subcamps were built, and the new prisoners were sent to them. A record 65,645 new prisoners were listed in the "book of numbers." At its height in 1944, the prisoner population reached 114,524. Beginning in May, the camp received large transports of Jews from "selections" (*Selektionen*) in AUSCHWITZ. In May and June, four such transports brought a total of 7,500 prisoners. On August 10, a shipment of 4,589 Jewish prisoners came from the PŁASZÓW camp. The last large transport in 1944 arrived in late September, bringing 6,449 prisoners, of whom half were Jews. According to the camp's records, a total of 13,322 Jewish males and 504 Jewish females entered Mauthausen in 1944. That year, 3,437 Jews died there.

On January 25, 1945, the first transport of Auschwitz evacuees reached Mauthausen. In one week, about 9,000 prisoners from various countries arrived, most of them Jews. Thousands of prisoners were also transferred from Sachsenhausen,

> In 1942, Mauthausen was designated the concentration camp destination for Nazi prisoners deemed to be "incorrigible" in other locations.

GROSS-ROSEN, and other camps. They were sent to the Mauthausen satellite camps. In April, another gigantic flow of Jewish prisoners, who had been transferred from their native **HUNGARY** to camps along the Austrian-Hungarian border, reached Mauthausen. A total of 24,793 new prisoners were recorded in the camp books in 1945.

Structure of the Camp

The entire Mauthausen camp covered about 37 acres (150,000 square meters). The camp was divided into the prison camp, the command area, and the **SS** dwellings. The prison camp occupied the main part of the camp area, with three sections. Camp No. 1 was the residential camp, with twenty wooden huts, including quarantine huts for incoming prisoners. Camp No. 2, the workshop area, contained four huts; from early 1944 onward, this was also a quarantine area. Camp No. 3, built in the spring of 1944, contained six huts at first. Beginning in the summer of 1944, the sick and debilitated prisoners were moved there before being killed. Each hut was designed to hold 300 prisoners, but usually double that number, or even more, were packed into them.

Opposite the main gate was the assembly ground. The prisoners had to gather there and stand for the morning and evening roll call, and certain prisoners were taken there to be killed in the presence of all the others. On one side of the assembly ground were three stone buildings. Two were used for the camp services (kitchen, showers, and laundry). The third housed the prison and the gas chamber, which was disguised as a shower (*see* **GAS CHAMBERS/VANS**). Beneath the prison was the crematorium, where dead bodies were burned. In a nearby cell, prisoners were shot.

Outside the camp enclosure was the "Russian camp," which was converted into the camp hospital in the spring of 1943. About a month before the liberation, in April 1945, a tent camp was set up outside the camp enclosure, with fourteen large tents. It was set aside for Hungarian Jews. It was also a place for Jews from the entire network of Mauthausen camps to stay in until they were taken to Gunskirchen.

Living Conditions

Until the war started in September 1939, the routine in Mauthausen resembled that of other concentration camps in Germany. Apart from the crushing labor, the conditions of Mauthausen were not so severe at that time. With the start of the war, the nature of the camp and its operation changed radically. Within a short time, the number of prisoners increased–from 994 in late 1938 to 2,666 in December 1939.

Mauthausen became a concentration camp and killing center for "undesirable political elements" in Nazi Germany. It also became a liquidation center for people opposed to the new regimes in the German-occupied countries. From mid-1940 onward, most prisoners were no longer German. The camp absorbed about 7,500 Spanish prisoners and members of the International Brigades who had fought alongside the republican soldiers in the Spanish Civil War. Eight thousand Polish prisoners were also brought to the camp, mainly from the intelligentsia. These arrests were part of the effort to paralyze the leadership in occupied **POLAND**. The same policy was adopted with the Czechs. With the change in the composition of the prisoners came a drastic worsening of conditions. Their treatment and punishments became more severe. The food rations were cut, and the prisoners were severely overcrowded. This caused a deterioration of the sanitary conditions, a spread of typhus and dysentery epidemics, and a consequent marked increase in the

Prisoner number 139,157 was recorded on May 3, two days before the liberation of Mauthausen.

In 1939, 445 prisoners died at Mauthausen and its satellite, Gusen. In 1940, the death toll rose to 3,846.

death rate. In 1939, some 445 deaths were recorded; in 1940, 3,846 prisoners died in the camps of Mauthausen and Gusen.

Another essential change occurred in the operation of the camp following a decision to expand military industry in the camps. Because of the severe shortage in the labor force, the Nazis needed more efficient work from the concentration camp prisoners. From the fall of 1943, most of the Mauthausen prisoners were put to work in the war industry. They worked mainly in digging underground tunnels to house factories for rocket assembly and production of plane parts. The camp population increased dramatically: from March to December 1943, the number of prisoners in Mauthausen and Gusen grew from 14,800 to 26,000. The maximum number, recorded in March 1945, was 84,000.

Most of the prisoners in Mauthausen who held supervisory and other posts were criminal offenders. The camp authorities encouraged them to treat the ordinary prisoners harshly. They had complete control over the lives of the inmates under their command. The main jobs held by prisoners were those of camp elder and his deputies, and camp registrar. The work in the camp was supervised by the **KAPO**s. The inmate blocks were under the authority of the block elders, block registrars, and room elders. All these prisoners were rewarded with a large number of privileges.

Prisoners by National Groups

The Poles were the largest national group at Mauthausen. The first Polish prisoners arrived on March 9, 1940. Another nine transports arrived that year. All were sent to Gusen. In 1944, after the **WARSAW** Polish Uprising was put down, the last groups of Poles arrived. Poles of German origin (**VOLKSDEUTSCHE**, or ethnic Germans) who declared their loyalty to the German race were released. The Polish students and members of the underground resistance in the first transports were killed in the fall of 1940. The camp's record of the dead lists 30,203 Poles, including many Polish Jews. Altogether, there were nearly 50,000 Poles in the Mauthausen camps.

Czech prisoners arrived mainly in 1941 and 1942. They were mostly political prisoners, including Jews, Communists, and intellectuals. In the first months of 1942, three transports arrived bringing 970 prisoners. They were soon killed by the block elders and the Kapos. After the shooting in Prague of Reinhard **HEYDRICH** by the Czech underground on May 29, 1942, some 253 Czechs were taken to Mauthausen and killed. The women among them were taken in groups to the gas chamber. Most of the Czech prisoners were murdered in the three months following Heydrich's assassination. Altogether, about 5,200 Czechs arrived at the camp. The number who survived is unknown.

The majority of the Soviets were prisoners of war. They lived in separate huts set up in an area known as the "Russian camp." Of the 5,000 who arrived in the first shipments, no more than 80 were still alive in March 1942. One group of Soviet inmates were the prisoners of Operation K—officers or noncommissioned officers who had escaped and been recaptured. At Mauthausen, these prisoners were held under particularly harsh conditions, and many died within a few weeks. In February 1945, about 500 of them rebelled. They succeeded in breaking out of the camp enclosure. In a rapid operation that took place with the participation of the local inhabitants, all the escapees were caught or killed, except for eight, who survived the war.

In addition, there were large groups of French, Italian, and Yugoslav prisoners in the camp at different times, as well as German prisoners. Of the 7,500 Spanish republicans, about 4,200 died in the camp in 1941 and 1942.

Six thousand naked prisoners being held in the Mauthausen camp courtyard. After 24 hours, 140 had died.

Fate of the Jews

Until the spring of 1941, only a few Jews arrived at Mauthausen. Most died within a short time, as a result of the work at the quarry and from maltreatment. Then entire groups of Jews began arriving. The first consisted of Czech Jews who were brought with the transports of Czech political prisoners. The SS officers, the Kapos, and the block elders treated this group of Jews harshly, and all soon died. In 1941, a second group, consisting of about 900 Jews, arrived from the NETHERLANDS. They had been taken as hostages after protests in the Dutch cities against the German occupation. Late in that year, only nine of this group remained alive. Not one of them survived until liberation.

From mid-1944 on, far larger groups of Jews began to arrive. The 6,000 Hungarian Jews brought to work in the Mauthausen camps after selections at Auschwitz in May and June were followed by 4,600 Jews from the Płaszów camp. These Jews too were treated far more harshly than the other prisoners. They worked digging tunnels for the munitions factories. The work was conducted in three shifts, at an extremely fast pace. No effort was made to spare the labor force. After a month or two, they were broken men who could hardly put one foot before the other. Each month, thousands of new prisoners arrived to replace those who had died. Because of the extremely bad conditions that the Jews were forced to live in, starvation and diseases accounted for more than 95 percent of the deaths.

> Jews were treated more harshly than other prisoners at Mauthausen and their extreme living conditions accounted for many deaths.

From January 25, 1945, with the general evacuation of Auschwitz, a second wave of transports began to arrive at Mauthausen. The majority of the 9,000 new prisoners were Jews. Most were sent to work digging underground tunnels at various subcamps. The last large group consisted of Hungarian Jews. Beginning in the fall of 1944, tens of thousands of Hungarian Jews had been sent to build a line of military fortifications along the border between Austria and Hungary. As the fighting front drew near in March and April 1945, the camps there were evacuated, and the prisoners were sent by foot to Mauthausen. Many died during the evacuation. They were housed in a tent camp, where they slept on the muddy earth in greatly overcrowded conditions. There was no running water or toilets, and they were given very little food. Epidemics of typhus and dysentery soon broke out, causing many deaths. On April 9, when there were already more than 8,500 prisoners in the tent camp, the transfer to this camp of all the Jewish prisoners in the main camp and in Gusen was begun. An estimated 3,000 prisoners died in the tent camp. On April 16, the first group of inmates was taken from there to the Gunskirchen camp, about 37 miles (60 kilometers) west of Mauthausen. The rest of the prisoners were transferred to Gunskirchen in two groups, a few days apart. They were taken by forced march. All who faltered on the way were shot down on the spot.

Liquidation Stage

In the second half of 1944, the stream of prisoners brought to Mauthausen increased. The death rate rose to huge dimensions. According to the official camp records, 24,613 prisoners died between January and May 1945. The actual number of dead was far greater, however, since the frequent transfers made exact record keeping impossible. Transports arrived from the camps that had been evacuated: Gross-Rosen, **Bergen-Belsen**, **Dora-Mittelbau**, **Neuengamme**, Buchenwald, **Ravensbrück**, Sachsenhausen, and other small camps. In late March and April 1945, the prisoners from the satellite camps were marched to the main camp. All those who could not march were killed with phenol injections, and their corpses were buried in the camps.

The main camp was now full to overflowing, a place of total disorder. The severe overcrowding and reduced food rations hastened the death of many. In the hospital, cases of cannibalism were documented. The crematoria could not burn all the corpses, and a gigantic grave was dug near the camp enclosure to hide 10,000 bodies. At the same time, the Germans began to burn documents. They also released favored prisoners, particularly criminal offenders, inmates of long standing, and those holding posts in the camp. Prisoners of Norwegian, Danish, Dutch, Belgian, and French nationality were released and handed over to the International Red Cross, which took them to Switzerland. The Jews were all transferred to Gunskirchen under the most severe conditions. The prisoners interpreted this act as a step toward their slaughter.

On May 3, a police unit from **Vienna** took over guarding the camp. The following day, work stopped, and the SS officers left the camp. One officer killed all the prisoners working in the crematorium and in the bunker, with a single exception. Late the next morning, American army tanks entered Mauthausen. The prisoners opened the gates and the camp was liberated.

It is estimated that 199,404 prisoners passed through Mauthausen. It is believed that 119,000 of them died, of whom 38,120 were Jews. This number includes the victims at the Hartheim castle. From August 1941 to October 1942, and from April 1944 to the end of that year, sick and debilitated prisoners and "undesirable" prisoners, including Jews, were regularly sent from the network of

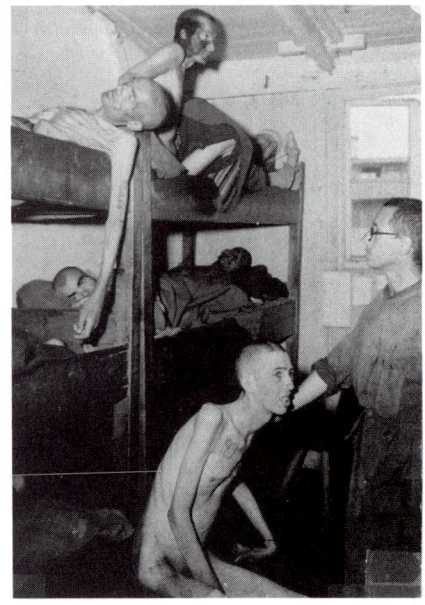

Tatooed survivors in a barracks in Mauthausen.

Mauthausen camps to the Hartheim castle near Linz, to be killed in the gas chamber there.

The suffering of the Mauthausen internees has been expressed in the Greek composer Mikis Theodorakis's *Ballad of Mauthausen*, based on a work by the Greek Jewish poet Jacob Kambanelis.

SUGGESTED RESOURCES

Frister, Roman. *The Cap: The Price of a Life.* New York: Grove Press, 2000.

Horwitz, Gordon J. *In the Shadow of Death: Living Outside the Gates of Mauthausen.* New York: Maxwell Macmillan International, 1990.

Weitz, Sonia Schreiber. *I Promised I Would Tell.* Facing History and Ourselves, 1993.

Mayer, Saly

(1882–1950)

Saly Mayer was a Swiss Jewish leader and a representative on the JOINT DISTRIBUTION COMMITTEE (JDC). He made his living as a lace manufacturer, and retired in the 1930s. An elected representative of a liberal-democratic party in his native Saint Gall in 1921, he was in municipal administration until 1933. Mayer was active in the Saint Gall Jewish community, founding a modern welfare organization there. He became secretary of the Federation of Swiss Jewish Communities (SIG; Schweizerischer Israelitischer Gemeindebund). He assumed the presidency of the SIG in 1936, and held the position until late in 1942, when he was forced out, due in part to the perception that he had not negotiated a generous enough immigration policy for Jewish refugees wishing to enter Switzerland. His close contact with the Joint Distribution Committee resulted in his being appointed its representative in Switzerland in 1940.

During Mayer's presidency, the SIG joined the WORLD JEWISH CONGRESS, and was actively involved in negotiations regarding the partition of Palestine in 1937. In 1938, following the occupation of Austria by German forces, a stream of 3,000 to 4,000 Austrian Jewish refugees began arriving in Switzerland. Mayer tried to negotiate to provide asylum to Jews fleeing Nazi persecution in Austria. Political and social circumstances were not in his favor. The Swiss Jewish community already numbered about 18,000, and Swiss public opinion strongly supported the anti-refugee stance held by the government. Despite his efforts on behalf of the refugees, Mayer was later criticized for not doing more to ease the restrictive Swiss policy on Jewish immigration.

As SIG president, Mayer was responsible for communicating with the JDC European office in Lisbon, and assisting refugees in Switzerland. Little money was available at first: $6,370 in 1940 and $3,030 in 1941. Mayer suggested that money be sent from the United States, through the Joint Distribution Committee, to support the increasing number of Jewish refugees in Switzerland. Mayer received $235,000 early in 1942 and $1,588,000 late in 1943. In 1944 he received $6,467,000, and between January and May 1945, another $4,600,000. Of this, he spent $1,913,000 in Switzerland in 1944, and about another $1 million in the first months of 1945, leaving something over $4,500,000 to spend for refugees elsewhere, primarily in Hungary, Romania, France, and Shanghai. But though funds had increased since earlier years, there was never enough to meet demand, and the refugee organizations in each country obtained much less for saving lives than they needed.

> A lonely, conservative, pedantic, and suspicious man, Mayer was independent and not known for maintaining good relationships with the leaders of various Jewish organizations in Switzerland and throughout Europe.

In the summer of 1942, the Slovak underground Jewish leadership approached Mayer requesting ransom money to save Jewish lives. In November and December of the same year, negotiations began in Slovakia for a larger ransom payment (the Europa Plan), which was supposed to save western and southeastern European Jews from deportation. Mayer at first saw these offers as simple extortion demands, but he changed his mind in the spring of 1943 and sought to provide the money. He did this illegally and without the support of other JDC leaders.

In 1944, Rezső **Kasztner**, the Hungarian Jewish negotiator, suggested that Mayer negotiate with the Nazis for the ransom of Hungarian Jews. Mayer was told by the United States authorities that he should negotiate but not offer either money or goods, and that he had to report to the United States legation on his moves. The Swiss gave him identical instructions, and forbade the Nazis to cross into Swiss territory. The JDC told him he was not their representative in these talks. Mayer nevertheless engaged in the negotiations between August 21, 1944, and February 5, 1945, with SS officer Kurt Becher and his representatives. Kasztner also attended most of these meetings. As a result of these efforts, Heinrich **Himmler** abandoned plans to deport the Jews of **Budapest**, and Mayer succeeded in arranging for a meeting between Becher and a representative of the American **War Refugee Board** in Switzerland on November 5, 1944.

After the war, Mayer was accused of acting without consulting the other Jewish organizations, and of not standing up for Jewish demands strongly enough. The Hungarian Jewish negotiators accused him of not supplying the money and goods that the Nazis demanded. These accusations seem to have little substance. Mayer turned his Hungarian Jewish colleagues into bitter enemies because he suspected them—wrongly—of financial dishonesty.

Mayer continued to serve as liaison for the JDC in central Europe after the war, and he sent food parcels to **Dachau** and other places in south Germany immediately upon their liberation. He also intervened, not always effectively, in the reconstitution of JDC committees in Hungary and Romania. Gradually, his role diminished, and although he was much praised by the JDC for his work, he retired. SS officer Kurt Becher and other Nazis had approached Mayer after the war, seeking his help to escape American justice, but he managed to evade them. He died before he could write his memoirs.

SUGGESTED RESOURCES

Bauer, Yehuda. *American Jewry and the Holocaust: The American Jewish Joint Distribution Committee, 1939-1945.* Detroit: Wayne State University, 1981.

Milton, Sybil, ed. *American Jewish Joint Distribution Committee, New York.* New York: Garland, 1995.

Medical Experiments

Experiments on human beings are an accepted practice in medical research. But they are generally governed by strong restrictions. They must not be intended for "pure" research—research that does not have the immediate purpose of developing a new medicine or treatment. They also must not have the sole purpose of advancing the researcher's career. Human beings may be involved only in those phases of an experiment for which they are absolutely essential. High-risk medi-

cines and experimental treatments may be tried out only when no cure exists and where an illness is already fatal. Under no circumstances may a person in good health be deliberately infected with a dangerous disease in order to try out a new medicine or treatment. Low-risk experimental medicines and forms of treatment may be tried out on people who are in good health. This may be done on a voluntary basis only, and the volunteer must be fully informed of all possible risks. Accidents do occur in medical experiments on human beings; the subject's health might be damaged, or even death may result. But under no circumstances may bringing about these results be a deliberate, essential element of the experiment.

In Nazi GERMANY and German-occupied countries, between 1933 and 1945, medical experiments were carried out in which these fundamental rules and the general standards of medical ethics were ignored. At least seventy pseudo-medical research projects of various kinds were conducted in Nazi CONCENTRATION CAMPS between September 1939 and April 1945. These projects involved medical experiments performed on human beings against their will. At least 7,000 people are known to have been subjected to these experiments; other cases are believed to have occurred, but neither documentary nor testimonial evidence has been presented to verify how many victims were affected.

Government medical services were involved in these experiments, as were the army medical corps and the medical services of the SS. As soon as Hitler came to power in 1933, he put all the health and medical services in Germany under a single national authority. In 1942, he named Karl Brandt, a member of his staff, chief of all medical services in the country, including those of the military and the SS. Hitler authorized Brandt to plan, direct, and supervise all medical services. Medical institutions conducted experiments and treatments that went against the code of medical ethics and were designed to serve Nazi ideology, which had a strong element of RACISM. This ideology promoted the exclusive advancement of the "Aryan" race. It rejected equality—and even the right to exist—of races and groups that were viewed as "inferior." Among these other groups were the Jews, the special target of Nazi hatred. (See also ANTISEMITISM.)

> The universal code of "medical ethics" is based on the equality of every person in human society. It morally and personally obliges every medical doctor to safeguard the health and life of every human being: "Strengthen my body and soul so that they may at all times be ready for untiring efforts, on behalf of the rich and the poor, the good and the bad, the beloved and the hated; let me see in every patient man only, for man he is." This passage, from the "Doctor's Prayer," is attributed to Maimonides (1135–1204)—a rabbi, philosopher, and physician.

Racisim and Nazi Medical Practice

The Nazis introduced racist-inspired measures relating to the field of medicine. A law was passed to prevent people with genetic diseases from having children. In 1935, a law was passed to protect the "German people's" genealogical heritage, as well as the Law for the Protection of German Blood and Honor. To satisfy this racist policy, German doctors and other medical personnel carried out the following measures:

1. The sterilization, between 1933 and 1937, of 200,000 young men and women who were found to have supposedly genetic diseases;

2. The killing of 90,000 mentally and chronically ill people in the EUTHANASIA PROGRAM;

3. The establishment of departments for genetic research and for genetic, anthropological and genealogical surveys of the entire "non-German" population to which the Law for the Protection of German Blood and Honor applied. The purpose was to identify people who qualified as being of "pure Aryan" blood.

Some 200 German medical doctors were stationed in the concentration camps where Nazi medical experiments took place. Universities and research institutes in Germany and AUSTRIA planned their research projects and advised the camp doctors in their work. Their laboratories received blood samples and human tissue for examination from these experiments.

MEDICAL EXPERIMENTS

Cruel and murderous experiments were performed by qualified and experienced doctors, in cold blood and in the name of science.

Every medical experiment had to have the approval of SS head Heinrich HIMMLER. At first, every application had to be submitted directly to Himmler. Beginning in 1944, Dr. Ernst Robert Grawitz, chief medical officer of the SS, screened the applications first. He solicited "expert" opinions before passing them on to Himmler. One, from a medical viewpoint, was from Dr. Karl Gebhardt, Himmler's personal physician and chief surgeon of the SS and police. The other opinion, from Richard Glücks and Arthur NEBE, had to do with the victims to be chosen for the proposed experiment.

The medical experiments fell into two broad categories: (1) experiments whose objectives satisfied professional medical ethics and the purposes of medical practice, but whose methods broke with moral law; (2) experiments whose very purposes violated medical ethics and that could not meet the accepted norms of medical research.

Immorality of Methodology

The first category of experiments consisted of two groups: experiments related to survival and rescue, and those involving medical treatment.

SURVIVAL AND RESCUE Survival and rescue experiments were designed to test the human potential for survival under harsh conditions and adaptation to such conditions, and to determine how to save lives. Experiments involved high altitudes, freezing temperature, and the drinking of seawater. They were conducted by the Luftwaffe (the German air force) in cooperation with the SS, on prisoners in the DACHAU camp.

High-altitude experiments were meant to learn the maximum altitude at which air crews of damaged aircraft could be saved. They also examined what equipment air crews needed in order to save themselves at an altitude of 13 miles (21 kilometers). (That was the maximum altitude reached by Allied aircraft at the time.) The victims of these experiments were put into pressure chambers that duplicated the conditions prevailing at 13-mile altitudes—low pressure and a lack of oxygen. The experiments were carried out with the knowledge that, for the most part, human beings cannot function properly at an altitude of 3.7 miles (6 kilometers) and above without a supply of oxygen. Under conditions that simulated parachuting from an altitude of 8 miles (13 kilometers) without an oxygen supply, the victims went through spasms and lost consciousness. Beginning at 9 miles (15 kilometers), they had breathing problems. There were cases in which victims stopped breathing altogether. Still, the experiments, without an oxygen supply, went on to an altitude of 13 miles. Some 200 Dachau prisoners were used for these experiments, and seventy to eighty lost their lives as a result. The experiments were carried out by Dr. Siegfried Ruff and Dr. Hans Romberg, civilian doctors from the German Experimental Institute of Aviation in BERLIN, and by Dr. Sigmund Rascher, an air force doctor and SS officer.

The freezing experiments were designed to learn the most effective method of treating people who were in a state of shock after prolonged immersion in freezing seas or exposure to dry cold. The victims of the first of these experiments were put into a tank of ice water and kept there for 70 to 90 minutes, or as long as it took for them to lose consciousness. At this critical stage, they were taken out of the freezing water. Attempts were then made to restore their normal body temperature, by various means. No painkillers were used to relieve the victims' suffering. About 300 people were used in these experiments. Eighty to ninety of them lost their lives.

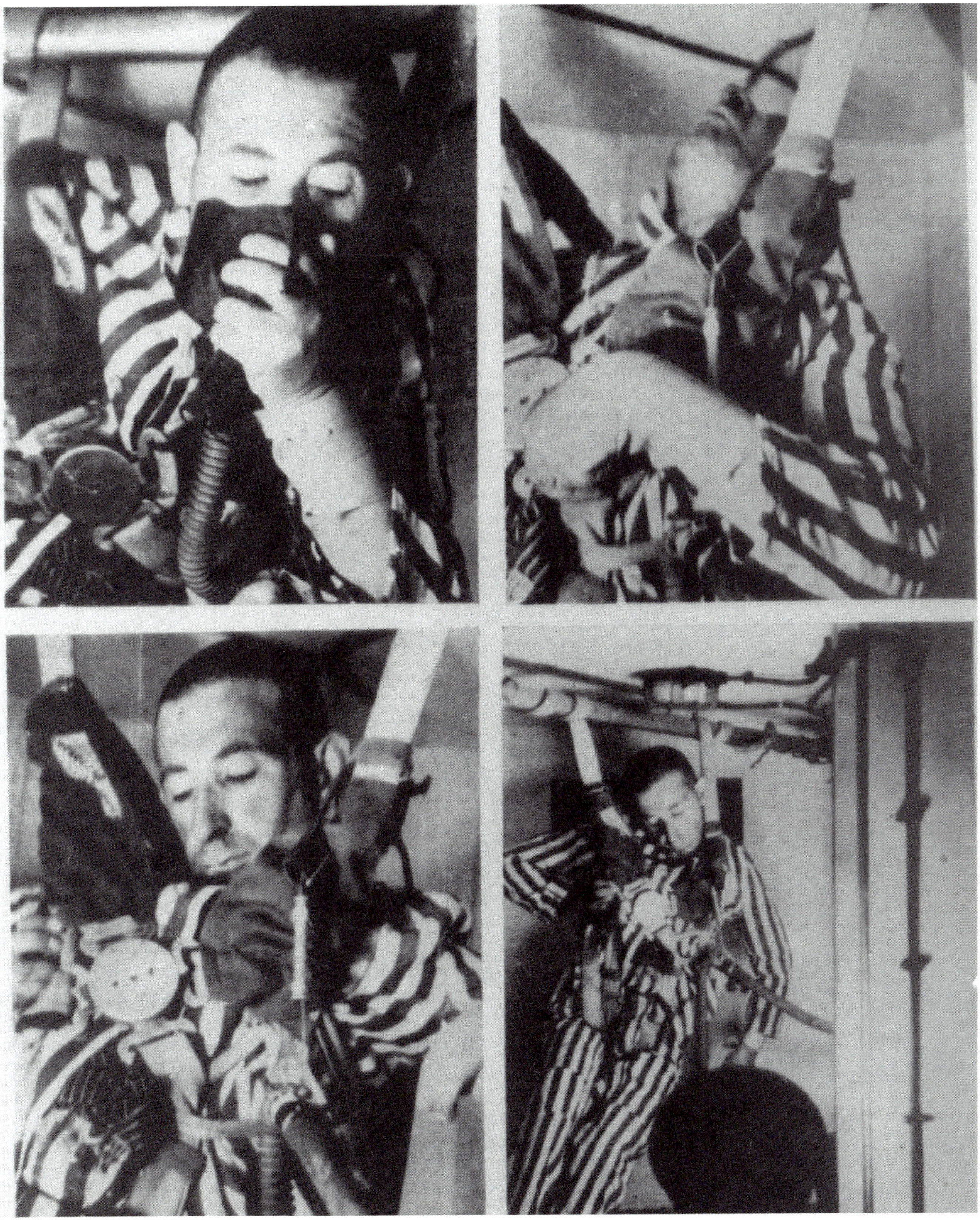

MEDICAL EXPERIMENTS

A prisoner in a parachute harness is deprived of oxygen during low-pressure experiments. Clockwise from top left: breathing through a mask in a decompression chamber; in convulsive seizures caused by anoxia (severe oxygen deficiency); limp stage; and unconscious in the chamber. These photographs are from the files of doctors at Dachau.

MEDICAL EXPERIMENTS

Some experiments explored humans' exposure to dry cold. The victims were put naked into the snow-covered courtyard of the experiment compound. They were kept there for nine to fifteen hours, from 6:00 in the evening to 9:00 the next morning, at a temperature of 8.4°F (–6°C). Their terrible screams of pain were ignored, and they were given no means of relief. But their screaming had the effect of forcing these experiments to be discontinued, because they disturbed the civilian population living near the Dachau camp. The dry-cold experiments were carried out by Professor Ernst Holzlöhner and Dr. E. Finke of Kiel University, who had been drafted to the air force for this purpose, and by Dr. Rascher. Experiments were performed on 60 prisoners, providing new information on the proper treatment of cold victims.

The experiment with salt water was designed to establish a reliable method of making seawater drinkable. The aim was to improve the chances for survival of air crew or naval personnel stranded in the sea. The experiment was conducted on 44 people, 41 of them **Gypsies** (Romani). The main purpose was to learn the chances of survival when the only liquid available to drink was seawater, or seawater whose taste had been improved by a chemical agent (named Berkatite), without any change in the salt content. The experiment was conducted in series of 15-day periods. During those times, the victims were forced to drink .53 to 1.06 quart (.5-1.0 liters) of seawater or Berkatite per day. Dr. Wilhelm Beiglböck, an air force adviser, was in charge. The experiment confirmed what was already known—that there was no difference between seawater and Berkatite as far as their dehydrating effect on human beings was concerned.

MEDICAL TREATMENT The Nazi experiments for medical treatment consisted of three main categories: (1) experiments relating to the treatment of battle injuries; (2) those relating to the treatment of victims of gas attacks; and (3) those testing immunization compounds or medicines for the prevention or treatment of contagious and epidemic diseases.

One experiment for the treatment of war wounds took place in the **Ravensbrück** camp. The victims were 75 Polish political prisoners, all women. The experiment's purpose was to establish the effectiveness of sulfanilamide in preventing infection and putrefaction from taking place in limbs as a result of wounds. The doctor in charge was Dr. Gebhardt, who had been the attending physician of Reinhard **Heydrich** after he was attacked by an assassin. When Heydrich died of his wounds, it was hinted that he could have been saved if enough sulfanilamide had been available. Himmler asked Gebhardt to prove, by experiment, that sulfanilamide was not effective against putrefaction caused by gangrene (the immediate cause of Heydrich's death). A special effort was made to induce severe infections in the bodies of the victims. When Dr. Grawitz learned that there had not yet been deaths in the experiment, he demanded that the infections be worsened. As a result, five women died because they were not given proper surgical treatment, since the experiment demanded that only sulfanilamide be used. The remaining women were ill for a long time and were disabled for life. Infection by gangrene bacilli is a frequent occurrence in battle wounds, so the purpose of the experiment was justifiable. But the methods used turned it into a criminal act.

Another series of experiments relating to war wounds involved the treatment of fractures and the transplantation of bones, muscles, and nerves. Dr. Gebhardt conducted these experiments on Polish women prisoners at Ravensbrück. The purpose was to find solutions to problems in the treatment of severe wounds in the upper and lower limbs. At first, the leg bones of physically sound young women were broken, and they were given various treatments. In later experiments, entire bones and other tissues were extracted in order to transplant them into patients at the SS hos-

pital in Hohenlychen. In fact, whole limbs were amputated from the prisoner victims for transplants. These amputations were carried out on mentally ill prisoners, who were then put to death. The experiment cost the lives of 11 out of the 24 victims; the rest were maimed for life.

Yet another war-wounds experiment tested the effectiveness of the biochemical treatment of infected wounds. In this experiment, pus was injected into the soft tissue of the victims in order to generate infected wounds. This took place in the Dachau hospital. The victims were 20 German prisoners and 40 prisoners of other nationalities, and cost the lives of 19 of them. Experiments relating to second- and third-degree burns were conducted at **AUSCHWITZ**, while **BUCHENWALD** was the scene of experiments dealing with phosphor burns caused by incendiary bombs.

Another experiment in the treatment of wounds was designed to test the effectiveness of blood-coagulating agents. This experiment was carried out by Dr. Rascher at Dachau. The specific substance being tested was Polygal 10, which is taken orally to stop bleeding resulting from wounds or after surgery. To conduct the experiment, four victims were shot point-blank in parts of the body that are prone to heavy bleeding, after they were forced to swallow a certain amount of Polygal. The victims died instantly. This bizarre experiment replaced the simple method, used by hospitals, of determining the effectiveness of a coagulating agent by measuring the duration of bleeding and the time it takes for the blood to coagulate.

Experiments on the treatment of chemical-warfare victims were conducted throughout the war. In March 1944, however, Hitler ordered Karl Brandt to intensify medical research on the effects of chemical warfare. As a result, all studies conducted in this field became part of Nazi Germany's overall research program on gas warfare. In 1939, experiments on the use of mustard gas were carried out in the **SACHSENHAUSEN** concentration camp by Dr. Walter Sonntag and Dr. Heinrich Baumkötter. At the same time, Dr. August Hirt was conducting experiments in this field, on a larger scale, at the Ganzweiler camp. Of the 220 persons he used as subjects, 50 died as a result of the experiments. Ganzweiler was also the scene of experiments in the treatment of phosgene poisoning. (Phosgene is a gas that causes suffocation; if absorbed in large doses, it leads to death by asphyxiation.) These experiments, which tested the effectiveness of hexamethylene tetramine, were carried out by Professor Otto Bickenbach, a member of the Strasbourg University faculty. At the **NEUENGAMME** camp, 150 prisoners were made to drink water containing chemical-warfare substances, as part of a research project for the purification of drinking water. There were other experiments in this field, but no details concerning them have come to light.

Another area of experiments had to do with the immunization and treatment of infective and epidemic diseases such as malaria, infective hepatitis, and typhus. The malaria experiment was a civilian venture. It was carried out at Dachau by Dr. Claus Schilling. The experiment used 1,200 prisoners, most of them Catholic priests, and cost the lives of 300 to 400 people. Of them, no more than 30 died of the disease itself. The others died from overdoses of the medicines that were being tried out on them. Infective hepatitis was the subject of experiments at Sachsenhausen, carried out by Dr. Arnold Dohmen, as well as at the Natzweiler and Buchenwald camps. In some of these experiments, it was expected that the human subjects would die. For these, Dr. Grawitz asked Himmler to put at his disposal Jewish prisoners, who were already condemned to death. Following the invasion of the **SOVIET UNION** by the Germans in June 1941, typhus fever became widespread among the German army. From 1941 to the end of the war, a broad program of experiments was conducted at Buchenwald and Ganzweiler to test the effectiveness of various immunization inoculations. Hundreds of prisoners were used in these experiments, and hundreds died as a result.

MEDICAL EXPERIMENTS

In the typhus experiments at Buchenwald, one group of "test persons" (TPs, in SS usage) was inoculated with various serums then in general use. A second "control" group was not inoculated. A third group was infected with the disease at the start of the experiment, to serve as a "bank" for live viruses to be used in the infecting of other victims with the disease. As a rule, typhus is transmitted by fleas, which carry the virus. When the experiments were started, the "natural" means of transmission was tried out. Later, the "test persons"—those who had been inoculated, as well as the control group, who had not been inoculated—were infected by having blood from a typhus patient injected into their bodies. Of the 729 people used in the experiment, 154 died as a result. Of the 120 people who had served as a live-virus bank, 90 died.

Another set of typhus-immunization experiments began at Ganzweiler in late 1943, by Professor Eugen Haagen of Strasbourg University. Haagen asked for 300 physically fit prisoners of military age, of whom he selected 90. Using a live-virus serum that he had developed, Haagen infected both the non-immunized control group and the immunized group. His experiments cost the lives of 30 people.

Among other experiments involving contagious and epidemic diseases was one related to yellow fever. This disease was widespread in North Africa, where German forces were fighting. In the experiment, 485 people were inoculated with a yellow-fever serum to test its effectiveness. Other experiments dealt with smallpox, paratyphoid A and B, cholera, diphtheria, and influenza. Tuberculosis experiments were conducted on 114 "test persons" at Dachau and on 100 men and 20 children at Neuengamme. Ganzweiler was the scene of immunization experiments on 1,700 people relating to diseases of an unknown nature.

The above experiments were for the most part carried out on behalf of the army or civilian health authorities, and at their request. Many other experiments, however, simply served the interests or the medical specialization of the doctor who devised and conducted them.

"Racial" Experiments

The second broad category of experiments—those that violated medical ethics—involved (1) experiments designed to provide biological and physiological findings to support the Nazi ideology based on differences between the "Aryan" race and other races; and (2) experiments to further the aims of Nazi Germany's ideological policy by medical means—that is, to bring about the destruction of the Jews.

Three types of experiments were conducted to provide biological evidence to support Nazi racist ideology: experiments on dwarfs and twins; serological (blood-related) experiments; and a study of the skeletons of Jews.

The experiments on dwarfs and twins were carried out by Dr. Josef MENGELE at Auschwitz. The only firsthand evidence on these experiments comes from a handful of survivors and from a Jewish doctor, Miklós Nyiszli, who worked under Mengele as a pathologist. The victims were twins and dwarfs, ages two and above. Mengele subjected them to clinical examinations, blood tests, X-rays, and anthropological measurements. In the case of the twins, he drew sketches of each twin, for comparison. He also injected his victims with various substances and dripped chemicals into their eyes (apparently in an attempt to change their color). He then killed them himself by injecting chloroform into their hearts, to carry out comparative pathological examinations of their internal organs. Mengele's purpose, according to Dr. Nyiszli, was to establish the genetic cause of the birth of twins. The goal was to develop a program to double the birth rate of the "Aryan" race. The experiments on twins affected 180 people, adults and children.

Mengele also carried out a large number of experiments in the field of contagious diseases (typhoid and tuberculosis) to find out how human beings of different races withstood these diseases. He used Gypsy twins for this purpose. Mengele's experiments combined scientific research with the racist and ideological aims of the Nazi regime.

The serological experiments, conducted by Professor Werner Fischer of the Koch Institute for Contagious Diseases and Dr. Karl Georg Horneck, were intended to prove that there were serological differences among the races—that is, differences in blood serum. The experiments were carried out on Gypsies in the Sachsenhausen camp. Similar experiments had been conducted earlier by the same doctors. In 1938, Fischer had made a comparative study of the blood serum of whites and blacks; and in 1941, Horneck had made such a study of black PRISONERS OF WAR.

The project on skeletons of Jews was carried out by Dr. August Hirt at Strasbourg University. His purpose was to prove the racial inferiority of "Jewish-Bolshevik commissars" by means of an anthropological study of their skeletons. For this experiment, 115 Jews in a good state of health were selected and killed in gas chambers. Their corpses were sent to the anatomical institute at Strasbourg University, where Hirt hoped to show that communism and Judaism affect the structure of the skeleton, and thus to demonstrate the inferiority of the human beings concerned.

Experiments designed to support Nazi ideological policy included those involving methods of mass sterilization and of killing individuals as well as masses of human beings. From the very beginning of Hitler's rule, sterilization was part of Germany's health policy. As early as 1933, a program was launched in Germany to sterilize all genetically diseased, retarded, and alcoholic individuals, so as to protect the well-being of the "Aryan" race. Similar programs were put into effect in some of the German-occupied countries.

> From the scanty information available, it appears that Mengele expected the victims' deaths and that this anticipated result formed a central element in his experiments.

Sterilization

Experiments in mass sterilization began in 1942. They were not designed as a means of installing the "Aryan" race as the future ruler of the world. Instead, they aimed to provide an alternative to the immediate destruction of the Jews and of other people who, according to Nazi racist ideology, should not be permitted to live. Such a method would also enable the Nazis to interfere as little as possible with the MISCHLINGE (persons of "mixed blood") and use them to meet labor requirements. The sterilization experiments were carried out on Hitler's own initiative, but Hitler was also responding to proposals made by several doctors who had a professional interest in them. They suggested to Hitler that sterilization could serve as a powerful weapon in the total war against Nazi Germany's enemies.

Dr. Horst Schumann, in Auschwitz, first sterilized men, women, and children by means of radiation. He exposed them to large doses of X rays, which caused severe burns. He then removed the men's testicles and sent them to a Breslau institute for examination. Dozens, perhaps hundreds, of people of different nationalities were used in these experiments. Most of them were sent to the gas chambers soon afterward, since their radiation burns made them unfit for work. Sterilization experiments were also conducted on women and children in Ravensbrück. Viktor Brack, the author of this group of experiments, suggested to Himmler that the method be used on 3 million Jews—out of the total of 10 million earmarked for extermination—provided they were fit and could be used as forced laborers (see FORCED LABOR).

Other sterilization experiments were carried out at this time by Professor Carl CLAUBERG at Auschwitz and Ravensbrück. Their aim was to study mass steriliza-

tion by one-time injection of a chemical substance into the womb. Thousands of women were used in this experiment; most of them Jewish, and the rest were Romani (Gypsy) women. Himmler had asked Clauberg how much time it would take to sterilize 1,000 women by means of an efficient, speedy, inexpensive, and dependable method. Clauberg found that by using the method he had devised and tested, a team consisting of one doctor and ten assistants could sterilize up to 1,000 people a day. Clauberg used a routine gynecological examination to inject a chemical into the womb that had the effect of totally destroying the lining membrane of the womb and severely damaging the ovaries. The second stage of the experiment was to surgically remove the damaged ovaries and send them to Berlin for study. Clauberg's experiment resulted in the permanent sterilization of the victims and in irreversible damage to their wombs and ovaries.

During the war, sterilization programs were also carried out in the occupied countries. These programs were based on racist grounds. In 1942, a number of doctors and political figures—including Clauberg—suggested to Himmler that non-surgical experiments in mass sterilization be carried out in the concentration camps. Mass sterilization, they argued, would be the answer both to the labor requirements for the war effort (by keeping the concentration camp prisoners alive for this purpose) and to the major objective of Nazi racist policy: the rapid and total destruction of all the Jews of Europe.

Military Tribunals

On October 25, 1946, The Medical Case, tried by the Nuremberg Military Tribunals, opened. Twenty-three defendants, including twenty doctors, were put on trial. Many had held senior posts in the administration or the army. Sixteen were found guilty under Allied Control Council Law No. 10, providing for the punishment of war crimes and crimes against peace and humanity. All the defendants were accused of CRIMES AGAINST HUMANITY, and of several other crimes under that law. They were found guilty of planning and executing experiments on human beings against their will, in a cruel and brutal manner involving severe torture, and of the deliberate murder of some of the victims, in cold blood and with full awareness of the seriousness of their deeds. The Nuremberg Military Tribunals found that the medical experiments were crimes that served the ideological objectives of the Nazi regime. They also found that none of the many experiments carried out by the Nazis was of any scientific value.

Five people who had played a central role in the medical experiments were not tried at Nuremberg. Ernst Grawitz committed suicide in 1945, Carl CLAUBERG was tried in the Soviet Union, Josef MENGELE escaped to South America, and Horst Schumann disappeared and has not been traced. Siegmund Rascher was executed on Himmler's orders in February 1945 for falsely claiming that his wife gave birth to children after age forty-eight.

During the 1950s and 1960s, other German physicians who had been involved in experiments in concentration camps were brought before German courts, tried, and in a number of cases, convicted. Among them was Dr. Heinz Baumkötter, former SS doctor at Sachsenhausen.

SEE ALSO TRIALS OF THE WAR CRIMINALS.

SUGGESTED RESOURCES

Aly, Gotz. *Cleansing the Fatherland: Nazi Medicine and Racial Hygiene.* Baltimore, MD: Johns Hopkins University Press, 1994.

Caplan, Arthur L., ed. *When Medicine Went Mad: Bioethics and the Holocaust.* Totowa, NJ: Humana Press, 1992.

In the Shadow of the Reich: Nazi Medicine [videorecording]. First-Run Features, 1997.

Lifton, Robert Jay. *The Nazi Doctors: Medical Killing and the Psychology of Genocide.* New York: Basic Books, 1986.

Matalon Lagnado, Lucette. *Children of the Flames: Dr. Josef Mengele and the Untold Story of the Twins of Auschwitz.* New York: Morrow, 1991.

Mein Kampf

Mein Kampf ("My Struggle") is volume one of a book written by Adolf HITLER when he was imprisoned in GERMANY in the mid-1920s, after he tried to take over the government. It was published in July 1925, under the title "A Reckoning" *(Eine Abrechnung)*. The second volume, "The National Socialist Movement" *(Die nationalsozialistische Bewegung)*, was published in December 1926 (although the book gives 1927 as the year of publication). Since 1930, all editions have been published as a single volume under the title, *Mein Kampf.* By 1945, some 10 million copies had been put in circulation, and the book had been translated into sixteen languages. Since then, it has appeared in several translations, but no new German edition has been published. Over the years, *Mein Kampf* went through some corrections, mostly of style and a few of fact, but only one substantial change was made: The editions that came out in 1930 and later state that the leaders of lower rank in the NAZI PARTY would no longer be elected but would be appointed by the next higher rank.

Volume one was meant to be Hitler's autobiography and volume two to show how the Nazi party came into being. The book as a whole, according to the preface, was to set forth Hitler's aims and beliefs. The autobiographical information, however, is largely untrue and incomplete. In the same way, the "history" of the Nazi party, described in the second volume, is altered by Hitler's ideological statements.

While the book deals with many aspects of politics, Hitler's views on Germany's foreign policy are described in detail. His goals were to first establish political alliances with ITALY and Britain, then to go to war against FRANCE. Through these alliances, Hitler hoped to create conditions that would allow Germany to capture territory in Eastern Europe and Soviet Russia that would serve as *Lebensraum* ("living space") for the German people.

The book also contains the basics of Hitler's deadly plans for the Jews. Beginning in 1919, Hitler had called for the removal of the Jews from Germany. By this he generally meant that they should emigrate or be expelled from the country. In the book, however, he demands that the Jews be killed, and he claims global significance for this demand: "No people can remove this fist 'of the international Jew'; from its throat, unless it uses the sword....; This must necessarily be a bloody process." Hitler complains that the German government missed the opportunity of "mercilessly exterminating" the Jews at the beginning of World War I. He also argues that Germany would not have lost the war if it had "used poison gas" on 12,000 to 15,000 Jews.

Opinions vary on the importance of *Mein Kampf.* Some scholars believe that the book was only propaganda. Others find that it contains a clear statement of Hitler's goals, especially when considered in the light of the policies he actually pursued after he rose to power in Germany in 1933.

SEE ALSO **ANTISEMITISM; RACISM.**

A bound copy of *Mein Kampf.*

SUGGESTED RESOURCES

Fleming, Gerald. *Hitler and the Final Solution.* Berkeley: University of California Press, 1984.

Hitler, Adolf. *Mein Kampf.* Boston: Houghton Mifflin, 1999.

Staudinger, Hans. *The Inner Nazi: A Critical Analysis of Mein Kampf.* Baton Rouge: Louisiana State University Press, 1981.

Wistrich, Robert S. *Hitler's Apocalypse: Jews and the Nazi Legacy.* New York: St. Martin's Press, 1985.

Mengele, Josef

(1911–1978?)

Josef Mengele was a German medical doctor and **SS** officer. Mengele was born in Günzburg, **GERMANY**. In 1935 he was awarded a Doctorate in Philosophy by the University of Munich, and in 1938 an M.D. degree from the University of Frankfurt. He was a member of Stahlhelm, an extreme right-wing and antisemitic organization, from 1931 to 1934. Mengele joined the **NAZI PARTY** in 1937 and the SS in 1938. From June 1940 he served in the Waffen-SS medical corps, and in August of that year he was appointed an *Untersturmführer* (second lieutenant). In May 1943 he was promoted to *Hauptsturmführer* (captain) and was posted to the **AUSCHWITZ** extermination camp, where he remained until its evacuation on January 18, 1945. Mengele spent much of his time on pseudoscientific **MEDICAL EXPERIMENTS** and also on the *Selektionen* (selection procedures) of Jews who were brought to the camp. In the course of these *Selektionen*, most of the Jews were immediately sent to their death in the **GAS CHAMBERS**. The rest were put on **FORCED LABOR** in **CONCENTRATION CAMPS**.

Mengele's pseudoscientific experiments, in which he used human beings as guinea pigs, dealt primarily with infants and young twins, and with dwarfs. The experiments involved the maltreatment of the prisoners in various ways, such as the excision of their genital organs and a variety of harmful injections into the veins or directly into the heart.

When Auschwitz was evacuated, Mengele was transferred to the **MAUTHAUSEN** concentration camp; when that camp was liberated on May 5, 1945, all trace of him was lost. In mid-1949 he turned up in Argentina, where he was given asylum. Mengele's criminal actions were documented at the Nuremberg Trial and in the trials of the Nazi criminals who had functioned at Auschwitz (*see* **TRIALS OF THE WAR CRIMINALS**). In 1959 the West German authorities issued a warrant for his arrest, and in 1960 the West German Foreign Ministry asked Argentina for his extradition, but Mengele succeeded in escaping to Brazil and from there made his way to Paraguay. According to some sources, he was drowned in December 1978, in Brazil, but the veracity of this has been questioned. In June, 1985, a coffin believed to be Mengele's was opened in Embu, Brazil. In 1992, an international panel of forensic experts declared the remains to be those of Josef Mengele.

SEE ALSO **OFFICE OF SPECIAL INVESTIGATIONS**.

SUGGESTED RESOURCES

Astor, Gerald. *The "Last" Nazi: The Life and Times of Dr. Joseph Mengele.* Chicago: D. I. Fine, 1985.

Josef Mengele: The Final Account [videorecording]. Set Productions, 1998.

A wanted poster for Josef Mengele, showing him as he appeared in his 40s, and in an artist's sketch of what he would look like at 74.

Matalon Lagnado, Lucette. *Children of the Flames: Dr. Josef Mengele and the Untold Story of the Twins of Auschwitz.* New York: Morrow, 1991.

Nyiszli, Miklos. *Auschwitz: A Doctor's Eyewitness Account.* New York: Arcade, 1993.

Posner, Gerald L. *Mengele: The Complete Story.* New York: McGraw-Hill, 1986.

Minsk

Minsk is the capital of Belarus, which from 1919 until 1991 was known as the Belorussian Soviet Socialist Republic (*see* **Belorussia**). In 1926 the Jewish population of Minsk was 53,686; by June 1941 the number had grown to 80,000, constituting one-third of the city's population. Only a number of Jews managed to escape from the city in the six days between the German invasion of the **Soviet Union** and the conquest of Minsk on June 28, 1941. German parachutists had been dropped east of the city, and they intercepted thousands of Jews who were trying to flee and forced them to return. When the civil administration was established by the Germans, Minsk became the headquarters of Wilhelm Kube, the *Generalkommissar* (general commissioner; chief administrator) for Belorussia.

On July 8, 1941, the Germans killed 100 Jews in Minsk, and thereafter, they murdered Jews singly or in groups daily. On July 20, the Germans ordered the creation of a ghetto made up of thirty-four streets and alleys, as well as the Jewish cemetery. Jews from Slutsk, Dzerzhinsk, Cherven, Uzda, and other nearby places were brought into the ghetto. Married couples with one non-Jewish partner were also put into the ghetto, as were their children. Altogether, 100,000 persons were rounded up and put behind the ghetto walls. The next month, 5000 Jews from the ghetto were seized and murdered. The surviving Jews were forced to pay ransom, to report every Sunday for roll call, and to wear a yellow badge (*see* **BADGE, JEWISH**) on their back and chest, as well as a white patch on their chest with their house number.

Shortly after the ghetto was established a **JUDENRAT** (Jewish Council) was put in place, with Eliyahu (Ilya) **MUSHKIN** at its head. Its seven departments—welfare, housing, supplies, health, workshops, labor, and registration—were responsible for meeting the day-to-day needs of the Jews as well carrying out German orders in the ghetto. Mushkin cooperated with the anti-Nazi underground movement, however, and in February 1942 he was arrested and hanged.

In an *Aktion* (operation) on November 7, 1941, the Germans rounded up 12,000 Jews and murdered them in nearby Tuchinka. Shortly afterward, the houses in which the murdered Jews had lived were filled with Jews recently deported from **GERMANY**. A second *Aktion* took place on November 20, in which the Germans murdered 7,000 Jews, also in Tuchinka. After the two *Aktionen*, the ghetto underground activists intensified their activities, preparing for escapes to the forests and widening its network of hiding places in the city.

On March 2, 1942, the Germans launched a third *Aktion*. They ordered the Judenrat to hand over 5,000 Jews, but on orders of the underground, the Judenrat did not comply. The Germans then began shooting Jewish workers on their way back from their places of work outside the ghetto and carried them off, killing more than 5,000 people, among them the children of the Shpalerna Street orphanage. When the Germans asked that the leader of the underground, Hersh Smolar, be surrendered to them, the Judenrat chairman produced Smolar's bloodstained identity card as proof that he was dead. The Germans also instituted night *Aktionen*, resorting to them with increasing frequency in the spring of 1942. In one such night *Aktion*, on April 2, about 500 people were murdered.

Between July 28 and 31, 1942, the Germans killed some 30,000 Jews, among them the German Jews who were in a separate ghetto in Minsk. The Germans forced Jaffe address the crowd and try to allay their fears, but when trucks with gas engines burst upon the square where they had assembled, Jaffe cried out: "Jews, the bloody murderers have deceived you—flee for your lives!" Jaffe and the ghetto police chief were among the victims of that *Aktion*, following which only 9,000 Jews were left in Minsk. The Germans replaced the Judenrat with an administrative committee that would carry out Nazi orders.

In August 1943 a transport of Minsk Jews left for the **SOBIBÓR** extermination camp. On September 10, 2,000 Jews were sent to the labor camp at **BUDZYŃ**, near **LUBLIN**. During the final *Aktion*, on October 21, 1943, the last four thousand Jews were killed, at Maly Trostinets. When Minsk was liberated on July 3, 1944, only a small number of those who had gone into hiding during the final *Aktion* remained alive.

The Ghetto Underground

In August 1941 an underground force was established in the ghetto, with Hersh Smolar as one of its founders. The founding group formulated the under-

The hanging of two partisans in Minsk in October, 1941. At left is Masha Bruskina, a 17-year-old Jewish girl.

ground's goal, which was to escape into the forests and fight in the ranks of the partisans. Initial activities included forming a network of underground fighters, finding ways to get news from the front, setting up a secret printing press, and developing contacts with sympathizers in the non-Jewish parts of the city. The ghetto underground had nearly 450 members, organized into cells. In this period the underground also hoarded weapons. At the beginning of September 1941 a representative of the partisans came to the ghetto and asked for money, which Mushkin, head of the Judenrat, supplied. In early 1942, regular contact was established with the partisans in the forests; the ghetto underground sent groups of its members out to establish its own partisan bases there. Following the third *Aktion*, in March 1942, the great escape into the forests began. The majority of the escapees headed to the southeast of Minsk, or to the northwest of the city, and set up partisan bases there. Most of the guides for the groups that fled the city were children from the ghetto, ranging in age from 11 to 14. Minsk Jews established seven partisan units. An estimated 10,000 Jews fled to the forests, the majority losing their lives on the way.

partisans
Anti-Nazi resistance fighters who carried out acts of sabotage and assassination.

Jews from the Reich in Minsk

Between November 1941 and October 1942, a total of 35,442 Jews from Germany and the Protectorate of **BOHEMIA AND MORAVIA** were deported to Minsk. Most of them were taken by train directly to Maly Trostinets and murdered there. The first of these transports arrived in Minsk in November 1941; it was made up of Jews from Hamburg, Düsseldorf, Frankfurt, **BERLIN**, Brünn (Brno), Bremen, and **VIENNA**. They were housed in a separate ghetto, adjoining the main Minsk ghetto.

The ghetto of the Reich Jews was divided into five sections, according to the places from which they came—Hamburg, Berlin, the Rhineland, Bremen, or Vienna. There was little contact between the main Minsk ghetto and the Reich ghetto. The German Jews were killed in the major *Aktion* of July 28 to 31, 1942; on March 8, 1943; and in the fall of 1943. Some were sent to the Budzyń labor camp. Only ten Reich Jews were still alive in Minsk when the city was liberated.

SUGGESTED RESOURCES

Rokhman, Leyb. *The Pit and the Trap: A Chronicle of Survival.* New York: Holocaust Library, 1983.

Smolar, Hersh. *The Minsk Ghetto: Soviet-Jewish Partisans Against the Nazis.* Washington, DC: U.S. Holocaust Memorial Museum, 1989.

A Teacher's Guide to the Holocaust: Resisters. [Online] http://fcit.coedu.usf.edu/holocaust/people/resister.htm (accessed on August 22, 2000).

Mischlinge (Part Jews)

The word *Mischlinge* (part Jews) literally means "hybrids." The **NUREMBERG LAWS** of September 1935 initially mentioned only Jews and Germans. But in November 1935, when the concept of a "Jew" was defined in the first implementation ordinance of those laws, a third group appeared: those who were neither Jews nor Germans—the *Mischlinge*. The census of 1939 showed that 72,000 *Mischlinge* of the first degree and 39,000 of the second degree were still living in **GERMANY**.

Categorizing *Mischlinge*

Mischlinge of the first degree, or half Jews, were those who had two Jewish grandparents, did not belong to the Jewish religion, and were not married to a Jewish person as of September 15, 1935. They had the rights of regular German citizens, although they were limited by a series of regulations. For example, they could marry only *Mischlinge* of the first degree. Marriage with a German or with a *Mischlinge* of the second degree required a special permit from the Ministry of the Interior and the party chancellery, which was almost never granted. As of 1940 *Mischlinge* of the first degree were excluded from military service and, as of 1942, from high schools. They were also barred from employment in the armaments industry and from taking part in Germany's trade representations abroad.

Mischlinge of the second degree, or quarter Jews, were those with one Jewish grandparent. They were subject to certain limitations in professions requiring full German origins, but were drafted into the army and were allowed to marry Germans, but not quarter, half, or full Jews. In all other matters they were treated like German "Aryans." This category also included mixed marriages. Consequently, as of April 8, 1940, soldiers married to *Mischlinge* of the second degree were treated like them, and those married to *Mischlinge* of the first degree or to Jews were treated like *Mischlinge* of the first degree.

At the end of 1941, proposals were made that all *Mischlinge* of the first degree be sterilized. The **WANNSEE CONFERENCE** considered a proposal of allowing those *Mischlinge* scheduled to be deported to remain in Germany if they submitted voluntarily to sterilization. The compulsory sterilization of all *Mischlinge* was also suggested at the conference. But the question of what policy should be adopted toward the *Mischlinge* was never resolved because of the Nazis' fears of the possible repercussions among the large number of German relatives of the *Mischlinge*. The only *Mischlinge* killed were inmates of the **CONCENTRATION CAMPS** who had been arrested in the 1930s. These people were transferred to **AUSCHWITZ** at the end of 1942.

A similar lack of consistency characterized the *Mischlinge* policy in conquered countries. When Dutch Jews were ordered to register in January 1941, the order also included those Dutch people who had one Jewish grandparent. Such quarter Jews were not relocated to Amsterdam or deported. Dutch Jews were allowed to

> Generally, the policy was to absorb the *Mischlinge* of the second degree into the German nation, whereas those of the first degree were equated with Jews.

petition the General Commission for Administration and Justice for the Occupied Netherlands Territory for exemption from the status of full Jew and half Jew. Countless applications flooded the commission. Many were handled by Dr. Hans Georg Calmeyer, who was extremely lenient and accepted 75 percent of the applications for serious consideration. He also recommended that those Jews whose applications were under consideration not be sent to a "Jewish camp" (that is, deported), because if their petitions were to be granted, all their property would have to be restored to them. Another aspect of the treatment of *Mischlinge* in the **NETHERLANDS** arose in the context of marriages between Jews and "Aryans." The 8,610 registered Jewish partners in these unions were essentially given the option of deportation or undergoing sterilization to prevent them from bringing further *Mischlinge* into the world. Nevertheless, while 2,562 submitted to sterilization, half of them men and half women, many were killed anyway. After the ghettoization of Polish Jewry, *Mischlinge* of all degrees were also put in the ghettos. In **SLOVAKIA**, however, they were exempted from deportation to **EXTERMINATION CAMPS**.

For Adolf Hitler, the question of the status of Germans of partial Jewish descent was of paramount importance because of his obsession with "racial purity."

Hitler's Interest in *Mischlinge*

Hitler's personal concern regarding the status of the *Mischlinge* in Germany rested on his racist belief that all *Mischlinge* were a menace and that the complete assimilation of foreign blood was impossible. "Families," he argued, "even if they have only a minute quantity of Jewish blood in their veins, regularly produce, generation by generation, at last one pure Jew." For this reason, applications made by Jews for a change in their status, a process known as "equalization," were handled by the Ministry of the Interior, and all potential approvals had to be referred to Hitler. His decision was then sent directly to the *Mischlinge*. For this reason too, on February 20, 1944, Hitler expressly ordered that all *Mischlinge* cases be dealt with by his deputy, Martin **BORMANN**, and submitted to himself for final approval. Hitler's intervention was also required when a number of *Mischlinge* received, compliant with the racial legislation, a racial classification different from that corresponding to their biological condition. In all these cases, Hitler's personal decision was needed to clarify the status of the individual concerned.

This was true also of mixed marriages involving *Mischlinge*. However, Hitler's personal intervention could still lead him at times to contradict his own principle. While saying in private conversations that he was convinced that Germany would harm itself by accepting *Mischlinge* into the army, and that exemptions from the status of full Jew or half Jew should therefore be reduced to a minimum, he exempted some 260 officers or their wives who were *Mischlinge* of the first degree. Similarly, by 1942, some 340 Jews had been equalized by him with *Mischlinge* of the first degree. By means of legal trickery, he also granted the status of half Jew to some 3,000 people considered Jews. After the attempt on his life on July 20, 1944, Hitler's obsession with Jewish influence intensified. As a result, he ordered that civil servants who were *Mischlinge*, or who were married to Jews or *Mischlinge*, could no longer hold high governmental office, even if their partners had previously been equalized with "Aryans." This new regulation affected a wide range of people in important posts, among them an ambassador and a high official in the Ministry of Churches.

The drafting of *Mischlinge* into the armed forces was of great concern to Hitler as well. A decree of April 8, 1940, declared that only he could grant permits to *Mischlinge* to serve in the army. The same motive inspired his order that a second-degree female *Mischlinge* required his permission to marry if the groom was in active service.

Hitler was obviously even stricter regarding membership in the **NAZI PARTY**, which was meant to be a mainstay of racial purity. The hunt for *Mischlinge* in the party ranks was much more thorough than demanded by state law, and expulsions from the Nazi party included *Mischlinge* even up to the fifth degree. However, those *Mischlinge* who had proved their merit prior to 1933 and when there was also only a small degree of Jewish blood were permitted to remain in the party. The problem was dealt with individually only in exceptional cases, as when the person involved had been unaware of his Jewish ancestry and had been active in the party for years. All applications for exemptions had to go through Hitler. Hitler also issued general instructions that the offspring of political leaders were not to marry *Mischlinge*, even if the latter had received equal status with Germans.

SUGGESTED RESOURCES

Koehn, Ilse. *Mischling, Second Degree: My Childhood in Nazi Germany.* Puffin Books, 1990.

Kuehn, Heinz R. *Mixed Blessings: An Almost Ordinary Life in Hitler's Germany.* University of Georgia Press, 1988.

Newman, Amy. *The Nuremberg Laws: Institutionalized Anti-semitism.* San Diego: Lucent Books, 1999.

Rosenstrasse Protest in Nazi Germany. W. W. Norton, 1996.

MIXED MARRIAGES. SEE MISCHLINGE.

Mogilev-Podolski

Mogilev-Podolski is a town on the Dniester River, in the Vinnitsa district of the **UKRAINE**, across the border from the Romanian district of Bessarabia. In 1926 Mogilev-Podolski had a Jewish population of 9,622, 41.8 percent of the total. On July 19, 1941, it was occupied by German and Romanian forces. Thousands of Jews were murdered. The town remained under Nazi control until the **SOVIET UNION** invaded in March of 1944, as part of the Allied war effort against Adolf **HITLER** and the Axis powers of **GERMANY**, **ITALY**, and the countries aligned with them.

Mogilev-Podolski was an assembly point for Jews expelled from Bessarabia and Bukovina, in Romania. It was also an important crossing point to the region between Romania and Ukraine known as Transnistria. The Romanian town of Atachi, through which the expelled Jews had to pass, faces Mogilev-Podolski on the Romanian bank of the Dniester. During the days preceding the Nazi occupation, tens of thousands of Jews tried to escape by migrating north from Bessarabia and Bukovina to the Soviet interior. Many were caught by advancing German forces and forcibly returned to the regions along the Dniester.

In the fall of 1941, when the first group of Jews from Romania was deported to Mogilev-Podolski, there were 25,000 Jews already in the town, including many who ended up there after their failed escape. By November many **columns** of Jews from Bessarabia and Bukovina had passed through the city. A total of 55,913 expelled Jews passed through Mogilev-Podolski between September 15, 1941, and February 15, 1942.

Thousands of people were packed into the transit camp at Mogilev-Podolski, which consisted of decrepit and filthy barracks. Conditions were so intolerable that every day many people committed suicide. The Romanian camp guards abused the Jews mercilessly. Thousands of Jews who were not permitted to stay in Mogilev-Podolski were driven out and forced to walk to villages and towns in the district or to cross the Bug River, where they faced conditions even worse than in Mogilev-

columns
Row after row of prisoners on forced marches.

Podolski. Some 15,000 expelled Jews stayed in Mogilev-Podolski, despite the ban imposed by the authorities, either by bribing authorities or because their work was beneficial to the local or district economy. The Jews who managed to stay organized themselves into groups, based on their community of origin. One of them, Shimon Jegendorf, from Rădăuţi, was an engineer by profession, and he was able to repair and reactivate the local electric power station, as well as a foundry and other factories. This led to many job openings, and 2,000 to 3,000 Jewish workers and their families were granted residence permits. The rest of the Jews in the city, numbering some 10,000, lived with the constant threat of deportation hanging over their heads.

The Romanian officials in charge in the district were hostile and cruel to the Jews. There were also German military units stationed in Mogilev-Podolski, supervising the Jews working on the construction of a bridge across the Dniester. These Germans mistreated the Jews and frequently executed them for minor offenses. About 2,000 male Jews were sent away on **Forced Labor**, escorted by Romanian police guards who treated them harshly. Some were transferred to areas under German control, and many perished or were shot to death.

In December 1943, the Mogilev-Podolski ghetto held 12,836 deportees from Bukovina, 348 from Bessarabia, and 3,000 local Jewish inhabitants. In March 1944 the Jewish leadership in Bucharest obtained permission to bring 1,400 orphans back to Romania. Most of the other deportees were unable to flee to Romania in time. When the city was liberated by the Soviet army, on March 20, 1944, many of the male Jews were drafted on the spot, given several weeks of training, and sent to the front or to work in coal mines. Of those who stayed in Mogilev-Podolski, many lost their lives when the Germans shelled the city. In the spring of 1945 most of the deportees were permitted to return to Romania; those who had survived the forced labor in the Soviet Union came back in 1947.

The number of survivors in Mogilev-Podolski was relatively large because of the town's proximity to Romania, the Jews' own self-help organization, and the aid they received from the Jews in Romania.

SUGGESTED RESOURCES

Arad, Yitzhak. *The Einsatzgruppen Reports: Selections from the Dispatches of the Nazi Death Squads.* Washington, DC: U.S. Holocaust Memorial Museum, 1989.

Gitelman, Zvi, ed. *Bitter Legacy: Confronting the Holocaust in the USSR.* Bloomington: Indiana University Press, 1997.

Monowitz. See Auschwitz.

Moravia. See Bohemia and Moravia, Protectorate of.

Moreshet. See Museums and Memorial Institutes.

Morgenthau, Henry, Jr.

(1891–1967)

Henry Morgenthau, Jr. was an American statesman. As secretary of the treasury of the **United States**, Morgenthau was the highest-ranking Jew in the administration of President Franklin D. Roosevelt. During the period of the **Holocaust**, Mor-

> Morgenthau's diaries show that he blamed the State Department for thwarting efforts to admit even the small number of Jews who were legally entitled to enter under the immigration law. His subordinates informed him of a deliberate effort to turn off the flow of information detailing the implementation of the "Final Solution." He complained to Secretary of State Cordell Hull, until he realized that Hull was uninformed and uninterested in the issue.

genthau influenced Roosevelt on the subject of the American rescue effort. In addition, he helped inspire the creation of the WAR REFUGEE BOARD in January, 1944.

Morgenthau was born in New York City into a prominent German Jewish family. After earning a fortune as a banker and real-estate developer, his father entered politics and was active in the Democratic party. The elder Morgenthau also served as American ambassador to Turkey from 1913 to 1916. Henry Morgenthau, Jr. studied agronomy at Cornell University. His family bought a large working farm in New York State, not far from the home of Roosevelt. A link between the Morgenthaus and Roosevelts had already been established through their common interest in the Democratic party. Years later, Morgenthau moved to the top of American politics as an integral part of the Roosevelt entourage, and a firm bond of friendship developed between the two men.

In 1928, after Roosevelt was elected governor of New York State, he appointed Morgenthau chairman of the agricultural advisory commission. Two years later he became conservation commissioner. Some of the innovative policies of the New Deal's agricultural program have their roots in this period. In 1933 Morgenthau was named to the Federal Farm Board and the Farm Credit Administration, and in 1934 he was appointed to the Cabinet as secretary of the treasury. His subordinates in the Treasury Department, John W. Pehle, Josiah E. DuBois, Jr., and Randolph Paul, alerted Morgenthau to the fact that the State Department was blocking refugee immigration (see UNITED STATES DEPARTMENT OF STATE), which ultimately led to some meaningful action on behalf of Jewish refugees.

Through the Treasury's control of export licenses, Morgenthau maintained a far-reaching influence in the foreign relations area, especially American policy toward the "New Order" in GERMANY. Early on, Morgenthau sensed the danger the National Socialists posed for world peace, and he advocated military preparedness. During the ambassadorship of William E. Dodd in BERLIN, Morgenthau refused to issue a license for the sale of helium to Germany. The later conflict between the State Department and the Department of the Treasury over rescue policy is best understood in the context of Morgenthau's intrusions into the foreign-policy area, resulting in a rivalry between him and Cordell Hull, the secretary of state. Although Roosevelt shared the view that the State Department was generally ineffective, he essentially agreed with the department on the low priority that should be given to the "Jewish question" during the war. After the EVIAN CONFERENCE in 1938, Roosevelt requested that Morgenthau chair the President's Advisory Committee on Political Refugees, but Morgenthau refused. At that time, Morgenthau was unaware of what Berlin had in store for European Jewry.

By the fall of 1942, as bits of news about the Nazi anti-Jewish depredations began to filter back to Washington, Morgenthau's uneasiness grew. By mid-1943, Morgenthau was showing signs that the destruction of European Jewry was having a considerable impact on him.

In January 1944, Morgenthau's assistant, Josiah Du Bois, Jr., handed him his "Report to the Secretary on the Acquiescence of This Government in the Murder of the Jews," which documented the State Department's "willful failure to act." After toning down the more dramatic phrasing of the brief, and changing its title to "A Personal Report to the President," Morgenthau convened Benjamin V. Cohen and Samuel Rosenman, two presidential advisers who were Jewish, to deliver the report together with him to the president on January 16, 1944. Following that visit Roosevelt established the War Refugee Board. Several Jewish organizations have claimed credit for mobilizing Morgenthau in the rescue cause. Whatever the case, it came too late to help millions of Jewish victims of the Nazi death machine.

Henry Morgenthau, Jr., at his desk in the U. S. Department of Treasury.

Shortly before Germany's surrender, Morgenthau published his book, *Germany Is Our Problem* (1945) where he explained his plan for the "pastoralization" of the former Reich. Morgenthau's fear was that a re-built Germany could bring on World War III. Roosevelt's successor, Harry S Truman, thought Morgenthau's plan was impractical. The recovery of Europe could not be managed without Germany playing its customary role.

Morgenthau soon resigned his post and became deeply involved in Jewish causes. He was recruited by Henry Montor to become general chairman of the United Jewish Appeal, a position he held between 1946 and 1950. Morgenthau is given credit for successfully organizing its first 100,000,000 dollar fund-raising campaign. He also drew much closer to the Zionist consensus that now held sway in the American Jewish community. In 1950 he accepted the chairmanship of the board of governors of the Hebrew University, and a year later he followed Montor to the Israel Bond Organization and the American Financial and Development Corporation for Israel. At the time of Morgenthau's death in 1967, he was fully immersed in Jewish causes.

SUGGESTED RESOURCES

Blum, John Morton. *Roosevelt and Morgenthau*. Boston: Houghton Mifflin, 1970.

Everest, Allan Seymour. *Morgenthau, the New Deal, and Silver; A Story of Pressure Politics.* New York: Da Capo Press, 1973.

Morgenthau, Henry. *Mostly Morgenthaus: A Family History.* New York: Ticknor and Fields, 1991.

Müller, Heinrich

(1900–?)

Heinrich Müller was a loyal **HITLER** supporter who became chief of the **GESTAPO**. After attending elementary school, Müller was apprenticed to the Bavarian Aircraft Works in Munich. In 1917 he volunteered for the air force; he became a

> As joint directors in the Gestapo organization, Gerhard Flesch and Heinrich Müller were responsible for Gestapo subdivisions overseeing a wide range of functions, including good-conduct certificates, the file registry, the identification service, the Nazi party and its affiliated organizations, the security of weapons and explosives, and special duties—surveillance and assassinations.

fighter pilot on the western front in April 1918, and was awarded several distinguished-service medals. In June 1919 he was discharged as a noncommissioned officer. He began working at the Munich police headquarters in December 1919. In the spring of 1929 he passed with distinction the examination for the intermediate level of the police force, and before long he was the Munich police headquarters expert in the fight against communism and related "leftist" movements.

Müller was a hard and ambitious worker who on occasion disregarded the law, according to evidence given by the **NAZI PARTY** district administration in 1936. Under the Weimar Republic, his political affiliation fluctuated between the German National Popular Party and the Bavarian People's Party; rumor had it that in 1933 he and some of his colleagues opposed handing over the Munich police administration to the **SA** (*Sturmabteilung*; Storm Troopers) and the **SS**.

Before long, however, Müller became one of the most important aides to Reinhard **HEYDRICH**, the new Bavarian police chief. This was a result of his intimate knowledge of the Communist party and of the German section of the Comintern (the Third Communist International), and his familiarity with Soviet police methods. Müller's reports also gained Heinrich **HIMMLER**'s attention; this won him promotion to the rank of senior police secretary, on May 1, 1933, and, on November 16, 1933, to senior secretary of the criminal police. In 1935, he was appointed controller of the criminal police. In 1936, to ensure that no problems arose in the relations between the Bavarian political police and the Gestapo and SS, Müller, who was not a party member, was appointed a member of the **SD** (*Sicherheitsdienst*; Security Service).

Soon afterward, Heydrich was appointed Gestapo chief, and he took Müller along with him, together with his former superior, Gerhard Flesch, appointing them joint directors responsible for the suppression of hostile elements. Flesch and Müller oversaw Gestapo action against organizations fully or partially associated with communism and Marxism, including the trade unions. They were also in charge of Gestapo subdivisions that monitored religious organizations, Jews, Freemasons, and emigrants; protective-custody and **CONCENTRATION CAMPS**; economic, agricultural, and social policies; and nonpolitical organizations.

Müller's phenomenal rise to power, however, began after the suppression of the so-called Röhm Putsch on June 30, 1934, the "Night of the Long Knives." Four days later Müller was promoted to SS-*Obersturmführer* (first lieutenant) and put in charge of senior officials. On January 30, 1935, Müller rose to the rank of SS-*Hauptsturmführer* (captain); on April 20, 1936, to SS-*Sturmbannführer* (major); and on January 30, 1937, to SS-*Standartenführer* (colonel). In June of that year, he was given the rank of senior administrative councillor and criminal police councillor, against the recommendation of the Munich-Upper Bavaria Police District Administration, although by then he had been in charge of the Gestapo office for a year. From September 1939 to the end of the war, Müller was head of Section IV (Gestapo) of the **REICH MAIN SECURITY OFFICE** (RSHA; *Reichssicherheitshauptamt*) and deputy commander of the Security Police and the SD. He was responsible to Heydrich and, after Heydrich's assassination, to his successor, Ernst **KALTENBRUNNER**.

Müller was one of the most powerful men in the Nazi state terror system, but he stayed out of the limelight. On April 20, 1939, he became an SS-*Oberführer* (brigadier general) and on December 14, 1940, an SS-*Brigadeführer* (major general); two days later he was also promoted to *Generalmajor* of the police. On November 9, both Müller and Arthur **NEBE** were appointed to the rank of SS-*Gruppenführer* (lieutenant general) and to the equivalent rank in the police.

On October 15, 1944, Müller, the ex-pilot, was awarded the Knight's Cross with crossed swords, the highest German award offered during World War II, in recognition of his services in the merciless pursuit of those who participated in the July 20, 1944, plot against Hitler. These included some of Müller's friends, such as Count Wolf Heinrich von Helldorf, Arthur Nebe, Hans Gisevius, and Friedrich Werner von der Schulenburg.

Müller remained loyal to Adolf **HITLER** to the end in the bunker where Hitler spent his last weeks. All trace of Müller was lost on April 29, 1945. Rumors that he had escaped to Brazil or Argentina persisted, and he was placed on a list of "most wanted Nazis" in 1973.

SUGGESTED RESOURCES

Douglas, Gregory. *Gestapo Chief: The 1948 Interrogation of Heinrich Müller* (3 vol.). Los Angeles, CA: Bender, 1996–98.

Gellately, Robert. *The Gestapo and German Society: Enforcing Racial Policy, 1933–1945.* New York: Oxford University Press, 1990.

Johnson, Eric A. *The Nazi Terror: Gestapo, Jews and Ordinary Germans.* New York: Basic Books, 1999.

Muselmann

Muselmann is German word that translates literally as "Muslim"; the term was widely used among prisoners in **CONCENTRATION CAMPS** to describe peers who were on the verge of death from starvation, exhaustion, and despair. Many prisoners reached this stage soon after their arrival in a camp, due to their inability to adapt to the conditions and the difficulties of accepting the harsh regime. Often, these individuals had belonged to the intelligentsia or the well-to-do classes, and had come to the camps from countries that still had a measure of economic well-being and individual liberty. The psychological shock of daily life in a concentration camp was as lethal to these men and women as the physical hardships were. Others fell victim to extreme hunger, physical overexertion, and corporal punishment. Many prisoners were sick, but they sought to hide their condition, fearing that their admittance to the camp hospital would lead to their being designated for death.

Muselmänner (the German plural form of *Muselmann*) were past the point of trying to hide their condition. They could be identified by such characteristics as a lack of flesh on their bodies, tight yellow skin over their bones, a dull and expressionless look in their eyes, and the inability to stand upright for any length of time. They were indifferent to their surroundings, apathetic, and listless. The Nazis in charge of the camps regarded them as undesirables, since they were incapable of working. Most of the prisoners avoided contact with *Muselmänner*, as well, afraid that this condition could be in store for them.

A person who had reached the *Muselmann* stage had no chance of survival, and did not remain alive for more than a few days or weeks. The origin of the term has not been established; some have attributed it to a certain similarity between a concentration camp *Muselmann* and the image of a Muslim prostrating himself in prayer.

SUGGESTED RESOURCES

Leipceiger, Nathan. "Remembering the Holocaust: A Concentration Camp Survivor Recalls His Liberation." *Maclean's,* Jan. 23, 1995.

Matzner, David. *The Muselmann: The Diary of a Jewish Slave Laborer.* Hoboken, NJ: Ktav, 1994.

> "By August many had deteriorated badly, both physically and mentally.... we could only guess at their state of mind, because they had stopped communicating with others and were locked inside themselves: they had become the living dead of the camps."
>
> Helen Lewis, A Time to Speak *(New York: Carroll & Graf) 1994, p. 71.*

MUSEUMS AND MEMORIAL INSTITUTES

Museums and Memorial Institutes

Holocaust Remembrance Day (Yom ha-Sho'ah) is observed according to the Jewish calendar on 27 Nisan, which falls during the period when the Warsaw Ghetto Uprising took place, late April to early May. In Israel this is an official memorial day. The main ceremony takes place at Yad Vashem, in Jerusalem, and other events are held throughout the country. Pupils in Israeli schools also commemorate the day. In the United States the day is observed in many cities, communities, and college campuses, with an official ceremony in Washington, DC. The Polish government sponsors a memorial ceremony on April 19.

In Israel, the UNITED STATES, and Europe, there are many museums and other memorial institutions devoted to the period of World War II and the HOLOCAUST. These memorial sites have been established by survivors' groups and soldiers' organizations, by synagogues and churches, by families and individuals, by private funds and public allocations. Some of the memorial sites have been built in response to the Jewish injunction to remember, others help fulfill a government's need to explain a nation's past to itself. The aim of many memorial institutions and occasions is to educate people of younger generations and to help them develop a sense of shared experience, destiny, responsibility, and meaning for the future.

The first memorial sites were the places of destruction themselves. In October 1944, Soviet liberators made the concentration camp at MAJDANEK, near LUBLIN in POLAND, the first memorial and museum of its kind. The only other extermination camp to be left partially standing, at AUSCHWITZ-Birkenau, was also made a state memorial. Its barracks were converted into national pavilions, and the ruins of its gas chambers were left untouched to recall their former reality.

In addition to the memorials and museums located at the sites of former camps in Poland and GERMANY, memorials ranging from elaborate statues and mausoleums to simple plaques now mark some of the sites of DEPORTATIONS, destroyed synagogues, and razed Jewish cemeteries throughout Europe. In many instances, survivors returned to their former homes in Poland and Germany only long enough to erect memorials to their lost families and communities, before moving on.

Among the most famous museums and memorial institutions are two in the United States—The United States Holocaust Memorial Museum and The Simon Wiesenthal Center—and one is in Israel—*Yad Vashem*.

United States Holocaust Memorial Museum

Located only 400 yards from the Washington Monument, at the heart of the National Mall in Washington, the United States Holocaust Memorial Museum (USHMM) is America's national institution for the documentation, study, and interpretation of Holocaust history. The world's largest and most comprehensive Holocaust museum, it also serves as the United States' memorial to the millions of people murdered during the Holocaust.

The museum, which came into being through a unanimous act of the United States Congress in 1980, is designed to be a permanent and powerful reminder to the American people and to the world that humankind must guard forever against the danger of another Holocaust. The museum is also an educational institution dedicated to teaching children and adults, through multimedia presentations, publications, and curriculum resources, and facilitating scholarship on the Holocaust through the Center for Advanced Holocaust Studies.

The USHMM's permanent exhibition, titled The Holocaust, tells the story of Nazi terror. While it focuses on the six million Jews who were murdered, the museum also tells the tragic story of GYPSIES, Poles, Soviet PRISONERS OF WAR, homosexuals, the handicapped, Jehovah's Witnesses, and other victims of Nazi persecution. In addition, it recognizes the American liberators of the EXTERMINATION CAMPS and tells another story—about the failure of the free world, including the United States, to stop the Holocaust. Changing exhibits focus on various Holocaust topics. The Wexner Learning Center offers research opportunities with access to text, images, maps, music, survivor testimony, and film, via multimedia computers. Special exhibits for children between the ages of eight and eleven are also available.

The USHMM opened its doors in 1993. Since then, it has become one of the most-visited museums in Washington, D.C. Located a half-block south of Independence Avenue, the building, adjacent to the Bureau of Engraving and Printing, extends the entire length of the block between Fourteenth Street SW and Raoul Wallenberg Place (formerly Fifteenth Street SW).

The building comprises 225,000 square feet of floor area on five levels above ground, and a below-ground concourse. The Hall of Witness serves as the museum's central gathering place, through which visitors pass to all parts of the building. This large, solemn hall, illuminated by natural light, resonates with symbolic references to the Holocaust. A deep crack, a symbol of the rupture of civilization during the Holocaust, runs down one wall of the hall.

The Hall of Remembrance, a hexagonally-shaped, skylit memorial projecting from the museum, is a spiritual space, designed as an area for contemplation and reflection as well as for public ceremonies. Along the hallway walls there are niches for candles —universal symbols of remembrance. The hexagon evokes the memory of the six million Jews murdered in the Holocaust.

The United States Holocaust Memorial Museum offers many internet-based resources and services, as well. The museum's internet website (*see* Suggested Resources, below) offers a comprehensive online learning center featuring free access to texts, bibliographies, timelines, and classroom curriculum materials. In addition, virtual exhibits from the museum's permanent and traveling collections, featuring multimedia interactive learning activities, are available.

The Tower of Faces in the permanent exhibition at the United States Holocaust Museum.

The Simon Wiesenthal Center

The Simon Wiesenthal Center, named for the Viennese Nazi-hunter Simon **Wiesenthal**, was established in Los Angeles in 1977 by its founder and dean, Rabbi Marvin Hier. In 1979 a museum developed by Holocaust historian Efraim Zuroff was opened. More than 20 years later, the Simon Wiesenthal Musuem of Tolerance is a hands-on, experiential learning center visited by thousands of students and individuals every year. Housed in a five-level structure that includes theaters, an auditorium, multimedia work stations and research areas, the Museum of Tolerance features permanent and traveling exhibitions.

The Simon Wiesenthal Center includes more than a museum. With offices around the world, the center is supported by more than 400,000 members in its work on behalf of Holocaust remembrance, the defense of human rights and the Jewish people. Since its establishment, the Wiesenthal Center has focused on political issues related to the Holocaust and has specialized in the use of mass media to educate the public about the events of World War II. Its major campaigns have included efforts to cancel the statute of limitations on war crimes in West Germany, and attempts to force South American governments such as those of Paraguay and Chile to surrender leading Nazi criminals (Dr. Josef **Mengele** and Walther **Rauff**). The center has also been instrumental in uncovering hundreds of Nazi collaborators of eastern European origin who escaped to Western democracies, and in convincing the governments of **Great Britain**, Australia, and Canada to investigate this issue and prosecute the criminals found in those countries. More recent efforts include work on behalf of Holocaust survivors who are entitled to, but have little ability to retrieve, financial reparations awarded to them.

In 1982, the Wiesenthal Center's documentary *Genocide* was awarded an Oscar as the best documentary film of the previous year. In 1997, the center produced an Academy Award-winning documentary called *The Long Way Home*, which examines the plight of Jewish survivors of the Holocaust trying to rebuild their lives during the post-war years of 1945–1948. The center has also videotaped more than four hundred hours of testimony by Holocaust survivors and liberators.

A key component in the outreach and education mission of the Simon Wiesenthal Center is its Internet-based Simon Wiesenthal Center Multimedia Learning Center Online (*see* Suggested Resources, below) featuring more than 3000 searchable text documents, tens of thousands of images, teacher and curriculum resources, virtual exhibits, special document collections, and access to many of the resources of the Museum of Tolerance.

Yad Vashem

Yad Vashem (The Holocaust Martyrs' and Heroes' Remembrance Authority) is an Israeli national institution that commemorates the Jews who fell victim to the Holocaust. Yad Vashem was first proposed in September 1942, by Mordecai Shenhavi. He recommended "the commemoration of the Holocaust in the Diaspora, and of the participation of the Jewish people in the Allied armies." He also proposed the name Yad Vashem (meaning "a monument and a name"), from Isaiah 56:5: "I will give them, in my house and in my walls, a monument and a name, better than sons and daughters; I will give them an everlasting name that shall never be effaced."

On May 2, 1945, Shenhavi submitted his idea to the Jewish National Institutions in Jerusalem. This led to a recommendation that a center in Jerusalem be established that would include an eternal light for the victims; a registry of their names; a memorial for the destroyed Jewish communities; a monument for the fighters of the ghettos; a memorial tower in honor of all the Jewish fighters against the Nazis; a permanent exhibit on the **CONCENTRATION CAMPS** and extermination camps; and a tribute to the **"RIGHTEOUS AMONG THE NATIONS"**.

In February 1946, Yad Vashem opened an office in Jerusalem and a branch office in Tel Aviv; preliminary planning was begun. The outbreak of the Israeli War of Independence in May 1948, however, brought Yad Vashem planning and operations to an almost complete standstill.

In 1950, planning for Yad Vashem resumed. A hill in west Jerusalem was chosen as the site for the memorial. A building to house the archives, the library, and the administrative offices was completed in 1957, and Yad Vashem moved in that same year. On April 13, 1961, the Hall of Remembrance was dedicated, symbolizing the 6 million Jews killed. The walls of the Hall of Remembrance are made of huge basalt slabs and it has a tent-shaped roof (hence its Hebrew name, *Ohel Yizkor*, or Tent of Remembrance).

Alongside the Tent of Remembrance is the Historical Museum, which contains a permanent exhibition of authentic photographs, artifacts, and documents relating to the Holocaust and heroism. The Hall of Names, which was dedicated on April 7, 1968, holds the pages of testimony in which the names of the Holocaust victims are registered by surviving relatives and friends. In 1982, the building with an art museum and an auditorium was opened to the public. Three years later, the Soldiers', Partisans', and Ghetto Fighters' Monument was dedicated. A monument to the millions of Jews who perished in the extermination camps is situated on the northwestern edge of the large plaza between the museum and the Hall of Remembrance. And in 1987, the Children's Memorial was dedicated, commemorating the 1.5 million Jewish children who perished in the Holocaust.

Yad Vashem Holocaust Memorial, Jerusalem, Israel.

The Yad Vashem Archive contains millions of pages of documents, testimonies, and memoirs in many languages. It is one of the largest and most important collections relating to the Holocaust. The library's volumes, mainly dealing with the Holocaust period, also include works on the growth of modern ANTISEMITISM, FASCISM, and Nazism; on the background of World War II; and on the fate of the Holocaust survivors.

Educational programs affiliated with Yad Vashem include the International School for Holocaust Studies, which opened in 1999, with course offerings in eight languages and more than 90 faculty members; seminars, conferences, and publications for educators; curriculum materials for classroom use; and online resources available through the Yad Vashem Internet website (*see* Suggested Resources, below).

One unique feature of Yad Vashem is the Avenue of the Righteous Among the Nations. A public committee was appointed by Yad Vashem to determine who was entitled to the "Righteous Among the Nations" medal. The award is given to those non-Jews who, at the risk of their own lives and for humanitarian reasons, saved the lives of Jews. Most of the trees along the avenue have been planted by the rescuers themselves; the first trees were planted on May 1, 1962.

The Yad Vashem site in Jerusalem continues to evolve in its mission to preserve the memories of the lives lost during the Holocaust. As part of an initiative called Yad Vashem 2001, the entire museum complex will be expanded in an area that is about three times larger than the current site. The new archive and library building, which opened in March 2000, will include more documents from Europe, additional videotaped interviews with Holocaust survivors and previously uncollected rare artifacts belonging to those who lived during the Holocaust era. In addition, the project calls new historical and art museum spaces, as well as for the complete computerization of Yad Vashem's documentation system, which includes millions of names of Jewish victims in the Hall of Names, making Yad Vashem's retrieval system among the most advanced and accessible to the public worldwide.

Yad Vashem has become a major national shrine, and more than 2 million people, from Israel and abroad, visit it every year. A visit to Yad Vashem is part of the program for official guests on state visits to Israel.

SUGGESTED RESOURCES

Abells, Chana Byers. *The Children We Remember: Photographs from the Archives of Yad Vashem, the Holocaust Martyrs' and Heroes' Remembrance Authority, Jerusalem, Israel.* New York: Greenwillow Books, 1986.

Arad, Yitzhak. *The Pictorial History of the Holocaust.* New York: Macmillan, 1990.

Cole, Tim. *Selling the Holocaust; From Auschwitz to Schindler: How History Is Bought, Packaged, and Sold.* New York: Routledge, 1999.

Gilbert, Martin. *Holocaust Journey: Traveling in Search of the Past.* New York: Columbia University Press, 1997.

Saidel, Rochelle G. *Never Too Late to Remember: The Politics Behind New York City's Holocaust Museum.* New York: Holmes and Meier, 1996.

The Simon Wiesenthal Center Online. [Online] http://motlc.wiesenthal.com/ (accessed on September 4, 2000).

United States Holocaust Memorial Museum. [Online] http://www.ushmm.org (accessed on September 4, 2000).

Weinberg, Jeshajahu. *The Holocaust Museum in Washington.* New York: Rizzoli International Publications, 1995.

Yad Vashem Online. [Online] http://www.yad-vashem.org.il/ (accessed on September 4, 2000).

Young, James Edward. *The Texture of Memory: Holocaust Memorials and Meaning.* New Haven: Yale University Press, 1993.

Mushkin, Eliyahu

(d. 1942)

Eliyahu Mushkin was the chairman of the Minsk JUDENRAT (Jewish Council) and a supporter of its underground and the local PARTISANS. A native of MINSK, Mushkin was an engineer and a member of the local government staff. Shortly after the Germans occupied Minsk at the end of June 1941, Mushkin was appointed Judenrat chairman because of his knowledge of German or, according to one version, because he was recommended for the post by a member of the city council.

Mushkin lost little time in establishing contact with the Minsk ghetto underground. He was helpful in aiding Jews to escape from the ghetto, and he supplied the partisan units in the area with money, medicines, and equipment. Mushkin exercised a decisive influence on the attitude of the other members of the Judenrat, which for all practical purposes became the executive arm of the underground and carried out its decisions. Mushkin was able to warn the underground of impending dangers, and the Jews respected him. His close contacts with the underground, coupled with the duties that the German authorities imposed on him, put Mushkin in a precarious situation. He had to be extremely careful, and could not afford to trust even some of his own staff.

In February 1942 Mushkin was arrested under circumstances that are not entirely clear. One report was that he was charged with attempting to bribe a GESTAPO officer to release a Jewish prisoner. According to another version, he was arrested when someone informed on the Judenrat to the Gestapo, revealing that the Judenrat was helping the partisans. A third version is that Mushkin had given refuge to a German officer who sought to avoid frontline service, and that it was this officer who gave him away. Mushkin was tortured and, a month after his arrest, he was hanged. The members of his family were killed during one of the night-time killing sprees known as "night Aktionen."

SUGGESTED RESOURCES

"Jews in the Soviet Union." *The Jewish Student Online Research Center.* [Online] http://us-israel.org/jsource/Holocaust/sutoc.html (accessed on September 4, 2000).

Smolar, Hersh. *The Minsk Ghetto: Soviet-Jewish Partisans Against the Nazis.* Washington, DC: U.S. Holocaust Memorial Museum, 1989.

Natzweiler-Struthof

Natzweiler-Struthof was a **CONCENTRATION CAMP** near the town of Natzweiler, in Alsace, **FRANCE**. One of the smallest concentration camps, it was located 31 miles (50 kilometers) south of Strasbourg, on a hill in the Vosges Mountains. It was established after Nazi official Albert Speer had been on an inspection tour of France, which **GERMANY** had recently occupied. While there, he noted the presence of granite deposits in the Natzweiler area. The German Earth and Stone Works Ltd., an **SS** company, promptly followed up on Speer's observations. By the fall of 1940, the company had launched a project to quarry the granite, with the work to be done by prisoners. The first batch of prisoners—300 German nationals—arrived on the site in May 1941. At that time, construction of the camp had not been completed. The prisoners were assigned temporary housing in the former Hotel Struthof. The number of prisoners increased at a slow pace, as compared to the rate of growth in other concentration camps. It was only on August 15, 1942, that Natzweiler became available for routine assignment of prisoners by the **REICH SECURITY MAIN OFFICE** (*Reichssicherheitshauptamt*; RSHA).

By the end of 1943, there were 2,000 prisoners in the main camp. Most labored in arms production. At no time were more than 500 inmates put to work in the quarries, a project that turned out to be costly. In the summer of that year, several sheds were erected in the quarry area. These served as workshops in which prisoners overhauled Junkers aircraft engines. In the same area, deep tunnels were dug to provide space for underground factories that would be safe from air attacks. The Natzweiler camp was expanded in 1944, as part of Nazi efforts to relocate vital armaments plants to underground facilities.

Natzweiler also had several new satellite camps on German soil, mainly in Baden-Württemberg. One of these camps was in Neckarelz, where a gypsum mine was converted into an intricate tunnel system. Daimler-Benz Aircraft moved its engine plant there from the **BERLIN** area. This was a joint project undertaken by Daimler-Benz, the Natzweiler camp, and the Ministry of Armaments. Another satellite was Leonberg, near Stuttgart, where, in the spring of 1944, the Messerschmitt Aircraft Company put an unused highway tunnel to new use. Leonberg started operations with 1,500 prisoners; their number rose to 3,000 within a year.

Yet another satellite was the Schörzingen camp, established in February 1944 to extract crude oil from oil shale. This was one of the Nazi regime's desperate, last-minute efforts to bounce back from the losses of raw materials caused by the ongoing German retreat from the East and by bombing from the air. At the end of 1944, more than 1,000 prisoners were working in Schörzingen, and the plan was to bring in another 4,000.

The total number of prisoners in the Natzweiler satellites in October 1944 was 19,000. In Natzweiler itself, the number had risen to between 7,000 and 8,000. During the course of 1944, members of the **French Résistance** were among the prisoners

French Résistance
An organized, underground effort on the part of French citizens to fight back against the German occupying forces in their country.

brought to Natzweiler. Most of them were killed immediately. In a special category were the so-called NN (*Nacht Und Nebel*) prisoners. They were chosen by the **SS** for road construction and work in the quarries, where conditions were at their worst. An RSHA order of September 24, 1944, had decreed that "all Germanic NN prisoners" were to be transferred to Natzweiler. The death rate was exceptionally high for this group, due to harsh working conditions and the abusive treatment of the prisoners.

In August 1943, a gas chamber was built in Natzweiler, in one of the buildings that had formed part of the hotel compound. The contractors for the project, Waffen-SS Natzweiler, left behind a rare document in which, unlike the coded terminology generally used by the Nazis, specific mention was made of "the construction of a gas chamber at Struthof." This clear language appears in a bill for the job that the SS sent to the Strasbourg University Institute of Anatomy. The director of that institute was Professor August Hirt. At least 130 prisoners were transferred from **Auschwitz** to be killed in the Natzweiler gas chamber for his collection of skeletons. Most of these prisoners were Jews. Another member of the Strasbourg University faculty, Professor Otto Bickenbach, also took advantage of the Natzweiler gas chamber, to conduct experiments on prisoners with antidotes of phosgene, a poisonous gas. These victims were **Gypsies** (Romani) who had been transferred from Auschwitz the previous year to serve as human guinea pigs for SS doctors experimenting with antityphus injections.

The main camp was disbanded in August and September 1944, but most of the satellites were evacuated only in March 1945. The prisoners were sent on **death marches**, in the general direction of **Dachau**.

In 1989, a memorial plaque was placed on the wall of the Natzweiler-Struthof crematorium in memory of the Jews who were put to death at the camp.

SUGGESTED RESOURCES

Koestler, Arthur. *Scum of the Earth.* New York: Hippocrene, 1991.

Weisberg, Richard H. *Vichy Law and the Holocaust in France.* New York: New York University Press, 1996.

Nazi-Deutsch. See Sprachregelung.

Nazi Party

The Nazi party was in power in **Germany** from 1933 to 1945. It was formally known as the National Socialist German Workers' party (*Nationalsozialistische Deutsche Arbeiterpartei*; NSDAP). Founded on January 5, 1919, the Nazi party had its origins in the Political Workers' Circle (*Politischer Arbeiterzirkel*), a small right-wing group. This group met beginning in November 1918 under the leadership of Anton Drexler, a locksmith, and Karl Harrer, a reporter. Rabid **antisemitism**—hatred toward Jews—characterized its meetings. This hatred of Jews, and the murderous governmental policies that eventually stemmed from it, would become more central to the Nazi party as time went on. In 1919, under Drexler, this circle became the German Workers' party (*Deutsche Arbeiterpartei*). Its foundation marked the beginning of the development of politically organized National Socialism. In early 1920, it was renamed the NSDAP.

Nazi party members fill a stadium at a party meeting in Nuremberg, 1937.

Adolf **HITLER** joined the party on September 12, 1919, and became its leader in 1921. The party was banned in 1923, as a result of Hitler's failed "Beer Hall Putsch"—his attempt to take over the German government. The ban lasted until 1925, when the Nazi party was re-founded. The party remained in existence until September 20, 1945. On that date, soon after Germany's defeat in World War II (1939–1945), the victorious Allies declared the party illegal.

The Nazi party had an authoritarian structure, based on what was termed the "leadership principle" *(Führerprinzip)*. All authority and responsibility flowed downward from the top levels. At its head stood the "leader" *(Führer)*, Hitler.

Hatred in a New Generation

After the death and devastation that Adolf Hitler and his Nazi party forced on millions of people in Europe, it is hard to believe that Nazism could be embraced by anyone. However, there are neo-Nazi groups—also called white supremacists, skinheads, Aryan supremacists, or white-rights groups—that have revived the spirit and harsh rhetoric of Nazism.

The Ku Klux Klan (KKK) is a long-established and well-known American hate group that attacks blacks, Catholics, and Jews. The group's primary target has historically been African Americans. In recent years, their message has focused on the perceived need for "white rights" protection from government policies of non-discrimination.

Neo-Nazi groups are generally located in the United States and Canada, in Germany, Austria, and France, and in Australia. Neo-Nazis focus most of their vitriol on Jews, praising the philosophy and tactics Hitler and his henchmen used to rid the world of people they considered inferior to themselves. As a rule, the Neo-Nazi groups do not have many members—perhaps a few thousand in each of the countries where organized groups exist—but their voices are widespread. They abuse the concept of

Beneath him was the leader's deputy. The political organization of the party was run by the eighteen highest-ranking party officials; most of them also held other high government posts. The next thirty-two highest-ranking Nazi party officials were responsible for the party's smaller, regional operations. Its affiliated groups included the SA (*Sturmabteilungen*; Stormtroopers) and the **SS** (*Schutzstaffel*, meaning "defense unit"; also called black-shirts). Another major Nazi group was the **Hitler Youth** (*Hitlerjugend*). There were also labor groups and teachers' unions. This diffuse and widespread organization helped Hitler to keep a firm grip on power. It led to harsh rivalry among the Nazi officials, which allowed Hitler to reserve all the main decisions for himself.

The Nazi party was of little political consequence in the early 1920s, but it grew steadily in the following decade. Germans were suffering from a loss of international prestige due to their defeat in World War I (1914–1918), and their economy was in shreds. Poverty and unemployment were widespread. Germans, desperate, began to look for different political solutions to their problems. Hitler and the Nazi party spoke to this deep dissatisfaction among the German citizens, bitterly criticizing the existing democratic form of government, the Weimar Republic.

The Nazi party also blamed "International Jewry" for Germany's economic woes, thus providing the Germans with a convenient scapegoat, or target, for their anger and frustration. The party's strength grew dramatically, and in January 1933, Hitler was named chancellor of Germany. In elections in March of that year, the Nazi party won control of the **Reichstag**. Shortly thereafter, Hitler declared all other political parties illegal.

Reichstag
German Parliament.

"free speech" to promote messages of hate in the media, through public demonstrations, and on the Internet.

The relative anonymity and virtually unlimited reach of the Internet has greatly increased hate groups' ability to spread their propaganda. They monitor discussions in public newsgroups and chat rooms to recruit members; they bash participants whose views differ from their own, and court those whom they believe can be manipulated. To spread their messages of hate, they prey especially on young people who seem lonely, confused, or emotionally fragile. The twisted arguments of Holocaust deniers and revisionists are used to try to persuade others to accept their point of view.

Wherever they are, and whatever names they are known by, these are all "hate groups." They promote intolerance, prejudice, and violence against people who are different from themselves. The most common targets are Jews, blacks, and immigrants, but Latinos, Asians, homosexuals, and Catholics may also be recipients of organized hatred when they constitute a minority in a country or region.

The Nazi party's membership among ordinary German citizens increased from some 6,000 in 1922 to 8.5 million in 1945. Much of the party's popularity was based on mass mobilization: rallies, demonstrations, and other forms of political expression. Under Hitler, the Nazi party was the only legal political party in Germany, and the Nazis' yearly rallies in Nuremberg became the public center of Germany's political life.

The party's "platform" of 25 major objectives was published in 1920. It was formulated by Hitler and Drexler and included militaristic, nationalistic, social, economic, and antisemitic clauses. Point 4 of the party program, for example, stated that only the German "people" (*Volk*) could be citizens of the state—and only people of "German blood," regardless of religious affiliation, could be *Volk*. This meant, among other things, that no Jew was regarded as a "member of the nation" (*Volksgenosse*). Other groups singled out for severe discrimination included GYPSIES and the disabled; Jews, however, were universally victimized with particular brutality. These Nazi policies were to lead eventually, in World War II (1939–1945) and the Holocaust, to the deaths of millions of people.

SUGGESTED RESOURCES

Brustein, William. *The Logic of Evil: The Social Origins of the Nazi Party, 1925–1933.* New Haven: Yale University Press, 1996.

Fischer, Klaus P. *Nazi Germany: A New History.* New York: Continuum, 1995.

Lace, William W. *The Nazis.* San Diego: Lucent Books, 1998.

Nardo, Don. *The Rise of Nazi Germany.* San Diego: Greenhaven Press, 1999.

Noakes, J., and Pridham, P., eds. *Nazism, 1919–1945: A History in Documents and Eyewitness Accounts.* New York: Schocken Books, 1990.

Nebe, Arthur

(1894–1945)

Arthur Nebe was an officer in the Reich criminal police. In World War I (1914–1918) he volunteered for the army and in 1916 he was promoted to the rank of second lieutenant. He was discharged from the army in March 1920 as a regimental adjutant in the engineering corps, with the rank of lieutenant. Nebe began studying law and legal medicine at Berlin University, and in April 1920 his candidacy to the criminal police was accepted. On July 1, 1923, despite initially failing the examination, he was appointed commander of the criminal police, thanks to the intervention of two officers, one of whom was Dr. Bernhard Weiss, deputy commandant of the Berlin police.

After World War I the criminal police in Prussia were not highly regarded, and the Nazi press, led by Joseph GOEBBELS, began to mock Weiss, who was of Jewish origin. Nebe, now dealing mainly with murder and drug cases, also made fun of Weiss behind his back. In June 1931 Nebe joined the SS, in July the NAZI PARTY, and in November the SA (*Sturmabteilung*; Storm Troopers). In 1932 he formed Nazi party groups among the Berlin criminal-police officers. A racist and nationalist career officer who joined the Nazis only after their impressive victories in the elections, Nebe tried to create the impression that he had always been an antisemite, and he took advantage of the political situation in order to advance to the top of the operative branch of the state police.

On April 1, 1933, Nebe was accepted to serve in the GESTAPO, with the rank of *Kriminalrat* (criminal-police commissar). About six months later, on October 1, he was promoted to the rank of *Regierungsrat* (government adviser), and two months later to the rank of *Oberregierungsrat* (chief government adviser). In 1936 Nebe rose to the rank of SS-*Sturmbannführer* (Major), and on June 30, 1937, to director of the Reich criminal police, thus becoming head of the united police (Kripo) of all GERMANY. In 1938 he rose to the rank of SS-*Obersturmbannführer* (Lieutenant Colonel), and then to that of SS-*Standartenführer* (Colonel). Nebe was made an SS-*Oberführer* (Brigadier General) on April 20, 1939. On December 14, 1940, Nebe rose to the rank of *Generalmajor der Polizei*, and about two weeks later, to that of *Brigadeführer* (Major General) in the SS.

Nebe volunteered as a participant in the OPERATIONAL SQUADS (*Einsatzgruppen*) that helped invade the SOVIET UNION, and in August 1941 he commanded Operational Squad B on the central front. The units under his command are estimated to have killed more than 45,400 people, mostly Jews, by late October of that year. Nebe's involvement in killing on behalf of the Nazis began with his role in the EUTHANASIA PROGRAM, which he was associated with from its outset. He personally transmitted Viktor Brack's instructions to Dr. Albert Widmann to help the Führer's Chancellery find suitable mass killing methods. In September 1941 Nebe again summoned Widmann, instructing him to find out whether explosives could be used as effectively as firearms in the mass killing of Jews in the MINSK vicinity, and whether this could be accomplished without attracting attention.

Nebe was perhaps not the loyal Nazi he appeared to be; he established and maintained contact with members of the German opposition movement, including

> **antisemite**
> A person who discriminates against those who are Jewish and their culture.

Ludwig Beck and, later, Hans Oster. Nebe eventually became one of the most important informers for the opposition movement. He retained this contact through his friend Hans Bernd Gisevius, who served in the Gestapo, the Ministry of the Interior, and the consular service in Switzerland, and who in 1943 and 1944 was an informer for the Americans.

After the failed attempt on the life of Hitler in July 1944, Nebe took part in the arrests of the conspirators, but after three days, on July 23, 1944, he disappeared. On January 16, 1945, after a simulated suicide attempt, he himself was arrested and implicated in the assassination attempt. He had already been expelled from the Nazi party on a charge of treason. He was first demoted to the rank of private in the SS, and then finally expelled. He was sentenced to death by hanging. Before the sentence was carried out on April 3, 1945, Nebe managed to leave perplexing "confessions" that implicated many acquaintances and associates in serious crimes.

SUGGESTED RESOURCES

Arad, Yitzhak. *The Einsatzgruppen Reports: Selections from the Dispatches of the Nazi Death Squads.* Washington, DC: U.S. Holocaust Memorial Museum, 1989.

Burleigh, Michael. *Death and Deliverance: "Euthanasia" in Germany 1900-1945.* New York: Cambridge University Press, 1994.

Thomsett, Michael C. *The German Opposition to Hitler: The Resistance, the Underground, and Assassination Plots, 1938–1945.* Jefferson, NC: McFarland, 1997.

NEO-NAZISM. SEE HOLOCAUST, DENIAL OF.

Netherlands, The

Jews have lived in the area known today as the Netherlands (often called Holland, which is actually a region of the country) for many hundreds of years. They were subjected to terrible persecution in the Middle Ages. But from the late 1600s, the Jews of the Netherlands enjoyed general tolerance and safety. At the time of its occupation by the Germans in 1940, the Netherlands had a Jewish population of 140,000, representing 1.6 percent of the total population.

Amsterdam, the capital city, had the largest Jewish community in the Netherlands—in 1940, about half of the country's total Jewish population. The Nazi treatment of the Amsterdam Jews and the status given to Amsterdam's Jewish Council (the *Joodse Raad; see also* JUDENRAT) affected all the Jews of the Netherlands. The growth of Nazism in GERMANY and of similar racist movements in other European countries also had an effect on the Netherlands, leading to manifestations of ANTISEMITISM.

The Netherlands.

From 1933 to 1940

After Adolf HITLER and his NAZI PARTY came to power in Germany in 1933, many people (Jews and non-Jews) from Germany moved to the Netherlands. Dutch Jews hated the Nazis and wanted to express their feelings with actions, not just words. To prevent them from taking potentially dangerous actions and to find a solution for the refugee problem, the Committee for Special Jewish Affairs was established. Before long, care of refugees and emigration assistance became the

> Through legislation and economic isolation, Jews were eventually excluded from the public life of the Netherlands in virtually every way.

committee's main activities. Refugees who had entered the country illegally were held in camps. In 1939, **WESTERBORK** was put up for this purpose, in the village of that name, to be maintained by the Committee for Special Jewish Affairs. From 1939 to 1940, a total of 34,000 refugees entered the Netherlands. Of these, 15,174 were still there when the Germans invaded the country in May 1940.

May 1940 to Mid-1941

On May 9–10, 1940, the Germans invaded the Netherlands. Great panic seized the Jews; many tried to flee to Britain or to the south, and several dozen Jews committed suicide rather than face the persecution they expected would take place. In the first few months, the Germans behaved in a restrained manner, trying to gain popularity among the Dutch population, who were stunned by the course of events. At Hitler's express order, a civil administration was installed in the Netherlands, under **SS** administration. A Dutch administration existed side by side with the German administration. Since Queen Wilhelmina and the Dutch government had fled to Britain and set up a government-in-exile there, the main secretaries of the government ministries constituted the highest Dutch authority in the Netherlands.

On November 4, 1940, an order was given for all Jewish civil servants to be "suspended" from their jobs. The Nazis ordered that Jewish-owned or -controlled businesses be registered. This registration was a first step toward **"ARYANIZATION"**—the transfer of all economic assets to non-Jewish ownership. On January 10, 1941, a decree was issued under which all Jews, and any person with a Jewish grandfather or grandmother, had to be registered. A total of 159,806 persons registered, 19,561 of them the offspring of mixed marriages (*see* **MISCHLINGE**). These measures, and others that followed, convinced the Jews that an authoritative body should be formed to serve as the leadership of Dutch Jewry. So in December 1940, the Jewish Coordinating Committee was created.

The German occupation of the Netherlands led to a decline in the economic situation and threw many people out of work. The Dutch administration, under pressure from the Germans, forced the unemployed to take up work in Germany. This caused much resentment among their families, and the clandestine and anti-Nazi Communist party sought to exploit this mood among the population by staging strikes and public demonstrations. Members of the Dutch Nazi party were also dissatisfied. They had hoped that the Germans would entrust the power in the Netherlands to them, thereby enabling them to purge the country of Jews. The German authorities, however, restrained the Dutch Nazis and did not permit them to run riot. In early 1941, the Dutch Nazis decided to take matters into their own hands, launching an anti-Jewish campaign of their own.

In the Jewish quarter, Jews and non-Jews organized to resist the Nazi attacks. In February 11, during a march organized by the Dutch Nazis, a clash took place that cost the life of one of the Nazi Storm Troopers. The Germans reacted by sealing off the Jewish quarter. A week later, German police entered a Jewish café. The owner, who mistook the police for Dutch Nazis, put into motion a prearranged plan, in which ammonium gas was sprayed on them. In the wake of that incident, the Jewish quarter was blockaded and young Jewish men were hunted down; 389 people were arrested and taken to **BUCHENWALD** concentration camp. Fifty of them died within three months, and the others were deported to **MAUTHAUSEN**. Of the whole group, only one person survived the ordeal. In September 1941 more Jews were arrested and sent straight to Mauthausen.

The arrests and the brutal treatment of the prisoners by the German police shocked the people of Amsterdam. Communist activists used the occasion to call a

Jewish books and ritual objects hidden behind a plastered niche in the Meijerplein synagogue in Amsterdam, uncovered by the Germans.

strike on February 25. The strike soon encompassed all sectors of the population, and the entire transportation system, the large factories, and the public services came to a standstill. It also spread to other cities in the region. The Germans were taken by surprise and sent out large forces to suppress it. This strike had far-reaching consequences. The German administration no longer had any doubts about the failure of their plan to gain support for Nazi ideology among the Dutch population. The events of February 1941 led to a harsher anti-Jewish policy.

Separation

The first step toward implementation of the Nazis' "FINAL SOLUTION" was the separation of the Jews from the general population. In the summer of 1941,

Jews in the Netherlands were barred from public places. A night curfew and limited shopping hours were imposed on them. Jews were allowed to use public transportation by special permit only, and then only if space was available. In August, all Jewish students were ordered removed from public schools and put into special Jewish schools to be set up for this purpose. As for the universities, no new Jewish students had been admitted since early 1941; the exclusion of Jews at this level would apply to those already enrolled in 1942. On September 15, 1941, Jews were barred from public assemblies, museums, libraries, public markets, the stock exchange, and so on. Certain halls, stores, and boardinghouses were designated for Jews only, and placed out of bounds to non-Jews.

Organized Plunder

The next step toward the "Final Solution" was to confiscate personal property and valuables from the Jews. The first German agency to embark upon this in the Netherlands was the Rosenberg Special Operations Staff. Alfred **Rosenberg**'s men were interested mainly in acquiring public and private Jewish libraries. Rosenberg also received Hitler's permission to seize the household furniture left behind by the Jews who were deported and to distribute it among the German population in the eastern territories. This operation (called Aktion M, for *Möbel*, furniture) was of enormous dimensions. From the Netherlands alone, in a single year, 17,235 apartments (9,981 in Amsterdam) were emptied of their contents. But Rosenberg's was an independent operation, not part of the plunder program carried out by the German administration in the Netherlands, which eventually stripped Jews of all their money and property.

Deportation

In late 1941, the Germans told the Jewish Council that camps were being opened to which "unemployed" Jews would be sent for work. In reality, this was a step toward eventual deportation. The camps were German **forced-labor** camps, and the Jews endured much harsher conditions than those of Dutch workers. Not only unemployed Jews were sent to the camps. Those with jobs were also affected, when the Germans canceled their work permits and thereby turned them into "unemployed" people. Strong pressure was put on the Jewish Council to fill the constantly increasing quota for workers. At first the Council refused to submit, but later it cooperated.

The deportation plan also provided for the removal of the Jews from all the provinces, with most to be gathered together in Amsterdam. This phase was launched on January 14, 1942, beginning with the town of Zaandam. The Dutch nationals among the Jews were ordered to move to Amsterdam, while those who were stateless were sent to the Westerbork camp. Not all the Jews were permitted to move to Amsterdam; a new camp was set up, near Vught, as an alternative to Amsterdam or Westerbork.

Another step designed to ensure that no Jew escaped the German net was the introduction of the yellow badges (*see* **Badge, Jewish**). All Jews were required to wear them; any person caught without the badge after the appointed day was threatened with deportation to Mauthausen. The Dutch population disapproved of this humiliation of the Jews, and some of them expressed their feelings by wearing, in public, a yellow badge of their own. This particular protest movement, however, did not last for long. The yellow badge was soon overshadowed by far more ominous developments.

Jews in Amsterdam on their way to the collection point for deportation (1943).

On June 26, 1942, the Germans declared that "the Jews of the Netherlands will be employed by the police in labor camps in Germany—men, women, and entire families." From that point on, the Nazi-administered **Central Office for Jewish Emigration** had the decisive say on Jewish policy. The German administration decreed that at first, young Jews, for the most part of German origin, would be sent to the labor camps; each would receive an individual notification and would have to register with the Jewish Council. The Amsterdam Jews panicked, and only a small number registered. In order to frighten the Jews into registering, a large manhunt was conducted when the date for the first transport drew near. In this manhunt, 540 Jews were arrested and held as hostages. Still, the quota that had been fixed for the first three transports was not filled. When the trains arrived at Westerbork and the camp commandant realized that he was 400 Jews short of the 2,000 he was to move to the Auschwitz-Birkenau **extermination camp**, he made up the shortage with prisoners from Westerbork. The removal of entire families, including the old and the very young, left no doubt that the term "employed by the police" was no more than an effort to camouflage what was really the deportation of Dutch Jewry.

Large sectors of the population reacted with fury to this development. The country's churches took an unprecedented unified stand in protest. They called upon all clergy to read the text of their protest at the following Sunday's services. The German administration put heavy pressure on the churches to call off the public protest, and the Protestant churches gave in. But the Catholic archbishop, Johannes de Jong, insisted that the protest telegram to the Germans' commissioner, Arthur Seyss-Inquart, be read out. The Germans retaliated by arresting all Jewish converts to Catholicism—201 people, some of them monks and nuns—and deporting them to Auschwitz.

The public protests had no effect on the Germans, who continued to send Jews to Westerbork and from there to **Auschwitz** and **Sobibór**. The German plans were helped by the Dutch agencies' readiness to cooperate. Despite the visible disapproval of some segments of the population, the municipal administration, railway workers, and Dutch police, with few exceptions, all contributed to the roundup of the Jews and their expulsion from the country.

> The Germans had a plan for relieving some of the congestion at Westerbork: in a single month, the Germans sent 7,463 Jews to their death in extermination camps in the East. Soon afterward, the deportations to Westerbork were resumed at an accelerated pace.

On October 2, 1942, a countrywide operation was launched to speed up the pace of deportation. All the Jewish men in labor camps in the Netherlands were transferred to Westerbork, where they were joined by their families from Amsterdam—a total of 12,296 people. The Westerbork camp could not possibly accommodate such a large number, and overnight, conditions there became utterly unbearable. To reduce the numbers of detainees at Westerbork, the Germans raised the quota for the trains taking Jews to the East. In May 1943, the rate of DEPORTATIONS was accelerated.

When the supply of Jews for deportation ran dry, another wide-ranging manhunt took place. In this operation, on June 20, 1943, some 5,524 Jews were arrested. By that summer, only a small remnant of Jews was left. On the eve of the Jewish New Year, September 29, 1943, the last roundup took place. At that time, 2,000 Jews, including the Jewish Council leaders and senior staff, were taken to Westerbork. The deportations were based on a systematic method and proceeded gradually, enabling groups or individuals to have their deportation postponed or speeded up. Very few Jews deported from the Netherlands survived the HOLOCAUST.

Hiding Out and Escaping

By the summer of 1942, Jews who had not responded to calls for deportation had to go into hiding. Their number grew, especially in 1943. In the early stages, they used their personal contacts with non-Jews to find hiding places. Later, groups and organizations were formed for the purpose. It is believed that about 25,000 Jews went into hiding, of whom about one third fell into German hands. Among these was the family of Anne FRANK. About 4,500 children were hidden; only a very few were discovered by the Germans. Non-Jews who were caught giving refuge to Jews in their homes were not executed, but they were sent to Nazi concentration camps, where many perished.

After the Holocaust

The reintegration of the Jews into Dutch society after the end of the war in 1945 was a lengthy and painful process. The Netherlands had suffered more from the German occupation than any other country outside Eastern Europe, and its shattered economy needed to be rebuilt. Antisemitism in government and business circles led to a tendency not to permit the Jews to regain the positions they had held before the war. The Jews also had to fight to recover their property.

A bitter struggle was waged over the war orphans. The groups that had specialized in hiding the children felt that they should be the ones to take care of them now that the war was over. They succeeded in having a royal decision passed in their favor, and then a law, authorizing a committee (made up largely of Christians) to determine which orphans should stay with the families that had saved them and which should be put under Jewish guardianship. Of the 3,481 children registered with the committee, 1,540 were restored to their parents, or to one of them. In the end, 360 children (17.5 percent of the orphans) remained with non-Jewish families. In two widely publicized cases, the Christian families refused to follow the courts' decision to give up the children, and smuggled them out of the country.

> **collaborated**
> Helped the enemy.

Several trials were held of Jews who had **collaborated** with the Germans. The resistance organizations and the Dutch government-in-exile had planned to conduct trials against Germans who had committed crimes in the Netherlands and against Dutch collaborators. However, due to the staggering number of suspects (130,000) and the conciliatory policy adopted by the postwar Dutch government,

only a fraction of these cases reached the courts. A total of 242 Germans were tried, of whom 203 were sentenced. Of these, 18 were sentenced to death; only five of them were actually executed. The death sentences of three defendants who had been tried for their crimes against the Jews were commuted to life imprisonment. But when the government wanted to release them in 1972, the storm of public protest forced the government to reverse the decision. In January 1989, the last two remaining prisoners, Ferdinand aus der Fünten, who oversaw mass roundups of Jews, and Franz Fischer, who was responsible for the deportation of 13,000 Dutch Jews to extermination camps, were granted amnesty by the Dutch government. This pardon led to angry demonstrations in many parts of the country. Of the Dutch collaborators, many of whom had tortured their victims, only four were executed. The collaborators who were sentenced to prison, including those sentenced to life terms, were pardoned after a relatively short time and released.

SEE ALSO **TRIALS OF WAR CRIMINALS**.

SUGGESTED RESOURCES

Camp of Hope and Despair: Witnesses of Westerbork, 1939–1945 [videorecording]. Ergo Media, 1994.

Frank, Anne. *Anne Frank: The Diary of a Young Girl.* Bantam Books, 1993.

Friedman, Carl. *Nightfather.* New York: Persea Books, 1995.

Hillesum, Etty. *An Interrupted Life: The Diaries of Etty Hillesum, 1941–1943.* New York: Pantheon, 1983.

Moore, Bob. *Victims and Survivors: The Nazi Persecution of the Jews in the Netherlands, 1940–1945.* New York: Arnold, 1997.

Neuengamme

Situated near Hamburg, **GERMANY**, Neuengamme was initially an annex of the **SACHSENHAUSEN** concentration camp. Eventually Neuengamme itself had many satellite camps.

The first group of prisoners arrived at Neuengamme on December 13, 1938; their task was to build the camp. They were housed in a former brick factory. That very factory was the reason for the establishment of a concentration camp in Hamburg, which before then had only temporary, small camps (Wittmoor and Fuhlsbüttel). The **SS** wanted to reactivate the brick factory and use its products in building the huge public structures that were being planned for the city.

In April 1940, the German Earth and Stone Works Ltd. (Deutsche Erd-und Steinwerke GmbH), an SS company, signed an agreement with the city of Hamburg that provided for a substantial expansion of the brick factory, the digging of a canal to connect the factory with a tributary of the Elbe River, and a train track siding to link it to the railway network. All of this work was to be done by prisoners. As a result of the agreement, barracks were put up and more prisoners were brought in, the total reaching about 1,000. Beginning in the fall of 1941, thousands of Soviet **PRISONERS OF WAR** were brought there as well. Soviet prisoners eventually became the largest national group in the camp, numbering 34,500, including 5,900 women.

Neuengamme became an independent concentration camp in June 1940. In 1942, private firms such as the well-known Walther weapons factory established branches at Neuengamme. Numerous annexes to the camp were set up at various centers of the armament industry, especially the Bremen and Hamburg shipbuilding and machine works. They were also established in Hannover and in the industrial area of Brunswick, which adjoined the Volkswagen Company (the current site of Wolfsburg) and the Hermann Göring Works (today the location of the town of Salzgitter).

By 1945, there were seventy Neuengamme annexes. Most of the new prisoners were put into these satellites. In 1944, the main camp had a prisoner population of 12,000; about twice that number were in its satellites. Beginning in the summer of 1944, large transports of Jewish prisoners were brought in, mainly from **HUNGARY** and **POLAND**. Some 13,000 Jews prisoners passed through the main camp and its annexes (among them 3,000 women) in 1944 and 1945.

It is estimated that 106,000 prisoners were sent to Neuengamme during its existence. The death rate there was high, in comparison to those of other **CONCENTRATION CAMPS** situated in Germany, and especially in the early years, when the brick factory was being reactivated. It is believed that at least 55,000 prisoners perished in Neuengamme and its annexes. The main camp was evacuated in the second half of April 1945, following the evacuation of most of the annexes.

SUGGESTED RESOURCES

Concentration Camp Memorial Neuengamme. [Online] http://www.hamburg.de/Neuengamme/welcome.en.html (accessed on September 5, 2000).

"Neuengamme." *The Jewish Student Online Research Center (JSource).* [Onlinel] http://www.us-israel.org/jsource/Holocaust/Neuengamme.html (accessed on September 4, 2000).

"NIGHT OF THE BROKEN GLASS." SEE KRISTALLNACHT

(NIGHT OF THE BROKEN GLASS).

Nisko and Lublin Plan

The Nisko and Lublin Plan was conceived by the Nazis as a territorial solution to the "Jewish question." The plan was to forcibly relocate the Jews living in the expanding Third Reich to the Lublin area in the eastern extremity of German-occupied **POLAND**. This idea dominated planning and policy-making in **SS** circles between September 1939 and March 1940.

The Nazi victory over Poland in September 1939 brought nearly 2 million Polish Jews under German control, including more than a half million in the "incorporated territories" that were annexed to **GERMANY** in early October, including Danzig, West Prussia, Poznań, and Eastern Upper Silesia. At the same time, the war made it more difficult for Jews to leave German-occupied territories through emigration. The Germans decided to use Polish territory as a "dumping ground" for Jews of the Third Reich, which then included **AUSTRIA**, the Protectorate of **BOHEMIA AND MORAVIA**, and the "incorporated territories."

In 1939 Adolf **EICHMANN** set up an agency in Prague to oversee the emigration of the Jews of the newly acquired Protectorate of Bohemia and Moravia (as he had done in **VIENNA**). Eichmann and Higher **SS** and Police Leader, Franz **STAHLECKER**,

NISKO AND LUBLIN PLAN

Nisko and Lublin, January 1940.

originated the idea of "resettling" Jews in Poland in September 1939. Reinhard **HEYDRICH** gave his approval. Other Nazi leaders, including Hitler, agreed.

When Heydrich met with Eichmann and the **OPERATIONAL SQUADS** (*Einsatzgruppen*) commanders on September 21, he told them Hitler had approved a plan to concentrate Polish Jews in the cities as a short-term goal. The secret, long-term goal was to deport them eastward into territory not intended for Germanization and even to expel some of them into Soviet territory.

On September 28, 1939, a new agreement between Nazi Germany and the **SOVIET UNION** made the Lublin region available to Germany, while yielding **LITHUANIA** to the Soviets. Immediately, this new extremity of the German empire became the target spot for relocating the Jews, and the concept of the "Lublin Reservation" emerged.

The plans for a Lublin Reservation were part of a wider scheme for the racial restructuring of eastern Europe. The Nazis intended to expel not only Jews and **GYPSIES** but also Poles from the incorporated territories, and resettle these regions with ethnic Germans (**VOLKSDEUTSCHE**) repatriated from the Soviet sphere. Himmler was charged with both repatriating (bringing back) the ethnic Germans and eliminating alien populations in the Reich.

In October, **GESTAPO** chief Heinrich **MÜLLER** instructed Eichmann to oversee the expulsion of 70,000 to 80,000 Jews to the designated areas. Eichmann arranged for **DEPORTATIONS** from Vienna and Mährisch Ostrau, (today called Ostrava), and Eastern Upper Silesia.

In Mährisch Ostrau, Jewish engineers, carpenters, and artisans were "recruited" and told to bring their tools with them. Jewish firms were to supply food and building materials. The Nazis tried to give the process a voluntary character and the evacuees were forced to sign a statement saying they had volunteered for a "retraining camp." In Vienna the Jewish leaders were also informed that they were to prepare a list of 1000 to 1200 working men for deportation.

Germanization
The Nazi plan to "convert" some populations to German culture by eradicating all aspects of the original culture and placing them under German rule.

NISKO AND LUBLIN PLAN

Hitler's goal of reassembling all "Aryan" Europeans on German soil would have led to the relocation of whole cities and villages of ethnic Germans from their homes outside Germany, with or without their permission, and the isolation of "undesirable" populations in remote regions of the Reich.

On October 18, the first transport of 901 Jews left Mährisch Ostrau. The deportees were marched from the train station at Nisko to a swampy meadow near Zarzecze and put to work setting up barracks. The next day, the best workers were selected from the group, and the rest were marched eastward and dispersed throughout the Lublin district. Transports of 875 Jews from Katowice and 912 Jews from Vienna departed on October 20 and were treated similarly upon arrival.

Eichmann believed that his experimental transports to the transit camp at Nisko were the prelude to a general deportation of all Reich Jews. By mid-October he was referring to "continuous" transports that would soon leave Germany itself as well. On October 19, however, Müller notified him that all deportations to Poland required explicit approval from **BERLIN**. When he inquired about the situation, Eichmann's deputy was informed that "every transport of Jews had to be stopped."

Eichmann hurried to Berlin, where he did secure approval for a transport of 672 Jews from Vienna that left on October 26, and a combined transport of 400 Jews from Mährisch Ostrau and 1,000 from Katowice that left on October 27, but that was all. No further transports were sent to Nisko, although the camp remained.

Eichmann blamed the abrupt halting of the Nisko experiment on the opposition of Hans **FRANK**, the governor-general of Poland, but this seems unlikely. Himmler later claimed he had made the decision himself, on the basis of "technical difficulties."

These "technical difficulties" were probably related to problems Himmler faced in finding jobs and housing for the ethnic Germans from the Baltic. The first contingent arrived in Danzig in mid-October 1939. At the end of that month, Himmler ordered that 550,000 Jews and 450,000 Poles be deported within four months in order to make room for the incoming Baltic Germans. In a swift and brutal operation that December, 87,000 Poles and Jews were deported from the Warthegau. This deluge of penniless refugees certainly aroused the opposition of Hans **FRANK**, leading to a temporary postponement of further Jewish deportations, as well as a curtailment of Polish deportations. Despite his objections, however, it is not likely that he was influential enough to cause this decision to be made.

At a meeting on February 12, 1940, with Hermann Göring, Frank, and Arthur Greiser, the Nazi district leader of the Warthegau, Himmler still spoke of the Lublin region as "destined to become the *Judenreservat*" (reservation for the Jews), and deportations were subsequently scheduled for August. But by March 1940 Hitler was expressing doubt about this plan. He noted that the "Jewish question" really was a space question that was difficult to solve, particularly since there was no space at his disposal. The establishment of a Jewish state around Lublin was not a solution. German attention thus shifted to the possibility of expelling the European Jews to a distant territory overseas, with particular focus on the island of Madagascar (*see* **MADAGASCAR PLAN**).

The inmates who were left at Lublin, when the Lublin Reservation plans collapsed in 1939, suffered through a winter of hard labor and harsh weather. In April 1940, higher SS and police leader in the **GENERALGOUVERNEMENT**, Friedrich Wilhelm **KRÜGER** ordered the camp dissolved. The remaining 501 Jews who had not been expelled throughout the Lublin area were returned to Austria and the Protectorate.

SUGGESTED RESOURCES

Hilberg, R. *The Destruction of the European Jews*. 3 vols. New York: Holmes and Meier, 1985.

Moser, Jonny. "Nisko: The First Experiment in Deportation." *Simon Wiesenthal Center Museum of Tolerance Online.* [Online] http://motlc.wiesenthal.com/resources/books/annual2/chap01.html (accessed on September 4, 2000).

Reynolds, Quentin James. *Minister of Death: The Adolf Eichmann Story.* New York: Viking Press, 1960.

Novak, Franz

(1913–)

Franz Novak helped Adolf EICHMANN in the deportation of Jews to their death. A native of Wolfsberg, in AUSTRIA, Novak joined the HITLER YOUTH in 1929 and became a NAZI PARTY member in 1933. In July 1934 Novak was involved in the Nazi-staged plot to overthrow the Austrian government, during which Chancellor Engelbert Dollfuss of Austria was assassinated. Novak had to flee the country, taking refuge in GERMANY. As punishment, the Austrian government took away his citizenship.

After Austria was annexed by Germany in 1938, Novak returned to VIENNA. There he was assigned to the SD (*Sicherheitsdienst;* Security Service) and became a senior staff member of the CENTRAL OFFICE FOR JEWISH EMIGRATION, which was headed by Eichmann. At the time, the office had the task of forcing Jews to emigrate from the country. Novak joined Eichmann in setting up similar offices in BERLIN and, later, in Prague.

When Eichmann was appointed head of a section of the REICH SECURITY MAIN OFFICE and launched the extermination of the Jews, Novak was put in charge of the transportation subsection. There he helped order the trains that took Jews from the ghettos and from western Europe to EXTERMINATION CAMPS and CONCENTRATION CAMPS. In 1944 he played a very active role in deporting the Jews of HUNGARY to their death.

After the war, Novak went into hiding in Austria under a false name. In 1957 he reverted to his real name, but the Austrian police took no action against him, even though his name was on the list of wanted war criminals. Several years later, during Eichmann's highly publicized trial in Israel for his war crimes, Novak's share in the "FINAL SOLUTION" was revealed. He was arrested in 1961. In 1964 he was sentenced to eight years' imprisonment; after that decision was appealed, the Austrian Supreme Court ordered a retrial. At the second trial, which took place in 1966, Novak was acquitted and set free.

Franz Novak.

SUGGESTED RESOURCES

"Testimony of Franz Novak," *The Nizkor Project* [Online] http://www.nizkor.org/hweb/people/e/eichmann-adolf/transcripts/Testimony-Abroad/Franz-02.html (accessed on October 1, 2000.

NOWAK, FRANZ. SEE NOVAK, FRANZ.

NSDAP. SEE NAZI PARTY.

Nuremberg Laws

The Nuremberg Laws legitimized the Nazis' campaign of antisemitic riots and arrests of Jews, which had been taking place prior to 1935. They also laid the foundation for all the decrees that would follow, leading ultimately to the point at which the Jews were no longer protected by any laws of the Reich.

The Nuremberg Laws were constitutional laws announced with great public fanfare at the annual **NAZI PARTY** rally in 1935. They became the basis for the progressive legal exclusion of Jews from German life and formed the foundation of the Nazis' anti-Jewish policy.

Two Laws

There were two Nuremberg laws, which were proclaimed at a special session of the Reichstag (the lower chamber of the German parliament). The first one, known as the Reich Citizenship Law, stated that only Germans or people with related blood could be citizens of the Reich, or German empire. German Jews lost their political rights through this law, while the "Aryan" Germans, who were supposedly descended from the ancient nomadic Aryans, were declared citizens of the Reich. The Reich Citizenship Law was supplemented by government orders issued between November 1935 and July 1943 that systematically excluded the Jews from German life. The second of the two laws, the Law for the Protection of German Blood and Honor, prohibited sexual intercourse and marriage between Jews and Germans, the employment of German maids under the age of forty-five in Jewish households, and the raising of the German flag by Jews. The new racial laws had a symbolic function, dramatizing the exclusion of Jews from German society.

The Nuremberg Laws have been described by some scholars as the result of a hasty, last-minute decision on the eve of the Reichstag convention in Nuremberg. According to a number of historians, Hitler had meant to deliver an address on foreign policy in front of the diplomatic corps. However, because of an unexpected change, this was not feasible. Hitler, needing to fill an empty time slot during this festive occasion, decided instead to devote his speech to the Jewish question. He ordered the laws to be drafted quickly. Nazi experts on the Jewish question were brought to Nuremberg and told to create a law regulating marriages between Jews and Germans. Hitler chose one out of four drafts. This theory of how the Nuremberg Laws originated is based on testimony by Bernard **LÖSENER**, the expert on Jewish affairs in the Ministry of the Interior. Lösener testified at the postwar Nuremberg trials, where an international court brought indictments against those accused of war crimes. It seems more likely, however, that the Nuremberg Laws, even if they were drafted hastily were not merely an improvisation, but rather the implementation of on-going policy. The laws were directly related to the Nazis' party platform and the principles outlined in Hitler's writings.

Classification of Jews a Priority

The need to clarify and define the status of the Jews in **GERMANY** had become urgent. Regional governmental officials and the **GESTAPO** had repeatedly asked for an official clarification of Germany's policy toward the Jews; the absence of a clear-cut policy had resulted in clashes between party activists and government officials. The unrest of the spring and summer of 1935 aroused expectations within the party that there would be antisemitic legislation. The situation became particularly pressing when anti-Jewish rioting erupted in the summer of that year. The party and the public were demanding that the Jewish question be explicitly defined and made public.

Three main issues dominated the discussion: the exclusion of Jews from German citizenship; marriage and sexual relations between "Aryans" and Jews; and the boycotting of Jewish enterprises. By early 1935 several leading Nazi officials, including Wilhelm Frick, the Reich minister of the interior, had announced that the government was going to revoke the citizenship of the Jews of Germany. Hjalmar Schacht, the minister of economics, hinted that various anti-Jewish Laws and decrees were being prepared in order to coordinate all governmental antisemitic measures. On September 12, the head of the Reich Medical Association, Gerhard Wagner, announced the intention of promoting a law for the protection of German blood. All of this took place before Hitler supposedly made a last-minute program change at the Reichstag convention in 1935 and had the Nuremberg Laws drafted. Regardless of the circumstances surrounding their origin, the passage of the Nuremberg Laws legalized anti-Jewish activity while controlling the violence, so to speak, and limiting anti-Jewish acts to those defined by laws and decrees. This led to frustration among the more extreme party members or followers, who wanted no limits placed on their behavior toward Jews. Their resentments were to break out in November 1938 with the renewed anti-Jewish riots known as **KRISTALLNACHT**.

SUGGESTED RESOURCES

Hecht, Ingeborg. *Invisible Walls: A German Family Under the Nuremberg Laws.* San Diego: Harcourt Brace Jovanovich, 1985.

Newman, Amy. *The Nuremberg Laws: Institutionalized Anti-semitism.* San Diego: Lucent Books, 1999.

Noakes, Jeremy, and Geoffrey Pridham. *Documents on Nazism 1919–1945.* New York: Viking Press, 1974.

"The Nuremberg Laws." American-Israeli Cooperative Enterprise. [Online] http://www.us-israel.org/jsource/Holocaust/nurlaws.html (accessed on September 5, 2000).

NUREMBERG MILITARY TRIBUNALS. SEE TRIALS OF THE WAR CRIMINALS.

NUREMBERG TRIAL. SEE TRIALS OF THE WAR CRIMINALS.

NYILASKERESZTES PÁRT. SEE ARROW CROSS PARTY.

Oberg, Carl Albrecht

(1897–1965)

Carl Albrecht Oberg was an **SS** officer. Born in Hamburg, Oberg served in World War I and earned several military decorations. In 1920 he took part in the nationalist attempt at a **coup d'état** (the "*Kapp putsch*"). In the early 1920s he was the liaison man in Schleswig between the nationalist organizations and the German army (*Reichswehr*). He worked for several months in 1926 at a tropical-fruit trading company and was then unemployed until 1930, when he acquired a tobacco stand in Hamburg.

In 1932 Reinhard **HEYDRICH** took Oberg along with him to Munich and then to **BERLIN**. Oberg became Heydrich's right-hand man in the **SD** (*Sicherheitsdienst*; Security Service). He rose quickly through the ranks and by 1935 was a *Standarten-*

coup d'état
Takeover of the government.

OFFICE OF SPECIAL INVESTIGATIONS

führer (Colonel). In 1938 he was the commanding officer of an **SS** battalion in Mecklenburg, and in January 1939 he became chief of police in Zwickau. In September 1941 he was appointed SS and Police Leader in the Radom district of the **GENERALGOUVERNEMENT**. There he was responsible for the massacring of Jews and the drafting of Poles for **FORCED LABOR**. He was promoted in March 1942 to Brigadier General, and on May 12 of that year he was posted to **PARIS** as Higher SS and Police Leader in occupied **FRANCE**.

Oberg was responsible for putting into effect the order for wearing the yellow Jewish badge (*see* **BADGE, JEWISH**), for severe measures against the French Résistance, and, above all, for applying the **"FINAL SOLUTION"** to the Jews of France. On Oberg's orders some 75,000 Jews from France were deported to the **EXTERMINATION CAMPS** in **POLAND**. Only a few thousand of them survived. In August 1944 he was promoted to SS-*Obergruppenführer* (Lieutenant General) and police general. In December of that year, Oberg was posted to the command of a military unit that was part of an army formation commanded by Heinrich **HIMMLER**.

In June 1945, Oberg was arrested by the Americans and sentenced to death. On October 10, 1946, he was extradited to France, and on October 9, 1954, was again sentenced to death. This was reduced to life imprisonment on April 10, 1958. Under a presidential amnesty his sentence was further reduced, on October 31, 1959, to 20 years' imprisonment with hard labor. In 1965 Oberg was granted a pardon by President Charles de Gaulle and was repatriated to **GERMANY**, where he died the same year.

SUGGESTED RESOURCES

Josephs, Jeremy. *Swastika Over Paris.* New York: Arcade, 1989.

Weisberg, Richard H. *Vichy Law and the Holocaust in France.* New York: New York University Press, 1996.

Office of Special Investigations

The Office of Special Investigations (OSI) was created by the U.S. Department of Justice in 1979 to investigate individuals accused of having committed **HOLOCAUST**-related crimes between 1933 and 1945. The OSI is responsible for detecting, investigating and taking legal action to denaturalize and deport or otherwise remove such individuals or prevent them from entering the **UNITED STATES**. (The United States lacks jurisdiction to prosecute these cases criminally, primarily because the events took place on foreign territory.) The unit assists the U.S. Immigration & Naturalization Service (INS) and the Department of State in screening applicants for entrance to the United States and petitioners for naturalized U.S. citizenship.

Axis criminals
Those who were associated with the Axis powers in World War II, including Germany, Italy, and Japan and their satellite nations.

The OSI is also responsible for helping to extradite accused Axis criminals found in the U.S. to stand trial abroad. Defendants in OSI cases are individuals against whom the unit has amassed proof of complicity in the Axis regimes' perpetration of acts of persecution, such as the mass murder of Jews, and other **CRIMES AGAINST HUMANITY**.

United States law prevents the entry into the United States of anyone who was involved in Nazi or Axis persecution, whether as immigrants or as visitors. As part of the OSI's responsibility to enforce these laws, the office has provided the names of more than 60,000 suspected Axis persecutors to the visa denial and border control "watchlists" maintained by the U.S. Immigration & Naturalization Service, the Department of State and the U.S. Customs Service.

Prior to the creation of the OSI, the federal government's efforts in Nazi cases were handled by INS and by U.S. Attorney offices around the country. However, in large part because these agencies lacked the historical and other highly specialized expertise to investigate these complex cases, their efforts were notably unsuccessful. In the 34 years between the end of World War II and the establishment of the OSI, just one Nazi persecutor was denaturalized (Hermine Braunsteiner-Ryan), and she and just one other Nazi persecutor (Ferenc Vajta) were removed from the United States by federal prosecutors; numerous cases were lost. Congressional hearings in 1977 and 1978 and two General Accounting Office (GAO) studies documented this history and also established that several federal agencies had even employed Nazi suspects and provided immigration assistance to some of them.

By contrast, the OSI has succeeded, to date, in denaturalizing more than sixty Nazi persecutors and in removing fifty such persons from the United States. It thought to be the most aggressive, effective, and successful Nazi-hunting organization in the world.

In 1987, the OSI placed former United Nations Secretary General Kurt Waldheim on its watchlist, which prohibits entry into the United States, after his 1986 election as president of **AUSTRIA**. In 1992, the unit also documented and verified the death of Dr. Josef **MENGELE**, the infamous Nazi doctor remembered for his **MEDICAL EXPERIMENTS** on prisoners at **AUSCHWITZ**.

Recent years have seen a continuing increase in the OSI's activity under its director, Eli M. Rosenbaum. During 1994, for example, the unit filed seven new cases in federal courts, its highest single-year total in a decade. The principal reason for this escalation has been the dissolution of communist rule in eastern and central Europe at the beginning of the 1990s, which resulted in the opening up to OSI personnel of archives previously sealed by communist authorities in the former **SOVIET UNION** and its satellites. These archives house what is probably the largest existing volume of captured Axis documentation. This wealth of evidence has suddenly and unexpectedly become available during the final years in which it can be put to law enforcement use, and OSI's multilingual personnel—like their counterparts in Germany, Canada, England and elsewhere—are involved in an unprecedented race against the clock to examine as many of these records as possible while the suspects are still living. These newly available records have enabled OSI to build compelling cases against existing suspects and also to locate additional suspects in the United States.

In 1996, the OSI undertook a large-scale research and investigative project in support of an initiative ordered by President Clinton to trace the fate of gold and other assets looted by the Nazis. The OSI has served as the lead Justice Department representative in that inter-agency effort, which has been led by Under Secretary of State Stuart Eizenstat. Most significant among the investigative breakthroughs made by the OSI is the uncovering of information at the U.S. National Archives that led to long-elusive proof that gold confiscated from Nazi victims was (1) transferred by Germany to Switzerland during the war; and (2) included in gold that was shipped to the Tripartite Gold Commission by U.S. occupation authorities in postwar Germany, for distribution to European central banks. The OSI also found captured German documents revealing that the Nazis devised and implemented a secret program of shipping to Switzerland jewelry taken from Jews. This jewelry (explicitly identified in the documents as "Jewish jewelry") was sent by diplomatic pouch to German diplomatic personnel in Berne, where it was retrieved by a German agent who then used it to purchase industrial diamonds essential to the German war effort. The OSI

Despite the OSI's increased and successful research and investigative activity since the mid-1990s, it is clear that the World War II investigation and prosecution program will eventually be phased out, as the pool of suspects and witnesses dwindles due to the unavoidable ravages of age and illness.

staff also succeeded in tracing the surviving records of the Reichsbank Precious Metals Department, which had been unseen for nearly five decades. In September 1997, OSI's "Holocaust Assets" team received the Assistant Attorney General's Award for Special Initiative, in recognition of their accomplishments.

The first inter-agency report on this 1996 initiative was publicly released in May 1997 by Under Secretary Eizenstat to near-universal worldwide acclaim. The second inter-agency report was released in June 1998, and it focused primarily on the wartime and postwar conduct of Sweden, Spain, Portugal, Turkey and Argentina, as well as on allegations that gold of the wartime Axis government of **CROATIA** had been transferred to the Vatican. Under Secretary Eizenstat praised OSI's work on the project as "pioneering and quite remarkable."

Following enactment in October 1998 of the Nazi War Crimes Disclosure Act (P.L. 105-246), the OSI undertook major responsibility within the newly-established Nazi War Criminal Records Interagency Working Group to assist in the unprecedented government-wide effort to locate, declassify and disclose to the public classified documents pertaining to Nazi criminals and to transactions in plundered assets of Holocaust victims. This compliance effort is an on-going process.

The OSI has won the Founders Award of the American Association of Immigration Lawyers and similar awards from numerous organizations representing Holocaust survivors, including the 1995 Holocaust Memorial Award of the Holocaust Survivors and Friends Education Center. In 1997, the Anti-Defamation League named OSI the first recipient of its newly established annual International Human Rights Award, created to recognize those who have "contributed in a profound and exemplary manner to the cause of justice on behalf of victims of human rights violations."

Among the most successful cases filed by the OSI have been the following: Otto Albrecht von Bolschwing (aide to Eichmann), Andrija Artukovic (Justice and Interior Minister of Croatia; the only cabinet-level Axis official ever known to have entered the United States after the war), Aleksandras Lileikis (Chief of the Lithuanian Security Police for the **VILNA** [Vilnius] Province), and Arthur Rudoph (Nazi slavemaster who later headed the Saturn V rocket program for NASA).

SUGGESTED RESOURCES

Ashman, Charles. *The Nazi Hunters.* New York: Warner Books, 1990.

Levingston, Steven. "The Executioner's Trial." *Boston Globe Magazine,* Nov. 8, 1998.

"Not Finished Yet: Hunting for Nazis." *The Economist,* Feb. 1, 1997.

Ohlendorf, Otto

(1907–1951)

Otto Ohlendorf was one of the Nazi administrators responsible for the extermination policy against the Jews. Born in the Hannover district, Ohlendorf studied law and economics, and joined the **NAZI PARTY** and the **SS** in 1925 and 1926, respectively. In the early 1930s he was a lecturer at several economics institutions, and was active in party organizational affairs and propaganda. He joined the **SD** (*Sicherheitsdienst;* Security Service) in May 1936 and took up a senior post. In September 1939 he became chief of the SD Inland (Interior) section in the **REICH SECURITY MAIN OFFICE** (RSHA; *Reichssicherheitshauptamt*).

Ohlendorf was appointed commander of Einsatzgruppe (Operational Squad) D in June 1941. He was often cited as a model young man who had dedicated himself and his abilities to the party and to Nazi ideology, and who had become head of an Operational Squad that had murdered at least 90,000 people. By June 1942 the unit under Ohlendorf's command had moved along the Black Sea coast and through the Crimea and Northern Caucasia, killing masses of Jews and other Soviet citizens as it went from place to place. For this service in the SOVIET UNION, the Armed Forces High Command awarded Ohlendorf the Military Service Cross, Class 1, with swords.

In November 1943 Ohlendorf was appointed deputy director general and chief of the foreign-trade section in the Reich Ministry of Economic Affairs, in addition to his SD post. A year later he was promoted to the rank of lieutenant general in the SS. After the war, Ohlendorf was the chief defendant in the Nuremberg Military Tribunals' Case No. 9, the Einsatzgruppen Case. In January 1946 he appeared as a witness in the Nuremberg Trial of major war criminals, tried by the International Military Tribunal at Nuremberg. In reply to the prosecutor's question as to what order the OPERATIONAL SQUADS (*Einsatzgruppe*) had been given, Ohlendorf replied, "The order was to liquidate the Jews and the Soviet political commissars in the Einsatzgruppen area of operations and on Russian territory." Asked whether "to liquidate" meant "to kill," Ohlendorf answered: "Yes, I mean to kill." In his own trial, Ohlendorf explained why the Jews had to be murdered. Asked whether Jewish children also had to be murdered, Ohlendorf's answer was that this was unavoidable "because the children were people who would grow up, and surely, being the children of parents who had been killed, they could constitute a danger no smaller than that of the parents."

Ohlendorf was sentenced to death, and on June 8, 1951, he was hanged in the Landsberg prison.

Otto Ohlendorf, SS major general of Himmler's Einsatz Commandos (standing in front of microphone, wearing headphones).

SUGGESTED RESOURCES

Arad, Yitzhak. *The Einsatzgruppen Reports: Selections from the Dispatches of the Nazi Death Squads.* Washington, DC: U.S. Holocaust Memorial Museum, 1989.

Gitelman, Zvi, ed. *Bitter Legacy: Confronting the Holocaust in the USSR.* Bloomington: Indiana University Press, 1997.

Mendelsohn, J. *Punishing the Perpetrators of the Holocaust: The Brandt, Pohl and Ohlendorf Cases.* New York: Garland, 1982.

Operational Squads

The Operational Squads (*Einsatzgruppen*) of the Security Service (*Sicherheitsdienst*; SD) and the Security Police (Sipo) were mobile killing units operating in German-occupied territories during World War II. Operational Squads were intelligence units of the police forces that accompanied the invading army. They made their first appearance during the Anschluss in March 1938.

They reappeared in the invasions of Czechoslovakia, in March 1939, and of POLAND, on September 1 of that year.

In the invasions of Austria and Czechoslovakia, the Operational Squads were to act as mobile offices of the SD and the Sipo until such time as these organizations established their permanent offices. They followed immediately behind the Wehrmacht military units, and, as in the Reich, they assumed responsibility for the

Anschluss
The annexation of Austria to Germany.

Wehrmacht
The regular German army.

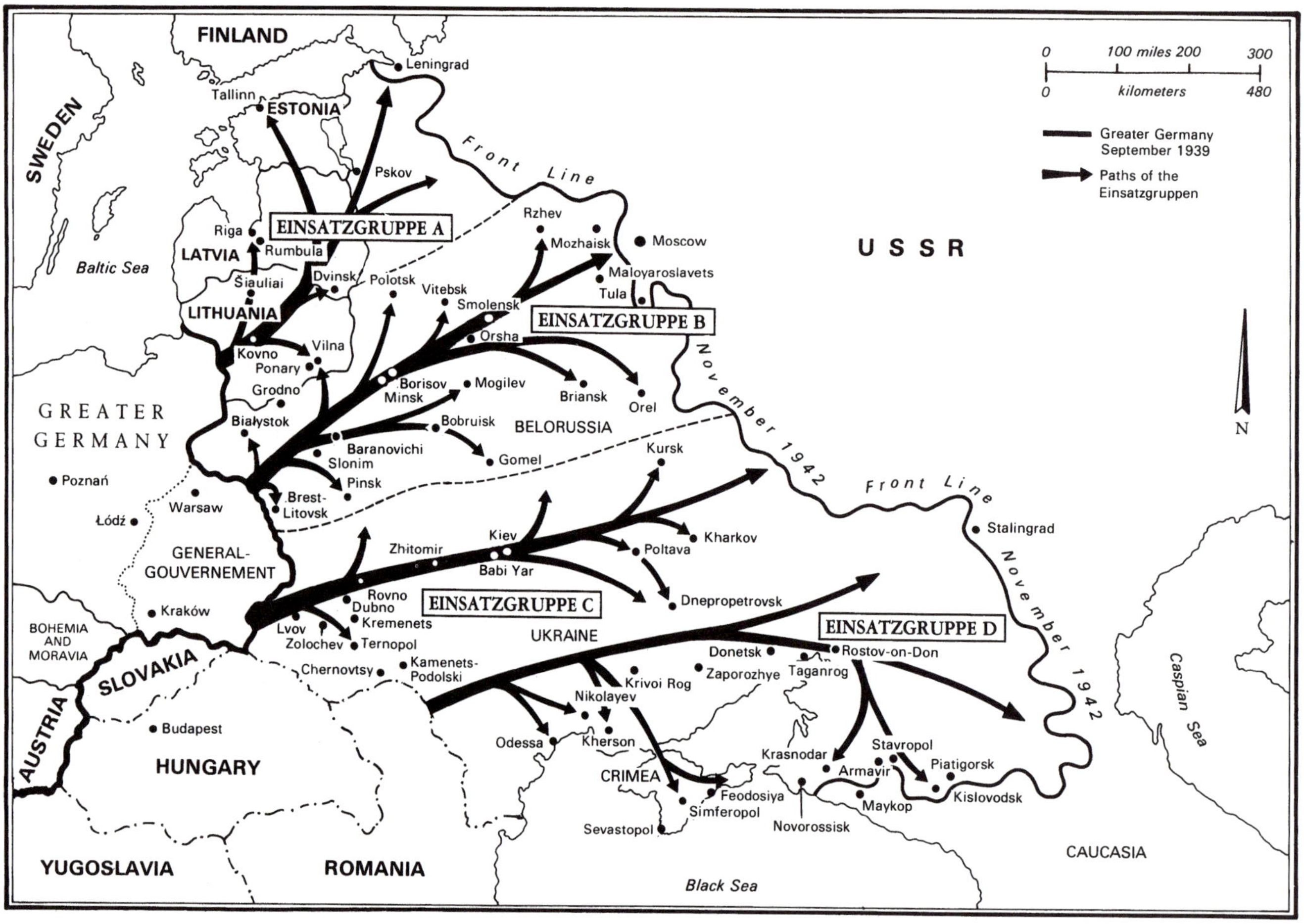

OPERATIONAL SQUADS

Einsatzgruppen (Operational Squads).

security of the political regime. In the Sudetenland (a part of Czechoslovakia), the Operational Squads worked with the military forces to find and imprison "Marxist traitors" and other "enemies of the state."

Preliminary Organization

Six Operational Squads were organized for use in the Polish invasion. Five were to accompany the invading German armies, and the sixth was to operate in the Poznań area, which was to be incorporated into the Reich and called the Warthegau. Each Operational Squad was subdivided into several *Einsatzkommandos*, one for every army corps. There were 15 *Einsatzkommandos*, each with 120 to 150 men. Operational Squad personnel were recruited from among the SD, Sipo, and **SS**, on a regional basis.

The Operational Squads followed foreign operations policies issued by the Sipo and SD. These had been developed as early as August 1939 by Reinhard **HEYDRICH**, head of the **REICH SECURITY MAIN OFFICE** (RSHA; *Reichssicherheitshauptamt*), and by *Generalquartier-meister* Eduard Wagner, the Wehrmacht representative in that office. The basic instruction was to fight hostile elements at the rear of the frontline units.

A more detailed description of the Operational Squads' mission appears in the following order of the day issued by the Eighth Corps: "To conduct counterespionage, to imprison political suspects, to confiscate arms, and to collect evidence that is of importance to police intelligence work." In practice, "combating hostile elements" came to mean carrying out terror operations on a grand scale against

Jews and the Polish intelligentsia. Around 15,000 Jews and Poles were murdered through these actions.

On September 21, 1939, Heydrich sent a high-priority note to the Operational Squad commanders outlining instructions for the treatment of Jews in the conquered territories. The Jews were to be rounded up and restricted in large communities situated on railway lines; Judenräte (Jewish councils; *see* **Judenrat**) were to be established; and operations of any kind against the Jews were to be coordinated with the civil administration and the military command.

On November 20 of that year, on orders from **Berlin**, the Operational Squads' functions were terminated; former members were absorbed by the permanent **SD** and Sipo forces in occupied Poland. However, when plans were made for the attack on the **Soviet Union**, they were reassigned among four Operational Squads that were reestablished as A, B, C, and D.

Invasion of the Soviet Union (June 1941)

During the planning of Operation "Barbarossa," Adolf **Hitler** emphasized that the impending war with the Soviet Union would be a relentless struggle between two completely opposed ideologies. It would require military victory, but also the ability to root out and destroy those who promoted the ideology of Communism. He specifically meant that anyone connected to the Soviet political and ideological system—commissars, as they were termed by Hitler—must be found and eliminated. Hitler entrusted this job to Heinrich **Himmler**, chief of the **SS** (*Reichsführer-SS*)and of all German police organizations. Decree 21, Hitler's order for Operation "Barbarossa," in the section "Instructions for Special Areas," states:

> In areas where military operations are being conducted, the *Reichsführer-SS*, in the name of the Führer, will assume the special duties required for setting up the political administration.... In the discharge of these duties the *Reichsführer* will operate independently and on his own authority.... The *Reichsführer* will ensure that the pursuit of his objectives will not interfere with military operations. Details will be worked out directly between the High Command and the *Reichsführer-SS*.

General Walther von Brauchitsch, the commander in chief of the army, ordered special units of the SD to fulfill those special security police assignments that went beyond the scope of military operations. The guidelines read, in part: "The special units will operate in the rear of the fighting forces and their task will be to seize archives, to obtain lists of organizations and anti-German societies, and to look for individuals such as exiled former political leaders, saboteurs, and the like; they will uncover any existing anti-German movements and liquidate them; and they will coordinate their activities in these areas with the military field-security apparatus." The order added that while the Sipo and the SD (including the Operational Squads) would be operating on their own responsibility, as far as logistics were concerned they would be attached to the armed forces and would depend upon the latter for housing, rations, transport, communications, and other matters. The order further provided that the special units were empowered to take administrative action against the civilian population, on their own responsibility but in cooperation with the military police, and with the approval of the local Wehrmacht commander.

Organizing and Training the Operational Squads

Early in May 1941, the candidates for the Operational Squads were assembled in the training school near the German border. Most had come from the RSHA,

With General von Brauchitsch's order, the Wehrmacht relieved itself of the task of carrying out mass murder, and restricted its involvement to logistics and military action. In reality, however, cooperation between the Wehrmacht and the Operational Squads occasionally went beyond the provisions of the agreement; sometimes regular military units had to stand guard over individuals or groups of persons who would soon die at the hands of the Operational Squads, or they guarded the sites where the executions would take place.

whose manpower division had ordered the SD and the Sipo to select suitable men for this purpose. Another group of candidates came from the Sipo senior officers' training school in Berlin. Yet another group, of 100 men, had been attending an officer candidates' school of the *Kriminalpolizei* (Criminal Police), and were sent from there.

The commanding officers of the Operational Squads—the *Einsatzkommandos*—and the **SPECIAL COMMANDO**s (*Sonderkommandos*) were chosen by Himmler and Heydrich from a list prepared by the RSHA. Most were senior officers of the SD. The radio operators, clerks, interpreters, drivers, and others of the Operational Squads were recruited from among the staff of the RSHA and the SS. Each of the reestablished Operational Squads had sub-units, which were usually either the *Einsatzkommandos* or the Special Commandos.

The first commander of Operational Squad A, SS-*Standartenführer* (Colonel) Dr. Franz Walter **STAHLECKER**, commanded about 1,000 men. Operational Squad A was attached to Army Group North. Its area of operations covered the Baltic States (**LITHUANIA**, **LATVIA**, and **ESTONIA**) and the territory between their eastern borders and the Leningrad district.

The first commander of Operational Squad B, SS-*Brigadeführer* (Brigadier General) Arthur **NEBE**, had 655 men under his command. The Operational Squad was attached to Army Group Center, and its operational area extended over **BELORUSSIA** and the Smolensk district, up to the outskirts of Moscow.

The first commander of Operational Squad C, SS-*Standartenführer* (Colonel) Dr. Emil Otto **RASCH**, had 700 men under his command. The Operational Squad was attached to Army Group South and covered the southern and central **UKRAINE**.

Operational Squad D, commanded by SS-*Standartenführer* (Colonel) Professor Otto **OHLENDORF**, had a complement of 600 men. It was attached to the Eleventh Army and operated in the southern Ukraine, the Crimea, and Ciscaucasia (the Krasnodar and Stavropol districts).

At first glance it appears that the relatively small units had a very large area to cover. However, when they were engaged in mass-murder operations, large forces of German police battalions and local auxiliary police battalions—Ukrainian, Belorussian, Latvian, or Lithuanian—assisted the Operational Squads. At times they also had Wehrmacht follow-up troops at their disposal.

In June 1941, Heydrich outlined the policy that was to guide the Operational Squads in carrying out their assignments, among them the implementation of the Führer's order to liquidate the Jews. On July 2, 1941, the senior SS and police officers that had been designated to act as Operational Squad commanders in the various parts of the Soviet Union received written instructions from Heydrich, which contained the following passage:

> The following is the gist of the highly important orders that I have issued to *Einsatzkommandos* of the Sipo and the SD, with which these two services are called upon to comply;…
>
> 4) *Executions.*
>
> The following categories are to be executed:
>
> Comintern officials (as well as all professional Communist politicians); party officials of all levels; and members of the central, provincial, and district committees; people's commissars; Jews in the party and state apparatus; and other extremist elements (saboteurs, propagandists, snipers, assassins, agitators, etc.).

German soldiers of the Waffen-SS and the Reich Labor Service stand and watch as a member of Einsatzgruppen D prepares to shoot a Ukrainian Jew kneeling on the edge of a mass grave filled with corpses, 1942.

The order regarding the "Jews in the party and state apparatus" affected, in practice, all the Jews in the Soviet Union. Operational Squad Report No. 111 of October 12, 1941, did in fact make it perfectly clear that the purpose was to kill all Jews.

The Operational Squads' Itineraries

The Operational Squads began their march into the Soviet Union, just behind the German army. Operational Squad A started out from East Prussia, and its units—the Special Commandos and *Einsatzkommandos*—rapidly spread out across Lithuania, Latvia, and Estonia. On June 25, Operational Squad A headquarters entered **Kovno** at the same time as the advance formations of the army, and at the beginning of July it moved to **Riga**. Next, Operational Squad A and several of its sub-units advanced toward Leningrad, to be able to enter the city along with the *Totenkopf* Division of the Waffen-SS. When the Leningrad front stabilized, Opera-

OPERATIONAL SQUADS

EYEWITNESS AT THE BABI YAR SLAUGHTER OF KIEV JEWS

From a statement of truck driver Höfer, a witness at Babi Yar:

"The Jews were led into a ravine which was about 150 meters long, 30 meters wide and a good 15 meters deep. Two or three narrow entrances led to this ravine .... When they reached the bottom of the ravine they were... made to lie down upon Jews who had already been shot. This all happened very quickly. The corpses were literally in layers. A police marksman came along and shot each Jew in the neck with a submachine gun at the spot where he was lying. When the Jews reached the ravine they were so shocked by the horrifying scene that they completely lost their will."

".... The moment one Jew had been killed, the marksman would walk across the bodies of the executed Jews to the next Jew, who had meanwhile lain down, and shoot him. It went on in this way uninterruptedly, with no distinction being made between men, women and children. The children were kept with their mothers and shot with them."

"The Good Old Days," in The Holocaust as Seen by Its Perpetrators and Bystanders, *Ernst Klee, Willi Dreesen, and Volker Riess, editors. (New York: The Free Press), 1991, pp. 64-65.*

tional Squad A was basically disbanded, and some of its personnel were used to establish and staff the regional SD and Sipo offices.

Operational Squad B started in **WARSAW**. Some of its units passed through **VILNA** and **GRODNO** on the way to **MINSK**, where they arrived on July 5, 1941. Other units belonging to Operational Squad B passed through Brest-Litovsk, Slonim, Baranovichi, and Minsk, and from there procceded to southern Belorussia: **MOGILEV-PODOLSKI**, Bobruisk, and Gomel, advancing as far as Briansk, Kursk, Orel, and Tula. All along their route, they murdered masses of people—Jews, **GYPSIES**, Communist activists, and **PRISONERS OF WAR**.

Operational Squad C made its way from Upper Silesia to the western Ukraine, by way of **KRAKÓW**. Two of its units, Einsatzkommandos 5 and 6, went to **LVOV**, where they organized a pogrom against the Jews with the participation of Ukrainian nationalists. Special Commando 4b organized the mass murders at **TERNOPOL** and Zolochev, and then continued east. On September 29 and 30, Special Commando 4a, commanded by Paul **BLOBEL**, committed the mass slaughter of Kiev Jews at Babi Yar. This unit was also responsible for the murder of **KHARKOV**'s Jews, in early January 1942. Einsatzkommando 6 marched to the east and liquidated numerous towns. Einsatzkommando 5 was then broken up into SD and Sipo teams and sent to Kiev and **ROVNO**, the capital of *Reichskommissariat Ukraine*. In Rovno, these teams launched a large-scale *Aktion* (Operation) at the beginning of November 1941, in which most of the Jewish inhabitants were murdered.

Operational Squad D was attached to the Eleventh Army. During its advance it carried out massacres in the southern Ukraine (Nikolayev and **KHERSON**), in the

Crimea (**Simferopol**, Sevastopol, Feodosiya, and other places), and in the Krasnodar and Stavropol districts (Maykop, Novorossisk, Armavir, and Piatigorsk).

Operation Squad Results

By the spring of 1943, when the Germans began their retreat from Soviet territory, the Operational Squads had murdered 1.25 million Jews and hundreds of thousands of other Soviet nationals, including prisoners of war. Jewish prisoners of war were separated from the rest and put to death. The Operational Squads shot their victims in ravines, abandoned quarries, mines, antitank ditches, or huge trenches that had been dug for this purpose. The shootings, especially of women and children, had a devastating effect on the murderers' mental state; even heavily drinking hard liquor (of which they were given a generous supply) could not alleviate this stress. This was one reason the RSHA in Berlin, in August 1941, chose to look for an alternative method of execution. This was found in the form of mobile gas chambers, or gas vans (*see* **Gas Chambers/Vans**)—heavy trucks with hermetically sealed chambers into which the trucks' exhaust fumes were piped. Within a short time these trucks were supplied to all the Operational Squads.

The Operational Squads performed their murderous work in broad daylight and in the presence of the local population. Only when the Germans began their retreat was an effort made to erase the traces of their crimes. This was the job of Special Commando 1005 (*see* **Aktion [Operation] 1005**): to open the mass graves, dig up the corpses, cremate them, and spread the ashes over the fields and streams.

Despite such efforts, the Operational Squads left behind an immense record of their deeds, in the form of summary reports drawn up in Berlin on the basis of detailed reports submitted by the various units in the field. Among the most comprehensive of these summary reports was the Report of Events in the USSR, which was first issued on June 23, 1941, and was continued until Report No. 195, dated April 24, 1942. Next, and in continuation, came the Reports from the Occupied Eastern Territories, which began on May 1, 1942, and were kept up until May 21, 1943. In addition, there were the reports on the operations and the situation of the SD and Sipo in the USSR, covering the period from June 22, 1941, to March 31, 1942.

After the War

After the war, the Operational Squad leaders were tried at the Subsequent Nuremberg Proceedings, in the ninth trial conducted by the Nuremberg Military Tribunals. The trial, *The United States of America* v. *Otto Ohlendorf et al.*, began on July 3, 1947, and ended on April 10, 1948; there were 24 defendants. Fourteen were sentenced to death, seven to periods of imprisonment ranging from 10 years to life, and one to the time already served. Two were not tried or sentenced. Four of the defendants were actually executed, and 16 had their sentences commuted or reduced to periods extending from the time already served to life imprisonment. One defendant was released, one died of natural causes, one committed suicide, and the execution of one was stayed because of the defendant's insanity.

Following the establishment of the Central Office of the Judicial Administrations of the *Länder*) at Ludwigsburg, West **Germany**, more than 100 additional indictments were handed down against Einsatzkommando commanders, officers, noncommissioned officers, and privates. In the ensuing trials no death sentences were passed, since the Federal Republic of Germany had abolished capital punishment.

See also **"Final Solution."**

SUGGESTED RESOURCES

Arad, Yitzhak. *The Einsatzgruppen Reports: Selections from the Dispatches of the Nazi Death Squads.* Washington, DC: U.S. Holocaust Memorial Museum, 1989.

"The Einsatzgruppen." *American-Israeli Cooperative Enterprise.* [Online] http://www.us-israel.org/jsource/Holocaust/einsatztoc.html (accessed on September 6, 2000).

Gitelman, Zvi, ed. *Bitter Legacy: Confronting the Holocaust in the USSR.* Bloomington: Indiana University Press, 1997.

OPERATION "ERNTEFEST." SEE "ERNTEFEST" (HARVEST FESTIVAL).

OPERATION 1005. SEE AKTION (OPERATION) 1005.

OPERATION REINHARD. SEE AKTION (OPERATION) REINHARD.

Oradour-sur-Glane

Oradour-sur-Glane was a French village in the Limoges area, the entire population of which was killed by **SS** men during the German occupation of **FRANCE**.

After the Allied landings in Normandy on June 6, 1944, there was an upsurge in anti-Nazi activity by partisan rebel groups all over **FRANCE**, and German army convoys traveling on French roads had to contend with extensive interference. The Germans resorted to deterrent and revenge operations in which they struck out at civilians before partisan groups in and around the villages could cause damage to roads, German troops, and railways. In one of these operations, on June 10, 1944, an SS unit arrived at Oradour, rounded up all the residents—634 men, women, and children—and forced them into the village church. Then they set the church afire, and all the people inside were burned to death. There were no survivors. After the war, Oradour was rebuilt and resettled. Its name became a symbol of the brutality that marked the German occupation of France.

SUGGESTED RESOURCES

Farmer, Sarah Bennett. *Martyred Village: Commemorating the 1944 Massacre at Oradour-sur-Glane.* Berkeley: University of California Press, 1998.

Kruuse, Jens. *War for an Afternoon.* New York: Pantheon Books, 1968.

Mackness, Robin. *Massacre at Oradour.* New York: Random House, 1989.

Organisation Schmelt

Organisation Schmelt is the name commonly used to refer to a system of **FORCED LABOR** for the Jewish population of Eastern Upper Silesia (a region of **POLAND** under German occupation). It operated from 1940 to 1944 in the ghettos and labor camps and was set up and administered by Albrecht Schmelt, Heinrich **HIMMLER**'s Special Representative of the *Reichsführer-SS* for the Employment of

These burned ruins were all that was left of Oradour-sur-Glane after the Nazis killed the inhabitants and set fire to their houses.

Foreign Labor in Upper Silesia. Schmelt, who was the chief of police in Breslau, was appointed to this post to coordinate all programs to exploit Jewish labor. Local authorities were under orders to support his efforts completely. By the end of 1940 Schmelt had forced certain Judenräte (Jewish councils) to draw up lists of all Jews who were fit to work, making the **JUDENRAT** members personally responsible for producing those on the list, under the threat of disbanding the Judenrat and dispatching its members to labor camps.

In 1940, Organisation Schmelt began setting up forced labor camps for Jews. These were located in the vicinity of important war-essential German industries in Upper Silesia and Zagłębie Dąbrowskie, or on their premises. Before long, Organisation Schmelt extended its operations beyond the borders of the region designated by Himmler, and organized labor camps in Lower Silesia and the Sudetenland as well. Schmelt had made agreements with each German plant specifying conditions of employment, wages, and the internal organization of the labor camps. The Jews chosen for these assignments typically had to report to a local transit camp and were threatened with arrest and withdrawal of ration cards from their families if they failed to comply.

In March 1941 Himmler decided to use labor from the Organisation Schmelt camps for constructing the plants that were under Albert Speer's administration. As a result, large numbers of Jews, eventually numbering four thousand, worked in the construction of the hydrogenation plant at Blechhammer. Additional forced-labor camps were established at Gleiwitz (Gliwice) for the construction of a soot-processing plant, at Miechowitz (Miechowice) and Ober Lazisk (Laziska Górne) for electronics factories, at Ratibor (Racibórz) for a light-metals plant, and at Fünfteichen (Miloszyce), near Breslau, for the construction of the Krupp Ordnance Factory (Bertha-Werk Fünfteichen).

Numerous camps were built at important railway junctions where new tracks were being built to serve military requirements. At least seventeen camps were established in the Opole district, along the projected route of the Breslau-Gleiwitz highway that was under construction.

> The Jews chosen for forced labor assignments through Organisation Schmelt were threatened with arrest and withdrawal of ration cards from their families if they refused their assignments.

By April 1942, forty forced-labor camps for Jewish prisoners were in existence and six more were being set up; the total number of prisoners in the camps was sixty-five hundred. While it existed, Organisation Schmelt established 93 forced-labor camps in Upper Silesia. Of these, 48 contained a fairly small women's section. Thirty-six camps were exclusively male, and six were exclusively female. Fifty camps were built in Lower Silesia and seventeen in the Sudetenland.

There were at least 160 Organisation Schmelt camps. In early 1943, 50,570 Jewish prisoners were employed in the enterprises of Organisation Schmelt. At first, only Jews from Zagłębie Dąbrowskie were sent to the camps, but when the Organisation Schmelt plants became more important for the military, Jews from the **GENERALGOUVERNEMENT** as well were dispatched to the Organisation's camps. In 1942, Speer obtained Himmler's consent to choose 10,000 Jews from the transports being sent from western Europe (from **DRANCY**, Mechelen, and **WESTERBORK**) to **AUSCHWITZ**-Birkenau.

Later, the Organisation Schmelt officials stopped such transports on their own initiative, to exchange Jews unfit for work—and, at times, dead Jews—for Jews in good physical condition. The Auschwitz camp commandant repeatedly protested, and Schmelt finally put a stop to it.

Jewish prisoners in the Organisation Schmelt camps usually shared the fate of all the other concentration camp inmates. From the beginning, these camps had been devised as a temporary measure. Late in 1941, in light of the order that had been issued to kill all Jews, it was expected that the camps, as well as the workshops employing Jews, would be targeted for liquidation and the Jewish prisoners would be sent to Auschwitz. Only when the military authorities intervened with the **REICH SECURITY MAIN OFFICE** (RSHA; *Reichssicherheitshauptamt*) and with Himmler was this liquidation postponed to a later date.

In 1943 Himmler decided to liquidate the plants and forced-labor camps and to deport the Jews working there to Auschwitz. An exception was made for camps whose prisoners were working for the most essential armament and ammunition factories, but these camps were now supervised by the administration of the **CONCENTRATION CAMPS** in Auschwitz or **GROSS-ROSEN**. Adolf **EICHMANN** supervised the entire process of liquidating the camps, which lasted until mid-1944. Twenty-eight camps in Lower Silesia and the Sudetenland were attached to Gross-Rosen. In Upper Silesia the prisoners of at least fifteen camps were put at the disposal of the Auschwitz camp authority. Jewish prisoners were transferred to Blechhammer from four of the other camps.

SUGGESTED RESOURCES

Axelrod, Toby. *In the Camps: Teens Who Survived the Nazi Concentration Camps.* New York: Rosen Pub. Group, 1999.

Browning, Christopher R. *Nazi Policy, Jewish Workers, German Killers.* New York: Cambridge University Press, 2000.

OSI. SEE OFFICE OF SPECIAL INVESTIGATIONS.

OŚWIĘCIM. SEE AUSCHWITZ.

PALESTINE. SEE ALIYA BET.

Paris

On the eve of World War II, Paris was the home of about 200,000 Jews. Only a quarter were French-born. The majority were eastern European Jews who had immigrated to **France** both before and after World War I (1914–1918); they had created a vast network of institutions in their adopted country, with a vibrant Yiddish cultural and political atmosphere. Several thousand refugees from **Germany**, **Austria**, and Czechoslovakia added additional diversity to the Jewish community in Paris after Adolf **Hitler**'s rise to power and his annexations. A heterogeneous community with a variety of political and cultural orientations, Parisian Jewry lacked unity as it entered World War II.

The German invasion that began on May 10, 1940, was followed by a massive exodus of citizens from northern France. Within six weeks France was defeated and an armistice agreement was reached that left the country divided: the north came under German occupation, while in the south, a new French government was established at the spa town of Vichy under the authoritarian leadership of Marshal Philippe Pétain. Believing in the Nazi promise of stability and normalcy for both parts of France under the Vichy leadership, hundreds of thousands of Frenchmen who had fled to the south decided to return to the occupied zone.

Some 20,000 to 30,000 Jews joined the migration back, among them community leaders and activists. Jewish organizations were slowly reestablished. Immigrant community activists, Zionists, and Bundists (Jewish socialists) were unified through the Fédération Des Societés Juives De France; this coalition was represented by the Amelot committee. The Communists formed a special underground organization known as Solidarité. The synagogues reopened, and schools run by the French Jews soon opened, as well.

By October 1940 the Vichy government began implementing antisemitic policies and issuing wide-ranging anti-**Jewish Law**s. In late September a required census of Jews showed that there were 150,000 Jews in Paris. This was followed by the **Aryanization** of Jewish enterprises—the forced transfer of ownership of business and financial assets from Jewish to non-Jewish control.

From September 1940 Theodor **Dannecker**, the Germans' "Jewish expert," began demanding the centralization of all the Jewish organizations. Prompted by awareness of the community's material needs and assured by Dannecker that he would not interfere, the Coordinating Committee (CC) of Jewish Welfare Societies was established in January 1941. All the organizations accepted centralization on this basis except for the Communists. In March, Dannecker brought in two men from **Vienna** to run the Jewish organization, causing a division among member groups of the CC. In May 1941 Dannecker ordered, on the basis of a Vichy law, the first internments: 3,700 Jewish men were rounded up and sent to Pithiviers and Beaune-La-Rolande (Loiret). Now, in addition to distributing 60,000 monthly meals, the CC's various agencies needed to help these men and their families. In August further tension ensued when the CC refused to fulfill Dannecker's demand for 6,000 men for **Forced Labor**. In reprisal, Dannecker ordered the internment of 4,300 French and immigrant Jewish men in the newly established camp at **Drancy**, northeast of Paris.

The continuous "Aryanization" of thousands of Jewish enterprises had already caused severe unemployment problems. These internments further contributed to the deteriorating economic situation of the community. The order to surrender radios, bicycles, and telephones, and the bombing of seven synagogues in October, heralded worse to come. The activities of the French Résistance led the Germans to

Throughout the nineteenth and twentieth centuries many Jews migrated to Paris, making it the center of Jewish life in France.

The order requiring Jews to wear yellow stars provoked widespread public resentment among the French, who found creative ways circumvent this discriminatory act against the Jews in their midst. Yellow became a fashionable color, and some people wore stars or other items to express solidarity with the Jews. Even the French police, not known for their courteous treatment of Jews, did not care to collaborate in this effort.

repatriated
Sent back to one's country of origin or citizenship.

take repressive measures against the Jews in December 1941: a fine of 1 billion francs was imposed and 750 French Jews were interned, from a group of 1,000 hostages who were being threatened with deportation. The Union Générale Des Israélites De France (UGIF), established by Vichy on November 29, 1941, on German orders, was held responsible for payment of the fine. When the year ended, Jews were no longer allowed to leave Paris or to change their address. By then, some 9,000 Jewish men had been interned and 10,000 had fled to the Vichy zone.

The year 1942 began with an ordinance forbidding Jews to leave their homes between 9:00 p.m. and 6:00 a.m. In March the first deportation took place, consisting of the 1,000 hostages; in June those previously interned were also deported. The **BERLIN** decision of June 1942, ordering preparations for mass **DEPORTATIONS**, led to new measures: Jews were ordered to wear the yellow star (*see* **BADGE, JEWISH**), and Jews were prohibited access to all public places. After detailed planning among German and French officials, the stage was set for a major operation in Paris. Mass arrests of foreign Jews, regardless of sex, age, or physical condition, began on July 16. Thousands of French police rounded up 13,000 Jews and interned them in the Vélodrome d'Hiver sports arena. They were taken to Drancy before being deported to **AUSCHWITZ**. Dannecker had expected to deport 28,000 Jews, but 15,000 had evaded arrest. Apart from escaping to the Vichy zone or hiding, the only way a Jew could survive was to obtain an identity card that served as a protective pass, either by working for German industry or through employment with the UGIF.

By early 1943 there were only 60,000 "legal" Jews left in Paris: 30,000 had been deported, thousands had fled or gone into hiding, and some 3,000 from Turkey, **HUNGARY, ITALY**, and neutral countries had been **repatriated**. As fewer Jews were available to meet deportation quotas, the Germans ordered arrests in children's homes, homes for the aged, and the Rothschild Hospital. Mid-1943 was a critical period: worker identity cards no longer provided protection, the UGIF was forced to release most of its foreign employees, and even Jews of mixed marriages were interned. Solidarité, committed to the armed struggle, had been decimated by the **GESTAPO**. The French Jewish group known as Amelot, which was dedicated to helping those in hiding, saving children, and distributing forged papers, was weakened by leadership losses. In June 1943, SS-*Obersturmbannführer* (Lieutenant Colonel) Alois Brunner increased the tempo of deportation, and took control of Drancy away from the French administration. When the UGIF refused to carry out Brunner's order to make arrests, its vice president André Baur and many of its longtime leaders and members were deported.

Early in 1944, when only 7,000 immigrant Jews and at least that many French Jews still resided openly in Paris, even French Jews, who had previously been exempt from deportation orders, filled convoys. Jewish organizations once again realigned and formed new umbrella committees, but the UGIF continued separately to offer certain services and maintain its network of children's homes.

The Allied armies landing on the coast of France in June 1944 held out hope for those remaining, but deportations continued unabated. On July 31, Brunner ordered the deportation of almost 300 children seized a week earlier from UGIF homes. On August 5, 1944, all but one of the children pictured at right were killed upon their arrival at Auschwitz. Paris was freed on August 25, 1944, and the remaining 1,400 Jews at Drancy were saved. Estimates of the number still left in Paris vary between 20,000 and 50,000. Of the 150,000 present at the October 1940 census, fully one third were no longer alive to celebrate the liberation.

Parisian Jewry demonstrated a very diverse response to the cataclysm of Nazi occupation and the Vichy collaboration. Hundreds fought in the August 1944 insurrection, and hundreds were executed or otherwise died after being deported

for engaging in resistance activities. More than 3,000 children and countless adults, had been saved through Jewish relief committees, while the UGIF continued to distribute aid until the very end. With the liberation, Parisian Jewry began to rebuild its shattered community and its organizational structure, returning to the political and ideological diversity that had marked it prior to World War II.

This picture was taken on December 18, 1943, in the courtyard of a public school in the Paris suburb of St. Mandé, the location of the girls' orphanage. Of the twenty children pictured here, only one survived deportation which occured in the early hours of July 31, 1944.

SUGGESTED RESOURCES

Aaseng, Nathan. *Cities at War: Paris.* New York: Macmillan, 1992.

Adler, Jacques. *The Jews of Paris and the Final Solution: Communal Response and Internal Conflicts, 1940–1944.* New York: Oxford University Press, 1987.

Josephs, Jeremy. *Swastika Over Paris.* New York: Arcade, 1989.

Neray, Ruth Bindefeld. *To Auschwitz and Back: My Personal Journey.* Sudbury, MA: Sudbury Press, 1997.

Partisans

In World War II (1939–1945), partisans—paramilitary fighting groups that fought against the Nazis in German-occupied Europe—operated mainly in Eastern

P artisans are self-organized fighting forces operating in enemy-occupied territory, usually using guerrilla tactics.

Europe and in the Balkan countries. This form of war-time resistance grew from the tension between having to obey and cooperate with the occupying power, and the reluctance to do so. For individuals, cooperation with the Nazis of **GERMANY** meant obeying their orders, working for them, and surrendering to them money and property. Such cooperation was widespread and unavoidable in occupied Europe. It took some time before the individual citizens of each occupied country came to feel the urge to upset the enemy's plans and interfere with them. When they reached that stage, they acted by evading orders, committing sabotage, failing to fulfill production quotas, and avoiding or refusing to go to Germany for **FORCED LABOR**. Such steps inevitably led to outright resistance. Many of those who offered resistance were motivated by hatred of **RACISM**, violence, **NAZI PARTY** ideology, and the methods used by the Nazis.

Organized resistance—on political, national, or religious grounds—passed through several phases. Since partisan groups were outlawed, they resorted to secret, "underground" operations. Political parties in the resistance movement began propaganda operations. They circulated underground newspapers, organized strikes, and tried to sabotage the enemy's efforts. There was generally little cooperation among the different groups. In the final stage of resistance—the stage of guerrilla warfare and armed struggle—these differences sometimes led to violent clashes.

In most places, the final stage of resistance began when the war reached a turning point in late 1942 and early 1943. The Nazis were suffering more defeats, and their forces were vulnerable to partisan activity. Anticipating the war's end, various national political movements began to jockey for position in the postwar era. Thus they intensified their respective armed confrontations against the occupier. The struggle for power among the political factions also led to more serious confrontations between rival movements, as occurred in Yugoslavia, Greece, and **POLAND**.

Partisan Organizations and Methods

In Poland, the **HOME ARMY** (*Armia Krajowa*), an underground military organization, was created at the very beginning of the occupation (in 1939). On more than one occasion its leaders decided not to put their main force into action. They preferred to save it for a decisive test against the Nazis, toward the end of the war. The Home Army was in sharp conflict with the Polish Communists when they set up their own underground organization, in early 1942. For the non-Communist Poles of the Home Army, there was no difference between the Germans and the Soviets—both were enemies who had occupied their land.

In some of the occupied countries, resistance to the Nazis was confined to attacks against specific Nazi officials, or to one-time special operations involving a sensitive security target. No attempt was made to train combat units and put guerrilla forces into the field on an ongoing basis, to take up street fighting, or to engage the enemy in some other form. In many countries, such as the Protectorate of **BOHEMIA AND MORAVIA**, the resistance avoided guerrilla warfare because of the great risk of retaliatory action, which would take many lives.

Polish partisans frequently operated in units that were called out for a specific mission or for a period of training. Afterward, they returned to their homes and civilian pursuits. They used the same methods to vanish from the scene when the Germans combed the forests in their search for partisans.

There were many Jews among the partisans of different countries. In some Eastern European countries, however, they faced overwhelming persecution by the general population. This situation made it very hard to be an effective partisan

fighter. For example, they did not dare to approach local people for food and information, as non-Jewish partisans could. And when they did join a partisan unit, they were not put on an equal footing with other partisans. Outside Eastern Europe, Jews who wanted to join the partisan forces faced a different situation. In the Balkan states (Yugoslavia, Bulgaria, and Greece), Jews were accepted as equals into fighting organizations. In Western Europe, including **France** and **Italy**, many Jews joined the underground fighters' ranks not particularly as Jews, but as citizens of the country fulfilling their duty, or out of loyalty to a particular political and ideological movement. When the stage of the **"Final Solution"** was reached, Jewish participation in partisan operations became part of a hopeless struggle and a determination for revenge.

Partisan activity by Jews was significant in the Baltic states and the **Vilna** area, in **Belorussia** and western **Ukraine** (which in the interwar period had been part of Poland). It is estimated that 20,000 to 30,000 Jews were in the partisan units in the forests of the region. A combination of factors made this possible. The heavily wooded terrain was suitable for establishing partisan bases in, and many of the Jews were from the area and knew it well. At a later stage of the war, most partisan units there were under Soviet command and accepted Jews into their ranks (except for Polish and Ukrainian units, which on occasion were hostile to Jews).

In June 1942, a central headquarters was established for the entire partisan movement in the Soviet territories occupied by the Germans. It became the channel through which means of communication, arms, equipment, and other supplies were provided to the partisans. The number of partisans grew rapidly, and their operations were now coordinated and mutually supportive. The partisans eventually reached a high standard of organization and discipline. They were well equipped and took part in many combat operations. The partisan units tormented the enemy by interfering with communications, attacking groups of soldiers, and punishing Nazi collaborators (people who helped the Nazis). Above all, they instilled fear into the German soldiers, giving them the sense of being surrounded by hostility. The partisans were increasingly effective fighters. In 1944, partisans in the East began to fight with military forces on the front, or tried to liberate areas in anticipation of the advancing Soviet army.

Belorussia

There were no partisan operations of large dimensions in the countries of Western Europe, except for France and Italy. Most partisan activity occurred elsewhere in Europe. Belorussia (present-day Belarus) had the largest concentration of partisans in Eastern Europe. Partisans began to operate there as early as the summer of 1941. Most of them were Soviet army troops whom the Germans had cut off and who were roaming the villages and forests. A few were Communist party activists who had fled their homes when the Germans entered the area. Belorussia's wide expanses of forest and swamp were ideal for large-scale partisan operations. By late August 1941, according to Soviet sources, some 230 partisan units were in existence. In late 1941, Belorussia had 5,000 partisans.

In the spring of 1942, thousands of automatic rifles and artillery pieces were supplied to the partisans in Belorussia from inside the **Soviet Union**. The partisan units soon formed into brigades, and a Belorussian partisan headquarters was set up. The partisan units provided a safe haven for some of the Belorussian people who were threatened with deportation or death by the Germans. The scope of partisan activities expanded greatly—in 1943, about 60 percent of Belorussia was an area of partisan actions. During the German retreat from Belorussia in the summer of 1944,

Guerrilla warfare is the war of the weak and oftentimes ill-armed against superior forces that have heavy and sophisticated arms at their disposal. Guerrilla forces, however, usually have the advantages of familiarity with the area, the sympathy of the population, and the ability to use hit-and-run tactics.

Group portrait of a Jewish partisan unit operating in the Lithuanian forests.

the partisans carried out large joint operations with the Soviet army. They blew up railway tracks in the German rear and harassed enemy units during their withdrawal.

By 1944, there were 374,000 partisans in Belorussia, of whom 91,000 were in family camps in the forests. The partisan movement in Belorussia included Belorussians, Russians, Jews, Poles, Georgians, Slovaks, and other groups. The number of Jewish partisans in the area ranged from 12,000 to 15,000—the largest concentration in the Jewish partisan movement.

Lithuania

In Lithuania, the partisan movement came into existence much later than in Belorussia. This relatively late development resulted from the deep hatred that most of the Lithuanian population had toward the Soviet Union. In addition, in the

early part of the war, Lithuania was far away from the fighting front in the East. It was from Lithuania, however, that the call rang out for Jews to rise up against the Nazis in the ghettos and to create a Jewish partisan movement. This call was contained in the manifesto that Abba Kovner published in the Vilna ghetto on the night of December 31, 1941. Three weeks later, the **UNITED PARTISAN ORGANIZATION** (*Fareynegte Partizaner Organizatsye*; FPO) was created in Vilna.

The Lithuanian partisan movement contained some 850 Jews, representing 10 percent of its total strength. The largest concentration of Jewish fighters from Lithuania came into existence in the Rudninkai Forest. The Jewish partisans were under the authority of the Soviet Lithuanian partisan movement. They sent couriers to the labor camps in Vilna to bring in more Jews from there. By the end of October 1943, there were 250 people at the Jewish partisans' base. They undertook sabotage actions against roads, bridges, and electricity and telephone poles. Jewish partisans also sabotaged Vilna's power station and water supplies. Some of their operations were designed to obtain arms and food supplies. On July 13, 1944, the Jewish partisans took part in the liberation of Vilna.

Ukraine

A large Soviet partisan movement arose in the northern part of Ukraine, with its wide expanses of forests and swamps. From the very first days of the occupation, these forest areas provided refuge to Jews who had fled the Nazis' extermination campaign, and to Jewish prisoners of war, who were also targeted by the Nazis for death. Both refugees and POWs joined the partisan units that began to organize in Ukraine as early as July 1941. Specific information on the role played by the Jews is scarce. Many Jews did not identify themselves as such, and so only a part of the story is known.

The Generalgouvernement

A large-scale underground movement existed in the Jewish communities and ghettos of Poland (part of the **GENERALGOUVERNEMENT**). While this movement showed initiative and daring in many areas, it did not have great success in guerrilla warfare or in the partisan struggle outside the cities. The reasons why the Jewish partisan struggle in Poland failed to reach large dimensions are complex. First, central Poland is thinly wooded, in comparison with the great forests of the East. Second, the strong military resistance (the Home Army) did not make use of guerrilla tactics early on against the Nazis, saving most of its strength for the final stages of the war. The Home Army did not encourage Jews to escape into the forests, and most unit commanders were not willing to accept Jews into their ranks. The fascist partisan faction National Armed Forces (*Narodowe Siły Zbrojne*)—which remained, for most of the period—outside the Home Army, was extremely anti-Semitic. Some of its members even murdered Jews who escaped to the forests. Some Home Army partisans were sincerely concerned about the fate of the Jews and tried to defend them in the forests, but their numbers were small and their power limited. The Polish Communists were more friendly to the Jews. Unlike the Home Army, the Communists wanted to begin an immediate struggle with the Nazis. The Jews were a natural ally in this goal. Also, the Communists and the political left in general were somewhat more sensitive to the fate of the Jews.

The third reason why Jewish partisan participation was limited in the Generalgouvernement was timing. While the Nazi extermination campaign was at its height (from the spring of 1942 to the spring of 1943), the partisan movement was still weak. By the

> During the extermination and murder of Jews that went on in the western Ukraine in the summer of 1942, many groups of armed Jews organized their own partisan units and escaped into the forests and mountains. In Volhynia, some 1,000 Jewish fighters, in 35 to 40 groups, kept fighting on their own before joining up with the Soviet partisan movement late that year. Some eventually died in heavy fighting.

Rachel Sacher Rudnitsky, a cantor's daughter from Warsaw who fought as a partisan in the forests near Vilna, shortly after its liberation.

time it gained in size and strength and included elements friendly to the Jews, very few Jews were left. Those still alive were imprisoned in labor and concentration camps.

According to data published by the Poles, about 25,000 people took part in the partisan movement in the Generalgouvernement. The number of Jews who succeeded in escaping and finding shelter in villages, forests, and mountains was apparently in the tens of thousands. Of them, only 2,000 ended up as armed fighters in the forests, and 3,000 wandered the forests and villages. The rest were caught and killed, or died in the wild.

Slovakia

In SLOVAKIA, the Zionist YOUTH MOVEMENTS, as well as members of the Communist party, played a key role in organizing resistance "cells." These groups were to go into action in the event of the resumption of deportations. Such cells existed in all the labor camps. In early 1944, contact was established between these cells and the Slovak National Council. When the SLOVAKIAN NATIONAL UPRISING broke out in late August of that year, the members of these cells joined it, along with other Jews who had not previously belonged to resistance cells. Twenty-five hundred Jews participated in the Slovakian uprising, of whom 1,566 were partisans, representing 10 percent of the total number of partisans in Slovakia. Five hundred Jews fell in the uprising; of these, 269 were partisans—that is, one out of every six Jewish partisans who took part.

Yugoslavia, Bulgaria, and Greece

In Yugoslavia, Bulgaria, and Greece, Jews were accepted into the ranks of the partisans as equals. No separate Jewish units, or units of a Jewish character, existed in these countries. The number of Jewish partisans there was relatively large, especially in Yugoslavia, where the partisan movement was the most important among all the German—occupied countries. The number of Jews who joined the Yugoslav partisans is especially impressive. They had to overcome great difficulties to make their way to the remote areas where the fighting took place. Also, by the time the Yugoslav partisans launched their struggle (in the fall of 1941 and, with greater strength, in the second half of 1942), most of the country's Jews had already been killed. The list of Jews who served in the resistance movement contains 4,572 names; of this number, 3,000 served in combat units. A total of 1,318 Jews fell in battle. Some 150 were awarded the First of the Fighters medal, and ten Jews received the National Hero award, the highest decoration that Yugoslavia had to offer.

SEE ALSO **RESISTANCE, JEWISH**.

SUGGESTED RESOURCES

Anflick, Charles. *Resistance: Teen Partisans and Resisters Who Fought Nazi Tyranny.* New York: Rosen Pub. Group, 1999.

Jewish Partisans of World War II [videorecording]. Aleph Productions, 1985.

MacLean, Alistair. *Partisans.* New York: Ballantine Books, 1984 (fiction).

Smolar, Hersh. *The Minsk Ghetto: Soviet-Jewish Partisans Against the Nazis.* Washington, DC: U.S. Holocaust Memorial Museum, 1989.

PART JEWS. SEE MISCHLINGE.

Pechersky, Aleksandr

(b. 1909)

Aleksandr (Sasha) Pechersky was the leader of the SOBIBÓR uprising. Born in Kremenchug, in the UKRAINE, as a child Pechersky moved to Rostov-on-Don, where he graduated from a music conservatory. He became a bookkeeper, but was

also active in drama and music circles. He served in the Red Army, holding the rank of second lieutenant.

When the Germans attacked the **SOVIET UNION**, Pechersky was drafted and posted to the front. In September 1941 he was promoted to lieutenant. He was taken prisoner the following month and contracted typhoid fever. Because the Germans shot all Soviet prisoners of war who were sick, he managed to conceal his illness and turn up for the prisoners' daily roll calls. In May 1942 Pechersky escaped, along with four other prisoners, but they were all caught. Contrary to the usual German procedure, they were not shot but were sent to a penal camp, in Borisov. It was there, when Pechersky had to undress, that he was identified as a Jew, a fact he had previously managed to hide from the Germans. On August 20, Pechersky was transferred to an **SS** camp in **MINSK**, in which some 100 Soviet Jewish prisoners of war were held, together with several hundred Jewish civilians from the Minsk ghetto. He stayed there for more than a year.

On September 18, 1943, the Minsk ghetto was liquidated and Pechersky was sent to the Sobibór extermination camp, with 2,000 Jews from the ghetto and the **SS** camp. They reached Sobibór on September 23. Pechersky was one of 80 Jewish prisoners of war who, on arrival in the camp, were selected for construction work. The rest of the transport was killed by exposure to lethal gas [*see* **GAS CHAMBERS/VANS**].

Shortly after Pechersky's arrival in Sobibór, he was contacted by the camp underground. As an officer, he agreed to take over the command of the underground and to lead it in an uprising. During the next three weeks Pechersky reorganized the underground, making the prisoners of war its core and planning the uprising. On October 14, 1943, under Pechersky's command, most of the **SS** men in the camp were killed and a mass escape from the camp took place. With a group of prisoners of war, Pechersky succeeded in crossing the Bug River, and on October 22, he made contact with Soviet **PARTISANS** in the Brest area. He joined the partisans and fought in their ranks until the summer of 1944, when the Soviet army advanced into the area and the partisans joined up with the regular army units. Pechersky, now fighting in the Soviet army, was badly wounded in August 1944, and was hospitalized for four months. On recovering, he was discharged and returned to his hometown, Rostov, where he settled.

Pechersky was the chief witness for the prosecution in the trial, held in Kiev in the spring of 1963, of 11 Ukrainians who had served as guards in the Sobibór camp. His account of the Sobibór uprising was published in Yuri Suhl's *They Fought Back* (1957) and in *The Fighting Ghettos*, (1967) edited by Meyer Barkai.

SUGGESTED RESOURCES

Escape from Sobibor [videorecording]. Live Home Video, 1991.

Rashke, Richard L. *Escape from Sobibor.* Boston: Houghton Mifflin, 1982.

Płaszów

Originally a forced-labor camp, the Płaszów camp was established in 1942 in a suburb of **KRAKÓW**. Its official designation was the Płaszów Forced-Labor Camp of the **SS** and Police Leader in the Kraków District. In January 1944, Płaszów became a concentration camp.

Jewish women pulling hopper cars of quarried stone at the Płaszów concentration camp, Kraków, Poland, 1944.

The construction of the camp began in the summer of 1942. It was built within the Kraków city limits, on a site that included two Jewish cemeteries, other Jewish community property, and the private property of Polish residents who had been evicted. From time to time the camp was enlarged. Its maximum size, in 1944, was 200 acres (81 hectares). It was encircled by an electric double-apron barbed-wired fence 2.5 miles (4 kilometers) in length. The camp was divided into several sections—the German quarters, the factories, and the camp itself. The camp was further divided into men's and women's sections, with separate subsections in each for Poles and Jews.

The Kraków ghetto was liquidated in 1943, on March 13 and 14. Most of the Jewish inhabitants were deported to **Bełżec**. During the liquidation, about 2,000 Jews were murdered in the Kraków streets (and buried in a mass grave in Płaszów). The rest of the Jews of the Kraków ghetto—some 8,000 people—were put into Płaszów camp. In early July, a separate camp for "retraining by work" was established within the Płaszów camp. This "retraining" camp was meant for Polish prisoners. Those Poles charged with disciplinary infractions were held there for several months; those charged with political offenses were given unlimited terms of "retraining." The Polish "retraining" camp also contained several dozen Romani (Gypsy) families, including small children (*see* **Gypsies**).

The number of prisoners held in Płaszów varied from time to time. Before the Kraków ghetto was liquidated, the camp contained 2,000 people. In the second half of 1943, however, 12,000 people were imprisoned there. In May and June 1944, the number of prisoners was at its height—22,000 to 24,000, including 6,000 to 8,000 Jews from **Hungary**. There were 1,000 Polish prisoners in the early stage; that figure jumped to 10,000 after the **Warsaw Polish Uprising**.

Płaszów also contained German criminal prisoners, who had various camp duties. The number of "permanent prisoners" (that is, inmates who were given per-

sonal numbers) is estimated to have been 25,000. There was also an unknown number of "temporary" prisoners and hostages. Amon Goeth, the camp commandant from February 1943 to September 1944 (one of five men to hold the post), was the person responsible for most of the heinous crimes committed in the camp, including mass murder, selections, working people to death, and individual murders.

Until 1944 most of the camp guards were Ukrainians in Nazi service. When Płaszów became a concentration camp, 600 **SS** men from the **SS Death's-Head Units** (*Totenkopfverbände*) took over.

While still functioning as a forced-labor camp, Płaszów was the scene of mass killing of Jews. When the SS took over, Poles who had been sentenced for political crimes were taken there and shot to death. It is estimated that some 8,000 people, individually and in groups, were murdered in Płaszów.

In mid-1944, as the **Soviet Union**'s Red Army was drawing near, work was begun on the breakup of the camp. Some of the surviving prisoners were transferred to other labor camps. Others were deported to **extermination camps**. In late May, 2,000 Jewish prisoners were deported to **Auschwitz**, where they were gassed to death.

In September 1944, the Polish section of the camp was liquidated. The SS also tried to erase the traces of the crimes that had been perpetrated in the camp. They had the mass graves opened, and the bodies were exhumed and then burned in heaps. On January 14, 1945, the last prisoners were evacuated from Płaszów and sent to Auschwitz.

SUGGESTED RESOURCES

Graf, Malvina. *The Kraków Ghetto and the Płaszów Camp Remembered.* Tallahassee: Florida State University Press, 1989.

Novac, Ana. *The Beautiful Days of My Youth: My Six Months in Auschwitz and Płaszów.* New York: Henry Holt, 1997.

Plotnicka, Frumka

(1914–1943)

Frumka Plotnicka was a leader of the **Fighting Organization of Pioneer Jewish Youth** (*He-Haluts ha-Lohem*) underground in **Poland**. Born in Plotnicka, near Pinsk, she was also a member of the youth movement *Freiheit* (*Dror*). Late in 1938 she worked at the *Dror* main office in **Warsaw**.

When World War II broke out, Plotnicka, along with most of the people in the *hakhsharot* (Zionist training farms), moved to Kovel, in Soviet-occupied eastern Poland, in the hope that from there they would find a way of reaching Palestine. In 1940 she was one of a group of *Dror* headquarters members who were asked to return to the German-occupied area to reorganize *Dror* as an underground movement. Basing herself in Warsaw, Plotnicka tried from the beginning of the invasion of the **Soviet Union** in June 1941 to consolidate and strengthen the *Haluts* underground movements throughout occupied Poland, even visiting nearly inaccessible ghettos. In September 1942 she went to Będzin on a mission for the **Jewish Fighting Organization** (*Żydowska Organizacja Bojowa*; ŻOB), to assist in setting up a self-defense organization there. She was in contact with several people and organizations in Switzerland and **Slovakia** and with the Rescue Committee of the Jewish

Agency in Turkey, to which she passed information about the situation in occupied Poland. Plotnicka rejected opportunities, such as moving to Slovakia or obtaining documents as a foreign national, to save her life. On August 3, 1943, she died in battle, together with the last group of fighters in Będzin.

SUGGESTED RESOURCES

Anflick, Charles. *Resistance: Teen Partisans and Resisters Who Fought Nazi Tyranny.* New York: Rosen Pub. Group, 1999.

A Teacher's Guide to the Holocaust: Resisters. [Online] http://fcit.coedu.usf.edu/holocaust/people/resister.htm (accessed on August 22, 2000).

POGROMS. SEE KIELCE; KRISTALLNACHT (NIGHT OF THE BROKEN GLASS).

Pohl, Oswald

(1892–1951)

Oswald Pohl was the head of the German ECONOMIC-ADMINISTRATIVE MAIN OFFICE (*Wirtschafts-Verwaltungshauptamt*; WVHA) during World War II. He joined the NAZI PARTY in 1926 and the SS in 1929, reaching the rank of *Standartenführer* (Colonel) in 1934. His organizational skills caught the attention of Heinrich HIMMLER, who brought Pohl to prominence in 1935 as chief of administration in the SS-*Hauptamt* (SS Main Office).

In 1939 Pohl was promoted to the rank of ministerial director of the Ministry of the Interior, where he rapidly developed SS economic enterprises with the help of sympathetic specialists from German industry. These activities were grouped together in 1942 as the WVHA, and Pohl's position made him one of the most powerful members of the SS structure. He was responsible for a work force of more than half a million concentration camp prisoners, some of whom were also "leased out" to private industry. Pohl was in charge of overseeing all the prisoner work programs.

In effect, it was Pohl who masterminded the "economic" aspect of the program to exterminate the Jews, as part of Himmler's emphasis on the effectiveness and financial independence of the SS. Pohl ensured that all the personal possessions of the murdered Jews—clothing, gold tooth fillings, wedding rings, jewelry, and so on—were sent back to GERMANY and turned into cash or otherwise utilized commercially. Under Pohl, prisoner labor was turned into a financial asset for the SS.

At the end of the war Pohl went into hiding, but he was found and arrested in May 1946. In 1947 he was condemned to death for CRIMES AGAINST HUMANITY, war crimes, and membership in a criminal organization. After a number of appeals he was executed in 1951.

SUGGESTED RESOURCES

Browning, Christopher R. *Nazi Policy, Jewish Workers, German Killers.* New York: Cambridge University Press, 2000.

Ferencz, Benjamin B. *Less than Slaves: Jewish Forced Labor and the Quest for Compensation.* Cambridge, MA: Harvard University Press, 1979.

Poland

The Poles are a Western Slavic people who created a unified state in the tenth century and adopted Roman Catholicism. In the course of Poland's thousand-year existence, its territory has alternately expanded and contracted. Numerous powers in the region, including Russia, **Austria**, and **Germany**, have ruled the country during its long, tumultuous history.

After World War I (1914–1918), Poland became an independent nation. But this status was fragile, and Poland was forced to seek alliances among the powers in Europe. In 1934, its leadership signed a treaty with Germany, meant to protect Poland's independence. But it did not take into account the fact that Adolf **Hitler**, the head of Germany and its **Nazi party**, viewed Poland only as a "satellite" or peripheral state at best. A violent clash between the two countries was inevitable.

Germany Attacks Poland

On September 1, 1939, Germany attacked Poland and World War II began. Germany had many advantages over Poland. The Polish state was surrounded by German military forces in the west, north, and south. In addition, Germany had superior military equipment. On September 3, 1939, **Great Britain** and **France** declared war on Germany, in response to the attack on Poland. However, they did not take any military measures that could have led to fighting on a second front and a reduction of the pressure on Poland. On September 6, Romania, an ally of Poland, declared itself neutral in the conflict. As a result, Poland stood alone in the face of German aggression and, despite its heroic resistance, was conquered. On September 28, **Warsaw** surrendered, and the last battle was fought in the early days of October.

A total of 66,000 Polish troops fell in the battles, and 133,000 were wounded. German losses were 16,000 dead and missing, and 30,000 wounded. Sixteen thousand Polish and Jewish civilians and **prisoners of war** were killed in more than 700 mass executions carried out by German military forces and the Nazis' **Operational Squads** (*Einsatzgruppen*). Despite their devastating defeat, however, the heads of the Polish government and army did not officially surrender.

Until October 26, 1939, German-occupied Poland was in the hands of a military administration. Thereafter, Germany annexed parts of western and northern Poland, and formed a civil administration, known as the **Generalgouvernement**, in the remaining areas of Poland held by Germany. More than 22 million inhabitants of Poland were now under German occupation. Over 10 million of them lived in the territories annexed by Nazi Germany, including 600,000 to 1 million Germans and 600,000 Jews. The rest, some 12 million people, including 1.5 million Jews, lived in the Generalgouvernement.

On September 17, Soviet forces entered eastern Poland, which the Soviets regarded as parts of **Belorussia** and **Ukraine**. By then, it was clear that the war had been decided in favor of the Germans. The Soviets met with little spontaneous resistance from Polish units. The Polish High Command had ordered the Polish army not to fight the Soviet army, except when Polish units were being attacked. An agreement between the **Soviet Union** and Germany, signed on September 28, fixed the final border between the two countries. The Soviets seized an area of 75,675 square miles (196,000 square kilometers), with a population of 4 million to 5

Administrative Divisions of Poland under German Occupation, 1939–1945.

million Poles and 1.2 million Jews. The non-Polish population, including the Jews, gave the Soviet units a warm welcome.

The Polish Leadership

On September 17, 1939, in view of the new situation that had arisen in their country, the top Polish leaders decided to leave and cross into Romania. There they were interned, as a result of German pressure. These leaders were then replaced by Polish leadership based in France. When France fell, in June 1940, the former leaders of the Polish government moved to Great Britain to form a government-in-exile. Most of the Polish army in France, however, did not escape in time. The Pol-

> Nazi policy in occupied Poland focused on eliminating Poland as a nation, through the destruction of Polish culture and society.

ish forces either fell into German hands or crossed the border into Switzerland, where the soldiers were interned.

Polish Government under Occupation

In September 1939, the central Polish government institutions dissolved. Before long, they were reestablished as underground organizations, by the Polish government-in-exile and the Polish underground authorities in Poland: the Delegatura (the Polish government's representation on Polish soil) and the National Council (*Krajowa Rada Narodowa*). As far as the Germans were concerned, the Polish state had ceased to exist both legally and politically. The Germans felt that they could thus rule at will, without taking into account the fact that the Polish government was continuing the war abroad. In the areas incorporated into Nazi Germany, the Polish administration, local government units, and all existing Polish organizations were liquidated, and new administrative units were established.

The men appointed by Hitler as governors were to "Germanize" the areas under their control, by expelling Poles and placing selected parts of the population on the Volksliste and accepting them as "ethnic Germans," or (Volksdeutsche). Germans were to be settled there. By the end of 1939, some 90,000 Jews and Poles had been expelled from the annexed areas into the Generalgouvernement. During the entire German occupation, 900,000 persons were expelled—not counting the Jews who were deported for extermination. In their place, 600,000 Germans from other parts of Poland and from other countries of Eastern Europe were settled in these areas, together with 400,000 Germans from the German state. The Poles who were temporarily permitted to stay were treated as subhumans. They were not allowed to live in the same place as Germans or to associate with them (except in their place of work), and they were robbed of all their property and personal belongings.

Nazi occupation policy was implemented by the administrations of the occupied areas; the SS, police, and Waffen-SS; and the Wehrmacht units stationed there. In 1942, these numbered 500,000 troops; in 1944, there were between 600,000 and 1.1 million. Neither side was prepared to cooperate with the other. The conquerors had no interest in such a relationship, since their plan was to transform Poland into German *Lebensraum* ("living space"). The Poles generally felt hatred toward their conquerors. The basic goal of Nazi policy was to destroy Polish society so that Poland would cease to exist as a nation. The means used to achieve this goal were: (1) the destruction of the Polish leadership; (2) the murder of people regarded as present or potential enemies of Nazi Germany; (3) the murder and extermination of "undesirable" racial and other groups (Jews, Gypsies, and sick people, the last by means of the Euthanasia Program); (4) the use of harsh measures against the population wherever the Nazis encountered resistance; (5) the provision of food in quantities just large enough to enable the Poles to perform hard labor; (6) the reduction of the population; and (7) the allotment of a role for the Poles in the "General Plan East"

The Jews were at first separated from the Polish population and imprisoned in ghettos and camps. Later, they were nearly all killed in the "Final Solution". The loss of life in Poland as a result of the fighting and of actions taken by the occupying authorities was 6 million—half of this number Jews. The expulsions affected 1.2 million people; 500,000 people were expelled after the Warsaw Polish Uprising. Some 2.5 million were sent to work in Germany. More than 2 million Poles were included in the *Volksliste*, which meant that the military draft was applied

Volksliste
A list of groups of people who were to be accepted into the Third Reich as Germans.

to them. The loss of life among the civilian population was ten times that suffered by the fighting formations.

The Church under the Occupation

The attempt to destroy the Polish nation also included the religious sphere of Polish life. In the eyes of the German authorities, the Catholic church in Poland was an integral element of the Polish people and the Polish state. For this reason, in the areas incorporated into Nazi Germany, the Polish elements in the church were liquidated, so that the church became a German institution. Many churches were turned into warehouses or stripped of their contents. During the war, close to 3,000 Christian clerics were killed in battle, 900 were shot to death, and 1,345 perished in CONCENTRATION CAMPS.

The Evangelical church, in the areas annexed by the Reich, was well disposed toward the Nazi authorities. Churchmen of German origin who were known for their loyalty to Poland, however, suffered harsh treatment.

> Worst among the crimes committed by Nazis in occupied Poland was the murder of the Jews.

Organized Terror

During the September 1939 fighting, terror was practiced on an organized basis, but its methods differed from place to place, depending on its purpose—short-range or long-range—and on the organization of the various occupation agencies. In the areas incorporated into Nazi Germany, the terror used against the Polish population between 1940 and 1945 was more or less uniform, with slight variations in its intensity. In the Generalgouvernement, there were marked differences in the degree of violence used, and also in the methods applied, depending on the military and political situations and the effectiveness of the methods used. The Generalgouvernement authorities employed terror on a large scale. When they could not control or suppress the population, the terror frequently took the form of mass beatings and manhunts. The German retreat from occupied Poland was also accompanied by the murder and massacre of prisoners.

The Nazis set up their largest internment camp system on Polish soil, including a number of EXTERMINATION CAMPS and concentration camps where Jews were systematically exterminated. The total included 1,798 labor camps and 136 refugee camps. Transit camps for deportees were also used as killing sites, as were several prisons and ghettos.

Poles were also imprisoned in nearly every concentration camp. The highly efficient Nazi camp system affected every aspect of the prisoners' lives, achieving its purposes by exposing prisoners to intolerable living conditions, forcing them to work to the very limit of their strength, meting out cruel punishments, holding lengthy roll calls in freezing cold, and generally seeking to humiliate the prisoners in every possible way.

Polish Areas Annexed to the Soviet Union, Lithuania, and Slovakia

The areas occupied by the Soviet Union after September 17, 1939, were incorporated into Belorussia and Ukraine. The land was confiscated, industry and banks were nationalized, and agriculture was **collectivized**. Soviet policy toward the various ethnic groups was designed to win the support of the non-Polish population. Most of the Jews rapidly adjusted to the new situation, and they took part in the new adminis-

collectivized
Transformed from a system of privately-owned farms to a government-supervised enterprise of production and distribution, generally under a communist system of government.

Polish resistance took the form of individual and public self-defense, and opposition to orders issued by the occupation authorities.

tration. The Poles, as a result, became distrustful of the Jews, which only added to the Poles' long-standing ANTISEMITISM. This attitude was exploited by Nazi anti-Jewish propaganda after the German attack on the Soviet Union in June 1941.

The areas that the Soviet Union had occupied in September 1939 were captured by the Germans during their invasion of the Soviet Union in 1941. A new territorial district, BIAŁYSTOK, was created, with a population of 1.7 million. It received a status similar to that of the Polish areas incorporated earlier into Nazi Germany.

On July 30, 1941, the Polish government-in-exile and the Soviet Union signed a treaty in which they agreed to cooperate in the war against the Germans. Agreement was also reached on the creation of a Polish army on Soviet soil. However, the expectations raised by this agreement were never fulfilled.

The Polish Resistance Movement

The German occupying forces suppressed the Poles with the utmost severity. After an initial period of uncertainty about how to respond to the German occupation, Polish resistance to the Nazis became widespread. More than 300 underground political and military groups were formed. There were two major underground political movements. One consisted of the Home Army (*Armia Krajowa*), together with the Delegatura. The other included the People's Guard (*Gwardia Ludowa*) and its successor, the People's Army (*Armia Ludowa*, together with the National Council (*Krajowa Rada Narodowa*).

Resistance by individuals and organized groups became a way of life. Economic sabotage reinforced patriotic feelings. Resistance activities included: (1) active sabotage, especially on lines of communication; (2) a well-organized military intelligence system; (3) PARTISAN units; (4) uprisings (such as the Warsaw Polish Uprising); (5) an underground press; and (6) an underground educational network.

The Jews in Poland

Jews have lived in Poland for a thousand years. Over the centuries, they have often been subjected to persecution, even massacres, resulting from intense antisemitism. After World War I ended, the Allied leaders had required Poland (and other countries in Eastern and Southeastern Europe) to sign a treaty for the protection of the ethnic and religious rights of minorities. The Polish struggle for independence from 1918 to 1920 was accompanied by anti-Jewish riots in hundreds of cities and towns.

Two basic elements determined the Polish attitude toward the Jews after World War I. One was the size of the Jewish population, which in the newly independent Poland constituted 10 percent of the total, rising as high as 30 percent in the major cities. The other issue was the key role allegedly played by the Jews in Poland's economy. Many Poles believed that a "Polonization" of economic life in the country's cities and towns was necessary. This hostility was heightened by the devastating worldwide economic depression of the 1930s, which hit Poland very hard. When the Polish leadership tightened the country's relations with Nazi Germany, it adopted a clear anti-Jewish policy. The government criticized brutal acts of violence against the Jewish minority—but gave its blessing to an anti-Jewish economic boycott. The pre-invasion Polish government assigned high priority to the accelerated emigration of Jews and reduction in the size of the country's Jewish population. More extreme groups tried using violent methods, such as starting anti-Jewish riots, to force the Jews to emigrate. Although broad political circles, composed of socialists and liberals, publicly attacked antisemitism and joined the Jews in the struggle

A Jew wearing a ritual prayer shawl, surrounded by Nazis. Two cut off his earlocks while others look on with amusement.

for their rights and in their self-defense actions, the idea of depriving the Jews, or at least a large proportion of them, of the right to live in Poland had wide support among the population in the second half of the 1930s. At the time of the German invasion of Poland, Jews became targets of violent discrimination by both their Polish neighbors and the German occupying forces.

World War II

Immediately after the Germans overwhelmed Poland in September 1939, a wave of riots and murders followed, perpetrated by the Operational Squads that accompanied the German forces. The "actions" (*Aktionen*) of the Operational Squads struck Poles, too. But even in their first blows, the Jews were singled out.

On the eve of the war, Poland had a Jewish population of 3.3 million, 1.2 million of whom lived in the areas that came under Soviet control. From early September 1939 to February and March 1940, there was an ongoing flow of refugees from the German-controlled part to the eastern, Soviet-held part. Several sources estimate that

In the summer of 1940, Jews were forbidden to emigrate from Poland. No more than 2,000 to 3,000 Jews were able to leave Poland legally. Most of them were well-to-do or had good connections.

POLAND

Early on, Jews were rounded up in city streets for jobs such as carrying loads, working in military barracks, and clearing the streets of the rubble caused by the air raids. The random seizures and assaults brought Jewish life to a virtual standstill. As a result, the Judenräte in large cities offered to supply the Germans with a fixed quota of workers, if the roundups in the streets were discontinued. This was the beginning of the Jewish labor gangs. They were paid for their work not by the Germans but by the Jewish community.

WHEN THE GERMANS CAME

Gerda Weissman Klein, who was a young Jewish girl in Poland at the time, remembers what happened when the Nazi occupation reached the street where she and her family lived in Bielitz.

… evening brought fury to the end of that last peaceful day. Sporadic shooting started from the rooftops, an attempt at delaying the enemy while our army retreated to Krakow. We looked for shelter in our cellar and sat there through the night. Toward morning the shooting stopped altogether and the vehicles of the Polish army ceased to roll. We came up from the cellar for a cup of tea in the living room. As I sat down on the couch near the window I could see people talking and laughing, carrying flowers, and everywhere the clicking of cameras.…

I looked out again. A swastika was flying from the house across the street. My God! They seemed prepared. All but us, they knew.

A big truck filled with German soldiers was parked across the street. Our neighbors were serving them wine and cakes, and screaming as though drunk with joy, "Heil Hitler! Long live the Fuehrer! We thank thee for our liberation!"

I couldn't understand it. I didn't seem to be able to grasp the reality of what had happened. What are those people doing? The same people I had known all my life. They have betrayed us.

Gerda Weissmann Klein, All But My Life *(New York: Hill and Wang), 1995, pp. 7–8.*

300,000 Jews, mostly young males, took this route. Some of the refugees returned to the west after a short stay, tired of living as refugees, or wanting to be reunited with their families. After this phase, and until the German attack on the Soviet Union in June 1941, the German-occupied part of Poland had a Jewish population of 1.8 million to 2 million, of whom 1.5 million were in the Generalgouvernement.

JEWISH POLICY The first directives about the treatment of the Jews in Poland were issued by Reinhard **HEYDRICH**, in a special letter addressed to the Operational Squad chiefs dated September 21, 1939. The policy on the Jews was to be implemented in two stages: an immediate operational stage, and a long-range stage defined as a "final aim" (*Endziel*). This second stage was not discussed in detail, though the Operational Squads chiefs were warned that the very existence of such a "final aim" must be kept strictly secret.

There were three immediate measures:

1. The expulsion of the Jews from the northwestern districts to the area that was designated to form the Generalgouvernement, and their concentration in the large cities, near major rail junctions;

2. The establishment of Ältestenräte ("councils of elders") or Judenräte (Jewish Councils) in the Jewish communities, to consist, when possible, of "influential personalities and rabbis," where such people were still to be found, to provide direct administration of Jewish life under the supervision of Nazi forces;

3. The taking into consideration of German economic interests, especially the requirements of the army, by the German officials in charge of the expulsions and evacuations. Jews whose continued presence was economically essential were to be left in place until further notice.

On November 25, 1939, Hitler officially announced the end of the military administration and the establishment of the Generalgouvernement, with Hans **FRANK** as its head. Frank began his term of office by issuing a series of anti-Jewish orders. In the late autumn, decrees were published that, among other things: (1) ordered all Jews ages ten and above to wear a white armband with a blue Star of David on the right sleeve of their inner and outer garments as of December 1; (2) prohibited Jews from changing their place of residence without permission from the local German administration; and (3) introduced **FORCED LABOR** for the Jews. Jewish stores and Jewish-owned enterprises had to be marked with a Star of David. In January 1940, Jews were barred from traveling by train except by special permit. The purpose of these decrees was to humiliate the Jews, restrict their freedom of movement, and isolate them from the rest of the population.

THE JUDENRAT Within a short time, Judenräte were established in all parts of German-occupied Poland. These Jewish Councils were the German authorities' main instrument for implementing their policy on the Jews. Most of the Judenrat members (some of whom had been forced to accept the appointment), as well as the Judenrat chairmen, believed that they would be able to serve the interests of their community and protect it as best they could. The Judenrat was the only institution permitted to appear on behalf of individual Jews and the Jewish community. It was the only channel of communication between the Jews and the authorities in a situation in which the Jews had lost all traces of their civil and legal status.

Each Judenrat operated on its own, in its respective community, and without any umbrella organization or other type of coordinating body. The Judenrat chairman were torn between protecting the people of the ghetto and protecting themselves; the Germans executed Judenrat chairmen who refused to carry out decrees designed to inflict grave harm upon the Jews. More information about the Judenräte and their role in Jewish communities in Poland during World War II can be found in the **JUDENRAT** entry.

FORCED LABOR AND PAUPERIZATION The history of the Jews of Poland under German occupation is divided into two distinct periods. The first was from the outbreak of war in September 1939 to the middle of 1941. At that point, the Germans launched their mass murder campaign, after their attack on the Soviet Union and the conquest of territories in the East. In the Generalgouvernement and the areas incorporated into Nazi Germany, the first phase lasted until early 1942. In parts of Zagłębie and Silesia, it lasted until the second half of that year. Once the German administration was installed in the occupied areas, the Jews there were smothered with decrees and regulations designed to humiliate, isolate, or rob them. Jews were confined to hard labor only. For this work they received minimal pay—if any—that was completely inadequate for the barest necessities of life.

The confiscation and liquidation of Jewish and Polish factories and businesses began as early as September 1939. In January 1940, the Jews were ordered to regis-

From its very start, the anti-Jewish campaign was not confined to official decrees. Other actions by the authorities were sometimes far worse. Soldiers in uniform rounded up Jews on the streets for various temporary jobs and often assaulted them, especially those wearing traditional garb. They also grabbed goods from Jewish homes and the shelves of Jewish stores without paying for them and seized Jewish apartments, evicting the rightful residents.

POLAND

Poland's largest Jewish communities on the eve of World War II.

Polish Jews tried to convince themselves that Germany was a nation with a civilized Western tradition that had exercised tolerance toward Jews during World War I. The first months of the new occupation soon made it clear that times had changed.

ter their property with the local authorities. In addition to factories, business enterprises, workshops, and houses, goods and valuables found in homes and in warehouses were also taken by the Nazis. Jews who did not own the kind of property that was officially subject to seizure were not safe from being robbed. Furniture, pianos, books, valuables, and artworks were removed from Jewish apartments. Even the apartments themselves were sometimes taken from their Jewish residents.

Most of the Jewish breadwinners in Poland who were salaried workers—laborers, business employees, clerks, teachers, and most of the professionals—were left without work or any alternative source of income. They had a hard time surviving on their savings and money from selling their valuables. From the very beginning of the occupation, refugees and the very poor suffered from hunger. On October 26, 1939, Hans **F**RANK issued a decree proclaiming that every Jewish male of working age was subject to forced labor. This became the basis for sending Jews to labor camps. At first many volunteered for the camps, assuming that they would receive the food they needed and a minimum standard of living conditions. When the true—and dreadful—situation in the Nazi camps became known, volunteering came to an abrupt end. Forced recruitment took its place. By early 1941 some 200 Jewish labor camps were in operation. Tens of thousands of Jews were forced to work there. The work consisted of flood control; construction of roads, defense works, and buildings; and agriculture. Because of the intolerable living and working

conditions, laborers in the camps were sapped of their strength. Epidemics broke out, and a high death rate resulted.

GHETTOIZATION Unlike the Judenräte, which were established under a central directive and on short notice, the process of confining the Jews to ghettos was a lengthy one. Sealed-off ghettos with an internal Jewish government of sorts, an economic life, and essential services were introduced only in Eastern Europe, the Baltic states, and the Soviet Union. The first ghetto of this era was established in October 1939, in Piotrków Trybunalski. For most of the time, it was an open ghetto. The first large ghetto, in **Łódź**, was sealed off in May 1940. In the Generalgouvernement, the ghettos were set up in 1940 and 1941—the Warsaw ghetto in November 1940, **Lublin** and **Kraków** in March 1941—and in Zagłębie, this happened as late as 1942 and 1943, when the Nazis' mass extermination of Jews was already well underway. Ghettos were generally set up in the occupied Soviet territories soon after the occupation in 1941.

Ghettos were guarded differently from place to place. German, Polish, and Jewish policemen were posted at the Warsaw ghetto gates. In Łódź, which was completely sealed off from non-Jewish areas, German police guarded the ghetto from the outside, and Jewish policemen patrolled inside the fence. Attempts to leave some closed ghettos were punishable by death. In the smaller ghettos, the guard consisted of one German policeman or several local policemen.

Living conditions inside the ghettos were largely determined by the degree to which the ghettos were segregated and sealed off, and by the size of their population. The worst off were the two most populated ghettos, Warsaw and Łódź; in 1940 and 1941, a total of 600,000 Jews were imprisoned in these two alone. In his diary, Nazi Joseph **Goebbels** called the ghettos "death boxes." But were the ghettos intended to be a primary tool for liquidating the Jews, or were they created as a Nazi tool of controlling the Jewish population?

In November 1941, Hans Frank noted that qualified Jewish workers in the Generalgouvernement could be useful for German industry. He and other senior Nazis argued that these Jews should be permitted to work, while "appropriate arrangements should be made" for the rest. In August 1942, Hans Frank declared: "Nothing much has to be said about the fact that we are starving 1,200,000 Jews to death; that is self-evident, and if the Jews do not die from hunger, anti-Jewish decrees will have to be speeded up, and let us hope that this is what will happen." By the time this was said, the "Final Solution"—the Nazis' plan to exterminate the Jews of Europe—was already underway.

This makes it difficult to state that ghettoization was meant as a consistent policy for eradicating the Jews. The local German authorities were not at all troubled by the huge death rate among the Jews (especially among Jews who were not working for them). But there is no evidence of a full-fledged, specific plan to bring about the physical liquidation of the Jews during the ghettoization stage—that is, in 1940 and 1941. In fact, in 1940, the Nazi top leadership was still toying with the idea of mass **deportations** of Jews to Madagascar (*see* **Madagascar Plan**). In any case, the definitive decisions on the fate of the Jews were made on the top level, in **Berlin**.

Jewish Ghetto Life

Most of the Polish Jews who had been leaders at various levels—in the parliament, the municipal government, and Jewish communal life—left Poland during

> Ghettos differed from one place to another, although the sites selected for the ghettos were almost always the most crowded and neglected sections of the cities. The Łódź ghetto was totally sealed by fences and barbed wire, and it had its own currency, which was totally worthless outside the ghetto. The Warsaw ghetto was enclosed with a wall, but it was possible (though dangerous) to get in and out. People took the risk in order to smuggle in food and manufactured goods. But in many smaller cities, the Jewish ghettos were open, with only a sign to indicate their boundaries.

At first, underground activities did not lead to confrontation with the Nazi authorities. The Germans were not interested in what the Jews were thinking, or in their political divisions. The Nazis evidently did not imagine that Jews were capable of forming an underground that could interfere with the occupation authorities. Only when they discovered that the Jews were maintaining contact with the Poles did the Nazis become furious.

the fighting in September 1939, or in the first few months of the occupation. They believed that they were endangered by their past activities, since the Nazi regime would likely first seek out those who had publicly expressed their anti-Nazi views.

As a group, the Jews who remained were well aware that the German Nazi regime was extremely anti-Jewish. Still, it was impossible for anyone to imagine where Nazi policy on the Jews would lead. And yet, after generations of discrimination and persecution, the Jews of Poland were better prepared for adversity than the Jewish communities in Western Europe.

SOCIAL WELFARE At the beginning of the occupation, Jewish political, social, and cultural organizations ceased to exist. Although no specific announcement to this effect was made, anything not expressly permitted had to be viewed as prohibited. The need for mutual help and social welfare prompted the first efforts to reorganize. Many Jews were called upon to take in refugees, to repair war damage, and to lend aid to the thousands of persons affected by the war. Social workers had not joined the exodus of public figures, and most of the leaders of the American Jewish **JOINT DISTRIBUTION COMMITTEE** (known as the Joint) had also stayed behind. As an American organization, the Joint was somewhat off limits to the Nazis, and it had funds at its disposal. Its officials began to set up aid centers, beginning with soup kitchens, where a bowl of soup and a piece of bread were given to the hungry. Welfare institutions for children and for the sick were also reactivated, and an aid network for refugees was established.

Representatives of the self-help organization sponsored by the Joint went out from Warsaw to the provincial cities, and representatives of remote Jewish communities came to Warsaw to seek help. At first the self-help effort was very important, but the money eventually ran out. The funds received up to late 1941 were not enough to cover even minimum welfare needs. After the **UNITED STATES** entered the war in late 1941, money from American sources could no longer be sent legally.

The financial assistance given by the Joint in 1940 was higher than in the following year, 1941—the year of distress, hunger, and mass starvation. But the Joint leaders did not give up. They appealed to Jews in the ghettos who had money hidden away to lend some of it to the Jewish Mutual Aid Society, with the assurance that the loan would be repaid when the war was over. This method was risky for both of the parties involved. Although it provided additional financial resources for the self-help organization, it could not meet the growing needs. Emanuel **RINGELBLUM** expressed the dilemma, writing in May 1942: "What to do? To give a spoonful to everybody, in which case nobody will stay alive, or to hand it out in generous portions—in which case only a few could benefit?"

CULTURAL ACTIVITIES Illegal cultural activities in the ghettos of Poland took many forms. In Warsaw, Kraków, and elsewhere, the authorities did not permit schools for Jewish children. Only in the 1941–1942 school year were elementary-school classes allowed in the Warsaw ghetto. In place of legal schools, a network of secret study "cells" operated, on the elementary and secondary levels. Warsaw also had clandestine secondary schools. Lectures on forbidden subjects were given in the ghettos, orchestras played and choirs sang, and theaters performed plays from the classical Jewish repertoire and sketches dealing with current life. Many diaries were kept in the ghettos. The diarists included writers, public figures, Jews who had never before tried their hand at writing, and even children. The diaries that have been preserved, written in different languages and styles, document the life of the Jews in the ghettos.

Jews in Occupied Poland

I realized that we were outsiders, strangers in our own home, at the mercy of those who until then had been our friends. Although I was only fifteen I had a strong feeling, . . . that our lives were no longer our own, but lay in the hands of a deadly enemy.

Gerda Weissmann Klein, All But My Life *(New York: Hill and Wang), 1995, p. 8.*

The Jews also refused to follow the Nazis' anti-religious decrees. In the Warsaw ghetto, public prayer services were prohibited. In Kraków, the synagogues were closed down. Still, the Jews continued to pray in prayer quorums and to observe the religion's dietary laws.

POLITICAL ORGANIZATIONS Many leadership functions were carried out by underground political organizations. Political party representatives were active in two spheres: political information and mutual help. Party activists maintained contact by means of postal services (which functioned to some degree in the ghettos), and they even established contact with foreign countries. The underground organizations also published clandestine newspapers.

More intensive and more important were the activities carried on by the **YOUTH MOVEMENTS** and the younger age groups of the political parties. Among them, the Zionists worked to train and educate the young generations for the challenges that lay ahead when the war was over. They also began to organize themselves for possible resistance, and they tried to persuade other Jews to join in that effort.

Jews and Poles

At first, contacts between the Jewish resistance and the main Polish underground were negligible. The central organs of the Polish underground—the Delegatura and the Home Army—had no contact with the Jews. Jewish citizens of Poland were not asked to participate in any way whatsoever in the Polish underground's institutions. Nor did the situation move the Polish underground to take any action on behalf of the Jews, even though it was active in many fields all over the country and had considerable human and financial resources. Individual Poles, in some cases, did maintain contact with their Jewish friends and helped them, as did some Polish groups that had contacts with Jewish organizations in the past. For the most part, the Jews of Poland were left to stand before the Nazis alone, unarmed, and without the support of the Poles.

Until the stage of total physical extermination, most of the Poles were indifferent to the fate of the Jews. This was due in part to the war conditions, the suffering, and the Nazi terrorization of Poles as well as Jews. Antisemitism also had an important impact on the behavior of the Polish population during the occupation. Apathy was not the only response, however. At one end of the spectrum were Poles eager to take over Jewish property and businesses. At the other were Poles who overcame their antisemitic attitudes toward the suffering Jews and supported them.

> Special soup kitchens for children kept them busy with games and some instruction.

> The largest and most dreadful deportation to take place on the soil of occupied Poland was from the Warsaw ghetto.

Preparations for the "Final Solution"

In late 1939 and early 1940, Jewish emigration from German-held territory was still allowed. An attempt was made to concentrate Jews in the Lublin Reservation (*see* NISKO AND LUBLIN PLAN). In the summer of 1940, the German Foreign Office and the GESTAPO produced the MADAGASCAR PLAN, under which the Jews of Europe were to be deported to that distant island in the Indian Ocean, to be held there under German control. But the Madagascar Plan was not feasible, due to the situation in the war zones and on the high seas. According to some sources, the Germans also considered a plan to deport the Jews into the remote expanses of the Soviet Union. This plan had to be abandoned when the German military advance was brought to a halt within European Russia. The Nazis in the occupied countries also did not show a clear-cut resolve in the first years to physically destroy the Jews.

It is clear, though, that for the Nazi authorities, the anti-Jewish measures and regulations that they were implementing at the time—the separation of the Jews from the general population, the elimination of Jews from economic life, the drafting of Jews for forced labor, and their imprisonment in ghettos—did not represent the limit of their planned actions against the Jews and their ultimate goal. Even the ghettos were no more than an intermediate station. More radical measures were being considered that could only mean the total elimination of the Jews. Generalgouverneur Hans Frank, whose statements on the fate of the Jews were always inspired by Hitler and other the top Nazi officials, remarked at a meeting of the Generalgouvernement in December 1941: "To be quite honest, the Jews have to be disposed of, one way or another."

Extermination Operations

The Germans attacked the Soviet Union in June 1941. For Hitler, this was the right moment to intensify his policy against the Jews, and the Operational Squads were sent to commit mass murder by shooting, which resulted in the deaths of hundreds of thousands of Jews. This marked the beginning of the utter destruction of European Jewry. From the Russian war front, the campaign of death was extended to Poland and the other German-occupied areas of Europe. The German authorities in each country participated, under a special task force responsible for planning and execution.

EXTERMINATION CAMPS On December 7, 1941, the first camp in which gas was used for killing was put in operation, at CHEŁMNO, northwest of Łódź, in a Polish area that had been incorporated into Nazi Germany. The first victims of that camp, Jews from the small towns of Dąbie, Sompolno, and Koło, were killed the next day. On December 15, the first Jews were deported from the Łódź ghetto to Chełmno, marking the beginning of a process that continued, with some breaks, until May 15, 1942. During this phase of deportations, 55,000 Jews were taken to Chełmno, in 66 transports. In October and November 1941, preparations began for the murder of the Jews in the Generalgouvernement, including the Jews of LVOV and Eastern Galicia—a total Jewish population of 2 million.

In the first half of 1942, three more extermination camps were established as part of AKTION (OPERATION) REINHARD: BEŁŻEC, SOBIBÓR, and TREBLINKA. The Jews of Eastern and Western Galicia were taken to Bełżec. The Jews of LUBLIN district were sent to Sobibór. The Jews of Warsaw and Radom districts and the Białystok district, for the most part, were deported to Treblinka. Bełżec, the first of these death camps, was put into operation on March 17, 1942. According to a Nazi report, about 50 percent of the Jews of Lvov district—a total of 252,989 people—had been deported by November 10, 1942. In March 1942, some 15,000 Jews from Lvov were deported, followed by another 50,000 in August 1942. During March and April 1942, Jews from a number of towns and cities in Galicia were deported, from such places as Stanisławów, Drogobych and Kolomyia. The second wave included tens of thousands of Jews from Przemyśl, **TERNOPOL**, and elsewhere.

DEPORTATIONS FOR DEATH OR FORCED LABOR Between mid-March and mid-April, the Jews of Lublin were deported, and that ancient Jewish community was liquidated. Some 2,500 to 3,000 people were murdered on the spot. Thirty thousand were deported, mostly to Bełżec. Four thousand Jews were left in the "residual ghetto," in the suburb of Majdan-Tatarski. On August 16, in an action against the Radom Jewish community, 18,000 Jews were deported.

At the Wannsee Conference on January 20, 1942, the Generalgouvernement state secretary, Dr. Josef Bühler, asked that the "Final Solution" begin in the Generalgouvernement.

In May 1942, the mayor of Kraków announced that only 15,000 Jews whose presence was essential for the economy would be permitted to stay there. The rest, some 40,000 people, were ordered to get out of the city within three months. During May and June 1942, about 6,000 Jews were deported to Bełżec. In a second wave of violent deportations in October, another 7,000 Kraków Jews were sent to Bełżec, and 600 were murdered on the spot. In the fall of 1942, similar events took place in the Białystok district. The first deportation from the city of Białystok was carried out in February 1943. The largest and most dreadful deportation to take place on the soil of occupied Poland was that from the Warsaw ghetto. It began on July 22, 1942, and lasted until mid-September. This operation cost the lives of 300,000 persons, with most of the victims sent to Treblinka.

In the towns and cities of Zagłębie, the Jews were subject to the forced labor operations of **ORGANISATION SCHMELT**. Beginning in late 1940, SS officer Albrecht Schmelt was in charge of the exploitation of the Jewish labor force on behalf of the SS. As chief of the organization that bore his name, Schmelt presided over a network of labor camps in Upper and Lower Silesia and the Sudetenland. Tens of thousands of Jews worked there. Organisation Schmelt also had at its disposal factories that had been put up in the cities and ghettos, in which Jews were working for the German war effort. Conditions in these camps and factories were very harsh, and the pay received by the Jews did not cover their minimum needs. But working for the organization protected the Jews for a relatively long time from deportation.

In May 1942, the extermination of the Jews of Zagłębie was launched. The method used by the "Schmelt men" was to purge the "unproductive elements" and deport them. This was a turning point for the Jews of Zagłębie. A general "selection" (*Selektion*) was made among the Jews of Będzin, Sosnowiec, and Dąbrowa Gornicza, and 11,000 of them were deported to the extermination camps. After this, most of the remaining Jews worked for Organisation Schmelt. The deportations were resumed in early 1943, and the Zagłębie Jewish communities were gradually liquidated, with the Jews deported to **AUSCHWITZ**. In August 1943, the last mass deportation took place. The few survivors who were left were also eventually sent to Auschwitz, and the liquidation came to an end by January 1944.

From April to September 1942, the Łódź ghetto was relatively quiet. This was the period when the ghettos in the Warthegau region were being emptied of Jews and liquidated. The Jews from those ghettos who were fit to work were moved to the Łódź ghetto. In September, the so-called Sperre Aktion was carried out in Łódź. In its brutality and severity, this action exceeded anything that had been experienced in other ghettos. The target figure for the deportation was 20,000, to consist of children under ten and elderly people over sixty-five. Babies were taken out of their mothers' arms,

Polish Response to the "Final Solution"

How did the Poles react to the murder, on Polish territory, of millions of Jews who were Polish citizens? The Polish underground did not carry out any military action to help the Jews or to sabotage the Nazi deportation and murder operations. But neither did it take any action to free the non-Jewish Poles from any of the camps where they were imprisoned. Tens of thousands of Jews escaped from the ghettos and sought refuge or some means of existence in Polish cities and villages. In and around Warsaw, for example, 20,000 Jews looked for a safe haven. For Poles, saving Jews was much more difficult and dangerous than in any of the occupied countries of Western Europe. Thousands of Jews also escaped to the forests. But because there was no organized Polish partisan movement, and because of the general hostility toward Jews in the rural areas, most of the escapees could not save themselves.

Before the fall of 1942, no public organization existed in Poland to extend help to the Jews. Whatever help was given was personal, political, or given in exchange for large sums of money. In late 1942 and early 1943 a provisional council for aid to the Jews was set up; this became the permanent Council for Aid to Jews (Rada Pomocy Żydom, known as Zegota). Several thousand Jews were taken care of and protected by Zegota. It was made up of Poles belonging to the Polish political Center and Left, some of whom were totally dedicated to their task. Thousands of Poles risked their lives to help Jews, and later they were officially recognized as "Righteous Among the Nations." Many Poles paid with their lives for saving Jews. People who helped Jews also jeopardized the members of their households. In many cases, the Germans killed family members of Poles who had saved Jews or had tried to do so.

For more information about Polish response to the plight of the Jews, see **Aid to Jews by Poles**.

German forces entered the Łódź ghetto, blocked off one section after another, and dragged the Jews out of their homes, choosing for deportation mainly those who were of no value as workers—young children, the elderly, and the ill. More than 16,000 Jews were then deported to Chełmno. Their survivors were left behind, heart-broken at the brutal loss of so many loved ones.

---

and when the action was over, 16,000 people had been deported. After the Sperre Aktion, the Łódź ghetto became a labor camp in which the entire population worked for the Germans. The German authorities in Łódź, and in the entire Warthegau, who at first had set their sights on a swift liquidation of the ghetto, were now benefiting from it. Not only were they in no hurry to evacuate or destroy it, they even resisted efforts by the SS to absorb the Łódź ghetto into its concentration camp system. As a result, the Łódź ghetto, which originally had been one of the first designated for liquidation, remained in existence longer than any other ghetto in Eastern Europe.

The liquidation of ghettos or parts of them in the Generalgouvernement continued throughout 1943. By the beginning of 1944, none of the ghettos were left. Under a special order issued by Hans Frank on June 3, 1943, the Jews and Jewish affairs were handed over to the Security Police (*Sicherheitspolizei*). This put an end to the tension

between the civil administration on the one hand, and the SS and police on the other, over the control of the Jews. With this order, Frank acknowledged that with the "Final Solution" underway, the SS and police were the sole authority determining the fate of the Jews. The only differences that still existed among the German authorities concerned the disposal of Jewish property—that is, which authority had the right to claim ownership of the possessions stolen from the Jews or left behind by them.

German factory owners were not happy about being deprived of the Jews' labor. They objected as best they could, but not much attention was paid to them. The German armed forces—the Wehrmacht—also benefited from the Jews' work, mainly the manufacture of items of equipment required by the military. In September 1942, the subject of Jewish manpower came up at a meeting held in Hitler's headquarters. On that occasion, Hitler agreed to permit Jewish workers to be kept in the Generalgouvernement on a temporary basis. As a result, the SS heads were forced to stop killing Jews regarded as essential or fit for work in late 1942 and early 1943. The condition, however, was that the Jewish workers had to be held in SS-supervised camps and that their wages would go to the SS. It was also made clear that this was a temporary arrangement and that these Jews, too, would have to be eliminated in the near future.

A number of camps now came into existence in which Jews were put to work—Poniatowa and **Trawniki** in the Lublin district; camps in the cities of Radom and Częstochowa; **Płaszów**, near Kraków; and the **Janówska** camp, near Lvov. In addition, in the concentration and extermination camps of Auschwitz-Birkenau and **Majdanek**, not all Jews were murdered on arrival. Some who were fit for work were assigned to concentration camps as manpower reinforcements. In early 1943, some 250,000 Jews of the Generalgouvernement were still being kept in camps (including 55,000 to 60,000 Jews in the Warsaw ghetto). The temporary exploitation of Jews as manpower, however, did not hold up the extermination process.

On November 3, 1943, all camps for Jews in the Lublin district were liquidated, including Poniatowa and Trawniki, in the action known as the **Erntefest** ("Harvest Festival"). According to official records, 42,000 Jews were murdered on the spot. Massacres continued into November 1944. By then, the hopeless situation of the Germans on the war front caused Heinrich **Himmler** to order a stop to the murders in Auschwitz-Birkenau, and to try to use the surviving Jews as a bargaining chip in negotiations with the West. All he had left to negotiate with were some tens of thousands of Jews, out of the millions who had been persecuted throughout Europe.

It is sometimes argued that the Germans deliberately chose Poland as the location for the extermination camps and implementation of the "Final Solution" because widespread antisemitism among the Poles held out the promise of local support for such deeds. There is no firm foundation for this argument, and other factors appear to have influenced the choice. Poland had a total occupation regime, under which no independent Polish authorities were allowed to function. The Germans did not have to ask the Poles or any Polish authorities whether they accepted the establishment of such camps on their soil. It may also be assumed that the Nazis chose Poland as the site for most of the extermination camps because millions of Jews were concentrated there and in other nearby countries of Eastern Europe. In addition, it was easier to keep atrocities secret from the general population in this geographic region than it would have been in Western Europe.

Resistance

Experience in modern times has shown that people are unlikely to rise up in rebellion against a totalitarian regime of unrestrained terror, under which there is no

The Aktion (Operation) Reinhard task force planned and organized the roundup of Jews and the deportations, and ran the extermination camps. The task force also robbed Jews of what was left of their property. At a later stage, it employed some of the Jews in the SS labor camps of the Lublin district, in workshops equipped with machinery and work tools that had once been the property of the victims.

> The question continues to be asked, "To what extent did the Jews of Poland know what was in store for them?" During the deportation stage, many of the victims had not yet heard the rumors about wholesale murder taking place in the camps. Or if such rumors had reached their ears, they did not trust them. Even those who had received reports on the extermination camps found it hard to believe that there was truly an elaborate program for the total destruction of the Jews of Europe.

chance of achieving any concrete result such as rescuing lives or overthrowing the oppressors. Such passive submission was widespread in Nazi-occupied countries, and not exclusively among the Jews. Even when the reality of the Jews' fate in death camps and labor camps became known, the majority of Jews were reluctant to stand up to the Nazis (*see* **Resistance, Jewish**). For one thing, many Jews had trouble believing that Hitler could actually intend to murder millions of Jews. In addition, devout Jews were reluctant to resort to the use of force. Finally, from a practical standpoint, what could unarmed, disenfranchised Jews do in the face of Nazi terror?

The idea of offering armed resistance, and being prepared to die in a last hopeless battle against the murderous enemy, was conceived by the Jewish youth movements in **Vilna**, and from there it spread. It led to the emergence of a strong resistance organization in Warsaw. Resistance activity there culminated in the **Warsaw Ghetto Uprising**.

The majority of the Jews admired the fighters' heroism and longed for revenge against the Nazis. But they were inclined to share the views of the Judenräte; or they felt that their first responsibility was to keep the family intact as long as possible. The great achievement of the ghetto fighters was that under conditions of the most extreme oppression and the disintegration of all public and social structures, the Jews were able to produce fighters who were motivated and guided by national and idealistic human imperatives.

Another way of fighting the Nazis was to join the **partisans** or family camps in the forests. Jews who had fought in the ghettos and had survived the final struggle there often took this as a next step in resistance. In addition, large numbers of Jews living close to extensive tracts of forests and swamp areas in eastern Poland joined partisan groups.

Another form of struggle waged by Jews came in the form of uprisings in the Nazi camps. Revolts were made by **Special Commando** (*Sonderkommando*) units. These were groups of Jewish prisoners who were forced to work in the extermination camps or in the killing installations at Treblinka, Sobibór, and Birkenau. In Treblinka and Sobibór, some members of groups that rebelled and broke out of the camps survived to tell the tale. The Birkenau rebels who operated in the vast Auschwitz camp complex were caught by the Nazis, and all were shot to death.

During the war, the Jews of Poland were able to maintain only loose contact with the free world. A few attempts were made to smuggle foreign citizenship papers (mainly South American passports) to Jews in the German-occupied areas. Some of the bearers of such documents were killed in Auschwitz.

After the War

At the war's end in May 1945, only 380,000 Jews of Poland had survived. This number includes Jews who managed to leave Poland at the beginning of the war for the West or for neighboring countries (excluding the Soviet Union), as well as several thousand who served in the Soviet army. This figure encompasses all the survivors among the Jews who were living on the soil of Poland when the war broke out and it represents less than 12 percent of the Jews of Poland.

The maximum number of Jews registered in Poland in the postwar period was 240,489, in June 1946. Many had no intention of staying in Poland; they planned to emigrate to other countries. After the war, Poland was the scene of sharp confrontations and strong antisemitism under the regime forced upon the country by the Soviet military and government. The violent post-war campaign against Jews reached its most serious point in a **pogrom** in **Kielce** in July 1946. Forty-two Jews

pogrom
A violent, organized, and often government-sanctioned attack against Jews and their property.

were murdered, including children and pregnant women. For the Jews, the Kielce pogrom was a traumatic event, and it greatly accelerated their emigration to the West. By the end of 1947, only 80,000 Jews were left in Poland.

SEE ALSO LITERATURE ON THE HOLOCAUST; MUSEUMS AND MEMORIAL INSTITUTES; TRIALS OF THE WAR CRIMINALS.

SUGGESTED RESOURCES

Hoffman, Eva. *Shtetl: The Life and Death of a Small Town and the World of Polish Jews.* Boston: Houghton Mifflin, 1998.

Kugelmass, Jack, ed. *From a Ruined Garden: The Memorial Books of Polish Jewry.* Bloomington: Indiana University Press, 1998.

Lasker-Wallfisch, Anita. *Inherit the Truth: A Memoir of Survival and the Holocaust.* New York: St. Martin's Press, 2000.

Schindler's List [videorecording]. MCA Universal Home Video, 1993.

Steinlauf, Michael. *Bondage to the Dead: Poland and the Memory of the Holocaust.* Syracuse, NY: Syracuse University Press, 1997.

Weiner, Miriam. *Jewish Roots in Poland.* Secaucus, NJ: Miriam Weiner Routes to Roots Foundation, 1997.

> In Poland, a country where Jews had been dwelling for a thousand years, only two Jews are left out of every thousand who lived there before the war broke out in 1939.

POLICE, GERMAN. SEE GESTAPO.

Ponary

Ponary is a site near VILNA, in LITHUANIA, where mass exterminations took place. Originally a resort, Ponary was situated in a wooded area 6.2 miles (10 kilometers) from Vilna, on the highway to GRODNO. In 1940 and 1941 the Soviet authorities excavated large pits at Ponary in which they planned to install fuel storage tanks, but they left the area before the project was completed. During the German occupation, the pits were used for the massacre of tens of thousands of Jews from Vilna and the surrounding area, as well as of Soviet PRISONERS OF WAR and other inhabitants who were suspected of opposing the Nazis.

The victims were brought to Ponary on foot, by road, and by rail, in groups of hundreds or even thousands, and were shot to death in the pits by SS men and German police, assisted by Lithuanian collaborators. The mass murder of Jews at Ponary was launched at the end of June or the beginning of July of 1941, and continued until the beginning of July 1944. During the early stages the victims were buried on the spot, in the existing pits. In September 1943 the Nazis began opening the pits and burning the corpses, in an effort to destroy the evidence of their crime. Some eighty Jewish prisoners were put on this gruesome job. On April 15, 1944, these prisoners made a daring escape attempt. Most of them were killed, but fifteen got away and joined the PARTISANS in the Rudninkai Forest. Estimates of the number of persons who were murdered at Ponary range from 70,000 to 100,000; the great majority of the victims were Jews.

SUGGESTED RESOURCES

Dawidowicz, Lucy S. *From That Place and Time: A Memoir, 1938–1947.* New York: W. W. Norton, 1989.

Gitelman, Zvi, ed. *Bitter Legacy: Confronting the Holocaust in the USSR.* Bloomington: Indiana University Press, 1997.

The killing operation at Ponary. Victims were herded into a narrow circular passage between the construction planks of an unfinished fuel-tank site. They were guarded by civilian Lithuanian collaborators.

PORTUGAL. SEE SOUSA MENDES, ARISTIDES DE.

Prisoners of War

A prisoner of war (POW) is someone who is captured during a war; the term is most often applied to a person in the armed forces who has been captured by the enemy. During World War II, the prisoners of war who suffered most at the hands of the Nazis were Jewish and Soviet soldiers.

Jewish Prisoners of War

During World War II approximately 200,000 Jewish soldiers belonging to the various Allied armies fell into German hands. The kind of treatment these Jewish

Identification tags for a prisoner of war interned in an unidentified German POW camp during World War II.

prisoners of war received depended on which army they were serving in. Jewish soldiers from the armies of Western countries (the **United States**, **Great Britain**—including the Jewish units from Palestine—**France**, Canada, and Australia) were treated no differently than their non-Jewish comrades. The Germans were far more cruel toward the Jewish POWs from the Polish army who were captured in September 1939, when Hitler invaded **Poland**. These Jews were systematically killed in stages and almost totally annihilated. Jews serving in the **Soviet Union**'s Red Army suffered immediate and total annihilation.

Jewish POWs from the Polish Army

Some 60,000 to 65,000 Jewish soldiers were taken prisoner by the Germans in September 1939. Wherever they were found they were terrorized by the Germans. Generally, they were separated from the rest of the prisoners while still at assembly points and at temporary transit camps. From these places, the prisoner soldiers were taken to POW camps for enlisted men.

In these camps, the Jews were separated from the other POWs and placed in a section where accommodations and food rations were greatly inferior to those

During the winter of 1939–1940 most of the Jewish prisoners of war were forced to stay in unheated and overcrowded tents without bathroom facilities.

in the rest of the camp. In fact, their conditions were no different from those of concentration camp prisoners. The food rations they received were extremely meager and left them constantly hungry. Thousands died from starvation. German camp guards tortured the Jewish POWs. A great many prisoners perished from cold and from torture. In late 1939 the Germans began releasing prisoners of war who had come from the German-occupied territories of Poland. The Jewish prisoners were taken to the ghettos then being established in occupied Poland. There they all perished together with the rest of the Jewish ghetto population when the ghettos were destroyed. Of the 60,000 Jewish enlisted men who were taken prisoner in the September 1939 battles, no more than a few hundred survived the war.

One thousand Jewish officers were taken prisoner in September 1939, and most of them were saved from extermination. Although they too were separated from their Polish fellow officers, they did not suffer the same fate as the enlisted men. The Jewish officers were put into POW camps for officers. Jewish officers were put into separate barracks or into a separate section of a barrack. Their situation was worse than that of the Polish officers, but most of them survived. In the last few months of the war, however, as the Allied armies approached, the Germans transferred the officer camps into the interior part of **GERMANY**. The prisoners were hurried along for hundreds of miles, they were starved and harassed, and the feeble and weak among them were shot to death. No figures are available for the number of officers killed on these **DEATH MARCHES**.

Jewish POWs from the Red Army

About 85,000 Jewish soldiers serving in the Red Army were taken prisoner. Once they were identified as Jews, they were all killed without exception, soldiers and officers alike. The killing of the Jewish POWs took place in various ways. Generally, as soon as a large number of prisoners had been taken, an identification roll call was held. Sometimes this occurred right before the soldiers were to be admitted to a camp. All those identified as Jews were killed on the spot, before the rest of the prisoners were taken in. Thousands of non-Jewish prisoners mistaken by the Germans for Jews were also killed.

Palestinian Jewish POWs

More than fifteen hundred Jews from Palestine who volunteered to serve with the British army were captured by Axis forces during World War II. The majority were captured during the fighting in Greece and Crete in the spring of 1941. Most of them eventually reached POW camps and labor detachments, where prisoners worked, in Germany. At first, the Germans were uncertain how to treat captive Jewish soldiers in British uniform. Eventually, with the support of their British comrades in the camps, Palestinian Jews were given the same treatment as all captured British soldiers. The Germans probably were afraid that if they harmed Palestinian Jewish POWs, the British would harm German POWs in revenge. As a result, the vast majority of Jewish Palestinian POWs survived their imprisonment. Most were liberated when Germany surrendered at the end of the war.

Soviet Prisoners of War

After Jews, Soviet prisoners of war (POWs) were the second largest group of victims of Nazi extermination policy. About 5.7 million Red Army personnel fell

into German hands between June 22, 1941, and the end of World War II. By January 1945, 3.3 million (57.5 percent of the total) had perished. By comparison, out of 235,000 Anglo-American POWs captured during the war, 8,348 (3.6 percent) were dead by the war's end.

German policy on the Soviet POWs could be rationalized by an existing legal issue. The Soviet Union had not approved the 1929 Geneva Convention on Prisoners of War. Nor had it committed itself to the 1907 Hague Convention on the Rules of War. Since the Soviet Union had not approved of these international agreements, the German government claimed that it was therefore under no obligation to treat Soviet prisoners of war according to these conventional standards.

One of Germany's major war strategies was to take advantage of Soviet agricultural resources. The Germans knew that as a result, millions of Soviet people would starve to death. Soviet POWs were destined to be the first victims. Even before the invasion of the Soviet Union was launched, the leadership of the Wehrmacht (German army) agreed that the Soviet prisoners would be given "no more than the bare essentials," as far as their food rations were concerned. Reports from the late summer and fall of 1941 show that in many prison camps, the desperate POWs tried to assuage their hunger by eating grass and leaves.

Tens of thousands of Soviet men lost their lives en route to the POW camps. Most of the prisoners captured in 1941 had to march across hundreds of miles, and thousands of prisoners who were too exhausted to continue were shot to death on the spot. When Soviet POWs were transported by train, the Wehrmacht's high command permitted only open freight cars to be used. This meant an enormous loss of life during the winter months.

Hardly any preparations were made for housing the POWs. All the Germans did was put up a barbed-wire fence around a designated camp site. The POWs were expected to construct their own housing, using the most primitive means. By February 1942, about 2 million of the 3.5 million prisoners captured in 1941 were dead.

From the very beginning, the treatment of Soviet prisoners was guided by Nazi opposition to Communist principles and philosophy. Red Army soldiers were described as dangerous and devious. German troops were called upon to take "energetic and ruthless action" and "use their arms" unhesitatingly "to wipe out any trace of resistance." Prisoners trying to escape were to be shot without warning. There is evidence that German Wehrmacht soldiers and civilians tried to improve the treatment of the Soviet prisoners. They were unable to prevail against Nazi orders, however.

In the middle of July 1941, General Hermann Reinecke, officer in charge of prisoner-of-war affairs in Wehrmacht leadership, and Reinhard **HEYDRICH**, as chief of the **REICH SECURITY MAIN OFFICE** (*Reichssicherheitshauptamt*; RSHA) came to an agreement regarding Soviet POWs. They decided that the Einsatzkommandos of the Security Police and the **SD** (*Sicherheitsdienst*; Security Service) would seek out the "politically and racially intolerable elements" among the Soviet prisoners, and kill them. This amounted to an enormous rise in the number of Soviet victims, since these "intolerable elements" included intellectuals, Communists, and Jews. Estimates of the number of victims of this operation range from at least 140,000 to 500,000. Under the Reinecke-Heydrich agreement, the Einsatzkommandos ultimately murdered all Jews among the Soviet POWs.

The **AUSCHWITZ**-Birkenau and **MAJDANEK EXTERMINATION CAMPS** had originally been constructed to handle Soviet POWs. But by January 1942, only a few hundred of the Soviet prisoners who had originally been brought to Auschwitz—

In many camps the Soviet prisoners of war were forced to live in holes dug in the ground or in huts made of foliage.

> Five factors can account for the extraordinarily high mortality rate among Soviet POWs: starvation; inhumane accommodations; extremely harsh transportation methods; excessively abusive daily treatment; and the deliberate murder, on orders from Adolf Hitler, of Soviet POWs.

out of a total of 10,000—were still alive. Heinrich HIMMLER decided to fill the camps with 150,000 Jews, instead, thus turning these camps into part of the machinery dedicated to the murder of the Jews.

In September 1941 Karl Fritzsch, the deputy commander of Auschwitz, killed approximately six hundred Soviet POWs in experiments with the ZYKLON B pesticide. Based on the outcome of his efforts, Zyklon B became the lethal gas of choice used to kill millions during the HOLOCAUST (*see* GAS CHAMBERS/VANS).

SUGGESTED RESOURCES

Bailey, Ronald H. *Prisoners of War.* Alexandria, VA: Time-Life Books, 1981.

Baron, Richard. *Raid! The Untold Story of Patton's Secret Mission.* New York: Putnam, 1981.

The Great Escapes of WWII [videorecording]. A&E Home Video, 1997.

Reid, P. R. *Colditz: The Full Story.* New York: St. Martin's Press, 1987.

PROTECTORATE OF BOHEMIA AND MORAVIA. SEE BOHEMIA AND MORAVIA, PROTECTORATE OF.

PROTEKTORAT BÖHMEN UND MÄHREN. SEE BOHEMIA-MORAVIA.

PROTESTANT CHURCHES. SEE CHRISTIAN CHURCHES.

Protocols of the Elders of Zion

The **Protocols of the Elders of Zion** is a forged document from the late nineteenth century that falsely claims to reveal a Jewish plot to take over the world. The term "protocols" means record of proceedings, as in minutes of a meeting. The document was adapted from a satire of Napoleon III written by Maurice Joly and published in Brussels in 1864. The *Protocols* have been reprinted many times, appearing with different introductions and commentaries.

According to the text and the commentaries, the Jews had a plan to achieve domination of the world. They would disrupt European society with the help of political and economic systems such as socialism, communism, and anarchy. At the same time, they would manipulate the price of gold to create a financial crisis, gain control of the media, and encourage prejudice against other religions. If they encountered opposition, the Jews would supposedly construct railways and underground passages from which cities could be blown up. Once in power, they would demand unswerving obedience to a Jewish king. In all of these schemes, the Jews were supposedly going to be aided by the Freemasons.

A novel with similar themes was published in 1868, a few decades before *Protocols* first appeared. Entitled *Biarritz*, it was written by Hermann Goedsche and published in BERLIN. The author was given the pseudonym Sir John Retcliffe (later changed to Readclif). In one chapter the representatives of the twelve ancient tribes of Israel have a gathering, held once every hundred years, where they report on the

>
> **Freemasons**
> Members of a fraternal order dating back to the 1700s that was committed to the ideas of religious tolerance and the equality of all people. Hitler banned the Masons in Germany, charging that they were responsible for economic distress and the events leading to World War I.

progress of their plot to take over the world. At the end of the session a speech is made by a represenative of the tribe of Levi. He expresses the hope that at the next gathering, one hundred years hence, the Jews will be the "princes of the world." This speech, which came to be known as the "Rabbi's Speech," was an important element of the *Protocols* and was published widely both before and after they became popular. Similar ideas were publicized in Russia at the end of the nineteenth century, especially in the books of Osman Bey.

The *Protocols* were apparently written in 1894 at the time of the widely publicized Dreyfus affair in **France**. This political scandal involved the wrongful conviction and imprisonment of Captain Alfred Dreyfus, a Jewish military officer accused of treason. The author of the *Protocols* was Pyotr Ivanovich Rachkovski, head of the foreign branch of the Russian secret police based in **Paris**. The French Right wanted a document showing that Alfred Dreyfus was part of a supposed conspiracy. Russians wanted to use the *Protocols* to support their antisemitic policies.

In 1903 a tsarist agent, Pavolaki Krushevan, published an abridged version of the *Protocols* in a pamphlet entitled *Program for World Conquest by the Jews*. The version that was to make the greatest impact was the one published in 1905 by Sergei Nilus in the third edition of his popular book *The Great in the Small: The Antichrist Considered as an Imminent Political Possibility*.

When opponents of the Russian Revolution fled to the West, they brought the *Protocols* with them. In 1919, a German-language edition of the *Protocols* was published under the pseudonym Gottfried zur Beck. Soon the Nazis began to make use of the book. Between 1919 and 1923 their propagandist, Alfred **Rosenberg**, also a Russian emigré, wrote five pamphlets about the conspiracy. A **Nazi party** edition was published in 1933.

In the 1920s the *Protocols* made their first appearance in the **United States**. A number of newspapers publicized their contents, linking the Jewish conspiracy to Russian communism. Among them was Henry Ford's paper, *The Dearborn Independent*, which published a series of articles based on the *Protocols* in the summer of 1920. The newspaper printed 500,000 copies of them in book form, and called it *The International Jews: The World's Foremost Problem*. In June 1927 Ford denied responsibility for the articles and tried to take the book out of circulation, but in the meantime it had been translated into six languages.

In Britain, the *Protocols* were published by most of the major newspapers in 1920. Even the *London Times* treated them seriously, publicizing them in their edition of May 8, 1920. But when their own correspondent showed the document to be a forgery, the *Times* published this revelation in a large headline on August 18, 1921. From then on the *Protocols* were discredited in **Great Britain**.

Between the world wars, numerous editions of the *Protocols* were published throughout the world in Polish, Romanian, Hungarian, Czech, Serbo-Croatian, Greek, Italian, Spanish, Portuguese, Flemish, Swedish, Latvian, and Arabic. During World War II, editions also came out in Norwegian and Dutch. Two trials were held before World War II in which the *Protocols* were declared to be a forgery: in Port Elizabeth, South Africa, in 1934; and in Bern, Switzerland, during 1934 and 1935.

The *Protocols* and the ideas contained in them became deeply rooted. It is clear that many leading Nazis, including Adolf **Hitler**, Heinrich **Himmler**, and Alfred Rosenberg believed them. For Hitler, with his perverse logic, the fact that Jews claimed the *Protocols* were a forgery was proof that they were genuine. Hitler once boasted that he had learned much from the *Protocols*: "political intrigue, techniques, conspiracy, revolutionary disruption, camouflage, diversion, and methods of organization." Alfred

Cover of a French edition of the *Protocols of the Elders of Zion*, c. 1934.

> The *Protocols of the Elders of Zion* provided a justification for the attempted annihilation of the Jewish people.

Rosenberg's philosophy, as set out in his book the *Myth of the Twentieth Century*, is also firmly rooted in his acceptance of the "truth" of the *Protocols*. Undoubtedly, such ideas brought many Germans and other Europeans into the Nazi way of thinking.

After World War II, the *Protocols* continued to be published throughout the world. The book fostered a hatred of Jews, particularly in the Middle East and the former Communist-bloc countries. New editions have also been published in many South American countries, as well as in Spain, ITALY, and Japan. The ideas put forth by the *Protocols* have been the staple of those who have sought to deny the HOLOCAUST (*see* HOLOCAUST, DENIAL OF).

SUGGESTED RESOURCES

Bronner, Stephen Eric. *A Rumor About the Jews: Reflections on Antisemitism and the Protocols of the Learned Elders of Zion.* New York: St. Martin's Press, 2000.

Segel, B. W. *A Lie and a Libel: The History of the Protocols of the Elders of Zion.* Lincoln: University of Nebraska Press, 1995.

Prützmann, Hans-Adolf

(1901–1945)

Hans-Adolf Prützmann was an SS officer. Born in Tolkemit, in the Elbing district of East Prussia, Prützmann joined the NAZI PARTY in 1929 and, a year later, the SS. He advanced rapidly in the police and in 1934 was promoted to the rank of major general. In 1938 he became a senator in Hamburg, and he was subsequently appointed the Higher SS and Police Leader in the Nordsee district. In April 1941 he was advanced to the rank of lieutenant-general of the police.

On the day of the German invasion of the SOVIET UNION, June 22, 1941, Prützmann was appointed Higher SS and Police Leader for the *Heeresgruppe* (Army Group) North. On October 31 of that year, he was transferred to the Southern Command in the UKRAINE. Two years later, on October 22, 1943, he also became Higher SS and Police Leader for the *Reichskommissariat* Ukraine (the portion of Ukraine under German control).

When the war was drawing to an end in the last quarter of 1944, Prützmann was given various special assignments, such as organizing the Werwolf bands and supervising the special intelligence service. He was also appointed commander in chief of CROATIA. At the end of the war he committed suicide after being captured by the British.

> **Werwolf bands**
> Paramilitary guerilla forces made up of uniformed Germans who went underground posing as resistance fighters in Allied-controlled territories. This operation was launched as Germany neared defeat in World War II.

SUGGESTED RESOURCES

Ezergailis, Andrew. *The Holocaust in Latvia, 1941–1944.* Washington, DC: U.S. Holocaust Memorial Museum, 1996. [Available in part online] http://vip.latnet.lv/LPRA/Ezergailis_preface.html (accessed on September 11, 2000).

PSYCHOLOGY OF SURVIVORS. SEE SURVIVORS, PSYCHOLOGY OF.

QUAKERS. SEE AMERICAN FRIENDS SERVICE COMMITTEE.

Racism

Racism is a belief that the race of an individual greatly influences his or her ability, inclinations, appearance, and behavior. According to this way of thinking, there are superior and inferior races. The word "race" has been used since the Renaissance to describe groups that have common physical characteristics, such as skin color, bone structure, or facial features.

The theoretical foundations of racism were laid during the eighteenth and the first half of the nineteenth centuries. Between the mid-nineteenth century and the end of World War I, racism gained in strength and acquired a clearer and better-defined direction. In the period between the wars, political mass movements in Europe, especially National Socialism (Nazism) in **GERMANY**, were heavily influenced by racist theory. Racism continued into the years following World War II. Its supporters were subdued, however, by the public's reactions to the crimes committed by the Nazis in the name of racism.

Early Concepts

At the end of the eighteenth century, **philologists** believed that language was an expression of a common past. Their research seemed to confirm that Sanskrit, an ancient language spoken in India, and ancient Persian, which was spoken in Iran, are related to many European languages. They believed that a people they called "Aryan" migrated long ago from Asia to Europe and brought a language with them, which these scholars called Indo-European or Aryo-European.

These scholars claimed that the Aryan past of contemporary Europeans was an indication of their superiority. A link was established between Germanic peoples, in particular, and Aryan prehistoric people. The philologists described the Aryans as courageous, manly farmers who led a solid family life. This historical myth of virtuous Aryan ancestors handily provided Europeans with "proof" of their moral and national superiority

Joseph-Arthur de Gobineau (1816—1882) repeated a version of this myth. He argued that the "pure" language of the Aryans proved they could rise above the materialistic aspects of life. At that time, Jews were did not enjoy full citizenship in many of the European nations in which they lived. Those who opposed making Jews full citizens argued that they were by nature incapable of speaking the language of the European nation in which they lived (they often spoke Yiddish). This trait, they said, had historical roots and reflected the Jews' materialistic character.

Philology and the historical myth of Aryan strength of character led to various conclusions. Some believed that any races that had not shared the Aryans' common past did not have the necessary qualities for self-government. In the **UNITED STATES**, the Anglo-Saxon myth was strong. Anglo-Saxons are descendants of the Germanic people who conquered England in the fifth century. Theodore Roosevelt, in his popular work *The Winning of the West*, praised the vitality of the Germans, who "went forth from their marshy forests" to conquer the American continent.

The study of race really belongs to the field of anthropology, rather than philology. Anthropologists came up with a more accurate definition of race, and at the same time made its own contribution to the rise of racism. The classification of mankind into races was introduced in the 1700s, when nations were first classified according to the color of their inhabitants' skin and the shape and size of their bodies. People who shared similar characteristics of color, size, and shape made up a

> **philologists**
> Scholars who study the roots of language and literature.

American athlete Jesse Owens, running in the 200 meter race at the 11th Olympics in Berlin, August 2, 1936. He won four gold medals and broke world speed records during the Games, but Adolf Hitler refused to recognize his accomplishments because he was black.

race. This, however, led to a more dangerous assumption: that a person's outward appearance and physical measurements reflected his spiritual qualities.

Growth and Spread of Racist Ideology

Gobineau's Essay on the Inequality of Human Races, written in the 1850s, was based on anthropology and philology. He claimed that the problems of the modern age were the result of racial corruption and that because the Aryan race was no longer pure, it was gradually losing its age-old superiority. As evidence of this racial corruption, he pointed to the worldwide rise of democracy and government by the majority. Gobineau's work foreshadowed the direction that racism would take during the twentieth century.

Carl Gustav Carus, a contemporary of Gobineau, took racist theory a step further. He was interested in identifying the ideal race, and he concluded that people of such a race were light-skinned, had blond hair and blue eyes, these qualities reflecting the forces of the sky and the sun. The notion of Aryan beauty based in part on the symbolism of nature gained particular significance in Germany.

From the second half of the nineteenth century, ANTISEMITISM served as the basis for racist views. The reason was simple: Jews were seen as embracing a foreign culture in the heart of Europe. They dressed differently, prayed differently, and spoke a different language (Yiddish). While they were restricted to living in ghettos

they had not aroused much interest. At the beginning of the nineteenth century, however, when Jews were given full civil rights, attitudes toward them changed.

When Jews were able to compete with their Christian neighbors in the same economic and social worlds, their enemies accused them of remaining distinct, despite their new freedom. Many Jews, both those who lived in the ghetto and those who had migrated to western Europe, chose to continue wearing their traditional clothes. The men wore beards and sidelocks, and they made a strange and mysterious impression on the peoples of central and western Europe.

Those who believed in racial differences and in the existence of a Jewish conspiracy tended to support the idea of a race war as well. The naturalist Charles Darwin's theory of evolution, which he proposed during the second half of the nineteenth century, seemed to provide a scientific basis for this notion. Some racists believed that humans enacted Darwin's principle of the survival of the fittest through race wars.

The French philosopher Vacher de Lapouge connected Gobineau's ideal of Aryan superiority with eugenics. Eugenics is a science that deals with improving hereditary qualities of a race or, in the case of animals, of a breed. In Germany, racial eugenics became popular, and many ideas were put forward as to how the superior race might reproduce under ideal conditions. This line of thinking reached its climax in Nazi Germany with the SS-sponsored Fountain of Life experiment. In order to ensure racial purity, carefully selected men and women who possessed authentic Aryan qualities were paired together for the sake of having children. Programs of this sort also considered the use of mercy killings. Under the Nazis (*see* **EUTHANASIA PROGRAM**), the mentally ill and the physically deformed were killed. The justification was that these individuals represented the degeneration of the superior race.

In the United States in the second half of the nineteenth century, blacks were the victims of the same types of charges that were leveled against the "inferior" Jewish race in Europe. Assumptions about character were made on the basis of external appearance. Fears of black men having children with white women led to lynchings, during which black men were killed by angry mobs.

Racism gathered strength everywhere before World War I, perhaps most of all in **FRANCE**, where national socialist movements appealed to the lower classes.

France's most significant contribution to racism during this period was the **PROTOCOLS OF THE ELDERS OF ZION**. The *Protocols* were supposedly the minutes of a secret meeting attended by the leaders of international Jewry. At that meeting, a plan was drawn up for for Jews to dominate the world "by cunning and by force." These minutes had in fact been created by Frenchmen in **PARIS** in collaboration with the Russian secret police. The purpose of the forgery was to provide "evidence" of a Jewish conspiracy. Theories about a Jewish conspiracy spread wildly after World War I. In the United States, for example, Henry Ford gave the *Protocols* a wide circulation. Refugees from Bolshevik (Communist) Russia introduced the *Protocols* into Germany, where they were adopted by the political Right. Hitler, for example, believed them to be true.

Racism and Politics

After World War I, attempts were made to put racist theories into practice. Political movements used racism as a tool for waging war against their enemies. In this respect there was no difference between National Socialism (*see* **NAZI PARTY**) in Germany, the Iron Guard in Romania, and the Ustaša in **CROATIA**. In the nineteenth century the racists had confined themselves to theory, but in the

> The Jews were accused of being "a state within a state," separate from the European cultures in which they lived.

Antisemitism was not just addressed toward culturally separate Jews. Assimilated Jews who adopted modern lifestyles were also looked upon as a subversive element. As the field of finance opened up during the 19th century, Jews became successful in this one area of professional life that was open to them. Jewish families such as the Rothschilds and the Pereiras were able to accumulate great wealth. Some Europeans, however, regarded this success as proof of the existence of a criminal Jewish conspiracy.

period after World War I, the leaders of racist movements took part in political action and resorted to violence. Leaders of racist movements were no longer content with removing the Jews from the economic and social life of their country. They called for their destruction. During the short period that the Iron Guard was in power in Romania (1940–1941), Anti-Jewish pogroms, or organized violence, were renewed. Similar atrocities committed by the racist political movements in **HUNGARY** and Croatia offer evidence that wherever racism flourished, violence followed.

In these countries, racist movements succeeded in attracting the lower classes to their ranks just as they were becoming a strong political force. In central Europe, which had strong Socialist and Communist parties, racism after the war attracted mainly the middle classes. But in **AUSTRIA** and Bohemia, the first large groups to join Hitler's National Socialism came from the working class.

The racist goal of **GENOCIDE** (mass murder) was achieved by the Nazis through a systematic process, rather than through uncontrolled and random violence. It is easy to identify the principal measures undertaken to create the first officially racist state in Europe. The **NUREMBERG LAWS** (1935) provided the legal basis for separating the Jews from everyone else. The laws also furthered the evolution of racism by precisely defining "Jewishness" on a genetic basis—something that had not been done before in racist doctrines. According to the Nuremberg Laws, a Jew was someone with at least three Jewish grandparents. A person who had two Jewish grandparents was defined as a *Mischling* (a person of mixed blood; *see* **MISCHLINGE**). This category was doomed to become extinct because *Mischlinge* were not allowed to procreate with either Jews or Aryans. The same laws also gave a legal definition of an "Aryan": a person whose paternal and maternal grandparents all belonged to the Aryan race. In order to become a member of the elite **SS** corps, a person had to provide evidence of pure Aryan ancestry dating back to the period before 1850. Racism thus became an integral part of the legal system of a major European nation.

As the Nazis began implementing the **"FINAL SOLUTION"**—the destruction of the Jews—they looked for cooperation from Germany's satellite states. It was a test of the strength of racisim in Europe during that period. The conservative-minded dictators in some of those states at first resisted Nazi demands to hand over their Jews. In Romania, Marshal Ion Antonescu issued orders for the deportation and extermination of Jews, but when it seemed the Nazis would lose the war, he reversed himself and tried to change the outcome of his earlier decisions. In Hungary, Admiral Miklós **HORTHY** held out against Nazi pressure until the German occupation of his country. In the West, Marshal Philippe **PÉTAIN** surrendered to the Germans the foreign Jews who had taken refuge in France, but tried to save the native French Jews from deportation.

In the West, resistance to racism was stronger, because Nazi influence on the fascist movements there had never struck deep roots. **FASCISM** in western Europe followed the example of **ITALY**, which had no racist policy before 1938. When the Italian dictator Benito Mussolini did adopt such a policy, the purpose was to revitalize his tired regime and cement an alliance with Germany. Although Italian Jewry went through difficult times and suffered many humiliations, the policy of genocide was carried out only under the German occupation. Italian public opinion never did accept racist ideas.

Among the Western Allies, Britain reserved its racist inclinations for the empire's colonial population. In Russia, antisemitism appeared sporadically during the war, but

Racism after World War II

After the World War II, racism was generally not an accepted element of any government's policy. One exception was South Africa, where racism became the official policy of the state. In the United States, racism was not a government policy, but the practice of segregation continued. The civil rights struggle in the 1960s finally obtained full voting rights and greater equality for blacks. Widespread anti-Jewish discrimination in employment and in hotels and vacation resorts ended earlier, in response to the HOLOCAUST. There were sporadic outbursts of anti-Jewish racism in France during the Algerian war. Racism was revived in both France and England as a result of immigration from their former colonies in Africa and Asia. In the Middle East, some Arab nations used racism as a weapon against the Jewish state of Israel.

Racist stereotypes continue to shape the attitudes of people worldwide, both overtly and subconsciously. Old historical roots still play a vital role in modern nationalism. People still view with suspicion and fear the differences they perceive between their own community and the outside world.

SEE ALSO **GENOCIDE**.

SUGGESTED RESOURCES

Bachrach, Susan D. *Tell Them We Remember: The Story of the Holocaust.* Boston: Little, Brown, 1994.

Jetzt—Nach So Viel Jahren [*Now—After All These Years*]. Arthur Cantor, 1982.

Massaquoi, Hans J. *Destined to Witness: Growing Up Black in Nazi Germany.* New York: W. Morrow, 1999.

Ross, Stewart. *Racism in the Third Reich.* Batsford, 1992.

As a nation, Germany embraced middle-class values, and respectability was a very important consideration. For the policy of race war to succeed, it had to be in the hands of a respectable movement, not one that supported a policy of pogroms, as did the Iron Guard. Instead, National Socialists began a process of dehumanizing the racial enemy. When attacks were finally launched, the victims no longer seemed to be human beings—they were the embodiment of evil.

Rasch, Emil Otto

(1891–1948)

An **SS** official and Operational Squad commander (*see* **OPERATIONAL SQUADS**), Emil Otto Rasch was born in East Prussia. Rasch served as a lieutenant in the German navy during World War I, and from 1918 to 1923 he studied at several universities, earning the degree of doctor of law and political affairs. For ten years he was an attorney for various companies. He became a member of the **NAZI PARTY** in September 1931, and in 1933 joined the SS.

When the Nazis came to power, Rasch was appointed mayor of Radeberg and then of Wittenberg. In 1936 he was taken on the staff of Section I of the **REICH SECURITY MAIN OFFICE** (RSHA; *Reichssicherheitshauptamt*). He became chief of the state police of Frankfurt am Main in 1938, and from March to May of that year he was also head of security for Upper Austria. For five weeks in early 1939, he headed the Security Police and **SD** (*Sicherheitsdienst*; Security Service) in Prague. After that he became chief of the Security Police and SD in Königsberg, East Prussia.

In May 1941, Rasch was appointed commander of Einsatzgruppe (Operational Squad) C. The next month his unit followed Army Group South on its way to the **UKRAINE**, where it carried out numerous operations in which tens of thousands of

Jews were murdered. The bloodiest and most infamous of these killing sprees was at **Babi Yar** in Kiev.

In September of that year Rasch was ordered back to **Berlin**, owing, he later claimed, to difficulties he had had with the *Reichskommissar* for the Ukraine, Erich Koch, and to differences with Heinrich **Himmler**. He became manager of the Continental Oil Company, a post he held until the end of the war.

After the war, Rasch was arrested and put on trial before the Nuremberg Military Tribunals. He died of natural causes in prison early in 1948, before the case ended.

SUGGESTED RESOURCES

Anatolii, A. *Babi Yar.* Cambridge, MA: Robert Bentley, 1979 (fiction).

Wiesenthal, Simon. *Babi Yar 1941–1991: An Educational Remembrance.* Out of print.

Rauff, Walther

(1906–1984)

Walther Rauff was a professional naval officer who became a Nazi official. He enjoyed a promising military career until a sordid divorce dimmed his career prospects and caused him to resign from the service in December 1937. He was then taken into Reinhard **Heydrich**'s **SD** (*Sicherheitsdienst;* Security Service) and was eventually made head of the section for technical affairs of the **Reich Security Main Office** (RSHA; *Reichssicherheitshauptamt*). It was in this capacity that he supervised, in late 1941 and early 1942, the outfitting and dispatch of some twenty gas vans (*see* **Gas Chambers/Vans**) in which at least 200,000 people were murdered. Rauff left **Berlin** to lead an SD Einsatzkommando in Tunis in late 1942, and he became the district **SS** and Police Leader for northern **Italy** when the Germans occupied that part of the country in September 1943.

After the war Rauff was held in a prisoner-of-war camp, from which he escaped in December 1946; he remained hidden in a monastery in Rome for eighteen months. He then made his way abroad, eventually settling in Chile. In 1963, an extradition request made by the Federal Republic of **Germany** was rejected in the Chilean Supreme Court on the ground that the crimes with which Rauff was charged were beyond the Chilean statute of limitations. He died in Santiago, Chile, in 1984.

SUGGESTED RESOURCES

"Gas Vans." *Simon Wiesenthal Center Museum of Tolerance Online.* [Online] http://motlc.wiesenthal.org/pages/t024/t02455.html (accessed on September 11, 2000).

The SS. Alexandria, VA: Time-Life Books, 1989.

Williamson, Gordon. *The SS: Hitler's Instrument of Terror.* Osceola, WI: Motorbooks International, 1994.

Ravensbrück

The Ravensbrück **concentration camp** was located near a village of that name on the Havel River. The site was two-thirds of a mile (1 kilometer) from the

Fürstenberg railway station and 56 miles (90 kilometers) north of **Berlin**. On May 15, 1939, a concentration camp for women was opened there. Three days later, 867 female prisoners were transferred to the camp from the Nazi concentration camp at Lichtenburg (present-day Prettin, in eastern Germany).

Two women, their prisoner numbers on their left sleeves, work in the spinning workshop, in Ravensbrück, Germany.

The camp structure was similar to that of other Nazi concentration camps, with 150 female supervisors (SS-*Aufseherinnen*) added to the men who served as guards and held administrative posts. The female supervisors were **SS** volunteers, or women who had accepted the post for the sake of the better pay and work conditions it offered, as compared to work in factories. In 1942 and 1943, Ravensbrück also had a training base for female SS supervisors. The 3,500 women who underwent training there worked at Ravensbrück and other concentration camps.

In late 1939, Ravensbrück had 2,000 prisoners. By the end of 1942, the number had grown to 10,800. In 1944, another 70,000 prisoners were brought to Ravensbrück. Most of them were transferred to one of Ravensbrück's thirty-four satellite camps. Some of these satellite camps were far away from Ravensbrück, in Mecklenburg, Bavaria, and the Protectorate of **Bohemia and Moravia**. Most of the satellite camps were attached to military industrial plants; one such plant was put up near Ravensbrück itself. In 1944, the main Ravensbrück camp had 26,700 female inmates, as well as several thousand girls in a detention camp for minors (*Jugendschutzlager*).

Andrei Vlasov was a Soviet army officer and Nazi prisoner of war who agreed to collaborate with the Germans against the Soviet regime between 1942 and 1945. The Nazis turned Vlasov over to the Soviet Union on May 15, 1945; he was executed by hanging for his treasonous actions.

In April 1941, a concentration camp for men was established near the Ravensbrück camp. Officially, however, it was a satellite of the **Sachsenhausen** camp. Approximately 20,000 male prisoners passed through this camp during the years of its existence, 16 percent of them Jews. In early 1945, Soviet prisoners in the men's camp were recruited for Andrei Vlasov's propaganda army, while German prisoners were drafted into Oskar **Dirlewanger's** SS brigade.

By early February 1945, some 106,000 women had passed through the Ravensbrück camp. Twenty-five percent of them were Polish, 20 percent German, 19 percent Russian and Ukrainian, 15 percent Jewish, 7 percent French, 5.5 percent Romani (Gypsy), and 8.5 percent others.

From the summer of 1942, **medical experiments** were carried out at Ravensbrück. One such project, directed by Professor Karl Gebhardt, made use of sulfonamide to treat festering wounds and bone transplants. Seventy-four inmates underwent these painful experiments; most of the victims were young Polish women suspected of belonging to the underground. Another experiment, conducted by Professor Carl **Clauberg**, involved sterilization; thirty-five women were the victims of the experiment, most of them **Gypsies** (Romani).

In the early stage of the camp's existence, the method used for killing prisoners was to shoot them in the back of the neck. In 1942, the inmates who were condemned to death were sent to institutions (such as Bernburg) that were involved in the **Euthanasia Program**, or to **Auschwitz**; or they were later murdered in Ravensbrück with phenol injections. Their bodies were burned at the nearby Fürstenberg crematorium. But the number of victims grew even further, so a crematorium was installed at Ravensbrück in April 1943, near the camp for minors. In late January or early February of 1945, gas chambers were constructed next to the crematorium. By the end of April, 2,200 to 2,300 people had been put to death in them.

In late March 1945, the order was given for Ravensbrück to be evacuated, and 24,500 prisoners, both men and women, were put on the road to Mecklenburg. Early in April, 500 women inmates were handed over to the Swedish and Danish Red Cross, and 2,500 German women were set free. On the night of April 29–30, Soviet forces liberated Ravensbrück, where they found 3,500 sick female prisoners being cared for by other inmates.

SUGGESTED RESOURCES

Gaulle-Anthonioz, Genevieve de. *The Dawn of Hope: A Memoir of Ravensbruck.* New York: Arcade, 1999.

Morrison, Jack G. *Ravensbruck: Everyday Life in a Woman's Concentration Camp, 1939–45.* Princeton: Wiener, 2000.

Ten Boom, Corrie. *The Hiding Place.* Tappan, NJ: Revell, 1971; Grand Rapids, MI: Chosen Books, 1996.

Rayman, Marcel

(1923–1944)

Marcel Rayman was a French Jewish underground fighter during the German occupation of **France**. Born in **Warsaw**, Rayman emigrated with his parents to France, where he became active in the Communist Jewish Workers' Sports Club.

In June 1940, when **Paris** was occupied by the Germans, Rayman joined the *Deuxième Détachement* (Second Company), a Yiddish-speaking unit that was under the command of the Communist partisan organization, the *Francs-Tireurs et Partisans* (Fighters and Partisans; FTP). He participated in numerous attacks on German soldiers and army installations in Paris. When the French secret service discovered and liquidated his company, Rayman was put into the "Manouchian Company," a Communist partisan unit led by the Armenian poet Missak Manouchian. On September 28, 1943, Rayman took part in a daring operation that resulted in the death of Dr. Julius von Ritter, the German official in charge of enlisting French laborers for work in **Germany**. Rayman fell into **Gestapo** hands a few days later and was one of the accused in a show trial, along with Manouchian and 21 other fighters, most of whom were Jewish. All of the accused, including Rayman, were executed.

SUGGESTED RESOURCES

Jewish Partisans of World War II [videorecording]. Aleph Productions, 1985.

Weisberg, Richard H. *Vichy Law and the Holocaust in France.* New York: New York University Press, 1996.

Refugees, 1933–1945

Since the mid-nineteenth century, the number of political refugees—individuals fleeing the land of their birth as a result of political, social, or economic persecution—has increased greatly. Large numbers of Jews left eastern Europe following the Russian pogroms of 1881, 1882, and thereafter. Then, World War I (1914-1918) and the subsequent social and the economic upheavals associated with the rise of totalitarian regimes in eastern Europe led to a refugee problem.

The First Wave, 1933–1938

Jews figured prominently in the first wave of refugees who fled **Germany** immediately after Hitler took power in January 1933. Different estimates, based on many sources, indicate that between 52,000 and 63,000 Jews left Germany in 1933; some 37,000 remained abroad. At first the German government did not prevent them from leaving; in fact, they encouraged them to do so. The pace of emigration slowed somewhat in 1934 and most of 1935, but accelerated notably after the **Nuremberg Laws** of September 1935 deprived Jews of German citizenship and civil rights.

Most of the emigrés went to neighboring countries, including **France**, the **Netherlands**, Switzerland, Czechoslovakia, and **Austria**. Many thought that the Nazis would not remain long in power and they could then return home. Often only individual family members left, while some remained in Germany to protect the family's interests. Some Jews remained in Germany to avoid the increasingly heavy emigration tax and because the laws strictly limited how much money they could take out of Germany. Up to 1938, the exodus remained limited to just over one-fourth of the 525,000 German Jews.

The Second Wave, 1938–1941

In 1938, thousands of frightened, impoverished German Jews, including entire families, flooded neighboring countries. During 1938, the Nazi policy clearly aimed

More Jews would have emigrated from Germany and its expanded territories had there been places for them to resettle. The outbreak of war in September 1939 created new obstacles for those who wanted to leave. By then, few could find space on a ship or secure the rare entry visas and other documents necessary to travel abroad.

to rid Germany of its Jews, in part because 200,000 additional Austrian Jews had become part of the Reich after Germany annexed Austria. To speed up the process, Nazi officials sent SS-Untersturmführer Adolf EICHMANN to VIENNA to organize forced expulsion. Between April and November of 1938, 50,000 Austrian Jews left the newly incorporated territory, over 30,000 more than left Germany in the same period.

With the recovery of the German economy and the end of unemployment, ARYANIZATION—the confiscation of Jewish property—intensified. A new wave of violence throughout Germany and Austria convinced many Jews that they had no future in Germany. In October, BERLIN expelled masses of Jews and dumped thousands of them in the Polish border town of Zbąszyń. The Polish government blocked their entry to POLAND. After KRISTALLNACHT, on November 9–10, 1938, many more Jews left. These refugees were joined by others from Czechoslovakia, part of which was absorbed into the Reich early in 1939.

In all, an estimated 150,000 additional Jews fled Germany after Kristallnacht. Some 71,500 Jews left the Greater German Reich between September 1939 and the end of 1941, when all exits were finally sealed. These represented about a fifth of the Jews remaining in the Reich. Most of them went to Britain, to the Western Hemisphere, to Shanghai, or to Palestine. The least fortunate remained in western Europe, where Nazism again engulfed them in 1940.

Closing the Doors

Throughout Europe and America, severe economic depression shaped immigration policies of the period. Hard times practically everywhere brought currents of ANTISEMITISM to the surface. Nations everywhere erected barriers against immigration. Western European countries did so in the early 1930s. The SOVIET UNION, under Josef Stalin, did not receive Hitler's victims, even those who were Communists. The British, faced with the Arab revolt in Palestine (1936–1939), began to limit entry just at the time when large numbers of Jewish refugees sought to go there. Restrictive policies governed Jewish immigration in Canada and the UNITED STATES, with only a few thousand permitted to immigrate each year.

Before 1938, however, temporary havens did exist in Europe, and refugees managed to leave. They had to pledge that they would not work in their host country and would eventually move on. But the international climate was cold and forbidding. The League of Nations, whose High Commission for Refugees had done important work during the 1920s, offered little help. Jewish agencies bore all the work and expense required to facilitate the passage of the increasing flow of refugees. The American Jewish JOINT DISTRIBUTION COMMITTEE (JDC) was the largest of these. It worked closely with the Jewish Colonization Association, Hicem (an amalgam, established in 1927, of several Jewish emigration and immigration organizations), the Jewish Agency for Palestine, and other groups.

After the Anschluss (annexation of Austria) in 1938, immigration officials around the world feared an unmanageable flood of unwanted refugees. Many of the fugitives from the Reich became stateless, having either lost their German nationality or been stripped of their Czech or Austrian citizenship. An international conference at Evian in July 1938 (see EVIAN CONFERENCE) widely publicized the plight of the refugees, but failed to achieve any loosening of restrictions. Jewish observers left the meeting feeling bitter and alone.

At the end of the 1930s, policymakers in the countries enacted further immigration restrictions. They realized that, because an equally great danger existed for the Jews in Eastern Europe, the tens of thousands of Jews from the Reich might

soon be joined by millions from Poland, **Hungary**, and Romania. Deepening anti-semitism in those countries, along with the severe impoverishment accompanying the Depression, exacerbated their fears.

In 1939 one traditional country of immigration after another shut its doors. After the Munich Conference, governments in the West grimly prepared for the war they had so long hoped to avoid. In 1939, the British placed severe limitations on Jewish access to Palestine. Panic-stricken Jews now sought any possible haven. Corrupt consular authorities sometimes sold entry permits to Latin American countries. About 17,000 German and Austrian Jews managed to reach the international port of Shanghai, practically the only place on the globe that required no visas or other documentation for entry, and later a haven for many Polish Jews as well. Other Jews, without legal means of staying in one country, continued moving from place to place.

Wartime Refugees

About 110,000 Jewish refugees were spread across Europe in 1939. When the war broke out, about 300,000 Jews, almost 10 percent of the entire Polish Jewish population, fled German-held territory in western Poland and crossed into parts occupied by the Soviets. During the following months, close to two million Jews came under Soviet rule for the first time, in parts of Poland and Romania as well

A group of Polish Jewish refugees on board the Japanese ship *Hikawa Maru* approximately six months prior to the Japanese bombing of Pearl Harbor in the United States. The ship set sail from Yokohama, Japan, on June 5, 1941, and arrived at Vancouver, Canada, on June 17.

Immigration limits everywhere hardened into firm barriers in the late 1930s, particularly after Germany annexed Austria.

in the Baltic states. Substantial numbers of them, deemed suspect and threatening to the new process of Sovietization, were uprooted and sent to the eastern regions of the USSR, along with many of their non-Jewish neighbors.

Meanwhile, in Poland, hundreds of thousands of Jews were also on the move. The Nazis planned to move vast numbers of Jews from the German-incorporated parts of Poland to the rest of the country under their control, called the GENERAL-GOUVERNEMENT—a kind of reservation they envisioned as a vast dumping ground for the people they had conquered in the east. Although these plans were halted after early DEPORTATIONS of Jews, the refugees continued to flow to towns and cities, where the Nazis set up ghettos. At least a million of Poland's three million Jews were torn loose from their homes by the effects of war and persecution during this period. Between 500,000 and 600,000 Jews—about one-fifth of Polish Jewry—died in ghettos and labor camps as a result of these Nazi policies.

In 1939 and 1940, Nazi strategists briefly planned to concentrate Jewish refugees in the LUBLIN area, part of the Generalgouvernement. This effort, known as the Lublin Plan (*see* NISKO AND LUBLIN PLAN), was seen as a temporary measure, after which its survivors would be dispatched even farther to the east, across Soviet territory. Tens of thousands of refugees were dumped into the Lublin region before the Nazis shelved this plan. In 1941 the Nazis, who were still searching for an answer to "the Jewish question," considered the MADAGASCAR PLAN as a way of ridding Europe of Jews, but no Jews were actually sent to that island in the Indian Ocean.

In the summer of 1941, following the Nazi attack on the Soviet Union, many communities of Polish and Soviet Jews were overrun too quickly for their inhabitants to become refugees. Eventually, OPERATIONAL SQUADS (*Einsatzgruppen*) and other Nazi forces massacred hundreds of thousands of them. On the Nazi side of the former border, about 10,000 refugees hid in so-called family camps in the often inhospitable countryside. About one and a half million Jews did manage to flee the German advance, ending up behind Soviet lines. Several hundred thousand were scattered throughout the Soviet Union, where they suffered greatly during the war.

Other Jews fled elsewhere in Europe. Oddly, two Axis countries protected significant numbers of Jewish refugees. Italian forces protected Jews in the parts of France, Greece, and CROATIA that they occupied. Hungary, although tied to Nazi Germany and committed to its own anti-Jewish program, nevertheless received Jewish refugees unofficially from neighboring Poland and SLOVAKIA. Occasionally, Jews managed to leave Bulgaria or Romania via the Black Sea. They hoped to reach Palestine, but refugee ships with this destination had to stop at Turkey to refuel and take on supplies. Turkish policy sought to avoid the use of a Turkish port for stopovers and very few Jews managed to land there.

About 21,600 Jews managed to enter Switzerland, but thousands more were turned back or deterred from attempting entry because of that country's harshly restrictive policy, tinged with antisemitism. The Spanish frontier was not officially open but Spain generally did not turn back those who managed to cross the Pyrenees. They did try to speed refugees out of the country, sending them on to the Portuguese port of Lisbon, from which thousands managed to leave for America. A substantial number of the 100,000 refugees who passed through Spain and Portugal during the war were Jews. Sweden received Jews from other Scandinavian countries, notably about 6,000 refugees from DENMARK who fled quickly in October 1943.

Outside Europe, Jewish refugees faced many obstacles, even though many foreign governments knew they were in grave danger. The gates to Palestine remained shut, and only 58,000 Jews managed to enter, whether legally or illegally (smuggled into the country by ALIYA BET). U.S. policy remained restrictive. (*See* UNITED

States Department of State). In April 1943, as public pressure mounted in Great Britain and the United States, the Allies held the Bermuda Conference to discuss the refugee problem. Neither government wanted to alter its policies, so the results were meager. More Americans protested against inaction, and finally, on January 17, 1944, Franklin D. Roosevelt agreed to establish an agency (the **War Refugee Board**) to address the refugee problem and rescue Jews. Despite the late response, representatives of the War Refugee Board managed to save many thousands of lives.

Elsewhere too, as the war neared its end, restrictions were eased and refugees could move about more freely. More Jews were now able to enter Switzerland and Sweden. Unfortunately, by this time few Jews were in a position to flee, and, for millions, it was too late.

See also **RESCUE OF CHILDREN**.

SUGGESTED RESOURCES

Feingold, H. *The Politics of Rescue: The Roosevelt Administration and the Holocaust, 1938–1945.* New Brunswick, NJ: Rutgers University Press, 1970.

Gruber, Ruth. *Haven: The Dramatic Story of 1,000 World War II Refugees and How They Came to America.* New York: Times Books/Random House, 2000.

Kaplan, William. *One More Border: The True Story of One Family's Escape from War-torn Europe.* Toronto: Douglas and McIntyre, 1998.

Marrus, M. R. *The Unwanted: European Refugees in the Twentieth Century.* New York: Oxford University Press, 1985.

Pomerantz, Jack. *Run East: Flight from the Holocaust.* Bloomington: University of Illinois Press, 1997.

Wolman, Ruth, ed. *Crossing Over: An Oral History of Refugees from Hitler's Reich.* New York: Twayne Publishers, 1996.

Reichenau, Walter von

(1884–1942)

A German field marshal, Walter von Reichenau fought in World War I and later served in the 100,000-man army of the Weimar Republic (and early Nazi years) known as the Reichswehr. He was the most ardent supporter of the **Nazi party** among the high-ranking officers of the German army. In his capacity as chief of a department in the Reichswehr Ministry, he was instrumental in the subordination of the armed forces under the Nazi leadership. He commanded an army in the attacks on **Poland**, **France**, and the **Soviet Union**. After the fall of France (June 1940), he was promoted to the rank of General Field Marshal.

In December 1941, Reichenau rose to the command of Army Group South in Russia. He issued a directive ordering and sanctioning the extermination of Soviet **prisoners of war** and Soviet citizens, especially Jews. The directive opened with the following sentences:

> There are frequent vague conceptions prevailing with regard to the behavior of the troops toward the Bolshevist system. The main object of the campaign against the Jewish Bolshevist system is the total destruction of their instruments of power and the elimination of the Asiatic influence from the cultural life of Europe. For this reason the troops are faced with

Walter von Reichenau.

> "Only thus can we fulfill our historic task to free the German people once and for all from the Asiatic-Jewish danger."
>
> —Walter von Reichenau, in a 1941 directive to troops under his command.

tasks which far exceed mere soldierly routine. In the eastern sector the soldier is not only one who fights according to the rules of warfare, he is at the same time the exponent of an uncompromising ideology and the avenger of all the bestialities that have been inflicted upon German and racially related people. Therefore the soldier must fully understand the necessity of meting out severe yet fair retribution to the Jewish subhumans [*Untermenschen*]. This retribution will also result in nipping in the bud any uprisings in the rear of the army, which, as experience has shown, have always been instigated by Jews.... Only thus can we fulfill our historic task to free the German people once and for all from the Asiatic-Jewish danger.

Hitler was greatly pleased with this order and directed that it be sent to all army commanders with a recommendation to issue similar orders. Reichenau died in Poltava on January 17, 1942, from a heart attack.

SUGGESTED RESOURCES

Bartov, Omar. *Hitler's Army: Soldiers, Nazis, and War in the Third Reich.* New York: Oxford University Press, 1991.

"A German Field Marshal Instructs the Wehrmacht on Its Role in the Soviet Union," in *The Holocaust: Selected Documents in Eighteen Volumes* (Vol. 10: The Einsatzgruppen or Murder Commandos). New York: Garland, 1982. [Online] http://www.assumption.edu/HTML/Academic/history/HI14Net/reichenau-english.html (accessed on September 11, 2000).

Reich Security Main Office

The Reich Security Main Office (RSHA; *Reichssicherheitshauptamt*) was the combined headquarters of the Nazi *Sicherheitspolizei* (Security Police; Sipo) and **SD** (*Sicherheitsdienst*; Security Service). The RSHA was the central office through which the Nazis' fight against the "enemies of the regime" was organized and coordinated with the police and state bureaucracy. Embodying the **SS** ideology, the RSHA was the principal tool in the regime's ideological, political, and racial warfare against its enemies.

Police Agencies, 1931–1939

Several SS institutions functioning during the period before the establishment of the RSHA may be considered its precursors. Chief among these was the SD and SS surveillance and intelligence apparatus, which was set up in 1931 by Heinrich **HIMMLER** and for which Reinhard **HEYDRICH** was responsible. Its primary tasks were to protect the Nazi leadership from the Weimar Republic's political police and to establish a secret espionage network to be used against party enemies, government agencies, and the party itself.

The second precursor of the RSHA was the **GESTAPO**, which was originally the political police of Prussia during the period of the **Weimar Republic**. In 1933 and 1934, Himmler used the SD as an instrument in his successful takeover of the political police of all the German states. These were formally unified with the Gestapo in 1936. Characteristically, Himmler kept the SD itself outside this new state bureaucracy. Moreover, he encouraged competition between the Gestapo and the SD.

Weimar Republic
German republic from 1918 to 1933.

A third precursor to the RSHA was the Criminal Police, or *Kriminalpolizei* (also referred to as Kripo), under Arthur **Nebe**. Nebe served first in the Gestapo. Then, eager to centralize and to use methods forbidden in a state observing the law, he took over the modern criminal police agencies of the German states and unified them to serve under the new regime. In 1936, the Gestapo and Kripo were reorganized as the Sipo. As state agencies, they came under Heydrich's control. Until 1939, the SD remained under his command as a separate SS main office.

The RSHA from 1939 to 1945

On September 22, 1939, the SD and Sipo were merged to become the RSHA. Once the personnel were all selected, the RSHA was ready to function as an instrument that would carry out future atrocities. Between 1939 and 1941 the RSHA developed into an enormous organization under Heydrich, who maintained his title as chief of the Sipo and SD. It came to comprise the following seven departments:

Dept. I, under Bruno Streckenbach (who would become acting RSHA chief for eight months following Heydrich's assassination in June 1942), was in charge of personnel.

Dept. II, originally under Dr. Werner **Best** and later under Dr. Neckmann, was in charge of organizations and law, including legislation, passports, and budget.

Dept. III, under Otto **Ohlendorf**, was essentially the former SD internal affairs department, and retained the same functions. Its main divisions dealt with economic matters, culture, and ethnic Germans.

Dept. IV, under Heinrich **Müller**, was the Gestapo, which was divided into fourteen divisions, plus the border police. The divisions dealt separately with political "enemies" (including Communists, Liberals, Catholics, and Protestants), and functionally with sabotage, counterintelligence, treason, and the like. Section IV B 4, under Adolf **Eichmann**, combined two areas of responsibility: evacuations and Jews.

Dept. V, under Nebe, was the Kriminalpolizei, which had four main divisions.

Dept. VI, officially under Heinz Jost and later under Walter Schellenberg, was called SD-Foreign, and was the foreign intelligence of the SS. Its six divisions dealt with German spheres of interest in the West. In reality, it was under the direct control of the chief of the RSHA.

Dept. VII, under Professor Franz Six, was the "ideological" branch of the RSHA, in charge of collecting, evaluating, and disseminating ideological material, mainly concerning Jews.

The basic structure of the RSHA remained the same following the assassination of Heydrich, his temporary replacement by Streckenbach, and his subsequent permanent replacement by Ernst **Kaltenbrunner** in early 1943. During Kaltenbrunner's era, the Gestapo department grew even larger. In the wake of the attempts on Hitler's life in 1944 and the subsequent breakup of the Abwehr (the Wehrmacht's intelligence service) because of its alleged involvement in the attempts, the SD's foreign department also became significantly larger.

The regional structure of the RSHA in the Reich itself was, by official design, under the control of the Sipo and SD inspectors in each military district. State police district offices in the larger cities and Gestapo branches and SD main and sectional offices were also theoretically subordinated to these inspectors. In reality, however, the Gestapo issued orders directly to its own branches. From 1941 on, the Gestapo often acted on its own against "enemies of the Reich," denounced and

> The Gestapo was the formidable backbone of the RSHA, combining surveillance, denunciation, and torture with its power to imprison people in concentration camps and execute them there.

arrested citizens, and supervised foreign workers who had been brought forcibly to **GERMANY** to fill the manpower gap.

In the occupied territories, a similar control from **BERLIN** was generally maintained. Here, the Gestapo, Kripo, and SD branches were under the control of the commanders of the Sipo and SD, although in the field the Gestapo, SD, and mobile killing units known as **OPERATIONAL SQUADS** (*Einsatzgruppen*) were largely autonomous. Himmler established an alternate line of command on May 21, 1941. The Higher SS and Police Leaders, whom Himmler had designated as his personal representatives on November 13, 1937, were allowed to bypass the regular chain of command and issue orders in Himmler's name directly to the Sipo and SD commanders, cutting out the RSHA.

Regardless of their professional training, the RSHA's served in a wide range of functions, both in the occupied territories and the Reich itself. Thus, Dr. Otto Ohlendorf, an economist, commanded Operational Squad (Einsatzgruppe) D; and the former SD man who became dean of the Faculty for Foreign Countries at Berlin University, Professor Franz Six, commanded Vorkommando Moskau of Operational Squad (Einsatzgruppe) B.

The primary victims of the Nazis, the Jews, became the special focus of RSHA activity under Eichmann's section, IV B 4. From late 1941 on, it directed the deportation of most of European Jewry to ghettos, slave labor, and **EXTERMINATION CAMPS**. The RSHA continued Hitler's extermination policies to the very end of the war.

SUGGESTED RESOURCES

Calic, Edouard. *Reinhard Heydrich: The Chilling Story of the Man Who Masterminded the Nazi Death Camps.* New York: Morrow, 1985.

Rurup, Reinhard, ed. *Topography of Terror, Gestapo, SS and Reichssicherheitshauptamt on the "Prinz-Albrecht-Terrain."* Berlin: Verlag Willmuth Arenhovel, 1989.

Rescue Committee of United States Orthodox Rabbis

The Rescue Committee of United States Orthodox Rabbis (Va'ad Ha-Hatsala) was a relief and rescue agency established in November 1939 by the Union of Orthodox Rabbis of the United States and Canada (the leading association of rabbis in the Orthodox community; otherwise known as the Agudat ha-Rabbanim). Its express purpose was to save the rabbis and rabbinical students who had escaped from **POLAND** to **LITHUANIA** following the outbreak of World War II.

During the initial two years of its existence, the Va'ad, led by its founder, Rabbi Eliezer Silver of Cincinnati, sent relief to the approximately 2,500 rabbis and students who had fled to Lithuania, among them practically the entire faculty and student body of such well-known **yeshivas** as those of Mir, Kletsk, Radin, Kamenets, and Baranovichi. The Va'ad assisted in the emigration of about 650 of these rabbis and yeshiva students during the period from October 1940 to June 1941. Several of the scholars emigrated to the United States (among them rabbis Aron Kotler, Avraham Yaphin, Reuven Grazowsky, and Moshe Shatzkes) and to Palestine (Eliezer Yehuda Finkel, Eliezer Shach and others), but the majority, approximately 500, ended up in Shanghai, where almost all remained for the duration of the war. In the

yeshivas
Rabbinical academies.

fall of 1941 the Va'ad obtained Canadian visas for 80 scholars, but only 29 succeeded in reaching Canada.

Several of the rabbis who arrived in the United States after the outbreak of the war, such as Abraham Kalmanowitz and Aron Kotler, played an active role in the Va'ad's activities. After the Japanese attack on Pearl Harbor and the American entrance into the war on December 7, 1941, the Va'ad initially concentrated on assisting the refugee scholars in Shanghai, as well as several hundred rabbis and yeshiva students in Soviet Central Asia. The latter were among the thousands of Polish citizens, deported by the Soviets to Siberia prior to the Nazi invasion, who were released in the wake of the Polish-Soviet agreement (the so-called Sikorski-Stalin Pact) of August 1941. The Va'ad sent these groups funds as well as parcels of food and clothing, and thereby enabled the scholars to maintain their unique lifestyle and continue their Talmudic studies despite the difficult conditions in Shanghai and Central Asia.

> The Va'ad helped to rescue several thousand Jews during the war and assisted thousands during the postwar period.

Following the revelation throughout 1942 of the mass annihilation of European Jewry, the Va'ad engaged in political activity designed to rescue Jews under Nazi occupation. The highlight was of these activities were a protest march of four hundred Orthodox rabbis to the White House on October 6, 1943, the only public demonstration by Jewish leaders in Washington during the war. The Va'ad also helped establish the **WAR REFUGEE BOARD** in the United States. In early January 1944, as the rabbis realized the scope of the disaster that had befallen European Jewry, the Va'ad officially decided to devote its subsequent efforts to rescuing all Jews, regardless of their religiosity or organizational affiliation. During 1944 and 1945 the Va'ad, through its branches in Switzerland, Sweden, Turkey, and Tangier, launched relief and rescue activities to assist the Jews under Nazi rule, and maintained contact with Orthodox leaders in **SLOVAKIA** and **HUNGARY**. The culmination of these efforts was the rescue of 1,200 inmates of the **THERESIENSTADT** concentration camp, who were sent to Switzerland in February 1945.

During the course of the war, the Va'ad's activities aroused considerable controversy within the American Jewish community, in large part due to the priority the Va'ad accorded to rabbis and yeshiva students. Most of the other **AMERICAN JEWISH ORGANIZATIONS** preferred to allocate equal resources to all Jews in distress. Moreover, the aid that the Va'ad provided for the refugee scholars in Shanghai, and to a lesser extent in Central Asia, was in addition to the regular assistance received by the refugees. This enabled the rabbis and yeshiva students to study on a full-time basis, while the other refugees had to work. Another issue that caused considerable controversy was that of rescue tactics. On various occasions the Va'ad used methods of transferring funds that violated the spirit, if not the letter, of American wartime restrictions. This policy was adamantly opposed by other Jewish organizations, primarily the **JOINT DISTRIBUTION COMMITTEE**, which throughout the war maintained a policy of strict adherence to United States governmental directives. The Va'ad's willingness during the final stages of World War II to transfer funds into Nazi hands in return for the release of Jews also aroused controversy. The final issue of debate within the community concerned the Va'ad's fund-raising activities. Shortly before the Va'ad was established, fund raising in the American Jewish community for domestic and overseas needs had been unified under the United Jewish Appeal. The Va'ad's decision to launch a separate fund-raising effort broke community unity.

After World War II, the Va'ad played an active role in rehabilitating survivors, aiding Jewish children, and providing for religious needs. During the period from its establishment in late 1939 until the end of 1945, the Va'ad spent more than $3 million on relief and rescue work.

> Holocaust survivor Klemak Nowicki recalls a close call with the Gestapo while he was a child hidden at a convent: "About three men were taking me out, and I remember that the bishop . . . said, If you take him, you'll have to take me. I don't know why, but they let me go. They usually didn't give a damn, they'd take everybody. But they left me alone. If it wasn't for the bishop's intervention, I would have been dead."
>
> *Howard Greenfeld,* The Hidden Children *(New York: Tucknor & Fields), 1993, p. 89.*

immigration quota
The limited number of citizens allowed to enter the United States as immigrants from any particular country.

SUGGESTED RESOURCES

Kranzler, David. *Thy Brothers' Blood: The Orthodox Jewish Response During the Holocaust.* Brooklyn, NY: Mesorah Publications, 1987.

Zuroff, Efraim. *The Response of Orthodox Jewry in the United States to the Holocaust: The Activities of the Va'ad ha-Hatzala Rescue Committee, 1939–1945.* Hoboken, NJ: KTAV, 2000.

Rescue of Children

The **NAZI PARTY**, led by Adolf **HITLER**, took power in **GERMANY** in 1933. **ANTISEMITISM**—hatred of Jews—was a fundamental part of the Nazis' beliefs, and they quickly started making laws that discriminated harshly against Jews. Some Jews realized that very dark times lay ahead for them in Germany and tried to emigrate to other countries. While some families left Germany together, others sent just their children to safer countries in Europe and overseas. In the period from 1934 to 1945, about 1,000 unaccompanied safer countries by Jewish refugees ages sixteen and below reached the **UNITED STATES**. Most of them were from Germany. They traveled to the United States either directly from Germany or after spending some time in a third country.

United States Efforts

The first organization to deal with the project of bringing the children to the United States and settling them there was the German Jewish Children's Aid (GJCA), established in New York in 1934. Another twelve or so organizations eventually came to play a role in the effort. Some of the groups, like the GJCA, were set up for this purpose. Others were existing organizations such as the American Jewish **JOINT DISTRIBUTION COMMITTEE**, the American Jewish Committee, and the United Hias Service.

Until 1941, the GJCA was able to bring 590 refugee children to the United States directly from Germany with the help of the children's emigration section of the German Jewish representative body, the Reich Representation of Jews in Germany (*Reichsvertretung der Juden in Deutschland*), and local American relief organizations. The United States immigration authorities accepted the GJCA's willingness to be responsible for the children, which relieved it of the need to find an individual sponsor for each child. But in all other respects, the children had to go through exactly the same procedure as adults who wanted to immigrate to the United States. They had to submit an immigration application, enclose medical certificates and security clearances, and wait for their turn in their country's  immigration quota.

Attempts were also made to have special laws passed to allow for the immigration of refugee children. In 1939, after the **KRISTALLNACHT** violence against Jews in Germany and **AUSTRIA**, a bill was introduced into Congress to allow 20,000 children—not necessarily Jewish—to enter the United States, over and above the immigration quota allowed for Germany. After a long struggle, however, the bill was taken off the congressional agenda.

British Child Refugees

In the summer of 1940, when the Battle of Britain was at its height, the idea of allowing British children to be brought to the United States on a temporary basis

was suggested. Within a few weeks, the **UNITED STATES DEPARTMENT OF STATE** made it possible for the children to enter the country as visitors, and thus to avoid the immigration regulations. Congress even passed a law permitting the children to be brought to the United States on American ships. This welcoming attitude of the government toward the transfer of British children to the United States contrasted sharply with its reluctance to admit refugee children from Germany. A special organization, the United States Committee for the Care of European Children (USCOM), was formed to deal with transporting the children from Britain and settling them in the United States. By the fall of 1940, when the "evacuation project" was called off, USCOM had brought in between 835 and 840 British children. The precise number of Jewish children among them is not known, but it is believed to have been no more than thirty or forty.

Jewish refugee children also went to the United States after a stay in **BELGIUM**, the **NETHERLANDS**, or **FRANCE**. Following the cancellation of the "evacuation project" from Britain, USCOM accepted the task of bringing these children to the United States. Between 1940 and 1942, volunteers from the Quakers (see the **AMERICAN FRIENDS SERVICE COMMITTEE**) helped to bring children from Jewish orphanages and from internment camps for foreign nationals in southern France, and to bring them to the United States. When they reached the United States, these children were placed under the care of the GJCA. From the summer of 1941

Four young members of the largest group of German-Jewish refugees arrive at Southampton (England) on the United States liner *Manhattan*. The refugees number nearly 250, including 88 children. March 24, 1939.

RESCUE OF CHILDREN

HIDDEN CHILDREN IN EUROPE

Jewish children rescued by non-Jews in Europe had very different experiences than those who were sent to the United States. Many of them spent their war years hiding from the Nazis.

Since her diary was first published in 1947, Anne Frank has been the human face of the Holocaust for millions of people. *The Secret Annex,* and later editions of Anne's *Diary of a Young Girl,* are among the most widely read books in the world. Many people do not know that there were thousands of hidden children during that period in history. Like Anne, not all survived. However, of the tens of thousands of Jewish children who were hidden, many did.

The First International Gathering of Children Hidden During World War II took place in New York City in 1991. Sixteen hundred people from around the world met to discuss their experiences as hidden children. For many, it was the first time they had spoken about that time in their lives.

Many had been physically hidden in attics, like Anne Frank, or in closets, basements, or underground tunnels. Children were hidden in forests and caves and even sewers. Others were given false identities and placed in convents and orphanages. Some children lived with non-Jewish families. Though not physically hidden away from the world, they adopted new names, observed different religions, lived apart from their real families, and otherwise hid their true identities.

Despite the diversity of their Holocaust experiences, the conferees discovered striking similarities among themselves. Perhaps most notable was the lasting impact of the desperate need to keep silent while in hiding. Whether they had to remain quiet in order not to be overheard, or they had to be careful not to reveal their Jewish roots, the hidden children practiced silence. Their lives—and those of their rescuers—depend-

to the end of the war in 1945, some 350 Jewish refugee children arrived in the United States after transit through France and Spain.

Upon arriving in the United States, most of the children were given physical and psychological examinations, and were then handed over to foster parents. The guidelines laid down by the American Children's Bureau for choosing the foster parents took into account their economic situation, their temperament and personality, and the reasons that had led them to apply to care for a refugee child. There also had to be religious compatibility between the child and the foster parents; United States law required that a child must not be placed in the care of foster parents belonging to a different religion. This meant that Jewish children were handed

ed on it. That wariness has stayed with many of the hidden children, often affecting their ability to form strong, trusting relationships.

Guilt was another shared characteristic of the now-grown hidden children. Some were told that they had no right to complain about their wartime experiences. For hadn't they lived? Hadn't they escaped the camps? Many who were forced to hide their Jewish origins suffered terrible guilt about denying the heritage for which their loved ones suffered and died. Survivor guilt was especially common—"Why did I survive when so many others died?"

Another common theme was enduring grief. Many families could not be reunited after the war; parents had been murdered, or their whereabouts could not be traced, or a child's real identity had been forgotten. Reunited families found, to their dismay that loved ones had been profoundly changed by the war, physically and psychologically. Some children were so young when they were hidden, they remembered their real families only vaguely, if at all. Hidden children had to mature quickly beyond their actual ages. Many survivors grieved the loss of childhood. Some felt abandoned by their parents, even while knowing they had been given up out of love and a desperate hope for a chance at survival.

The legacy of the hidden-child experience endures. Perhaps as a way to compensate for the deficiencies of their childhoods, many of the hidden children have become over-achievers. Some still fear persecution. Some don't know their real names or birthdays. Some are only now learning of their Jewish heritage. Since the fall of communism in Eastern Europe, previously unavailable documents are still revealing new details. Many who have always known had never before discussed their past with their own children.

Why did they come forth after decades of silence? To satisfy their families' curiosity. To heal. Perhaps most of all, to bear witness to the Holocaust.

over only to Jewish foster parents, unlike the situation in other countries, where Jewish refugee children were put into the hands of any family that was prepared to care for them. According to research conducted during the war and afterward, most of these Jewish refugee children integrated rapidly and well into American life.

SUGGESTED RESOURCES

Fox, Anne L. *Ten Thousand Children: True Stories Told by Children Who Escaped the Holocaust on the Kindertransport.* West Orange: NJ: Behrman House, 1998.

Giddens, Sandra. *Escape: Teens Who Escaped from the Holocaust to Freedom.* New York: Rosen Pub. Group, 1999.

Group of Jewish parachutists, resistance fighters from Palestine, sitting behind enemy lines.

Greenfeld, Howard. *The Hidden Children.* New York: Tucknor & Fields, 1993.

Kustanowitz, Esther. *The Hidden Children of the Holocaust: Teens Who Hid from the Nazis.* New York: Rosen Pub. Group, 1999.

Matas, Carol. *Greater Than Angels.* New York: Simon & Schuster Books for Young Readers, 1999.

Resistance, Jewish

Overview

In the Nazi system, Jews were faced with a process of dehumanization that ended in death. Any act that opposed that process can be regarded as resistance. Before and during the **HOLOCAUST**, there were many cases of planned or spontaneous opposition to the Nazis and their collaborators by individual Jews or groups of Jews. Jewish resistance took many forms and worked on many different levels.

Organized armed resistance is regarded as the height of opposition to the Nazis. Many instances of Jewish armed struggle throughout Europe have been documented; the most famous is the **WARSAW GHETTO UPRISING** of the spring of

1943. Virtually every attempt by armed Jewish fighters to confront Nazi forces ended in the defeat of the Jews. Most of the fighters themselves generally did not expect to be victorious; they fought for other reasons, such as to avenge the murder of other Jews, or to let future generations know that Jews had resisted the Nazis with arms to defend Jewish honor.

Among the Jewish PARTISANS, who did try to save lives through their efforts, fighting and survival went hand in hand. In addition to the partisan fighting units that committed acts of sabotage against the Nazi war effort, family camps were often created in forests for Jews who had escaped from ghettos or camps but were unable to engage in combat fighting. These camps were protected by the partisan fighters.

Resistance through Rescue

In most of the countries of Europe, the focal point of Jewish resistance was rescue, rather than armed confrontation. This was especially true in BELGIUM, the NETHERLANDS, HUNGARY, and GERMANY. In FRANCE, however, there was significant Jewish participation in organized armed resistance, along with rescue activities. In 1942, the Jewish underground in France crystallized, and the united Jewish forces established the Jewish Army (Armée Juive). The Jewish Army took part in many operations. It took revenge on traitors; attacked German airplanes, transport vehicles, and trains; and sabotaged factories producing materials for the Axis war effort.

Rescue was an important factor in the Slovakian national uprising (see SLOVAKIA. The Jewish fighters taking part in it hoped that the remaining Slovakian Jews would be saved by the toppling of the Nazi-oriented government from power. In Algeria, a defense group was organized by young Jews, under the guise of a sports club. The group played a key role in easing the entry of Allied forces into Algeria in 1942, by helping to seize and hold strategic positions in the cities.

Other forms of resistance may also come under the heading of rescue. Many Jews tried to escape from the Nazis by crossing borders to safer lands with the use of false identity papers, or by hiding (with non-Jews, or in any place where conditions permitted). For instance, some 350,000 Jews fled to Soviet territory from POLAND in the wake of the advancing German forces. Tens of thousands escaped from the WARSAW ghetto to the "Aryan" side of the city and were among the tens of thousands more who hid throughout Poland. Similarly, the rescue of Jewish children in France and Belgium, and the smuggling of Jews from France to Spain and from ITALY to Switzerland—all operations in which the Jewish YOUTH MOVEMENTS took part—come under the heading of resistance as well as rescue.

Spiritual Resistance

Also of great importance was spiritual resistance, called by the Jews "sanctification of life" (*Kiddush Ha-Hayyim*). Jews responded to their deteriorating circumstances and dehumanization with spiritual resistance. The creation of schools, theaters, and orchestras helped Jews retain their dignity despite Nazi oppression in the ghettos. Similarly, Jewish religious observance in the face of laws or rules that forbade it was an important aspect of the sanctification of life in ghettos and camps. Underground meetings of Zionist youth groups served this purpose as well. In many of the ghettos, notably those of Warsaw and KRAKÓW, underground Jewish newspapers and pamphlets were printed and distributed. This Jewish press gave information about events and analyzed them. It also strengthened morale by publicizing poems, fiction, and jokes. Finally, it also called for acts of armed resistance.

The foundation of Jewish resistance, especially in the ghettos and the Nazi camps, was the struggle to stay alive. The smuggling of food, clothing, medicine, and other necessities kept many Jews alive, at least for a while. Jews also traded with non-Jews whenever possible. In this way, an active underground counter-economy was maintained, which often meant the difference between life and death.

RESISTANCE, JEWISH

> Underground groups faced severe obstacles. They somehow had to smuggle arms into the ghetto, train fighters under ghetto conditions, and find a way to put fighters on battle alert in case of a surprise action by the Germans. The insurgents did not have the slightest chance of forcing the Germans to put a stop to the extermination. Their primary purpose was to offer resistance for its own sake.

Individual noncompliance with specific Nazi demands was another form of resistance. Many Jewish leaders who refused to follow Nazi directives were killed for their defiance. The first chairman of the **JUDENRAT** (Jewish Council) of **LVOV**, Dr. Joseph Parnes, was arrested and killed by the Nazis for refusing to hand Jews over to them for **FORCED LABOR**. Moshe Jaffe, the last leader of the **MINSK** Judenrat, defied the Nazis and told the Jews to flee for their lives. He was killed soon afterward.

Armed Resistance

Armed resistance by Jews in the Holocaust years differed from the resistance offered by the general populations of occupied Europe in World War II. Armed struggle by Jews was carried on under conditions in which the Jews were the object of general, absolute extermination. It was carried out by people spread out over hundreds of ghettos and hundreds of camps—none of which had any contact with the other. Its underground groups had very few possibilities open to them to prepare for an armed uprising. The Jews had to enter into armed confrontation with the Germans without having had a chance to train for it. They had to do this at a time when German military might was at its height, and to do so without any outside support. The timing of these armed resistance actions was dictated by the dates fixed by the Nazis for the transports of Jews to **EXTERMINATION CAMPS**.

ARMED RESISTANCE IN THE GHETTOS In approximately 100 ghettos in Poland, **LITHUANIA**, **BELORUSSIA** (present-day Belarus), and **UKRAINE**, armed Jewish underground organizations came into being. Their purpose was to stage uprisings, or to break out of the walled-in ghetto by the use of armed force. After escaping, they wished to engage in partisan operations on the outside. The two forms often combined, with the uprising being followed by an escape from the ghetto. There were also cases in which uprisings were spontaneous or improvised.

The largest single revolt by Jews was the Warsaw Ghetto Uprising of the spring of 1943. By then, 300,000 Warsaw Jews had either been murdered on the spot or deported to **TREBLINKA**; no more than 60,000 Jews were left in the ghetto. Dozens of survivors managed to escape from the ghetto through the city sewers. They reached the Wyszków Forest, where they tried to link up with partisans in order to keep up their fight against the Germans. Inside the ghetto, which by then was destroyed, several small groups maintained resistance throughout the month of June 1943. This struggle is commemorated worldwide on Holocaust Remembrance Day (Yom ha-Sho'ah) in late April or early May each year.

Several other ghettos in Poland formed Jewish Fighting Organizations. Some were inspired by the **JEWISH FIGHTING ORGANIZATION** (*Żydowska Organizacja Bojowa*; ŻOB) in Warsaw. The **UNITED PARTISAN ORGANIZATION** (*Fareynegte Partizaner Organizatsye*; FPO), in **VILNA**, became active as early as January 1942. Not content with local operations, the FPO made great efforts to stir up resistance across Eastern Europe. It was from Vilna that Abba Kovner made his famous appeal for armed struggle against the Nazis ("Not to Go like Sheep to the Slaughter"). The FPO did not succeed in staging a revolt inside the Vilna ghetto, but it did manage to get several hundred fighters out to join the partisans' struggle in the Rudninkai and Naroch forests. Similar to the FPO in style and action was the Antifascist Organization, which came into being in the **KOVNO** ghetto in January 1942. It operated until the liquidation of the ghetto in the summer of 1944. There, too, no open revolt took place inside the ghetto. However, many fighters were able to join the partisans in the area.

In Kraków, the Jewish fighting organization gave up the idea of staging a revolt inside the ghetto, maintaining that under the circumstances it did not stand a chance. Instead, the organization decided to move the fight against the Germans to the "Aryan" side of the city, and it launched several attacks against the Germans in the streets. Of these, the most famous was a raid on the German officers' club in the city, on December 22, 1942.

On October 25, 1941, when the Germans were about to put up ghettos in Starodubsk and Tatarsk, they were met with armed resistance by the local Jews. There were no survivors in this fight, and the events that took place came to be known from Nazi records only. On July 21, 1942, the Jews of Kletsk rose up in revolt, setting their houses on fire and breaking out of the ghetto by force. On the same day, the Jews of Nesvizh rose up; on August 9, 1942, the Jews of Mir; on September 3, 1942, the Jews in the Lachva ghetto; on September 9, 1942, the Jews in the Kremenets ghetto; and on September 24, 1942, the Jews in the Tuchin ghetto.

UPRISINGS IN THE CAMPS For the Jewish resistance movement, the Nazi camps were an extraordinary place in which to fight. Conditions there posed far greater problems for organizing resistance and for actual fighting than in the ghettos. The ghetto population, in relative terms, enjoyed freedom of movement within the confines of the Jewish quarter. The concentration camp inmates had only their barracks or place of work in which to move and keep in touch with one another—and even there, they were almost constantly under the supervision of the camp administration.

Conditions for resistance varied greatly throughout the system of camps that the Germans had created—**EXTERMINATION CAMPS**, **CONCENTRATION CAMPS**, forced-labor camps, and prisoner-of-war camps. But they also had certain features in common.

One enormous difficulty faced by the resistance movement was the incredible terror to which camp inmates were exposed. They had no means of defending themselves. They were completely at the mercy of the camp administration, guards, and officials. Any prisoner could be subjected to the most brutal torture and murder for even the slightest offense, or without having committed any offense at all. The possibility of offering resistance was severely limited, far more than in the ghettos, by chronic starvation and harsh living conditions.

Another factor that stood in the way of resistance initiatives was the principle of "collective responsibility." This meant that when prisoners committed some "wrong," not only those who had taken part were punished, often with their lives, but also other prisoners, who had not been involved. The success of one group of prisoners—for instance, in breaking out of the camp—in most cases led to the punishment of other prisoners. Civilians outside the camps were subject to the death penalty, more often than not without trial, for helping a prisoner to escape or offer resistance. This made it very hard to establish contact with civilians living in the vicinity of the camps and receive any help from them.

Despite all these difficulties, the prisoners succeeded in organizing uprisings in a number of camps. In several dozen camps, they organized escapes to join partisan operations in the area. In several camps, notably **SOBIBÓR**, **TREBLINKA**, and Birkenau (*see* **AUSCHWITZ**), Jewish members of the **SPECIAL COMMANDO** (*Sonderkommando*) units started uprisings. All were brutally put down. In Birkenau, all the rebels were killed. However, in Sobibór and Treblinka, a small number of Jews managed to escape. These were the only organized acts of Jewish armed resistance carried out against the Nazis in the concentration and extermination camp network.

Other uprisings took place in Kruszyna, Mińsk Mazowiecki, Krychów, and **JANÓWSKA**. There was an exceptionally successful escape from the prisoner-of-war

> In the smaller ghettos, preparing a force for a revolt was much more difficult than in a large place like Warsaw. It was harder to keep the preparations secret, undetected by the watchful eyes of the Germans who surrounded the ghetto. Still, notable instances of armed resistance occurred in smaller ghettos including Białystok, Częstochowa, Będzin, Sosnowiec, and Tarnów.

camp in LUBLIN, in the wake of which partisan operations were organized. Other successful escapes that were followed by partisan operations took place in Kraśnik, MAJDANEK, and Ostrowiec-Świętokrzyski.

SEE ALSO **ANIELEWICZ, MORDECAI; RINGELBLUM, EMANUEL; ROBOTA, ROZA; SZENES, HANNAH.**

SUGGESTED RESOURCES

Flames in the Ashes [videorecording]. Ergo Media, 1987.

Gurewitsch, Brana, ed. *Mothers, Sisters, Resisters: Oral Histories of Women Who Survived the Holocaust.* Tuscaloosa: University of Alabama Press, 1998.

Rescue and Resistance: Portraits of the Holocaust. New York: Macmillan Library Reference USA, 1999.

Resistance During the Holocaust. Washington, DC: United States Holocaust Memorial Museum, 1998. Reproduced in part at http://www.igc.org/iearn/hgp/aeti/aeti-1998-no-frames/resistance.htm (accessed on September 11, 2000).

Warsaw Ghetto Uprising [videorecording]. Ergo Media, 1993.

REVISIONISM. SEE HOLOCAUST, DENIAL OF.

Riegner Cable

An urgent telegram message, or cable, was sent on August 8, 1942, by Dr. Gerhart Riegner, the representative of the WORLD JEWISH CONGRESS (WJC) in Geneva. The intended recipients were Stephen S. WISE in the UNITED STATES and Sidney Silverman, member of Parliament, in Britain. The cable read as follows:

> Received alarming report that in Führer's headquarters plan discussed and under consideration according to which all Jews in countries occupied or controlled Germany numbering 3 1/2–4 million should after deportation and concentration in east be exterminated at one blow to resolve once and for all the Jewish question in Europe. Action reported planned for autumn; methods under discussion including prussic acid. We transmit information with all necessary reservation as exactitude cannot be confirmed. Informant stated to have close connections with highest German authorities and his reports generally speaking reliable.

The cable was transmitted through British diplomatic personnel to Silverman, and Howard Elting attempted to transmit the message through the American vice-consul in Geneva to the UNITED STATES DEPARTMENT OF STATE. In view of the apparently unsubstantiated nature of the information, the State Department refused to inform Wise. However, Silverman sent the cable to Wise from London, and it reached him on August 28. On September 2, Wise sent the cable to Under Secretary of State Sumner Welles, who invited Wise to meet with him, asking that he not publish the cable until it had been confirmed. Wise agreed, but he informed high-ranking officials in the United States including a number of Cabinet members and President Franklin D. Roosevelt. He also contacted Christian clergymen. On September 3, Jacob Rosenheim, president of Agudat Israel (the ultra-Orthodox Jewish movement) in New York, received a similar cable from Isaac Sternbuch of the RESCUE COMMITTEE OF UNITED STATES ORTHODOX RABBIS in Switzerland. As a result, Wise approached Rosenheim and formed a temporary emergency committee of Jewish leaders to decide what to do with the information and how to address the situation. On November 24, when the American government finally became convinced that Jews were being mass murdered in Europe, Wise broke the news of the cable, together with much supporting information, to the press.

After many years of investigation, historians discovered that the anonymous information on which Riegner's cable was based had been provided by Eduard Scholte, a Leipzig businessman who had official business in Switzerland and used the opportunity to transmit information to the western Allies. He contacted a Swiss intermediary, who in turn informed Dr. Benjamin Sagalowitz, a Jewish journalist who ran the Swiss Jewish press agency. Sagalowitz conveyed the information to Riegner on August 1.

The sources on which Scholte based his information are not known. The information itself was inaccurate: mass murder of Jews had been going on since June 1941, and gassings, first in vans, with carbon monoxide, and later in gas chambers (*see* **Gas Chambers/Vans**) had been taking place since September 1941. While the cable spoke of a future "blow" under "consideration," the ongoing extermination process had already begun. Moreover, the cable itself indicated that the information may not have been true. The last sentence had been introduced into the cable at the insistence of Dr. Paul Guggenheim, a senior member of the WJC living in Geneva. Nevertheless, the cable was a breakthrough, because it confirmed previously inconclusive information about the mass murder of Jews that had previously reached the West.

SUGGESTED RESOURCES

Laqueur, W., and R. Breitman. *Breaking the Silence.* New York: Simon & Schuster, 1986.

Peck, Abraham J., ed. *The Papers of the World Jewish Congress 1939–1945.* New York: Garland, 1991.

Wyman, D. S. *The Abandonment of the Jews: America and the Holocaust, 1941–1945.* New York: Pantheon Books, 1984.

Riga

Riga is the capital of **Latvia**. It was founded in the thirteenth century, and at various times it was under German, Polish, Swedish, and Russian rule. From 1918 to 1940 Riga was the capital of independent Latvia. In June 1940 Latvia became part of the **Soviet Union**, and Riga became the capital of the Latvian Soviet Socialist Republic.

Jews first settled in Riga in the seventeenth century. They were expelled from the city in 1742, but a few decades later Jews were living there again. In 1935 the Jewish population of Riga was 43,000, about half the total number of Jews in Latvia, and 11 percent of the city's total population. With Jewish schools, a rabbinical academy, a theater, and three Yiddish daily newspapers, Riga was the political and cultural center of Latvian Jewry.

On July 1, 1941, nine days after their invasion of the Soviet Union, the Germans occupied Riga. Several thousand Jews managed to get out of the city when it was being evacuated, but most were caught there. On the first day of the occupation, Latvian volunteer military units began arresting and killing Jewish males by the thousands. On July 4 the Latvian volunteers set fire to the city's central syna-

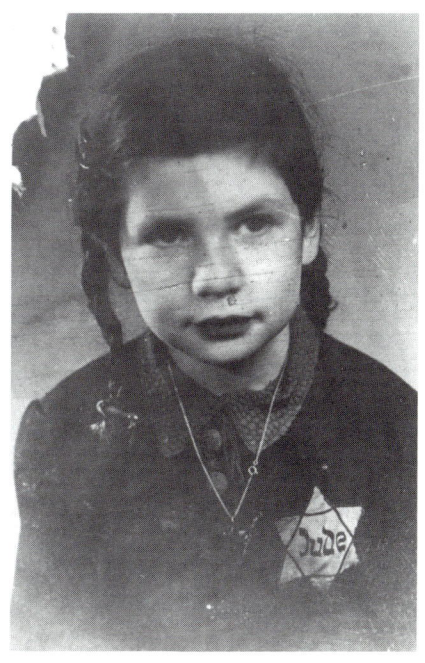

A young Jewish girl from Munich who was deported to Riga.

In a pogrom launched shortly after the German occupation of Riga, Jews were raped, chased away from food distribution lines, denied treatment in the hospitals, and rounded up for forced labor. Many were driven out of their homes to make room for Germans, and their money, furnishings, and valuables were confiscated.

gogue, the Chor synagogue, and later burnt down all the other synagogues in the city except for one. During the rest of July, several thousand more Jewish males were shot to death in the Bikernieki Forest and at other locations. Jewish doctors and a few skilled craftspeople, however, were spared and released.

Between July and October 1941 the Germans issued a series of anti-Jewish decrees. Jews had to wear a Star of David. They were not allowed to walk on the sidewalk, frequent public places, attend any educational institution, or practice a profession—except for doctors, who were permitted to have Jewish patients only. In mid-August all Jews were ordered to enter the ghetto, which had been set up in a suburb north of Riga. By the time the ghetto was sealed off, 29,602 Jews were concentrated there. A high fence was erected around it, and Latvian guards were posted at its gates to supervise the residents' exit and entry. The ghetto was extremely crowded, most of the houses were dilapidated, and sanitary conditions and water supplies were totally inadequate.

A Council of Elders was appointed, and a **JEWISH GHETTO POLICE** was formed. The Council of Elders tried to improve living conditions in the ghetto, establishing a hospital, a home for the aged, and a variety of other services. The ghetto supplied the Germans with Jewish forced labor: the unskilled were employed in backbreaking work, and the skilled artisans, in their regular occupations. Occasionally groups of Jews were sent to work outside the ghetto, in peat bogs, on farms, or on the nearby construction of the Salaspils concentration camp.

On November 19, 1941, the Germans separated the 5,000 Jews who were employed from the remaining ghetto inhabitants. The working Jews were moved to a fenced-in area in the northeast corner of the ghetto, which became known as the "small ghetto." On the night of November 30 the "large ghetto" was surrounded by German and Latvian guards. The next morning the inhabitants were taken to the **RUMBULA** Forest, 5 miles (8 kilometers) from Riga, where they were shot to death next to large pits that had been prepared beforehand. By early December, the entire population of the large ghetto, about 25,000 people, had been killed, including most of the members of the Council of Elders and Rabbi Menahem Mendel Zak, the Chief Rabbi of Riga.

After emptying the large ghetto of its inhabitants, the Germans filled it with Jews whom they had deported from **GERMANY**, **AUSTRIA**, and the Protectorate of **BOHEMIA AND MORAVIA**. This came to be known as the "German ghetto." Between December 1941 and the spring of 1942, 16,000 Jews from the **Reich** were brought to the German ghetto.

Reich
Germany, Austria, and the Protectorate of Bohemia and Moravia.

Most of the people who lived in the small ghetto worked outside, and some began living where they worked. The official food rations were too meager to live on. When almost 700 Jews arrived from **KOVNO**, in **LITHUANIA**, they set up a secret grocery and bakery. They also helped organize classes for the few children left in the ghetto.

In early January 1942 the first steps were taken to organize an underground—a secret military operation. Eventually there were between two and three hundred members, including 28 of the ghetto's 40 policemen. The ghetto underground organization contacted groups on the outside in the hope of joining the partisan (guerrilla) fighters. The members' main goal was to acquire weapons, which would be smuggled in by Jews working in the German storehouses, where captured weapons were kept.

Near the end of October, 1942 the Riga underground made an effort to join a group of partisans outside the ghetto in Belorussia. When this plan failed and Jewish fighters were killed outside the ghetto, there were swift repercussions for those left inside. Jews, many of whom had taken no part in either the escape or the underground movement itself, were arrested immediately and 108 uninvolved Jews were killed on October 31 in an act of reprisal against the underground movement.

On November 1, the small ghetto was incorporated into the larger German ghetto. Once the Nazi authorities discovered the underground, more and more Jews began living at their places of work, and the ghetto was gradually emptied of its inhabitants. In the summer of 1943 the Germans transferred some ghetto residents to the **Kaiserwald** camp and others to their places of work or to labor camps. That November the Germans carried out large-scale violence against Jews in the Riga ghetto. By December the process of clearing the ghetto of its inhabitants had been completed, and the Germans returned the area to the government of Riga.

In 1944, while the Soviet army was advancing toward the Latvian border, the Germans tried to erase evidence of the crimes they had committed. Groups of Jewish men were ordered to reopen the pits containing the mass graves of Riga's Jews and burn the corpses; then they, too, were killed. By June the Soviet army had reached the Latvian border. The Germans decided to slaughter many of the Jewish prisoners in Kaiserwald and other Latvian camps. The remaining Jews were sent to **concentration camps** outside the country, chiefly to the **Stutthof** camp, near Danzig. On October 13, the Soviet army liberated Riga. The remaining Jews in the city, about one hundred and fifty, including a few children, came out of their hiding places.

After the war the Soviet authorities encouraged citizens from the Soviet interior, including a large number of Jews, to settle in Riga. In 1947 Riga had a Jewish population of 10,000; by 1959 it had grown to 30,267. Some were remnants of Latvian Jewry who had taken refuge in the Soviet Union, or had survived concentration camps. Most were from the Soviet interior.

In 1962 a group of Riga Jews worked to establish a special memorial for the Jewish victims of the **Holocaust** on the field of slaughter in the Rumbula Forest. The site became a garden with a memorial to the murdered Jews. In the late 1960s and the early 1970s Riga was one of the centers of the Jewish national reawakening in the Soviet Union. Many Jews emigrated to Israel, which sharply reduced the Jewish population of Riga.

SUGGESTED RESOURCES

Ezergailis, Andrew. *The Holocaust in Latvia, 1941–1944.* Washington, DC: U.S. Holocaust Memorial Museum, 1996. Reproduced in part online at http://vip.latnet.lv/LPRA/Ezergailis_preface.html (accessed on September 11, 2000).

Press, Bernhard. *The Murder of the Jews in Latvia, 1941–1945.* Evanston, IL: Northwestern University Press, 1999.

Schneider, Gertrude. *Journey into Terror: Story of the Riga Ghetto.* New York: Ark House, 1979.

"Righteous among the Nations"

The record of the events and uprisings of the **Holocaust** would be incomplete without the inspiring chapters—unique points of light—recorded by individuals within the nations under Nazi rule who did not stand aside and accept the fate of the Jews with indifference. In comparison with the needs of the masses of Jews requiring aid and rescue in occupied Europe, the "Righteous among the Nations"—those who

---

On October 28, 1942, ten underground members left the ghetto in a truck driven by a Latvian, who was headed for the Belorussian border in order to join the partisans there. In a German ambush, most of the Jews were killed. The German security authorities lost no time in taking further punitive action. Later that day large numbers of suspects were arrested, and on October 31, 108 Jews who had nothing to do with the underground were executed.

"RIGHTEOUS AMONG THE NATIONS"

The Certificate of Honor awarded to "Righteous among the Nations."

risked life, freedom, and safety to rescue one or more Jews without the expectation of financial or other compensation—were few. Yet their acts show that aid and rescue were possible, and that more could have been done had there been more individuals who saw assistance to fellow beings in danger as a human obligation.

The title, "Righteous among the Nations," has come to describe the non-Jews who extended aid and comfort to Jews during the Holocaust. The name comes from a Hebrew phrase, *hasidei ummot haolam*, that means: "The righteous among the nations of the world have a place in the world to come." In general, the term "Righteous among the Nations" can apply to any moral person who extends sympathy, kindness, and assistance to Jews in times of trouble and trial. However, in the context of the Martyrs' and Heroes' Remembrance Law, the designation "Righteous among the Nations" is applied to specific individuals who risked their own lives for the life a Jew.

The Martyrs' and Heroes' Remembrance (Yad Vashem) Law, passed by Israel's **Knesset** in 1953, charged the Yad Vashem Remembrance Authority with establishing and perpetuating a memorial to "the Righteous among the Nations who risked their lives to save Jews." Since 1963, the Yad Vashem Remembrance Authority in Jerusalem has sponsored a commission to identify and name the "Righteous among the Nations." For decades, many of the commission members have themselves been Holocaust survivors. The commission is headed by an Israeli Supreme Court judge. Every instance of a rescuer being submitted for recognition as a "Righteous among the Nations" is carefully examined by the committee. Nomination materials include personal testimony or other evidence from the rescued person or persons that indicates what action the nominee took on behalf of the rescued, under what circumstances and threats, and for what (if any) compensation or benefit to the rescuer.

Knesset
Israel's Parliament.

There are three main criteria for recognition of a rescuer as a "Righteous among the Nations": (1) a concrete rescue action or aid in rescue, (2) rescue carried out at personal risk, and (3) remuneration neither requested nor received by the rescuer for the action or aid.

More than 16,000 individuals have been recognized as "Righteous among the Nations." Designees identified during the 1960s, 1970s and 1980s were each entitled to plant a tree along the avenue on Har ha-Zikkaron (the Yad Vashem Memorial Hill). Now, due to space considerations, designees are recognized with their names inscribed on the Wall of Honor in the Garden of the Righteous at Yad Vashem in Jerusalem. Each is also awarded a certificate of honor and a medal engraved with his or her name and the Talmudic maxim "He who saves one life is considered as having saved the whole universe." As one of its commemoration activities, Yad Vashem decided to issue a lexicon of "Righteous among the Nations," giving a brief description of the rescue act of each of them. The importance of this project transcends the aim of commemoration: no less important is the public dissemination of the stories of rescue and self-sacrifice so that future generations will be educated to understand the significance of the term "humanity."

> The greatest collective rescue activity was in Denmark. More than 7,000 of the nearly 8,000 Jewish inhabitants of the country were smuggled in small boats to Sweden while, at the same time, ships were waiting at Copenhagen to transport them to the extermination camps. The rescue was made possible by the universal willingness of the Danish population to take part in the operation.

Rescues and Rescuers

The majority of the rescues involved concealment in the home or yard of the rescuer, most often by building a bunker within the house or a warehouse; those in hiding had to remain there for weeks, months, and even years, usually without seeing the light of day. The food supply was a special problem in the wartime conditions of scarcity, and at times the needy rescuer shared a scant slice of bread with the people that he or she was concealing. This kind of rescue was perhaps the most dangerous because of the long period of concealment, the frequent searches for people in hiding, and, at times, denunciation by collaborators with the Germans. Others found a way to rescue by providing forged papers that allowed a Jew to live as a non-Jew outside the ghetto or camp, or by helping to smuggle Jews over the border to another area or country, such as unoccupied **France**, Spain, Portugal, and Switzerland. One teenage girl working in a munitions factory deprived herself of a slice of bread every day, month after month, giving it to the Jewish prisoner working next to her.

For the most part, the "Righteous among the Nations" worked as individuals, each one guided by the dictates of his or her conscience, out of purely humane motives, and at times from profound religious convictions. In several cases, as in Norway and the **Netherlands**, and to a certain extent in France and in **Belgium**, the anti-Nazi underground also helped persecuted Jews in different ways, mainly by finding hiding places.

Some individuals also developed broad rescue networks, saving many endangered Jews. The bold enterprise of Raoul **Wallenberg** in **Hungary** is one of the most famous; his passion to rescue was boundless. His initiatives were designed to prevent continuation of the **deportations** of **Budapest** Jews to **Auschwitz**, and they were largely successful. Wallenberg was always present where assistance was required and spared no activity to reduce the suffering, he also encouraged others with his initiative. Oskar **Schindler** took approximately 1,200 Jews working in his factory under his protection, made their living conditions easier, and looked after them until the liberation by the Red Army. In the Nazi nerve center of **Berlin**, Elisabeth Abegg courageously extended aid to persecuted Jews, concealing them in her apartment close to the Nazi command headquarters. Irena Adamowicz, a member of the Catholic scout movement in **Warsaw**, worked for the pioneering youth movement underground, traveling to many ghettos on dangerous missions. In 1942, she even reached the distant ghettos of LITHUANIA, where she reported on events in the Jewish communities throughout the occupied countries in eastern Europe. She won the trust of the Jews through her devotion and deep identification with their fate, and she prompted some of the members of her movement to work for the Jewish underground.

Rescue efforts even occurred in the extermination camps themselves. Herman Langbein and Ludwig Worl, who were interned at Auschwitz, came to the aid of Jewish prisoners there and worked to ease their wretched conditions. Julius Madritsch and Raimund Titsch manifested concern for the Jewish internees employed in the factories at the PŁASZÓW camp, obtaining food supplements for them and defending them from the ill treatment of the commandant, Amon Goeth, and his murderous helpers. The French doctor Adelaide Hautval was sent to Auschwitz as punishment for protecting Jews who were to be deported. When she arrived at the block where experiments were carried out on Jewish girls, she refused to participate in murder and cared for the Jewish prisoners with great devotion.

By their acts, the "Righteous among the Nations" saved not only Jewish lives but the honor of humanity in the terrible period of the Holocaust.

SUGGESTED RESOURCES

Bauminger, Arieh L. *The Righteous Among the Nations.* Tel Aviv: Am Oved, 1990.

"Righteous Among the Nations." *Yad Vashem Online.* [Online] http://www.yad-vashem.org.il/righteous/index.html (accessed on September 11, 2000).

A Teacher's Guide to the Holocaust: Rescuers. [Online] http://fcit.coedu.usf.edu/holocaust/people/rescuer.htm (accessed on September 11, 2000).

Ringelblum, Emanuel

(1900–1944)

Emanuel Ringelblum was an historian and Jewish public figure, and the founder and director of the clandestine archive *Oneg Shabbat*. Ringelblum was born in Buczacz, Eastern Galicia, into a middle-class merchant family. In World War I the family suffered economic setbacks and moved to Nowy Sącz. In 1927 Ringelblum earned a doctorate from the University of Warsaw for his thesis on the history of the Jews of WARSAW in the Middle Ages. From an early age, Ringelblum was a member of *Po'alei* Zion Left and was active in public affairs. For several years he taught history in Jewish high schools.

In 1930 he took on part-time employment with the JOINT DISTRIBUTION COMMITTEE. He established close working relations and personal ties with Yitzhak Gitterman, one of its leaders in POLAND, which he maintained during the war years as well. In November 1938 the Joint sent Ringelblum to the Zbąszyń camp, where 6,000 Jews were gathered—Polish citizens who had been expelled from GERMANY at the end of October. The five weeks that Ringelblum spent there, as the person responsible for the fortunes of the refugees, left an indelible impression on him.

In his professional capacity Ringelblum belonged to the third generation of historians of the Jews of Poland, a generation educated and trained in independent Poland. In 1923 a number of these historians formed a group, with Ringelblum as

Emanuel Ringelblum.

one of its outstanding scholars and organizers, which eventually was associated with Yivo (*Yidisher Visenshaftlikher Institut*; Institute for Jewish Research). Ringelblum was one of the editors of the publications issued by the group—*Yunger Historiker* (1926–1929) and *Bleter far Geschichte* (1934, 1938). In his research work Ringelblum concentrated on the history of the Jews of Warsaw, which he planned to bring up-to-date. Most of his writings are based on original archival material and cover a wide range of subjects. By 1939 he had published 126 scholarly articles.

During the war, Ringelblum was engaged in four spheres of activity in the Warsaw ghetto: (1) working in an institute for social self-aid among Warsaw Jews; (2) working in the political underground, with emphasis on its cultural affairs sector; (3) establishing and administering the clandestine *Oneg Shabbat* Archive; and (4) keeping an up-to-date chronicle of events. He also wrote articles on specific subjects, concerning the life of the Jews during the German occupation of Poland, especially Warsaw, covering the period from the beginning of the war up to his own arrest on March 7, 1944.

Ringelblum was in charge of the "public sector" in the self-aid organization. He ran a network of soup kitchens for the desperately impoverished Jewish population and organized and promoted the growth of "House Committees" (*Komitety Domowe*), made up of volunteers with no previous experience of public activity.

Ringelblum and his associates made the soup kitchens—in which tens of thousands of soup portions were dispensed every day—into clubs, under the patronage of the political underground. With his friend Menahem Linder, Ringelblum founded in the Warsaw ghetto a society for the promotion of Yiddish culture (*Yidishe Kultur Organizatsye*). They arranged lectures, observances of anniversaries of Jewish writers, and meetings with writers and scholars in the ghetto.

Ringelblum's most outstanding achievement was the secret *Oneg Shabbat* Archive, which he launched in the first few months of the war. In the initial stage, Ringelblum and a small group of friends concentrated on collecting testimonies and reports on events by Jews who came to Warsaw from the provinces to solicit assistance from the self-aid organization. He attracted a large circle of friends and activists to the archive, and succeeded in gaining the support of writers and underground activists representing the various political groups. As reported by Hirsch Wasser, the secretary of the underground archive (and the only surviving member of the team): "Every item, every article, be it long or short, had to pass through Dr. Ringelblum's hands.… For weeks and months he spent the nights poring over the manuscripts, adding his comments and instructions."

During the last stages of the ghetto's existence, Ringelblum and his associates collected every document and piece of evidence relating to the **DEPORTATIONS** and the murders and passed them on to the Polish underground, which in turn transmitted the information to London. This was how the Polish underground and London learned for the first time about the **CHEŁMNO**  extermination camp and came in possession of a detailed report on the deportation of 300,000 Jews from Warsaw. The archive also circulated in the ghetto a bulletin, *Yediot* (News), which enabled the underground to keep current with events.

Ringelblum himself kept a running record of events and important items of information, at first on a daily basis, and then, after July 1942, on a weekly and monthly basis. It was not a diary but rather a chronicle of events, enhanced by the author's own appraisals and the historical associations that the events brought to his mind. Ringelblum's notes are full of abbreviations and allusions. He obviously regarded them as the raw material for a comprehensive work that he would write after the war. After the mass deportation, Ringelblum's method of writing under-

> Emanuel Ringelblum was aware that there was no precedent for what was happening to the Jews under the occupation; he believed "it was important that future historians have available to them accurate records of the events that were taking place." The ghetto archive *Oneg Shabbat*—also known as the Ringelblum Archive—is the most extensive documentary source about Jews under the Nazi regime.

went a change. He no longer put down information in the form of a digest, but instead dealt with the broad and pressing issues of the time, in an attempt to evaluate the events he was witnessing and to comprehend their meaning. His writings also convey his bitter resentment and fear. In addition he composed biographical notes on many of the outstanding Jewish personalities who had gone to their death in the deportations and the struggle, with details of their accomplishments and of their fate under the occupation and in the ghetto. He dealt extensively with the lives of Yitzhak Gitterman, Mordecai **Anielewicz**, Ignacy (Yitzhak) Schiper, Meir Balaban, and Janusz **Korczak**. Ringelblum continued writing up to the last months of his life, which he spent in hiding with Poles. It was in that period that he wrote his work on Jewish-Polish relations, an attempt to cover a multifaceted subject without the help of written sources or reference materials.

Ringelblum's works have been translated and published, in full or in part, in Yiddish, Polish, English (*Notes from the Warsaw Ghetto*; 1958), Italian, French, German, and Japanese. He was the model for the hero of John Hersey's *The Wall*.

After the great deportation from the Warsaw ghetto, Ringelblum became an advocate of armed resistance, and the archive was put under the protection of the civilian arm of the **Jewish Fighting Organization** (*Żydowska Organizacja Bojowa*; ŻOB). In March 1943 Ringelblum accepted an invitation that he had repeatedly received from the Polish side, and with his wife and 13-year-old son left the ghetto and went into hiding among the Poles. On the eve of Passover 1943 he entered the ghetto on his own and walked straight into the uprising. What happened to him during the deportation and the fighting is not known, but in July 1943 he was found in the **Trawniki** labor camp. Two members of the Warsaw underground—a Polish man and a Jewish woman-smuggled him out of Trawniki and took him to Warsaw, in the guise of a railway worker. With his family and another 30 Jews, he hid in an underground refuge—and continued writing. A group of Jews trying to rescue others Jews in hiding among the Poles sought to enlist Ringelblum for their operation and to utilize his non-Jewish appearance. On March 7, 1944, however, before Ringelblum had decided whether to leave the hideaway, the place was discovered and all the Jews and Polish-protected persons there were taken to Warsaw's Pawiak Prison. According to one report, Jewish prisoners who were working in the prison as skilled craftsmen proposed that Ringelblum join their group, but when he realized that there was no chance for his family to be saved, he rejected the offer. A few days later Ringelblum, his family, and the other Jews who had been with him in the hideout were shot to death in the ruins of the ghetto.

SUGGESTED RESOURCES

Ringelblum, Emanuel. *Notes from the Warsaw Ghetto; the Journal of Emmanuel Ringelblum.* New York: Schocken Books, 1974.

Ringelblum, Emmanuel. *Polish-Jewish Relations During the Second World War.* Evanston, IL: Northwestern University Press, 1992.

Robota, Roza

(1921–1944)

Roza Robota was an activist in the Jewish underground in the **Auschwitz**-Birkenau camp. Born in Ciechanów, **Poland**, Robota was a member of the Ha-Shomer ha-Tsa'ir Zionist underground in her town. In 1942 she was taken to

Auschwitz, as part of a transport from Ciechanów, and was among the first prisoners to be put into the women's camp in Birkenau. A Jewish underground group set up in Auschwitz in 1943 contacted Robota, and she became the channel through which the group was able to develop support in the Birkenau women's camp.

In 1944, with Robota's help, minute quantities of explosives were smuggled out of the Union ammunition factory in the camp. They were handed over to the underground in Auschwitz I and to the **Special Commando** men employed in the Birkenau crematoria. In the wake of the investigation held after the Special Commando mutiny of October 1944, Robota and three other young female prisoners working in the Union factory were arrested. Robota was the only one who knew the names of the core group that ran the operations of the underground and its channels of communication, but despite the torture that she underwent, she did not reveal a single name. On January, 6, 1945, just a few weeks before the camp was evacuated, Roza Robota and three comrades—Ella Gartner, Tusia, and Regina—were hanged.

SUGGESTED RESOURCES

Langbein, Hermann. *Against All Hope: Resistance in the Nazi Concentration Camps, 1938–1945.* New York: Paragon House, 1994.

Resistance During the Holocaust. Washington, DC: United States Holocaust Memorial Museum, 1998. Reproduced in part at http://www.igc.org/iearn/hgp/aeti/aeti-1998-no-frames/resistance.htm (accessed on September 11, 2000).

"Rosa Robota: Heroine of Auschwitz." [Online] http://www.datasync.com/~davidg59/rosa.html (accessed on September 11, 2000).

A Teacher's Guide to the Holocaust: Resisters. [Online] http://fcit.coedu.usf.edu/holocaust/people/resister.htm (accessed on September 11, 2000).

Roza Robota.

Rosenberg, Alfred

(1893–1946)

Alfred Rosenberg was a Nazi ideologist and the head of the **Nazi party**'s foreign-policy department. Born in Revel (now Tallinn) in Estonia, Rosenberg came from a family of Baltic Germans. He studied architecture at the universities of **Riga** and Moscow. Fleeing to **Germany** in 1918, he settled in Munich, where he associated with White Russian reactionary expatriate circles and joined the ultranationalist and semi-occult Thule Society. He was already becoming known for his antisemitic and anti-Bolshevik views through such works as *Die Spur der Juden im Wandel der Zeiten* (The Track of the Jews through the Ages) and *Unmoral im Talmud* (Immorality in the Talmud), both published in 1919.

Rosenberg joined the German Workers' party following Adolf **Hitler**, whom he impressed with his theories of a Judeo-Bolshevik-Masonic conspiracy constantly engaged in "undermining the foundations of our existence." Rosenberg was one of the principal distributors of the **Protocols of the Elders of Zion**, a forgery of the tsarist police that appealed to his belief in the active working of occult powers to subvert civilization. In 1921 he became chief editor of the party newspaper. He participated in the abortive Munich Beer-Hall Putsch of November 1923 and was protected by Hitler from the attacks of other leading Nazis, who were offended by Rosenberg's Baltic origins and his intellectual arrogance.

Alfred Rosenberg.

Rosenberg's role as chief Nazi ideologist was enhanced by his founding, in 1929, of the *Kampfbund für Deutsche Kultur* (Fighting League for German Culture) and, above all, by his major work, *Der Mythus des 20. Jahrhunderts* (The Myth of the Twentieth Century; 1930). As an expression of Nazi philosophy this book had an influence comparable to that of Hitler's **MEIN KAMPF**. Rosenberg's book was enormously popular, and by 1942 had sold over a million copies. The book incorporated the racial theories of Joseph-Arthur de Gobineau and proclaimed that race was the decisive factor determining art, science, culture, and the course of world history (*see* **RACISM**). *Mythus* outlined several doctrines. The Teutons represented the "master race" of "Aryans," whose task was to subdue Europe. This belief was combined with denunciation of Judaism and Christianity, whose ideals of compassion and charity must yield to the neo-pagan Teutonic sense of honor. The swastika was the symbol of blood and soil, and denoted the worship of Wotan and the ancient Norse gods. The Jews had threatened the ideal of race with their internationalism and a religion of humanity destructive of the Teutonic spirit. With doctrines such as these, Rosenberg's *Mythus* sought to systematize Nazi ideology.

> **Reichstag**
> The German Parliament.

In 1930 Rosenberg was elected to the **Reichstag** as Nazi deputy for Hesse-Darmstadt, and he made a rapid ascent to positions of influence after 1933. In 1934 Hitler appointed him the "Führer's delegate for the supervision of the whole intellectual and philosophical education and training of the National Socialist party." From 1933 to 1945 he also headed the party's foreign-affairs department, which gave him access especially to fascist parties in eastern Europe and the Balkans. In 1939 he established in Frankfurt the *Institut zur Erforschung der Judenfrage* (Institute for the Investigation of the Jewish Question). Rosenberg declared in his inaugural address there that the "Jewish question" would be considered solved "only after the last Jew has left the Greater German living space." The institute's principal task was to ransack the libraries, archives, and art galleries of European Jewry to promote its "research." After the fall of **FRANCE**, Rosenberg and his staff spearheaded the seizure of French art treasures and sent them to Germany.

In November 1941 Rosenberg was appointed Reich Minister for the Occupied Eastern Territories, where his policy differed in detail but not in principle from the extermination policy achieved by Heinrich **HIMMLER**, Reinhard **HEYDRICH**, and the **REICH SECURITY MAIN OFFICE** (*Reichssicherheitshauptamt*; RSHA). Condemned to death at Nuremberg as a major war criminal, he was hanged in 1946.

SUGGESTED RESOURCES

Cecil, Robert. *The Myth of the Master Race: Alfred Rosenberg and Nazi Ideology.* New York: Dodd, Mead, 1972.

Dutch, Oswald. *Hitler's 12 Apostles.* Freeport, NY: Books for Libraries Press, 1969.

Whisker, James B. *The Philosophy of Alfred Rosenberg.* Newport Beach, CA: Noontide Press, 1990.

Rovno

Rovno (in Polish Równe) is a city in the northwestern **UKRAINE**, capital of the oblast (district) of the same name.

> **Interwar period**
> The years between the end of World War I and the beginning of World War II.

In the **interwar period**, Rovno belonged to the Volhynia (in Polish, Wołyń) district of **POLAND**. Jews had been living in the town since the sixteenth century.

A German police officer shoots Jewish women still alive after a mass execution of Jews from the village of Mizocz, southwest of Rovno.

On the eve of World War II, it had a population of nearly 57,000; about 25,000 were Jews. In September 1939 Rovno was occupied by the **Soviet Union**, and thousands of Jews from German-occupied Poland found refuge there. By June 1941, the Jewish population had grown to over 30,000.

In the battle for the city following the German attack on the Soviet Union in June 1941, the city center and the railway station were bombed and shelled and were heavily damaged or destroyed. Three thousand to four thousand people were killed, many of them Jews. Several thousand Jews fled the city to the east, either during the mobilization and general flight or in the evacuation organized by the local Communist party secretary.

On June 28, six days after the invasion, Rovno was occupied by the Germans. In the course of July and August, some 3,000 Jews were murdered under various pretexts. By order of the military government, a **Judenrat** (Jewish Council) was set up whose members included men active in community affairs during the prewar period. Two of the appointees to the Judenrat—the chairman, Dr. Moshe Bergmann, and a lawyer, Leon Sukharchuk—committed suicide rather than become the Nazis' helpers. The Jews were ordered to wear an armband with a blue Star of David on a white background (later replaced by a yellow badge; *see* **Badge, Jewish**). They were sent on **forced labor** and had to hand over their valuables and pay a ransom, in large sums of money and in gold.

On September 1, 1941, the Ukraine was put under the control of the civil administration known as the Reichskommissariat Ukraine. The *Reichskommissar*, Erich Koch, established his headquarters at Rovno, and apparently for this reason he sought to speed up the purge of its Jews. The planning of the *Aktion* was in the hands of Higher **SS** and Police Leader Friedrich **Jeckeln** of Army Group South. Its implementation was entrusted to the **SD** (*Sicherheitsdienst*; Security Service) forces in Rovno as well as to Ukrainian auxiliary police (*see* **Ukrainian Military Police**). The German military administration also took part.

On November 5, the Rovno district *Kommissar* informed the Judenrat that Jews who had no work permits would be moved to other locations for work. Notices to this effect were posted in the streets, ordering the Jews to report on November 7 with a minimum of luggage. On that day and the next, 21,000 Jews were rounded

up and taken to a pine grove at Sosenki, 4 miles (6 kilometers) away, where they were all shot standing next to trenches that had been dug in advance for their burial.

About 80 percent of Rovno's Jews were murdered in this operation. In postwar reports, members of the Soviet underground claimed that they had learned from Soviet PRISONERS OF WAR about the trenches that were being dug and tried to warn the Jews of their fate, but the Jews would not believe what they were told. There has been no confirmation of this report by any Jewish source.

The 5,000 surviving Jews were moved into a ghetto set up in the Wola quarter of Rovno, with seven families to an apartment. Though the ghetto was not sealed off from the outside, the inhabitants were severely restricted in their movement and in effect were confined to the ghetto area. They were assigned to forced labor, with several hundred working for the Jung construction firm.

The murder of Jews, singly or in small groups, went on without interruption until the final destruction of the ghetto. Occasionally, individual Jews offered resistance, sometimes even using firearms. In one case four Jews—Syma Gimberg, Isaac Schneider, Nyonya Kopilnik, and a woman by the name of Dvoricz—fought a group of Germans and Ukrainians face to face, killing some and themselves falling in the battle.

On July 13, 1942, the ghetto was surrounded by German and Ukrainian police. Force was used to round up the Jews, who were taken to the railway station. All of them—some 5,000 people—were packed into freight cars and sent northeast, toward Kostopol. When the train reached its destination, a wood northwest of the town, the Jews were taken out, lined up along prepared trenches, and shot.

While the ghetto was under siege, dozens of its inhabitants tried to flee; there were also some who jumped off the train while it was in motion. Most of the escapees were young people, who formed into groups or roamed the woods on their own. Before long they joined up with Soviet partisan units.

On February 5, 1944, Rovno was liberated in a combined operation of the Soviet army (Thirteenth Army and Eighteenth Cavalry Corps) and the partisan forces, who made their assault on the city from the west. The number of Jewish survivors in the city did not exceed a few dozen. They were joined by survivors and returnees from small towns in the district, where their lives had been endangered by Ukrainian nationalist PARTISANS of the Ukrainian Insurgent Army. The Jewish partisans obtained permission to establish a religious community and were given a building for a synagogue. They made this into a center where all new Jewish arrivals in the city reported and were given food and clothing.

In the summer of 1944, on the initiative of Zionist activists Abraham and Eliezer Lidowski, a clandestine organization was set up to establish escape routes to Palestine. The organization contacted a similar group in VILNA and devised a joint plan to move the Jews in the direction of Bucharest, where the pro-German regime had fallen in August 1944. When this plan failed, the Rovno and Vilna groups concentrated their efforts on central Poland, encouraged by the fact that an official repatriation program of Polish nationals—among them many Jews—had just been launched. By the fall of 1944, as many as 1,200 Jews had gathered in Rovno. Most of them left the city, moving toward destinations in the west.

SUGGESTED RESOURCES

Huneke, Douglas K. *The Moses of Rovno.* New York: Dodd, Mead, 1985.

Równe. See Rovno.

Rudninkai Forest. See Partisans.

Rumbula

Rumbula (also Rumbuli) was the site of a massacre in a wooded area near the railway station of the same name, 5 miles (8 kilometers) from **Riga**, the capital of **Latvia**. From November 29 to December 9, 1941, 38,000 Jews were murdered at Rumbula: 28,000 from the Riga ghetto and 10,000 who had been transported by train from **Germany**, **Austria**, and the Protectorate of **Bohemia and Moravia**.

After World War II the site was neglected, and there was no sign to commemorate the massacre that had taken place. In 1962 a group of Jewish activists placed a wooden sign there that read: "On this site the voice of thirty-eight thousand Jews of Riga was stilled, November 29–30, 1941 to December 8–9, 1941." The Soviet authorities, disapproving of any memorial sign that specifically mentioned Jews, removed it from the site. After persistent public pressure, a memorial stone was erected with inscriptions in Russian, Latvian, and Yiddish: "To the memory of the victims of the Nazis, 1941–1944."

The site has since become a place of Jewish assembly, particularly on the anniversaries of the Rumbula massacre and the **Warsaw Ghetto Uprising**, and on the Jewish high holidays. These gatherings have also become, to some extent, an expression of the national rebirth of the remnants of the Jewish population in Soviet Latvia.

SUGGESTED RESOURCES

Mikhelson, Frida. *I Survived Rumbula.* Washington, DC: United States Holocaust Memorial Museum, 1982.

Press, Bernhard. *The Murder of the Jews in Latvia, 1941–1945.* Evanston, IL: Northwestern University Press, 1999.

Russia. See Soviet Union.

Index

A

Abegg, Elisabeth, **3:** 179
Adamowicz, Irena, **2:** 165, **3:** 179-180
AFSC. *See* American Friends Service Committee (Quakers)
AGFA Camera Company, **2:** *14*
Aid to Jews
    by Allies after the War, **1:** 167
    by Belorussians, **1:** 91
    by Catholic church in Belgium, **1:** 66
    donations of foreign currency for travel, **1:** 51
    by Poles, **1:** 1-3, 91**4:** 128
    by Ukrainians, **1:** 55
    See also Non-Jews who aided Jews
    See also Rescue of European Jews
Akiva, **4:** 148
    in Kraków, **2:** 170
Aktion, **4:** 28
Aktion, Itelligenz, **2:** 169
Aktion "Erntefest." *See* Erntefest ("Harvest Festival")
Aktion 1005, **1:** 4-6
    at Babi Yar, **1:** 55
    map of, **1:** *5*
Aktion M ("Operation Furniture"), **3:** 88
Aktion Reinhard, **1:** 6-9
    See also Erntefest ("Harvest Festival")
Aktion T4. *See* Euthanasia Program
Algeria, **3:** 171
Aliya Bet, **1:** 9-13
Allied Control Council Law No. 10, **4:** 75
Allies
    definition of, **1:** 64
    effect on Jews of Allies' German policy, **2:** 69
    efforts to aid displaced persons, **1:** 167, **4:** 90
    liberation of Jews in southern Italy, **2:** 120
    postwar disunity among, **1:** 155-156
    refusal to bomb Auschwitz, **1:** 47
    responses to Jewish refugees, 1942-1945, **4:** 95

American Friends Service Committee (Quakers), **1:** 13-14, **3:** 167
American Jewish Committee, **1:** 15, 17
American Jewish Conference, **1:** 16
American Jewish Congress, **1:** 14, 17, **4:** 143
American Jewish Distribution Committee. *See* Joint Distribution Committee
American Jewish literature about the Holocaust, **3:** 11-12
American Jewish organizations, **1:** 14-16, 17
    founded by Stephen Samuel Wise, **4:** 140-*141*
    Rescue Committee of United States Orthodox Rabbis, **3:** 164-166
    for rescue of Jewish children, **3:** 166
    See also Joint Distribution Committee (JDC)
American Jews
    advisors to Franklin D. Roosevelt, **1:** 17-18, **3:** 69-*71*
    and the Holocaust, **1:** 16-19
    and the Joint Distribution Committee (JDC), **2:** 138-139
    Orthodox Rabbis, **3:** 165
    and the Rescue Committee of the United States
American press and the Holocaust, **1:** 20-21
American Quakers' reaction to Nazism, **1:** 13
American zone
    denazification, **1:** 154
    displaced persons' camps, **1:** 168
    United States Army role, **4:** 90-92
Amsterdam, **3:** 85, 86-87
    deportations from, **3:** 89
    Anne Frank's life in, **2:** 26-33
Anielewicz, Mordecai, **1:** 21-24, *22*, **4:** 155, 196
Anne Frank Foundation, **2:** 32
Anne Frank house, **2:** 31-*32*
Annex, The (Anne Frank), **2:** 30
Anschluss, **1:** 50-51
    historical context of, **2:** 54
Anti-Defamation League (ADL), **1:** 15
Antifascist Bloc, **2:** 130

Antifascist Struggle Organization, **2:** 165
Anti-Gypsy legislation, **2:** 81, 82-84
Anti-Jewish boycotts, **1:** *102*-104
Anti-Jewish legislation
    Croatia, **1:** 139
    France, **2:** 135-136
    Germany, **1:** 24-27, **2:** 51, 52, 54
    Hungary, **2:** 108
    Italy, **2:** 120
    "Jewish Code" in Slovakia, **4:** 12
    Lösener, Bernard, **3:** 28
    Nazi marriage laws, **1:** 25, **2:** 90, **3:** 66, 96, **4:** 180-181
    by Ustaša in Croatia, **1:** 139
    See also Nuremberg Laws
Anti-Jewish measures
    Austria, **1:** 50, 52-*53*, **2:** 171-174
    Belgium, **1:** 64-65
    Berlin, **1:** 84-86
    Bohemia and Moravia, **1:** 97-98
    Budapest, **1:** 109
    Croatia, **1:** 139
    Dvinsk, **1:** 174
    France, **2:** 22-23
    by French police, **2:** 35-36
    Generalgouvernement, **2:** 40
    German-occupied countries, **2:** 56
    Germany, **2:** 50-55, 56-57, 171-174
    Hungary, **2:** 109-110, 113, 114
    Kovno, **2:** 164
    Łódź, **3:** 20
    Lublin, **3:** 30
    Lvov, **3:** 37
    Netherlands, **3:** 87-88
    Order Banning the Emigration of Jews from the Reich **4:** 188-189
    Paris, **3:** 111-112
    Poland, **3:** 131-132
    Prague, **1:** 99
    Riga, **3:** 176
    Slovakia, **4:** 12
    by Soviets, **1:** 72, **4:** 22
    Tarnów, **4:** 52-53
    Ternopol, **4:** 55-56
    Ukraine, **2:** 109-110

INDEX

Anti-Jewish measures (continued)
    Vienna, **4:** 99
    Vilna, **4:** 102-103
    Warsaw, **4:** 115, 117-118
    See also Curfews and restrictions on Jews in public
    See also Economic measures against Jews
    See also Mass murders by Nazis
    See also Public humiliation of Jews
    See also Seizures of Jewish possessions
    See also Synagogues, destruction of
Anti-Judaism, Christian-inspired, **1:** 119
Anti-Nazi coalition, Baum Gruppe, **1:** 62-63
Anti-Polish measures, **2:** 40, **3:** 127
Antisemite and Jew (Sartre), **1:** 29
Antisemitism, **1:** 27-34
    of the Catholic saint who rescued Jews, **2:** 157
    definition of, **1:** 27
    effect on Jews in America, **1:** 18
    and fascism, **2:** 4
    in France, **2:** 18-19, *20*
    in Germany, **2:** 48-49
    of Goebbels, **2:** 67
    of Hitler, **2:** 93-94, 95
    impact on Jewish partisans, **3:** 114-115, 117
    importance for the Nazi Party, **3:** 80
    in Italy, **2:** 119-120
    in Lithuania, **3:** 16
    in Lvov, **3:** 36
    postwar, **1:** 167, **2:** 171
    postwar Poland, **2:** 153
    postwar Soviet Union, **4:** 25
    postwar Ukraine, **4:** 86
    relationship to racism, **3:** 151
    in Slovakia, **4:** 12
    of Stricher, Julius, **4:** 37-38
    in the United States, **4:** 94
    See also Holocaust: denial of
    See also Pogroms
    See also Protocols of the Elders of Zion
"Antisemitism of reason," **2:** 8
Antwerp, Zionist youth movements in, **1:** 67
Antwerp pogrom, **1:** 66
Apartments
    Budapest refuges for Jews, **1:** 110, **3:** 35, **4:** 110
    designated by Nazis for Jews, **1:** *108*, **2:** 57, **4:** 12, 114
    Nazi seizures of Jews', **1:** 36-37, 38, **4:** 99, 100, 109
Appeasement of Nazi Germany, **2:** 69-70
Arajs Commando, **3:** 3
Archives. *See* Books; Documents of the Holocaust; Museums
Arendt, Hannah, **3:** 13
Arisierung. *See* Aryanization
Armbands
    of Jewish ghetto police, **2:** *133*
    swastika, **2:** *93*
    white, with blue Star of David, **4:** 117

Armed resistance by Jews, **3:** 170-171, 172-174
    assassination attempts on Nazis, **2:** 74, 170
    in Belgium, **1:** 68
    decisions about, **2:** 170
    Liebeskind's famous quote about, **3:** 9
    origins of, **3:** 140
    in Poland, **2:** 6-7
    in Warsaw, **4:** 125, 130-131
    by youth movements, **4:** 148-149
    Zuckerman, Yitzhak, views about, **4:** 154
    See also Jewish Fighting Organization (ŻOB)
    See also Uprisings
Armia Krajowa. *See* Home Army (Armia Krajowa)
Arrow Cross Party, **1:** 34-35, **2:** 112-113
    activity in Budapest, **1:** 109
Art works belonging to Jews, **1:** 50, 65, **3:** 184
Aryanization, **1:** 35-38
    Austria, **1:** 50-51
    Belgium, **1:** 65
    Berlin, **1:** 84
    Bohemia and Moravia, **1:** 98
    definition of, **1:** 35
    following Kristallnacht, **2:** 174
    Netherlands, **3:** 86
    Paris, **3:** 111-112
    Poland, **3:** 131
    Slovakia, **4:** 12
    by Vichy government, **2:** 22
Aryans
    Alfred Rosenberg's writings about, **3:** 184
    Aryan clause in bylaws of German organizations, **1:** 25
    history of, **3:** 149
    Nazi classification of Mischlinge as, **3:** 67-68
    Nazi definition of, **3:** 152
    Nazi notion of Aryan beauty, **3:** 150
    Nazi research to identify, **3:** 53
    See also Non-Jews
    See also Pregnancy experiments by Nazis
Asiatic-Jewish-Bolshevik threat, **3:** 164
Asocials
    Nazi classification of groups of people as, **1:** 126
    Nazi view of Gypsies as, **2:** 82
Assassinations and attempted assassinations
    of German officers in Kraków, **2:** 170
    of Grodno ghetto commanders, **2:** 74
    of Hitler, **2:** 29, 67, 73, 85
Association for Jews in Germany, **2:** 58
Association of Jews in Belgium (AJB), **1:** 64
Atlas, Yeheskel, **1:** *38*
"Atonement payment," **1:** 37
Attacks on Jews. *See* Anti-Jewish measures
Auerswald, Heinz, **1:** 39
Auschwitz, **1:** 40-*49*
    entrance to, **1:** 127
    gas chambers at, **2:** 39, 43, 45
    I. G. Farben relationship with, **2:** 116
    survivor accounts of, **1:** 129, **3:** 6-7

    See also Zyklon B
Auschwitz Protocols, **4:** 14
Australia's position at Evian Conference, **1:** 190
Austria, **1:** 49-54
    antisemitism in, **1:** 31
    Central Office for Jewish Emigration, **1:** 51, 112
    Jewish youth movement, **4:** 145-146
    map of annexed, **1:** *50*
    Mauthausen, **3:** 45-51
    See also Vienna
Austrian Nazis, **1:** 50
Autobiographies
    Holocaust survivors, **3:** 14
    Hoss, Rudolf, **2:** 108
    Wise, Stephen Samuel, **4:** 141
    Zuckerman, Yitzhak, **4:** 154
Axis criminals, definition of, **3:** 98
Axis powers, **2:** 110
    anti-Jewish legislation in, **1:** 27
    Hungary's entry into, **2:** 111

B

Babi Yar, **1:** 54-56
    account of an eyewitness, **3:** 106
    escape of prisoners from, **1:** 5
"Babii Yar" (Yevtushenko), **1:** 56
Bach-Zelewski, Erich von dem, **1:** 56-57
Badges
    for categories of Jews in ghettos, **1:** 58
    pink triangle, **2:** 105, **4:** *2*
    for Polish and Russian laborers, **2:** 15
    for prisoners, **1:** 61, 131
    swastika, **2:** *93*
    See also Armbands
    See also ID cards
    See also Jewish badge, **1:** 57-61
Balkan states
    deportations of Jews from, **1:** 165
    partisan activity by Jews, **3:** 115
    See also Bulgaria
    See also Greece
    See also Yugoslavia
Ballad of Mauthausen (Theodorakis and Kambanelis), **3:** 51
Baltic states
    Gypsies, **2:** 86
    Lohse, Hinrich, **3:** 28
    partisan activity by Jews, **3:** 115
Bank accounts, Nazi seizure of Jews', **1:** 37
Banks, Nazi seizures of Jews', **1:** 35
Barbie, Klaus, **1:** *61*-62
Barth, Karl, **1:** 119
BASF (German company), **2:** 115, 117
Battle of Britain, **2:** 68
Baum Gruppe (Anti-Nazi organization), **1:** 62-63
Bayer (German company), **2:** 115, 117
Beer-Hall Putsch, **2:** 33, **3:** 81
Belarus. *See* Belorussia
Belgium, **1:** 63-69
    Catholics, **1:** 121
    deportation of Jews from, **1:** 164
    Jewish Brigade Group activities, **2:** 128

position at Evian Conference, **1:** 190
protest of Jewish badge, **1:** 66
Belorussia, **1:** 69-73
    Grodno, **2:** 73-75
    Hitler's plan to resettle, **2:** 42
    Lohse, Hinrich, **3:** 28
    map of, **1:** *70*
    Minsk, **1:** 72-73, **3:** 63-66, **4:** 21
    partisans, **3:** 115-116
    Vitebsk, **4:** 105-106
Bełżec, **1:** 7, 73-77
Benoît, Marie, **1:** *78*-79
Bereza-Kartuska, **2:** 5
Bergen-Belsen, **1:** 79-83
    postwar displaced persons' camps, **1:** 82, 168
Bergen-Belsen Trial, **4:** 74
Bergson Group, **1:** 19
Berlin, **1:** 83-87
    anti-Nazi coalition, **1:** 62-63
Bermuda Conference, **1:** 191-192, **3:** 161
Best, Werner, **1:** 87-88
Betar, **4:** 147, 148
Białystok, **1:** 71, 88-92
    underground groups in, **2:** 74, 75-76
Biarritz (Goedsche), **1:** 30
Biebow, Hans, **1:** *92*-93
Bielski, Tuvia, **1:** *93*-94
Birkenau, **1:** 41-42, 194
Black people
    forced sterilization of, by Nazis, **1:** 186-187
    Jesse Owens in Germany, **3:** *150*
    medical experiments on/about, by Nazis, **3:** 59
    parallels between American racism and Nazi antisemitism, **3:** 151
Blechhammer camp death marches, **1:** 151
Blobel, Paul, **1:** *94*-95
Blood, Nazi experiments about, **3:** 59
"Blood for Goods," **1:** 181, **2:** 148, **4:** 142
Blum, Abraham, **1:** 95-96
Bʾnai Bʾrith, **1:** 14-15
Bodies. *See* Corpses
Bogaard, Johannes, **1:** 96-97
Bohemia and Moravia, Protectorate of **1:** 97-99
    Gypsies, **2:** 85
    Jewish badge, **1:** 58
    Jews deported to Minsk, **3:** 65
    map of annexed, **1:** *98*
    mass murder of Jews from, **1:** 72
    Nazi expulsions of Jews from, **4:** 57
    Nazi plan to deport Jews to Poland, **3:** 92-93
    Nazi treatment of intellectuals, **3:** 47
    Volksdeutsche, **4:** 107
    youth movements, **4:** 149-150
Bolshevik Revolution, **1:** 30
Bolzano camp, **2:** 121
Books
    antisemitic, **3:** 146-148
    antisemtic children's, **1:** *32*
    book-burning, Goebbels' role, **2:** 66
    book-burning, in Berlin, **1:** *85*
    clandestine libraries, **4:** 122

hidden from Nazis by Jews, **3:** *87*
Nazi ban on Jews' ownership of, **2:** 164
Nazi seizure of Jews' libraries, **3:** 88
See also Literature of the Holocaust
Bormann, Martin, **1:** *100*-101
Bosnia, Jews in, **1:** 139
Bothmann, Hans, **1:** 101, 114
Boycott against Nazi Germany, **1:** 102, 103, **4:** 140, 143
Boycotts of Jewish businesses, **1:** 35, *36*, 102-104
    Nazi discussions about, **3:** 96-97
Brandt, Karl, **1:** 188, **3:** 53
Britain. *See* Great Britain
British military
    enlistment of Jews in, **2:** 73
    Jewish Brigade Group, **2:** 125-127
    lack of preparedness, **2:** 67-68
British zone
    denazification, **1:** 154
    displaced persons' camp, **1:** 168
Brussels, Zionist youth movements in, **1:** 67
Buber, Martin, **2:** 91
Buchenwald, **1:** 105-107
    death marches from, **1:** 151-152
Budapest, **1:** 107-110
    death march, **1:** 151
    ghetto, **2:** 114
    Jewish resistance groups, **2:** 170
    mass murder of Jews by Nazis, **1:** 34
    Relief and Rescue Committee, **2:** 148-149
Budzyń, **1:** 110-111
Bulgaria
    deportation of Jews from, **1:** 165
    Jewish badge, **1:** 60
    partisans, **3:** 119
Buna-Monowitz (Auschwitz III), **1:** 41
Bund, **1:** 63
Bund leaders
    Blum, Abraham, **1:** 95-96
    Feiner, Leon, **2:** *4*-5
    in Warsaw ghetto, **2:** 129-130

C

Camp conditions, **1:** 129, 130
    Bergen-Belsen in April 1945, **4:** 75
    Budzyń, **1:** 111
    Dachau in its last days, **1:** 147
    Gross-Rosen, **2:** 77
    Gurs (detention camp), **2:** 80
    Majdanek, **3:** 44, 47
    Mauthausen, **3:** 47-48
    for prisoners who worked, **2:** 77
Camp layout and facilities
    Auschwitz, **1:** 40-41
    barracks at Dachau, **1:** *146*
    barracks at Theresienstadt, **4:** 58
    barracks in Majdanek, **3:** *45*
    Bełżec, **1:** 75
    Bergen-Belsen, **1:** 79-80, *81*
    Buchenwald, **1:** 104, *106*
    Chełmno, **1:** 114
    Drancy (transit camp), **1:** 172
    Majdanek, **3:** 43

maps of, **1:** 74, **4:** *16*, *64*
Mauthausen, **3:** 47
Płasów, **3:** 121
Skarżysko-Kamienna, **4:** 10
Sobibór, **4:** 15
Treblinka, **4:** 63-*64*
See also Crematoriums
See also Gas chambers
Camp procedures for prisoners
    Auschwitz, **1:** 42-44
    Bełżec, **1:** 75-76
    Chełmno, **1:** 115-116
    in concentration camps, **1:** 130-131
    Dachau, **1:** 145-153
    Drancy (transit camp), **1:** 173-174
    at extermination camps, **2:** 38-39
    Sobibór, **4:** 16-17
    Treblinka, **4:** 65-67
Camps
    for displaced persons after the war, **1:** 82, 166-170
    survivors' reactions to, **4:** 47-48, 138
    tent camps, **3:** 47, 50
    types of Nazi, **1:** 124, 127
    See also Concentration camps
    See also Detention camps
    See also Extermination camps
    See also Labor camps
    See also Liquidation of camps
    See also Prisoners
    See also Transit camps
Camp staff
    Auschwitz, **1:** 45-45, **3:** 146
    Bełżec, **1:** 73
    Bergen-Belsen, **1:** 79, 81-82
    Chełmno, **1:** 114-115
    Dachau, **1:** 143-144
    Death's-Head Units, **4:** 31-32
    Drancy (transit camp), **1:** 172
    of extermination camps, **1:** 194
    Mauthausen, **3:** 48
    Płasów, **3:** 122
    Ravensbrück, **3:** 155
    Skarżysko-Kamienna, **4:** 10
    Sobibór, **4:** 15
    Stutthof, **4:** 42-43
    Treblinka, **4:** 64-65, *66*
    Westerbork, **4:** 135
    See also Trials of war criminals
Canada's position at Evian Conference, **1:** 190
Carbon monoxide gas, **2:** 37, 39, **4:** 156
"Cartload of Shoes, A" (Sutzkever), **3:** 10
Carus, Carl Gustav, **3:** 150
Catholic church
    aid to Jews in Belgium, **1:** 66
    in Amsterdam, **3:** 89
    attitudes towards Nazi persecution of Jews, **1:** 119-121
    in Croatia, **1:** 140-141
    denunciation of the Nazis, **2:** 54
    in France, **2:** 18, 23
    Holocaust saint, **2:** 156
    in Italy, **2:** 120
    Nazi medical experiments on priests, **3:** 57
    Nazi persecution of, **1:** 121

INDEX

Catholic church (continued)
    in Poland, **3:** 127
CDJ (Jewish Defense Committee), **1:** 68
Central Europe, antisemitism in, **1:** 28-29
Central Office for Jewish Emigration, **1:** 51, **3:** 89, 95, 98, 111-112
Central Union of German Citizens of Jewish Faith, **1:** 112-114
    Hirsch, Otto, and, **2:** 91-92
Central Union of Jews in Germany, **1:** 114
Certificate of Honor to Righteous Among the Nations, **3:** *178*
Certificates of employment for Jews, **3:** 38, 39, **4:** 103-104, 112, 123, 185
Chamberlain, Houston Stewart, **1:** 33
Chamberlain, Neville, **2:** 67, 70
Chambon-sur-Lignon. *See* Le Chambon-sur-Lignon
Chapters from the Legacy (Zuckerman), **4:** 154
Chełmno, **1:** 114-118
Chemical-warfare experiments by Nazis, **3:** 57
Children
    abandoned in Austria, **1:** 51
    antisemitic books for, **1:** *32*
    deported from Białystok, **1:** 71, 91
    deported from Izieu, France, **1:** 62
    deported from Paris as Allies landed, **3:** 112, *113*
    deported from Warsaw, **4:** 124
    detention camp for, **3:** 155
    exterminated at Chełmno, **1:** 116
    feelings of one deported from Łódź, **3:** 22-23
    hidden among Catholics, **1:** *120*
    hidden by the Dutch, **3:** 90
    Janusz Korczak's work with, **2:** 159-162
    number who perished in the Holocaust, **3:** 76
    orphaned, **1:** 175, **2:** 25, **3:** 64, 90, **4:** 100, 153
    parents forced to choose among, **4:** 103-104
    Polish, **4:** 152
    prisoners who became partisans, **1:** 111
    refugees, German Jewish, **3:** *167*
    refugees, in Great Britain, **2:** 72, 73
    role in the resistance, **3:** 65
    saved in Budapest, **1:** 110
    smugglers in the ghetto, **4:** 121-122, 123
    soup kitchens for, **3:** 135
    of survivors, **4:** 49-50
    working, **2:** 16
    See also Frank, Anne
    See also Rescue of Jewish children
Children's Block 66 (Buchenwald), **1:** *106*
Choms, Władysława, **1:** 118-119
Christian churches, **1:** 119-123
    contribution to antisemitism, **1:** 28
    protests against antisemitism, **1:** 119
    See also Catholic church
Christian X (King of Denmark), **1:** 160
Chronicles of the Łódź ghetto, **3:** 25-27

Churchill, Winston
    as Great Britain's war leader, **2:** 68, 69, 70
    and the Jewish Brigade Group, **2:** 127, 128
    postwar denazification efforts by, **1:** 154
Citizenship Law, Reich, **1:** 25, 26
Class and racism in Germany, **3:** 152
Clauberg, Carl, **1:** 123-124, **3:** 59-60
Cohen, Alfred, **1:** 15
Cohen, Judy, **1:** 40-41
Cohn, Marianne, **1:** *124*
Collaborators
    French, **3:** 4-5
    investigations of, **3:** 75, 98
    Italian, **2:** 122-123
    Judenräte, **2:** 142
    Kapo, **2:** 147-148
    Lithuanian, **3:** 19, **4:** 102, 141, *142*
    resistance actions against, **2:** 132
    Soviet, **3:** 156, **4:** 25
    Ukrainian, **4:** 84
    Volksdeutsche, **4:** 107-108
Collective farms
    See Kibbutzim
Colleges, Nazi laws prohibiting Jews from, **1:** 25
Commissars
    Nazi experiments on the bodies of, **3:** 59
    Nazi orders to kill, **2:** 158-159, **3:** 104
Committee for Special Jewish Affairs, **3:** 85-86
Communism
    definition of, **3:** 127
    Nazi views about, **3:** 103, 163-164
Communists
    alliances with Jews in Poland, **3:** 117
    Amsterdam strike by, **3:** 87
    in Baum Gruppe (anti-Nazi organization), **1:** 62-63
    in Belgian resistance movement, **1:** 66
    in concentration camps, **1:** 106, 126
    in France, **2:** 80
    in the French Resistance, **3:** 157
    in Latvia, **3:** 3
    Operational Squad searches for, **3:** 102
    relationships with Zionist groups, **2:** 74, 165
    in the Warsaw ghetto, **2:** 130
    Wittenberg, Yitzhak, **4:** 88, 89-90
    Yelin, Haim, **4:** 144
    See also Commissars
    See also Soviet partisans
    See also Soviet prisoners of war
Compulsory Aryanization, **1:** 36-38
Concentration camps, **1:** 124-134
    Bereza-Kartuska, **2:** 5
    Bergen-Belsen, **1:** 79-83
    Bolzano, **2:** 121
    Buchenwald, **1:** 105-107
    Budzyń, **1:** 110-111
    Croatia, **1:** 139-140
    Dachau, **1:** 143-145
    death marches from, **1:** 149-153

    definition of, **1:** 124
    Dora-Mittelbau, **1:** 170-172
    Fossoli, **2:** 121
    Gestapo relations with, **2:** 61
    Gross-Rosen, **2:** 76-79
    Gypsies in, **2:** *82, 84*
    Himmler's role in, **2:** 90
    in Italy, **2:** *119,* 120-122
    La Risiera di San Sabba camp, **2:** 121-122
    Majdanek, **1:** 86, **2:** 39, **3:** 42-45
    map of, **1:** *125*
    Mauthausen, **3:** 45-51
    Natzweiler-Struthof, **3:** 79-80
    Neuengamme, **3:** 91-92
    Płasów, **3:** 120-122
    Ravensbrück, **3:** 154-156
    Sachsenhausen, **4:** 1-2
    Stutthof, **4:** 42-44
    See also Auschwitz
    See also Camp conditions
    See also Camp layout and facilities
    See also Camp staff
    See also Death marches
    See also Economic-Administrative Main Office
Concentration camp syndrome, **1:** 133
Conferences. *See* Evian Conference; Wannsee Conference
Confessing Church, **1:** 121
Contacts abroad. *See* Reports to the outside world
Corporations. *See* German companies; SS companies
Corporatism, **2:** 2
Corpses
    Jews massacred at Kamenets-Podolski, **2:** *145*
    Nazi efforts to conceal, **1:** 4-6, **3:** 50, **4:** 68, 77, 122, 177
    Nazi medical experiments on, **3:** 58-59
Council of Elders of the Kovno Jewish Ghetto Community, **2:** 164
Cracow. *See* Kraków
Crematoriums
    Bełżec, **1:** 77
    Bergen-Belsen, **1:** *83*
    Natzweiler-Struthof, **3:** 80
Crimes against humanity, **1:** 134-137, **4:** 72, 76
    definition of, **2:** 45
    medical experiments as, **3:** 60
    relationship to genocide, **2:** 44
    U.S. Office of Special Investigations, **3:** 98
Crimes against peace, **1:** 134-135, **4:** 72, 73, 136-137
Crimes against the Jewish people, **2:** 45
Criminal organizations, **4:** 73
Criminal Police, **3:** 162
Croatia, **1:** 137-141
    deportation of Jews from, **1:** 164
    Gypsies, **2:** 86
    map of, **1:** *138*
    racist political movements in, **3:** 152
Crystal Night. *See* Kristallnacht

INDEX

Cultural Society of German Jews, **2:** 53
Curfews and restrictions on Jews in public, **1:** 26, **3:** 87-88, **4:** 102, 112, 117
    See also Ghettos
    See also Jewish badge
CV. *See* Central Union of German Citizens of Jewish Faith
Czechoslovakia. *See* Bohemia and Moravia; Slovakia
Czech police, **4:** 57
Czech underground, **1:** 6, **3:** 48
Czerniaków, Adam, **1:** 39, *141*-143
    diary entries, **1:** 143, **4:** 117, 123, 125, 198-199

D

Dachau, **1:** 143-147
Daimler-Benz Aircraft, **3:** 79
Dannecker, Theodor, **1:** 147-148
    role in Paris, **3:** 111
Darquier de Pellepoix, Louis, **1:** 148
Darwin, Charles, **3:** 151
Darwin's theory of natural selection, **1:** 22
Daugavpils. *See* Dvinsk
Death camps. *See* Extermination camps
Death marches, **1:** 149-153
    columns, **3:** 68
    photographs of prisoners on, **1:** *150, 152*
    rescue of Jews on, **3:** 35-36, **4:** *110*
    from Stutthof, **4:** 43
    survivor account of, **2:** 83
Declaration of the Boycott by the Nazi Party Leadership, **4:** 173-77
Deffaugt, Jean, **1:** 153-154
DEGESCH (German Vermin-Combating Corporation), **4:** 157
De Gobineau, Joseph-Arthur, **3:** 149, 150, 184
DEMAG (German company), **4:** 1
Demjanjuk, John (Iwan), **4:** *70*
Denazification, **1:** 154-157
Denial of the Holocaust
    by Jews deported to Poland, **3:** 140
    postwar, **2:** 100-104
Denmark, **1:** 157-161
    Best, Warner, **1:** 87-88
    deportation of Jews from, **1:** 165
    Jewish badge, **1:** 60
    Jewish refugees from, **3:** 160
    Protestants, **1:** 122
    rescue of Jews in, **1:** 27, **3:** 179
Department of State. *See* United States Department of State
Deportations, **1:** 161-165
    after emigration of Jews stopped, **1:** 161, 180
    Aktion Reinhard, **1:** 7, 8
    from Austria, **1:** 51-52
    from Belgium, **1:** 65, 66-67
    from Berlin, **1:** 86
    from Białystok, **1:** 91
    from Bohemia and Moravia, **1:** 99
    from Budapest, **1:** 109, **3:** 52
    of Croatian Jews, **1:** 140

Dannecker letter requesting permission to deport children from Paris, **4:** 191
    from Denmark, **1:** 159-160
    from Dvinsk, **1:** 175
    effect on Jewish resistance groups, **2:** 130-131
    "The Foot March," **1:** 109
    from France, **2:** 22-23
    of Germans in mixed marriages, **3:** 29
    from Germany, **2:** 57-58
    from Great Britain, **2:** 73
    from Grodno, **2:** 74
    of Gypsies, **2:** 83, 84-86
    from Hungary, **2:** 114, 115, 146
    Instructions for the Deportation of Jews from the Palatinate (Pfalz) **4:** 187-188
    Jews chosen first for, **3:** 26
    of Jews in Italy, **2:** 121
    of Kraków Jews, **2:** 168-171
    during Kristallnacht, **2:** 173
    of Lithuanian Jews by Soviets, **3:** 17
    from Łódź, **1:** 116, **3:** 20-21, 22-23
    from Lublin, **3:** 31-32
    from Lvov, **3:** 39
    from Minsk, **3:** 64
    Nazi euphemisms for, **4:** 28
    from Netherlands, **3:** 88-90
    from Paris, **3:** 112
    from Poland, **3:** 137-139
    of Poles, **1:** 162, **2:** 10, **3:** 126, **4:** 152
    of refugees from Austria, **1:** 52
    role of Central Office for Jewish Emigration, **1:** 112
    role of Jewish ghetto police, **2:** 134
    from Slovakia, **4:** 12
    to Sobibór, **4:** 17-18
    SS officer responsible for, **1:** 147-148
    from Starachowice, **4:** 35
    from Tarnów, **4:** 53
    from Ternopol, **4:** 56, 57
    to and from Theresienstadt, **4:** 58
    from Vienna, **4:** 99, 100-101
    from Warsaw, **4:** 123-124, 125-126
    from Warsaw Transfer Point (Umschlagplatz), **4:** 61-62
    from Westerbork, **4:** 135-137
    See also Drancy
Deportation ships
    Arandora Star, **2:** 73
    Exodus 1947, **1:** *12*
    See also Refugee ships
Deportation trains
    Aktion Reinhard, **1:** 7
    armed attack by Jews against, **1:** 68
    to Auschwitz, **1:** 42
    at Chełmno, **1:** 115
    cleaning, **4:** 66
    conditions on, **4:** 18
    Jews being loaded onto, **1:** *115, 164*
    logistic support for, **1:** 163, 180
    Novak, Franz, **3:** *95*
    Warsaw Transfer Point (Umschlagplatz), **4:** 62
Deportees

    in Amsterdam, **3:** *89*
    being loaded on trains, **1:** *115, 164*
    from Budapest, **1:** 110
    escape attempt by, **2:** 74
    finding destinations for, **1:** 162-163
    from Hungary, **1:** 34
    killed in Latvia, **3:** 4
    loss of possessions by, **1:** 37-38, 51
    in Lublin, **3:** 30
    in Minsk, **3:** 65
    in Mogilev-Podolski, **3:** 68, 69
    photographs of, **1:** *173,* **2:** *154,* **3:** *175,* **4:** *136*
    from Warsaw ghetto, **4:** *5*
Destruction of Jewish property. *See* Anti-Jewish measures; Synagogues, destruction of
Detention camps
    Bergen-Belsen, **1:** 79-80
    in France, **3:** 111, 112
    in Great Britain, **2:** 73
    Gurs, **2:** 79-81
    Kistarcsa, **2:** 154-155
    Lublin, **3:** 31
    Mauthausen, **3:** 46
    Theresienstadt, **4:** 57
    Westerbork (Netherlands), **3:** 88, 89, 90
Diaries
    Czerniaków, Adam, **1:** 143, **4:** 117, 123, 125, 198-199
    Frank, Anne, **2:** 28-31, **3:** 12-13
    Frank, Hans, **2:** 35
    Franz, Kurt, **4:** *67*
    ghetto, **3:** 134
    Goebbels, Joseph, **2:** 102
    Kaplan, Chaim A., **2:** 142, **4:** 117, 198
    Korczak, Janusz, **2:** 161
    prisoners at Auschwitz, **1:** 47
    Rudashevski, Yitskhok, **4:** 102, 105
    Tenenbaum, Mordechai, **4:** 54
    Warsaw ghetto, **4:** 120, 126
    Zelkowicz, Josef, **3:** 22-23
    See also Autobiographies
    See also Literature of the Holocaust
Dictatorship, appeal of, **2:** 3
Diels, Rudolf, **2:** 60, 61
Dirlewanger, Oskar, **1:** 166
Diseases
    in ghettos, **4:** 60
    Nazi experiments about, **3:** 56, 57-58, 59
    at Skarżysko-Kamienna, **4:** 10
    Warsaw ghetto, **4:** 120
Displaced persons, **1:** 166-170
    support by Joint Distribution Committee (JDC), **2:** 138-139
    United States Army and, **4:** 90-92
Documents for Jews
    forgeries by underground groups, **2:** 74, **3:** 35
    smuggling into Poland of forged, **3:** 140
    Vatican assistance in providing, **1:** 120
    See also ID cards
    See also Protective documents for Jews

193

INDEX

Documents of the Holocaust
  accumulated by Polish courts, **4**: 81-82
  Anne Frank house archives, **2**: 32
  from the Białystok and Warsaw ghettos, **1**: 90
  chronicles of the Łódź Ghetto, **3**: 25
  collected for postwar trials in Germany, **4**: 78
  Conversations with an Executioner (Moczarski), **4**: 41
  efforts to declassify and publicize, **3**: 99, 100
  Getto Walczy (The Ghetto Fighters) (Edelman), **1**: 96
  hidden in Oneg Shabbat archive, **3**: 180
  Himmler's "Some Thoughts on the Treatment of Alien Populations in the East," **3**: 40
  Hitler memo, **1**: *187*
  Jewish Historical Institute, **4**: 129
  Kaltenbrunner reports, **2**: 144
  the most revealing, **2**: 102
  Nazi Party platform objectives, **3**: 83
  Nuremberg Trial, **4**: 73-74
  from Operational Squads, **3**: 107
  Polish-Soviet Nazi Crimes Investigation Commission, **3**: 44
  proving construction of gas chamber, **3**: 80
  questions about reliability of, **2**: 101, 102
  speeches by Arthur Seyss-Inquart, **4**: 8
  Tenenbaum collection, **4**: 54, 55
  Wannsee Protocol (Eichmann), **4**: 113
  Wisliceny, Dieter, affidavits, **4**: 142
  See also Diaries
  See also Museums
Dominican Republican Settlement Association, **4**: 95
Domincan Republic's position at Evian Conference, **1**: 190
Donat, Alexander, **3**: 44
Don't Trust a Fox in the Chicken Coop or a Jew at His Word (Bauer), **1**: *32*
Dora-Mittelbau, **1**: 170-172
  death marches from, **1**: 153
Dora-Nordhausen. *See* Dora-Mittelbau
Drancy, **1**: 172-174
Dreyfus, Alfred, **3**: 147
Dror (Deror), **4**: 147
Drumont, Eduard, **1**: 30-31
Dünaburg. *See* Dvinsk
Dutch Nazis, **3**: 86
Dvinsk, **1**: 174-176

E

Eastern Belorussia, **1**: 71-73
Eastern Europe
  Nazi anti-Jewish legislation for, **1**: 27
  Nazi treatment of laborers from, **2**: 15
  youth movements in, **4**: 146-149
Eastern Galicia. *See* Lvov
East Germany trials of war criminals, **4**: 79

Economic-Administrative Main Office, **1**: 176-177
  administration of Auschwitz-Birkenau, **1**: 194
  administration of Bergen-Belsen, **1**: 70
  contradictory goals, **4**: 31
Economic boycott against Nazi Germany, **1**: 102, 103, **4**: 140, 143
Economic measures against Jews
  ban against possessing cash, **2**: 164
  Nazi boycott of businesses, **1**: 102, 103
  as precursor to "Final Solution," **2**: 9
  seizures of Jew's apartments, **1**: 36-37, 38, **4**: 99, 100, 109
  See also Aryanization
  See also Fines on Jewish communities
  See also Forced labor
Economic structure in Warsaw ghetto, **4**: 121-122
Edelman, Marak, **1**: 96
Edelstein, Jacob, **1**: *177*-178
Education, Jewish. *See* Schools
Eichmann, Adolf, **1**: 178-181
  conflict over deportations to Kistarcsa, **2**: 155
  duties in SD, **4**: 6
  impact of his trial, **3**: 13
  and Madagascar Plan, **3**: 41
  photographs of, **1**: *178*, *180*
  plan to deport Third Reich Jews to Poland, **3**: 92-93
  in Prague, **1**: 98
  role in emigration of Jews from Austria, **1**: 51-52
  search for way to exterminate Jews, **4**: 156
  strategy for deportations, **1**: 163-164
Eicke, Theodor, **1**: 181-182
  role in SS-Death's-Head Units, **4**: 32, 33
Einstein, Albert, **1**: 30
Elizabeth (Queen of England), **1**: 66-67
Elkes, Elchanan, **1**: *182*-183
El Salvadoran protection of Hungarian Jews, **3**: 35
Emigration of Jews
  after the war ended, **1**: 168-170
  from Austria, **1**: 51-52
  barriers to, **3**: 158, **4**: 98
  from Bohemia and Moravia, **1**: 98
  expulsion of Polish Jews from Germany, **2**: 54
  financial assistance for, **1**: 51
  Generalplan Ost, **2**: 41-43
  from Germany, **1**: 86, **2**: 51, 55-56, 106
  loss of property during, **1**: 37, 51
  Nazi euphemisms for, **4**: 28
  Nazi prohibition of, **1**: 26
  Nazi promotion of, **2**: 8-9
  Nazi resettlement plans, **3**: 40-41
  from Poland, **3**: 129
  as precursor to deportations, **1**: 161, 180
  to Siberia, **2**: 42
  through Mogilev-Podolski, **3**: 68

  See also Aliya Bet
  See also Madagascar Plan
  See also Nisko and Lublin Plan
Employment. *See* Jobs
Endlösung. *See* "Final Solution"
Endre, László, **1**: 183-*184*
England. *See* Great Britain
Enterdungsaktion. *See* Aktion 1005
Erdöl Raffinerie (German company), **1**: 42
Erntefest ("Harvest Festival"), **1**: 184-186
  as end of Aktion (Operation) Reinhard, **1**: 8
Escapes and escape attempts
  Aktion 1005 prisoners, **1**: 95
  Auschwitz, **1**: 46-47, 48
  to Belorussian forests, **1**: 73
  Bełżec, **1**: 77
  Chełmno, **1**: 116
  by children at Budzyń, **1**: 111
  by Danish Jews, **1**: 159
  from deportation trains, **1**: 68
  Drancy (French transit camp), **1**: 173
  Dvinsk, **1**: 175
  France, **2**: 23, 24
  Gesia Street concentration camp, **4**: 134
  Grodno ghetto, **2**: 74
  Jakuba Street camp in Łódź, **3**: 24
  by Jews who built Hitler's staff quarters, **3**: 34
  Kielce ghetto, **2**: 153
  Kraków ghetto, **2**: 170
  by Lithuanian Jews, **3**: 17, 18
  Lvov ghetto, **3**: 39
  Majdanek, **3**: 43
  Minsk, **3**: 65
  Netherlands, **3**: 90
  Ponary, **3**: 141
  from prison, **2**: 7
  by prisoners, **3**: 173-174, **4**: 65
  by prisoners at Babi Yar, **1**: 55
  by prisoners of the Sonderkommando 1004, **1**: 4-5
  by protectors of Frank, Anne **2**: 28
  Riga, **3**: 176-177
  Rovno, **3**: 186
  Skarżysko-Kamienna, **4**: 10
  Slovakia, **4**: 13
  Sobibór, **4**: 18
  to the Soviet interior, **1**: 72
  by Soviet prisoners of war, **3**: 48
  Starachowice, **4**: 36
  Treblinka, **4**: 65, 68-69
  in Ukraine, **4**: 86
"Essay on the Inequality of Human Races" (Gobineau), **3**: 149, 150
Estonia camps, **3**: 17-18, **4**: 105
Ethics, universal code of medical, **3**: 53
Ethnic Germans. *See* Volksdeutsche
Ethnic Germans' Welfare Office (VoMi), **4**: 106
Eugenics, **3**: 151
Europa Plan, **3**: 52, **4**: 13, 142
Europe
  antisemitism in, **1**: 28-29, 30-32

INDEX

Nazi dilemma of what to do with Jews in, **2:** 10
roots of fascism in, **2:** 1-2
treatment of Gypsies in, **2:** 84-87
Euthanasia Program, **1:** 186-189
    legal rationale for, **3:** 53
    testimony of Victor Brack regarding termination of mentally disabled in Germany, **4:** 199-200
    See also Zyklon B
Evacuation of the Soviet Union, **4:** 22-23
Evian Conference, **1:** 189-192
Evil, American fascination with Nazis', **3:** 13
Executions by Nazis
    Aryans who aided Jews, **1:** 2
    partisans, **3:** *65*
    prisoners at Auschwitz, **1:** 40
Exodus 1947 (ship), **1:** *12*
Experiments, Nazi, **3:** 52-61
    See also Nazi doctors
Expulsion of Jews. *See* Emigration of Jews
Extermination camps, **1:** 192-194
    Aktion Reinhard, **1:** 6-7
    Bełżec, **1:** 7, 73-77
    Birkenau, **1:** 41-42, 194
    Chełmno, **1:** 114-118
    Globocnik, Odilo, **2:** *65-66*
    Janówska, **2:** 124-126
    Majdanek, **1:** 184-186, **2:** 30, **3:** 42-45
    map of, **1:** 193
    in Poland, **3:** 136-137
    processing of prisoners at, **2:** 38-39
    rescue efforts for prisoners in, **3:** 180
    Sobibór, **1:** 7, **3:** 119-120, **4:** 15
    Treblinka, **1:** 7, **4:** 63-69
    See also Auschwitz
    See also Concentration camps
    See also Gas chambers
Extermination plan for Jews. *See* "Final Solution"
Extermination vans. *See* Gas vans

F

Fascism, **2:** 1-4
    definition of, **1:** 34
    fascist partisans in Poland, **3:** 117
    fascists' rise to power in Italy, **2:** 118-120
    in Great Britain, **2:** 71
Fascist Doctrine, The (Mussolini), **2:** 2
Federal Republic of Germany, trials of war criminals by, **4:** 76-81
Feiner, Leon, **2:** 4-*5*
Fiction. *See* Literature of the Holocaust
Fighting Ghetto, The, **3:** 120
Fighting Organization of Pioneer Jewish Youth, **2:** 5-7, **3:** 9
    Aharon Liebeskind's role, **3:** 9
    Frumka Plotnicka's role, **3:** 122-123
Films about Nazis, **3:** 13, 76
"Final Solution," **2:** 7-13
    applied to Italy, **2:** 120
    in Baltic and Belorussian areas, **3:** 28
    effect on American Jews, **1:** 19

Eichmann's role, **1:** 180
Erntefest ("Harvest Festival"), **1:** 184-186
exclusion of Scandinavian countries from, **1:** 158
financing for, **1:** 38, **4:** 8
in France, **2:** 23
in the Generalgouvernement, **1:** 6
Germans' attitudes about, **2:** 58-59
Göring orders Heydrich to prepare a plan for the "Final Solution," **4:** 190
Heydrich's role, **2:** 89
Himmler's role, **2:** 90-91
Hitler bans public reference to, **4:** 191
Hitler's role, **2:** 95-97
Hitler Youth's role, **2:** 99
Hoss' recollections about, **2:** 107
Hungarian Labor Service System and, **2:** 110
in Hungary, **2:** 114
impact of Madagascar Plan on, **3:** 40
Jewish badge and, **1:** 59
Korherr Report, **2:** 162
legally defined stages of, **4:** 75-76
Nazi acceptance of, **2:** 11
Nazi regulations that permitted, **1:** 27
Nazis' reasons for using Poland for, **3:** 139
origins in antisemitism, **1:** 33
outside world's knowledge of, **1:** 20
in Poland, **3:** 136-139
role of deportations, **1:** 164-165
SS role, **4:** 30-31
use of Auschwitz and Majdanek for, **1:** 129
Wannsee Conference, **4:** 113-114
West German courts' view of, **4:** 80-81
See also Anti-Jewish legislation
See also Anti-Jewish measures
See also Concentration camps
See also Deportations
See also Extermination camps
See also Ghettos
See also Liquidation of camps
See also Liquidation of ghettos
See also Mass murders by Nazis
See also Nazi deceptions
See also SD
See also Victims and survivors
Financial reparations
    current status of, **4:** 80
    excuses for not paying, **4:** 48-49
    from Germany, **2:** 139
    paid by I. G. Farben, **2:** 117
    Simon Wiesenthal Center role, **3:** 75
    U.S. Office of Special Investigations role, **3:** 99-100
Fines on Jewish communities
    in Austria, **4:** 98
    kinds of payments accepted Nazis, **3:** 34
    for murder of German diplomat, **1:** 26, 37
    Nazi uses of the payments, **4:** 87
    Paris, **3:** 37

Vienna, **4:** 100
Vilna, **4:** 103
See also Ransom payments to Nazis
Flick (German company), **2:** 115, 117
Food deprivation by Nazis
    among German troops, **1:** 187
    among Poles, **2:** 40
    cannibalism as result of, **3:** 50
    at Drancy (French transit camp), **1:** 173
    in Dvinsk ghetto, **1:** 175
    Frank, Hans, statement about, **3:** 133
    Jew's response to, **3:** 176, **4:** 115
    in Kharkov, **2:** 150
    in Kovno, **2:** 164
    in Łódź, **3:** 21
    by Lohse, Hinrich, **3:** 28
    Warsaw ghetto, **4:** 121
Forced labor, **2:** 13-18
    Auschwitz, **1:** 42-43
    Belgium, **1:** 65
    Dachau, **1:** *145*
    defined as a crime, **4:** 76
    and forced sterilization, **3:** 59
    of French workers, **2:** 19
    Gross-Rosen, **2:** 77
    Himmler's role, **2:** 90
    of Hungarian Jews, **2:** 108-110
    Italy, **2:** 121
    of Jewish conscripts in Hungary, **2:** *109*
    Jews in Warsaw ghetto, **4:** 121
    Judenräte role, **2:** 141-142
    Kovno, **2:** 163-164
    Organisation Schmelt, **3:** 108-110
    Poland, **3:** 131-133, 137-139
    postwar reparations to laborers, **2:** 117
    reliance of German army on Jews, **1:** 8
    See also Jewish prisoners' tasks
    See also Labor camps
Forced marches. *See* Death marches
Forced sterilization by Nazis
    of Germans with black fathers, **1:** 186-187
    of Gypsies, **2:** 82, 84
    of Jewish women, **1:** 123-124
    medical experiments with, **3:** 59-60
    and Nazi concept of Mischlinge, **3:** 66, 67
    Nazi rationales for, **3:** 53, 59
    numbers of persons subjected to, **1:** 188
    Proposal for the Sterilization of 2-3 Million Jewish Workers, **4:** 189-190
Foreign workers in Germany, **2:** 13, 14-15
Fossoli camp, **2:** 121
Fountain of Life, **3:** 151, **4:** 30
France, **2:** 18-26
    antisemitism in, **1:** 28, 30-31
    Benoît, Marie, **1:** *78-79*
    Catholics, **1:** 120
    concentration camps in, **3:** 79-80
    deportation of Jews from, **1:** 164
    Drancy (transit camp), **1:** 172-174
    fascist groups in, **2:** 4
    Gurs (detention camp), **2:** 79-81

INDEX

France (continued)
French police, role of, **2**: 35-36
Great Britain, relationship with, **2**: 68
Gypsies, **2**: 85
Jewish badge, **1**: 59, 61
Jewish underground groups, **3**: 171
Jewish youth movements, **4**: 150-151
Le Chambon-sur-Lignon, **3**: 5-6
map of Vichy and occupied, **2**: *19*
Oberg, Carl Albrecht, **3**: 98
policy about deportations, **3**: 152
Protestants, **1**: 122
racism in, **3**: 151
SS destruction of entire village, **3**: 108, *109*
See also Paris
See also Vichy government
Frank, Anne, **2**: *26-33*, 27
at Bergen-Belsen, **1**: 82
Frank, Hans, **2**: *33-35*
initiation of "Final Solution" in Generalgouvernement, **3**: 138-139
policies in the Generalgouvernement, **3**: 131-133
role in Nisko and Lublin Plan, **3**: 94
statement about disposing of Jews, **3**: 136
Frank, Margot, **1**: 82, **2**: 2627
Frank, Otto, **2**: 26-27, 28, 30, 32
Freemasons, **3**: 146, 183
Freezing, Nazi experiments on, **3**: 54, 56
Freight cars. *See* Deportation trains
French communists, **2**: 80
French Jews, deportations of, **2**: 23
French police, **2**: 35-36
French Resistance, **1**: 62, **2**: 19
French police and, **2**: 36
prisoners taken by Germans, **3**: 79-80
French Resistance leaders
Cohn, Marianne, **1**: *124*
Deffaught, Jean, **1**: 153-154
Rayman, Marcel, **3**: 156-157
French zone denazification, **1**: 154
Freudiger, Fülöp, **2**: 36-37
Fritsch, Werner Freiherr von, **2**: 105
Fritz Schulz Works, **4**: 62

G

Gas chambers, **2**: 37-3
Auschwitz, **1**: 41-42
Bełżec, **1**: 74-75, 76-77
construction at Auschwitz, **1**: 45
Dachau, **1**: 147
dismantling of, **1**: 48
documented construction of, **3**: 80
extermination of Jews at Auschwitz, **1**: 46
extermination of Jews at Bełżec, **1**: 75-76
Himmler's decision to use, **2**: 80
Majdanek, **2**: *38*, **3**: 43
Natzweiler-Struthof, **3**: 89
Sobibór, **4**: 15
Treblinka, **4**: 64, 66-67
See also Zyklon B

Gassing experiments on Germans, **4**: 139
Gas vans, **2**: 37
at Chełmno, **1**: 115-116
Nazi account of **4**: 189
survivor account of, **4**: 71
use in Belorussian ghettos, **1**: 72
use in Kharkov, **2**: 150
use in Ukraine, **4**: 86
See also Zyklon B
Gas-warfare experiments by Nazis, **3**: 57
Geburtenrückgang (Decline in the Birthrate) (Korherr), **2**: 162
Geheime Staatspolizei. *See* Gestapo
Generalgouvernement, **2**: 39-41
capital of, **2**: 167
compulsory labor laws, **2**: 16
Erntefest ("Harvest Festival"), **1**: 184-186
Hitler's plan for, **2**: 95
Krüger, Friedrich Wilhelm, **2**: 174
map of, **2**: *40*
partisans, **3**: 117-118
refugees from, **3**: 160
Ukrainian part, **4**: 85
See also Kraków
See also Lublin
See also Lvov
See also Radom
See also Warsaw
General Jewish Fighting Organization, **2**: 165
Generalplan Ost, **2**: 41-43
Genetic research by Nazis, **3**: 53, 58
Genocide, **2**: 43-46
legal standards applying to, **4**: 79
Nazi process of, **3**: 152
Genocide (Wiesenthal Center film), **3**: 76
Gens, Jacob, **2**: *46-47*
leadership in Vilna, **4**: 104, 105
relation with Josef Glazman, **2**: 64-65
and Vilna Communists, **4**: 89
German Armament Works, **2**: 124
German Christians movement, **1**: 121
German companies
factories inside ghettos, **2**: 170, **3**: 21, **4**: 121, 123
protests of loss of Jews' labor, **3**: 139
that built gas chambers, **1**: 45
that employed Jews from the ghetto, **2**: 17
use of forced labor, **1**: 42, **2**: *14*
use of Jewish prisoners, **1**: 176, **2**: 77, 116
use of prisoners, **3**: 79, **4**: 9, 91-92
See also I. G. Farben
See also SS companies
German Democratic Republic trials of war criminals, **4**: 79
German Earth and Stone Works, Ltd., **2**: 76, **3**: 79, 91
German girls' organization, **2**: 99
German invasion of the Soviet Union, **3**: 103
British reaction to, **2**: 68
and the "Final Solution," **2**: 11
Hungarians' role in, **2**: 111

Germanization, definition of, **3**: 93
German Jewish Children's Aid (GJCA), **3**: 166
German Jews
Central Union of German Citizens of Jewish Faith, **1**: 112-114
"equalization" with Germans, **3**: 67
Hirsh, Otto, leadership of, **2**: 91-92
Hitler's plans for resettlement of, **2**: 9
in Minsk, **3**: 65
murder of, by Nazis, **1**: 72, **3**: 64
privileges afforded by Nazis to, **1**: 51
German laws against Jews. *See* anti-Jewish legislation
German military
initial opposition to Nazis, **2**: 54
Luftwaffe, **2**: 68, **3**: 54
Mischlinge in, **3**: 67-68
Nazi medical experiments on behalf of, **3**: 54-58
recruitment tactics, **2**: 99
Reichenau, Walter von, **3**: 163-164
role in "Final Solution," **4**: 31
temporary halt of murders of Jews by, **3**: 139
See also German weapons factories
See also Operational Squads
See also Ukrainian Military Police
German occupation
Belgium, **1**: 63-65
Białystok, **1**: 88-89
Bohemia, Moravia and Silesia, **1**: 97
Croatia, **1**: 139
Denmark, **1**: 158
Dvinsk, **1**: 174
France, **2**: 19, 21, 23
Grodno, **2**: 73
Hungary, **1**: 107, 109, **2**: 112
Kovno, **2**: 163
Kraków, **2**: 167-168
Latvia, **3**: 2-3
Lithuania, **3**: 15-16, 17-18
Łódź, **3**: 19-21
Lublin, **3**: 30
Lutsk, **3**: 33-34
Lvov, **3**: 37
Netherlands, **3**: 86-87
northern Italy, **2**: 120-121
Paris, **3**: 111
Poland, **3**: 124-125, 130
Riga, **3**: 175
Rovno, **3**: 185
Soviet territories, **4**: 22, 23
Tarnów, **4**: 52-53
Ternopol, **4**: 55
Vilna, **4**: 103
Vitebsk, **4**: 106
Warsaw, **4**: 117
Western Belorussia, **1**: 70
Zamość, **4**: 152
German-occupied territories
anti-Jewish legislation in, **1**: 27
anti-Jewish measures in, **2**: 56
centers of Aktion 1005 activity in, **1**: 5-6

INDEX

concentration camp prisoners from, **1:** 128
cooperation with and resistance to Nazis in, **3:** 114
Gypsies, **2:** 85
map of Operational Squads in, **3:** *101*
Mischlinge policy in, **3:** 66-67
Nazi tolerance of homosexuality in, **2:** 105
Volksdeutsche, **4:** 107
See also Generalgouvernement
German organizations classified as criminal by the IMT, **4:** 72
German police. *See* Gestapo
German prisoners
    criminals, **3:** 121-122
    Jewish, **1:** 132-133
    at Mauthausen, **3:** 46
    Nazi medical experiments on, **3:** 57
    NN (Nacht Und Nebel) prisoners, **3:** 80
    political prisoners, **1:** 104
    status of, **1:** 131
German prisoners of war, Jews classified as, **2:** 110
Germans
    attitudes towards Nazi treatment of Jews, **2:** 58
    Hitler's plan to resettle in the east, **2:** 41-43
    married to Jews. *See* Mixed marriages
    See also Mischlinge
    See also Volksdeutsche
German Vermin-Combating Corporation (DEGESCH), **4:** 157
German war effort
    Aktion Reinhard impact on, **1:** 7-8
    forced-labor and, **2:** 13-18
German weapons factories
    at Dachau, **1:** *145*
    at Dora-Mittelbau, **1:** 170, *171*
    at Gross-Rosen, **2:** 78
    at Lublin, **3:** 31
    at Lvov, **2:** 124
    at Sauchsenhausen, **4:** 1
    in Silesia and Sudetenland, **3:** 109
German women, Nazi ideal of, **2:** 99
Germany, **2:** 47-59
    antisemitism in, **1:** 28-30, 32-33
    British appeasement of, **2:** 69-70
    Catholics, **1:** 119-120
    concentration camps in, **1:** 133
    imported laborers, **2:** 13
    Jewish badge, **1:** 60-61
    Jewish refugees from, **3:** 157-158
    Jewish youth movements, **4:** 145-146
    map of, 1938, **2:** *48*
    map of, 1942, **2:** *57*
    Protestants, **1:** 122
    reaction to trials of war criminals, **4:** 76
    Weimar Republic, **1:** 84, **2:** 49-50
    See also East Germany
    See also West Germany
Germany Is Our Problem (Morgenthau), **3:** 71

German youth, ideological training of, **2:** 99
Gestapo, **2:** 59-62
    murder of Jewish women, **3:** *185*
    photograph of, **2:** *60*
    "preventative" arrests by, **2:** 82
    relationship to French police, **2:** 36
    relationship to SD, **4:** 4
    relationship with Reich Security Main Office (RSHA), **3:** 161-163
Getter, Matylda, **2:** 63
Ghetto Fighters' Museum, **4:** 155
Ghettos, **3:** 26-27
    "A" and "B" in Grodno, **2:** 73
    alternatives used in Germany, **2:** 57
    armed resistance in, **3:** 172-173
    badges for categories of Jews, **1:** 58
    Belorussia, **1:** 71, 72
    Białystok, **1:** 71, 89-91
    Budapest, **1:** 109, **2:** 114
    Budapest international, **1:** 110, **3:** 36
    Derechin, **1:** 38
    Dvinsk, **1:** 174-175
    for German Jews in Minsk, **3:** 64, 65
    Jewish cultural activities, **3:** 134-135, **4:** *103*, 122, 171
    Jewish youth movements in, **4:** 147-148
    Kharkov, **2:** 150
    Kherson, **2:** 150-152
    Kielce, **2:** 152
    Kovno, **2:** 163-164, **4:** 145
    Kraków, **2:** 5-7, 167-169
    in Lithuania, **3:** 17
    Łódź, **3:** 21, 25-27
    Lublin, **3:** 31-32
    Lublin "small ghetto," **3:** 32
    Lutsk, **3:** 34
    Lvov, **3:** 37-38
    Minsk, **1:** 72-73, **3:** 64
    Mogilev-Podolski, **3:** 69
    Nazi burning of, **4:** *130*, 132
    Nazi euphemism for, **4:** 28
    Nazi managers of, **1:** 39
    Operational Squad role, **3:** 103
    Order by Ludwig Fischer on the Establishment of a Ghetto in Warsaw, **4:** 197-198
    photographer of, **1:** 182
    photographs of, **3:** *20*, **4:** *120*, *127*, *130*
    in Poland, **3:** 133-135
    psychology of survivors from, **4:** 47-48
    Riga, **3:** 176
    Riga "German," **3:** 176
    Riga "small," **3:** 176, 177
    Rovno, **3:** 186
    sale of possessions by Jews in, **2:** *169*
    Tarnów, **4:** 53
    Ternopol, **4:** 56
    Theresienstadt, **4:** 56, 57-61
    turned into concentration camps, **2:** 164-165
    turned into labor camps, **3:** 23, 38
    Vilna, **4:** 102, 104-105
    Vilna No. 1 and No. 2, **4:** 103
    Vitebsk, **4:** 106
    Warsaw, **4:** 119-121

    See also Apartments
    See also Certificates of employment for Jews
    See also Forced labor
    See also Jewish ghetto police
GJCA (German Jewish Children's Aid), **3:** 166
Glazer, Gesja ("Albina"), **2:** 165
Glazman, Josef, **2:** 63-65, *64*
Globocnik, Odilo, **2:** *65*-66
Goebbels, Joseph, **2:** *66*-67
    activities in Berlin, **1:** 84
    use of Nazi euphemisms, **4:** 27
Goedsche, Hermann, **1:** 30
Goldszmit, Henryk. *See* Korczak, Janusz
Gordonia, **4:** 147
Government control of the individual, **2:** 1-2
Graz, **1:** 52
Great Britain, **2:** 67-73
    declaration of war on Hungary, **2:** 111
    effect of World War II on its Empire, **2:** 69
    evacuation of children to the U.S., **3:** 166-167
    immigration policy, **2:** 71-72
    impact of *Protocols of the Elders of Zion*, **3:** 147
    policy towards Jewish refugees, **3:** 160-161
    position at Evian Conference, **1:** 190
    Protestants, **1:** 122
    racism in, **3:** 152
    reaction to Madagascar Plan, **3:** 42
    restrictions on immigration to Palestine, **1:** 10-11, 17
    See also British military
    See also British zone
Great Depression and U.S. response to Holocaust, **1:** 18, **4:** 93
Greece, deportations of Jews from, **4:** 142
Greek Jews
    deportation from Bulgaria, **1:** 165
    medical experiments on, **1:** 44
Greek partisans, **3:** 119
Greiser, Arthur, **2:** 44-45
Grodno, **2:** 73-75
Grojanowski, Jacob, **1:** 116
Grosman, Haika, **2:** 75-76
Gross-Rosen, **2:** 76-79
    death marches, **1:** 151-152
Grüninger, Paul, **2:** 79
Guards in camps. *See* Camp staff
Guards in Polish ghettos, **3:** 133
Gurs, **2:** 79-81
Gusen, **3:** 46
Gustav V (King of Sweden), **4:** 108
Gypsies, **2:** 81-87
    at Chełmno, **1:** 116, 117
    deportation from Austria, **1:** 53
    extermination at Auscahwitz, **1:** 46
    family camp at Auschwitz, **1:** 41, **2:** 84
    in Latvia, **3:** 3
    medical experiments on, **3:** 156
    murdered at Bełżec, **1:** 77
    Nazi classification of, **1:** 144, **2:** 84

197

INDEX

Gypsies (continued)
    Nazi medical experiments on, **3:** 56, 59, 60
    Nazi murders of at Babi Yar, **1:** 55
    photographs of, **2:** *82, 85*
    at Płasów, **3:** 121
    Ustaša extermination of, **1:** 140

H

Haavara Agreement, **4:** 140
Hachenburg, Hanus, **4:** 59
Haluts youth movements. *See* Youth movements
Harrison, Earl G., **4:** 91
"Harvest Festival." *See* Erntefest ("Harvest Festival")
HASAG (German company), **4:** 9
Ha-Shomer ha-Tsa'ir, **1:** 21,*22,* 23, **4:** 145, 149
    in Kraków, **2:** 170
He-Haluts Ha-Lohem. *See* Fighting Organization of Pioneer Jewish Youth
Heinkel Works (German company), **4:** 1
Hepatitis experiments by Nazis, **3:** 57
Hermann Göring Works, **3:** 92, **4:** 35
Herzegovinan, **1:** 139
Herzl, Theodore, **1:** 10
Heydrich, Reinhard, **2:** 87-89
    Aktion named for, **1:** 6
    decision to murder Soviet prisoners of war, **3:** 145
    deportation order for Gypsies, **2:** 83
    effect on the Gestapo, **2:** 61
    guidelines for Judenräte, **2:** 139-140
    instigation of the Jewish badge, **1:** 58
    instructions for measures against Jews **4:** 186-187
    Jewish policy for Poland, **3:** 130-131
    photograph, **2:** *88*
    powers over Jews, **1:** 26, 37
    role in establishing ghettos, **3:** 103
    role in Generalplan Ost, **2:** 41
    role in Nazi medical experiments, **3:** 56
High-altitude experiments by Nazis, **3:** 54, 55
Himmler, Heinrich, **2:** *89-91*
    cancellation of Nisko and Lublin Plan, **3:** 94
    effect on the Gestapo, **2:** 61
    negotiations with Allies over Jews, **3:** 139
    plan for expelling Jews and Poles, **3:** 40
    policy on Gypsies, **2:** 83, 86
    powers in Austria, **1:** 50
    release of Jewish prisoners in 1944, **2:** 149
    role in construction of Auschwitz, **1:** 40
    role in "Final Solution," **2:** 10
    role in Generalplan Ost, **2:** 42
    role in Nazi medical experiments, **3:** 54
    and the SS, **4:** 30
    visit to Sobibór, **4:** 18
    visit to Treblinka, **4:** 68
Hindenberg, Paul von, **2:** 50
Hirsch, Otto, **2:** 91-92
Hitler, Adolf, **2:** 92-97
    assassination attempt on, **3:** 29, 67, 73, 85
    bodyguards, **4:** 28
    construction of staff quarters, **3:** 34
    construction of underground home for, **2:** 77
    document from, **1:** *187*
    interest in Mischlinge, **3:** 67-68
    and the Madagascar Plan, **3:** 41
    Mein Kampf, **3:** *61-62*
    opinion about *Protocols of the Elders of Zion*, **3:** 147-148
    photographs of, **2:** *3, 93*
    Political Testament, **4:** *177-179*
    practice of "institutional Darwinism," **2:** 33
    promotion of emigration of Jews, **2:** 9-10
    relationship with I. G. Farben, **2:** 115-116
    relationship with the Nazi Party, **3:** 81
    rise to power, **2:** 50-55, 69, 94
    statements about the "Jewish question," **2:** 8, **3:** 61, 94
    views about Communism, **3:** 103
Hitlerjugend. *See* Hitler Youth
Hitler's *Political Testament*, **4:** 177-179
Hitler Youth, **2:** 97-99
Hoescht (German company), **2:** 115, 117
Holland. *See* Netherlands
Holocaust
    denial of, **2:** 100-104
    the enigma of, **4:** 45-46
    legally defined stages of, **4:** 75-76
    origin of the word, **2:** 100
Holocaust literature. *See* Literature of the Holocaust
Holocaust Martyrs' and Heroes' Remembrance Authority. *See* Yad Vashem
"Holocaust 1944" (Ranasinghe), **4:** 46
Holocaust Remembrance Day in the United States, **4:** 137
Holocaust survivor accounts
    about Auschwitz, **1:** 40-41
    about children in hiding, **3:** 166
    by a Gypsy, **2:** 83
    Majdanek, **3:** 44
    a mass murder by Nazis, **1:** 185
    stories, **3:** 13-14
    Stutthof **4:** 43, 44-45
    See also Autobiographies
    See also Diaries
    See also Poems of the Holocaust
Holocaust survivors
    in Austria, **1:** 54
    in Budapest, **1:** 110
    documentary (*The Long Way Home*), **3:** 76
    photographs of, **1:** *42, 80,* **3:** *50*
    psychology of, **4:** 45-50
    viewed as heroes/heroines, **3:** 14
    who emigrated to Palestine, **1:** 12-13
    See also Displaced persons
    See also Victims and Survivors
Holocaust (TV series), **4:** 78
Home Army (Armia Krajowa), **1:** 1, 2, **2:** 170, **3:** 114, **4:** 88-89, 117
    aid to Jews, **4:** 130
    Warsaw Polish uprising by, **4:** 134
Home purchase agreement, Nazi, **1:** 37
Homosexuality in the Third Reich, **2:** 104-105
Homosexuals, badges for suspected, **1:** 61, **4:** *2*
"Horror propaganda," **1:** 102
Horthy, Miklós, **2:** *105-106*
    intervention at Kistarcsa, **2:** 155
    ouster by Arrow Cross Party, **2:** 112
    role in invasion of Yugoslavia, **2:** 111
Höss, Rudolf, **2:** *107-108*
    fictional account of, **3:** 13
    quoted about Auschwitz, **1:** 44-45
    quoted about extermination procedures, **1:** 43
    search for way to exterminate Jews, **4:** 156
Hotel Royale, **1:** *191*
Hull, Cordell, **3:** 70
Human rights principle, **1:** 136, **3:** 100, 137
Hungarian army, **2:** 1-8,110, 113
Hungarian Jews
    attitude towards resistance, **2:** 148
    mass murder of at Kamenets-Podolski, **2:** 145-146
    at Mauthausen, **3:** *49-50*
Hungarian Labor Service System, **2:** 108-110
Hungarian police, **2:** 83, *112*
Hungary, **2:** 110-115
    antisemitism in, **1:** 31
    assistance to Jewish refugees, **3:** 160
    Catholics, **1:** 121
    companies that used forced labor, **2:** 108
    deportations of Jews from, **1:** 165, **4:** 142
    Eichmann's extermination of Jews in, **1:** *182-183*
    Gypsies, **2:** 86
    Jewish badge, **1:** 60
    Jewish leader Fülöp Freudiger, **2:** 36-37
    Lutz, Carl, rescue of Jews in, **3:** 34-36
    Nazi leader, László Endre, **1:** *183-184*
    Protestants, **1:** 122
    racist political movements in, **3:** 152
    Volksdeutsche, **4:** 108
    War Refugee Board and, **4:** 96, 114
    See also Arrow Cross Party
    See also Budapest
    See also Horthy, Miklós, **2:** *105-106*

I

ID cards
    ghetto soup kitchen, **2:** 152
    Hitler Youth, **2:** *98*

INDEX

for Jews, **2:** *53*
  Jews' use of fake Aryan papers, **4:** 13
  See also Certificates of employment for Jews
  See also Documents for Jews
I. G. Farben, **2:** 115-118
  investment in Zyklon B gas, **4:** 157
  use of Jewish prisoners, **2:** 77
Immigration to Palestine. *See* Israel; Palestine
Immunization experiments by Nazis, **3:** 58
IMT. *See* International Military Tribunal (IMT)
"In Auschwitz-Birkenau" (Cohen), **1:** 40-41
Institute for the Investigation of the Jewish Question, **3:** 184
Intellectuals, Nazi persecution of, **2:** 10, **3:** 40, 47
Intergovernmental Committee on Refugees (ICR), **1:** 190-191
International crimes, **1:** 136
"International" ghetto, **1:** 110, **3:** 36, **4:** 110
International law
  principles of, **1:** 136
  regarding legal wars, **4:** 74
  regarding prisoners of war, **2:** 13
International Military Tribunal (IMT), **1:** 134
  See also Nuremberg Trial
International Red Cross operations, **1:** 160, **3:** 50, **4:** 60-61, 174
Internet and the Holocaust, **3:** 76, 83
Internment camps. *See* Detention camps
Isolationist policy of the U.S., **4:** 93
Isolation of Jews. *See* Anti-Jewish measures; Ghettos
Israel
  founding of, **1:** 10-11
  immigration of displaced Jews to, **1:** 169, **4:** 91
  laws concerning genocide, **2:** 45
  survivors in, **4:** 49
  Yad Vashem memorials and museum, **3:** 76-77
Israeli attitudes towards the Holocaust, **3:** 14
Italians, rescue of Jews by, **1:** 140
Italy, **2:** 118-124
  assistance to Jewish refugees, **3:** 160
  deportation of Jews from, **1:** 165
  fascism, **2:** 1-4
  Gypsies, **2:** 85-86
  Jewish Brigade Group activities, **2:** 128
  map of concentration camps, **2:** *119*
Itelligenz Aktion, **2:** 169

J

Jäger, Karl, **2:** 124
Jakuba Street camp, **3:** 24
Janówska, **2:** 124-126
Japan, antisemitism in, **1:** 33
Japanese assistance to Jewish refugees, **3:** *159*
  Sempo Sugihara's role, **4:** 44-45
Jasenovac, **1:** 139

JDC. *See* Joint Distribution Committee
Jeckeln, Friedrich, **2:** *126*-127
Jeckeln Aktion, **3:** 3
Jehovah's Witnesses, **1:** 144, **2:** 108
Jewish Army, **3:** 171
Jewish badge, **1:** 57-61
  French responses to, **3:** 112
  with Jews' house numbers, **3:** 64
  photographs of, **1:** *59, 60*
  protests in Belgium, **1:** 66
  protests in the Netherlands, **3:** 88
  See also Anti-Jewish measures
Jewish Brigade Group, **2:** 127-129
  in postwar Belgium, **1:** 68
Jewish buildings. *See* Apartments; Aryanization
Jewish businesses. *See* Economic measures against Jews
Jewish Christians, **1:** 58, 61
Jewish collective farms. *See* Kibbutzim
Jewish conspiracy. *See* Protocols of the Elders of Zion
Jewish Coordinating Committee (Netherlands), **3:** 86
Jewish Councils. *See* Judenräte
Jewish cultural activities as spiritual resistance to Nazis, **3:** 171
Jewish Defense Committee (CDJ), **1:** 68
Jewish Diaspora, **1:** 10
Jewish emigrants. *See* Emigration of Jews
Jewish Fighting Organization (ŻOB), **2:** 129-132
  Anielewicz, Mordecai, his influence on, **1:** 23
  origins, **4:** 148
  support from Home Army (Armia Krajowa), **1:** 2
  at Trawniki, **4:** 62-63
  at Warsaw, **4:** 125, 126
  Zuckerman, Yitzhak, **4:** 153-155
Jewish ghetto police, **2:** 132-136
  Białystok, **1:** 89
  Lublin, **2:** *133*
  photographs of, **3:** *20*
  relationships with Jewish resistance groups, **2:** 134, 135, 165
  role in Nazi Aktionen in Vilna, **2:** 46
  roles in Lvov, **3:** 37, 38, 39
  Warsaw, **2:** 130, **4:** 119-120, 124, 132
  Westerbork (transit camp), **4:** 135-136
Jewish Law (Statut des Juifs), **2:** 135-136
Jewish Military Union (ZZW), **1:** 2, **2:** 131
Jewish National Committee, **2:** 131, **4:** 155
Jewish newspapers, **2:** 55, **3:** 171, 181
  in the United States, **1:** 21
Jewish organizations
  Association for Jews in Germany, **2:** 58
  Association of Jews in Belgium (AJB), **1:** 64
  Bergson Group, **1:** 19
  in Berlin, **1:** 62-63, 84
  Central Union of German Citizens of Jewish Faith, **1:** 112-114, **2:** 91-92
  Committee for Special Jewish Affairs, **3:** 85-86

Cultural Society of German Jews, **2:** 53
General Jewish Fighting Organization, **2:** 165
German Jewish Children's Aid (GJCA), **3:** 166
  in Germany, **2:** 55
  in Great Britain, **2:** 72-73
Jewish Coordinating Committee (Netherlands), **3:** 86
Jewish Military Union (ZZW), **1:** 2, **2:** 131
Jewish National Committee, **2:** 131, **4:** 155
  in Kraków ghetto, **2:** 168
Nazi consolidation of in Paris, **3:** 111
  in Polish ghettos, **3:** 134-135
  in postwar Poland, **2:** 171
  in postwar Warsaw, **4:** 128-129
  refugees' reliance on, **3:** 158
Reich Representation of German Jews, **1:** 84, **2:** 51-52, 55, 56
  in the Warsaw ghetto, **4:** 118-119
  in Weimar Republic Germany, **2:** 49-50
"Working Group" in Slovakia, **4:** 12-13
World Jewish Congress, **3:** 51, **4:** 143-144
  See also American Jewish organizations
  See also Jewish Fighting Organization (ŻOB)
  See also Joint Distribution Committee
  See also Judenräte
  See also Youth movements
  See also Zionist Groups
Jewish partisan leaders
  Bielski, Tuvia, **1:** 93-94
  Grosman, Haika, **2:** 75-76
  Szenes, Hannah, **4:** 51-*52*, 150
  Yelin, Haim, **4:** 144-145
Jewish partisans, **3:** *116, 118*
  in Soviet territories, **4:** 24, 86
  from Vilna, **4:** *89*
Jewish policy
  under Hitler, **2:** 95-97
  in Poland, **3:** 130
Jewish possessions. *See* Seizures of Jewish possessions
Jewish prisoners
  acts of kindness to, **3:** 179
  at Buchenwald, **1:** 104-106
  at Dachau, **1:** 144-145
  employed in Organisation Schmelt, **3:** 110
  at Mauthausen, **3:** *49*
  Nazi medical experiments on, **3:** 57-58, 60
  psychology of survivors, **4:** 48
  relative disadvantage of, **1:** 132-133
  role in Aktion Reinhard, **1:** 7
  Special Commando units with, **4:** 26
  usefulness for German war effort, **1:** 178
  who were nationals of neutral countries, **1:** 79-80
  See also Prisoners
Jewish prisoners of war, **3:** 143-155

199

INDEX

Jewish prisoners' tasks
    at Bełżec extermination camp, **1:** 75-76, 77
    with no practical purpose, **2:** 125
    sorting possessions of victims, **1:** 8
    See also Forced labor
Jewish professionals
    Nazi boycott, **1:** 103
    Nazi laws forbidding, **1:** 24-25, 26, 35
Jewish Protestants, **1:** 121
Jewish Religious Congregation (JRC) of Prague, **1:** 99
Jewish religious practices
    at Budzyń (labor camp), **1:** 111
    at Drancy (French transit camp), **1:** 173-174
    Nazi restrictions on, **1:** 25
    in Polish ghettos, **3:** 134-135
    as spiritual resistance to Nazis, **3:** 171
    at Theresienstadt, **4:** 59
    in Vienna, **4:** 100
Jewish resistance group leaders
    Anielewicz, Mordecai, **1:** 21-24, *22*, **4:** 155
    Kaplan, Joseph, **2:** *146*-147
    Liebeskind, Aharon, **3:** 9-11
    Plotnicka, Frumka, **3:** 122-123
    Zuckerman, Yitzhak, **4:** 153-155
    See also Tenenbaum, Mordechai
Jewish resistance groups
    Auschwitz-Birkenau, **3:** 182-183
    Belgium, **1:** 67-68
    Belorussia, **1:** 71
    Berlin, **1:** 86
    Budapest, **2:** 115
    France, **2:** 24, **4:** 151
    Grodno, **2:** 74
    Hungary, **3:** 35
    Jewish Military Union (ZZW), **1:** 2, **2:** 131
    Kovno, **2:** 165
    Kraków, **2:** 170-171, **3:** 9
    Łódź, **3:** 23-24
    Lublin, **3:** 30
    Minsk, **1:** 72, **3:** 64-65
    Netherlands, **3:** 86
    parachutists from Palestine, **3:** *170*, **4:** 14, *51-52*
    and the Polish underground, **3:** 135
    relationships with Jewish ghetto police, **2:** 134-135
    relationships with Judenräte, **2:** 142-143, **4:** 89, 104, 164-165
    relationships with partisans, **2:** 170
    relationship with Jewish youth movements, **4:** 147-148
    Riga, **3:** 176-177
    Ringelblum, Emanuel, **3:** *180*-182
    Slovakia, **4:** 14
    Soviet Union, **4:** 24
    Tarnów, **4:** 53
    Ukraine, **4:** 86
    United Partisan Organization (FPO), **4:** 88-90
    Warsaw ghetto, **4:** 122-126, 129-131
    weapons used by, **4:** 89, 131

    See also Armed resistance by Jews
    See also Jewish Fighting Organization (ŻOB)
    See also Resistance by prisoners
    See also Underground groups
    See also Youth movements
Jewish women
    forced labor by, **1:** 8, **2:** 114, **3:** *121*
    forced sterilization of, **1:** 123-124
    Gross-Rosen camps for, **2:** 78
    Nazi medical experiments on, **3:** 60
    photographs of, **3:** *18, 121, 185*
    prisoners' work in the camps, **2:** 78
    See also Women
Jewish youth movements. *See* Youth movements
Jews
    among partisans, **3:** 114-115
    betrayal by neighbors, **3:** 130, 135
    conscription in France, **2:** *21*
    determination to survive, **4:** 128
    fascist policy towards, **2:** 119
    in France, **2:** 20-21, 23-24
    German reasons for fearing, **1:** 29-30
    in Germany, **2:** 47-48
    at Gross-Rosen, **2:** 76-78
    in Hungary, **2:** 113-115
    idea of homeland, **1:** 10
    in Lithuania, **3:** 16
    married to Germans. *See* Mixed marriages
    Nazi classification system for, **1:** 25, **3:** 95-97
    Nazi racial experiments on/about, **3:** 58-59
    Nazi resettlement plans for, **3:** 40-41, 94
    in Poland, **3:** 128-129
    postwar identity of, **3:** 11-12, 14
    registration of, **2:** 16, **3:** 22, 46, *53*, 86
    stages in Nazi persecution of, **4:** 75-76
    stereotypes, **1:** 28, **2:** 52, 153
    Vichy government definition of, **2:** 136
    See also Mischlinge
Jews in hiding
    accounts by survivors, **3:** 166
    blackmailers of, **1:** 2
    children, **3:** 168-169
    Frank, Anne, and family, **2:** 26-33
    non-Jews who aided, **3:** 179
    postwar stress experienced by, **4:** 49
    Warsaw ghetto bunkers, **4:** 126, 131, 132, 133
Jobs
    Austrian dismissal of Jews and spouses from, **1:** 50
    certificates of employment, **3:** 38, 39, **4:** 103-104, 112, 185
    Jewish retraining courses for emigrants, **4:** 98, 100
    Nazi laws prohibiting Jews from working, **1:** 35, **4:** 36
    pay rate for forced labor, **2:** 17
    See also Economic measures against Jews

Joint. *See* Joint Distribution Committee (JDC)
Joint Distribution Committee (JDC)
    aid to Belgian Jews, **1:** 67
    aid to refugees in Budapest, **1:** 108
    conflict with Rescue Committee of the United States Orthodox Rabbis, **3:** 165
    donations to emigrants, **4:** 98
    efforts in Polish ghettos, **3:** 134
    Federation of Swiss Jewish Communities (SIG) and, **3:** 51-52
    support by American Jews, **1:** 18
Joint Rescue Committee, **2:** 137
Journalists who reported the Holocaust, **1:** 21
Judenräte, **2:** 139-143
    Białystok, **1:** 89
    Council of Elders of the Kovno Jewish Ghetto Community, **2:** 164
    duties in the Generalgouvernement, **2:** 16
    Jewish Religious Congregation (JRC) of Prague, **1:** 99
    Kielce, **2:** 152
    Łódź, **3:** 20, 23, 25
    Lublin, **3:** 30-31, 32
    Lvov, **2:** 125, **3:** 37, 38, 39
    Minsk, **3:** 64
    Nazi replacements for, **2:** 170, **3:** 39
    opposition of Jewish youth movements to, **4:** 147
    Poland, **3:** 131
    Regulation for the Establishment of the Judenräte, **4:** 184
    Rovno, **3:** 185
    Silesia, **3:** 109
    Tarnów, **4:** 52
    Ternopol, **4:** 56, 57
    Theresienstadt Council of Elders, **4:** 59
    Union Générale Des Israélites De France (UGIF), **3:** 112, 113
    Vilna, **4:** 103, 104
    Vitebsk, **4:** 106
    Warsaw, **4:** 118, 121
Judenrat "gardens," **1:** 89
Judenrat leaders
    duties the Nazis gave them, **2:** 140, 141-142
    Edelstein, Jacob, **1:** 177-178
    Elkes, Elchanan, **1** 184-185
    Freudiger, Fülöp, **2:** 36-37
    Glazman, Josef, **2:** 63-65, *64*
    Mushkin, Eliyahu, **3:** 78-79
    killed for defiance of Nazi orders, **2:** 169-170, **3:** 37, **4:** 105, 38, 172
    photographs of, **1:** *182*, **2:** *141*
    relationships with Jewish ghetto police, **2:** 132, 135
    relationships with Jewish resistance groups, **2:** 164-165, **3:** 64, **4:** 89, 104
    suicide by, **3:** 185, **4:** 123
    See also Czerniaków, Adam
    See also Gens, Jacob

INDEX

Judges at Nuremberg, **4:** *73*
Judgment at Nuremberg, **4:** 72
Jüischer Centralverein. *See* Central Union of German Citizens of Jewish Faith

K

Kadushin, Zvi, **1:** 182
Kaltenbrunner, Ernst, **2:** 144-145
Kamenets-Podolski, **2:** 145
Kaplan, Chaim Aaron, **4:** 117
Kaplan, Josef, **2:** *146*-147
Kapos, **2:** 147-148, **3:** 48, **4:** 68
Kasztner, Rezső, **2:** 148-149
Kaunas. *See* Kovnof
Kharkov, **2:** 149-150
Kherson, **2:** 150-152
Kibbutzim
    Ghetto Fighters' Kibbutz, **4:** 155
    in pre-war Kherson (Ukraine), **2:** 151
    Zionist, **1:** 10, **2:** 153, **4:** 154
Kielce, **2:** 151-152
Kiev. *See* Babi Yar
Kings
    Christian X (Denmark), **1:** 160
    Gustav V (Sweden), **4:** 108
    Leopold III (Belgium), **1:** 63-64
Kistarcsa, **2:** 154-155
Klein, Gerda Weissmann, **3:** 130, 135
Koch, Ilse, **2:** *155-156*
Koch, Karl Otto, **2:** *155-156*
Kolbe, Maximilian, **2:** 156-158, *157*
Kommissarbefehl (Commissar Order), **2:** 158-159
Kommissariat, **2:** 170
Kook, Hillel, **1:** 19
Koppe, Wilhelm, **2:** 159
Korczak, Janusz, **2:** 159-162, *160*
Korherr, Richard, **2:** 162
Kovno, **2:** 163-166, **4:** 145
Kowalski, Wladyslaw, **2:** 166-167
Kraków, **2:** 167-171
    deportations of Jews from, **3:** 137
    ghetto entrance, **2:** *168*
    Jewish Fighting Organization (ŻOB), **2:** 170
    Płasów (camp), **3:** 120-122
    synagogues, destruction of, **2:** 168
Kramer, Josef, **1:** 82, **2:** *171*
Krasnodor Trial, **4:** 71
Kristallnacht, **2:** 54-55, 171-174
    in Berlin, **1:** 85
    effect of Nurenberg Laws on, **3:** 97
    map of, **2:** *56*
    response by the Quakers, **1:** 13-14
Krüger, Friedrich Wilhelm, **2:** *174-175*
Krumey, Hermann, **2:** 175
Krupp (German company), **2:** 77, **3:** 109, 115, 117
Kulmhof. *See* Chełmno

L

Labor camps, **2:** 16-17
    Auschwitz III, **1:** 41-42
    Bełżec, **1:** 73
    Budzyń, **1:** 110-111
    coercion of Jews into, **3:** 109
    at Gross-Rosen, **2:** 77-78
    Janówska, **2:** 124-126
    for Jewish farmers from Kherson, **2:** 150-152
    Kielce, **2:** 153
    in Latvia and Estonia, **3:** 17-18
    in Lithuania, **3:** 17-18
    Łódź ghetto, **3:** 23
    Lutsk, **3:** 34
    Lvov ghetto, **3:** 38-39
    for Lvov Jews, **3:** 37
    Płasów, **3:** 120-122
    Poland, **3:** 139
    in Silesia and Sudetenland, **3:** 109-110
    Skarżysko-Kamienna, **4:** 9-11
    Starachowice, **4:** 35-36
    Ternopol ghetto, **4:** 56
    Trawniki, **4:** 62-63
    Vienna, **1:** 53-54
    Vilna, **4:** 105
    See also Kapo
Labour Party of Great Britain, **2:** 69
Lampshades from Jews' skins, **2:** 156
Language
    and antisemitism, **3:** 149
    of the Nazis. *See* Sprachregelung
La Risiera di San Sabba camp, **2:** 121-122
Latin American countries' positions at Evian Conference, **1:** 190
Latvia, **3:** 1-4
    Dvinsk, **1:** 174-176
    Gypsies, **2:** 86
    map of, **3:** *2*
    Riga, **3:** 175-177
Latvian military, **3:** 175-176
Latvian police, **3:** 3
Latvian resistance groups, **3:** 3
Laval, Pierre, **3:** 4-5
Laws. *See* International law; Laws, Nazi; Legal principles
Laws, Nazi
    banning economic activity by Jews, **1:** 36
    empowering the Gestapo, **2:** 60-61
    The Enabling Law, **2:** 50
    First Ordinance to the Riech Citizenship Law, **4:** 181-183
    Law against the Overcrowding of German Schools and Institutions of Higher Learning, **1:** 25, **4:** 179-180
    Law for the Protection of German Blood and German Home, **1:** 25, **3:** 53
    Law for the Protection of German Blood and Honor, **3:** 96, **4:** 180-181
    Law for the Restoration of the Professional Civil Service, **1:** 24-25
    Measure for the Elimination of Jews from the German Economy, **1:** 26
    See also Anti-Jewish legislation
    See also Marriage laws, Nazi
Leadership Principle, Nazi, **2:** 95, **3:** 81
Le Chambon-sur-Lignon, **3:** 5-6
Legal principles
    Allied Control Council, **4:** 75-76
    International Military Tribunal (IMT), **4:** 72-75
    Polish courts, **4:** 83
    West German courts, **4:** 79
Lemberg. *See* Lvov
Lenard, Philipp, **1:** 30
Leopold III (King of Belgium), **1:** 63-64
Levi, Primo, **3:** 6-8, **4:** 33
Libraries. *See* Books; Documents of the Holocaust; Museums
Liebehenschel, Arthur, **3:** *8*
Liebeskind, Aharon, **3:** 9-11
Liquidation of camps, **3:** 44, 50
    Auschwitz, **1:** 47
    Bełżec, **1:** 77
    Buchenwald, **1:** 107
    Budzyń, **1:** 111
    death marches from the camps, **1:** 149-153
    Dora-Mittelbau, **1:** 171
    in the Generalgouvernement, **1:** 184-186
    Gross-Rosen, **2:** 78-79
    Janówska, **2:** 126
    Majdanek, **1:** 184-186
    Mauthausen, **3:** 50
    Natzweiler-Struthof, **3:** 80
    Organisation Schmelt labor camps, **3:** 110
    Płasów, **3:** 122
    Poland, **3:** 139
    Ravensbrück, **3:** 156
    Sobibór, **4:** 19
    Starachowice, **4:** 36
    Stutthof, **4:** 43
    Ternopol, **4:** 56
    Trawniki, **4:** 62-63
    Treblinka, **4:** 68, 69
    Vilna area, **4:** 104
    See also Erntefest ("Harvest Festival")
Liquidation of ghettos
    Belorussia, **1:** 71
    Białystok, **1:** 90-91
    Budapest, **4:** 110
    in Croatia, **1:** 141
    Derechin, **1:** 38
    in the Generalgouvernement, **2:** 40, **3:** 138-139
    Gestapo role in, **2:** 62
    Kharkov, **2:** 150
    Kielce, **2:** 152-153
    Kovno, **2:** 165-166
    Kraków, **3:** 121
    Łódź, **1:** 117, **3:** 23, 24
    Lublin, **3:** 33
    Lvov, **3:** 39
    Reichskommissariat Ostland, **4:** 104-105
    Riga, **3:** 3, 177
    Riga "large," **3:** 176
    Starachowice, **4:** 35
    Vilna, **2:** 47, **4:** 90, 105
    Vilna area, **4:** 103
    Vitebsk, **4:** 106
    Warsaw, **4:** 40-41, 127

201

INDEX

Literature, antisemitic, **1**: 30, *32*
Literature of the Holocaust, **3**: 11-15
   Levi, Primo, **3**: 6-8
   Ringelblum, Emanuel, **3**: 181-182
   Szenes, Hannah,**4**: 51-*52*, 150
   Yelin, Haim, **4**: 144
   Wiesel, Elie, **4**: *137*-138
   Wiesenthal, Simon, **4**: 139
   See also Diaries
   See also Holocaust survivor accounts
   See also Poems of the Holocaust
Lithuania, **3**: 15-19
   annexation of Polish areas, **3**: 127-128
   Gypsies, **2**: 86
   Jewish communities, **1**: 69
   Kovno, **2**: 163-166, **4**: 145
   United Partisan Organization, **4**: 88-90
   Vilna, **3**: 16, **4**: 88-90, 101-105
Lithuanian Jews, **2**: 73
   extermination by Karl Jager, **2**: 124
Lithuanian partisans, **2**: 165, **3**: *116*-117
Lithuanian soldiers and police, **3**: 17
Łódź, **3**: 19-24
   deportations from, **3**: 137-138
   deportees, **1**: *115*, 116, 117
   Jewish Special Commando, **4**: 26
   See also Biebow, Hans, **1**: 92
Łódź ghetto, chronicles of the, **3**: 25
Lohse, Hinrich, **3**: 28
Lösener, Bernard, **3**: 28-29
Lublin, **3**: 29-33
   Budzyń, **1**: 110-111
   failure to solve "Jewish question" with, **2**: 10, **3**: 94
   plans for deportations of Jews to, **1**: 161-162, **3**: 92-95
   See also Majdanek
   See also Nisko and Lublin Plan
Łuck. *See* Lutsk
Luftwaffe, **2**: 68
Lutheran Church and antisemitism, **1**: 119, 121
Lutsk, **3**: 33-34
Lutz, Carl, **3**: 34-36, *35*
Lvov, **3**: 36-40
   labor camp, **2**: 124-126
Lyons, Butcher of, **1**: *61*-62

M

Madagascar Plan, **3**: 40-42, **4**: 184-186
   relation to "Final Solution," **2**: 10
   See also Nisko and Lublin Plan
Majdanek, **3**: 42-45
   gas chambers, **2**: 39
   liquidation of, **1**: 184-186
Malaria experiments by Nazis, **3**: 57
Marches. *See* Death marches
Marriage laws, Nazi, **1**: 25, **2**: 90, **3**: 66, 96
Marshall Plan, alternatives to the, **3**: 71
Martyrs' and Heroes' Remembrance Law, **3**: 178
Masons (organization), **3**: 146, 183
Mass graves. *See* Corpses, Nazi efforts to conceal

Mass murders by Nazis, **2**: 145
   Babi Yar, **1**: 54-56, **3**: 106
   the beginning of, **1**: 192
   Belorussia, **1**: 70-71, 72
   Białystok, **1**: 88
   of British prisoners of war in France, **1**: 182
   Budapest, **1**: 34, 109
   by burning victims alive, **1**: 171, **3**: 108, 176
   by carbon monoxide gas, **2**: 37
   Croatia, **1**: 140
   by electrocution, **2**: 39
   with the Euthanasia Program, **1**: 186-189
   Gypsies, **2**: 86-87
   Kharkov, **2**: 150
   Kovno, **2**: 163-164
   Kraków ghetto, **2**: 169
   Latvia, **3**: 3-4
   Lithuania, **3**: 17
   Łódź ghetto, **3**: 22-23
   Lublin, **3**: 32, 43
   Lutsk, **3**: 33, 34
   Lvov, **1**: 8, **3**: 38, 39
   Mauthausen, **3**: 46
   methods used for, **2**: 12, **4**: 23-24, 113
   Minsk, **3**: 64
   by Operational Squads, **3**: 104-*105*
   by phenol injection, **1**: 82
   photographs of, **1**: *135*, **3**: *105*, *142*
   Płasów, **3**: 122
   of Poles, **4**: 152
   Ponary, **3**: 141-*142*
   prisoners at Dachau, **1**: 146-147
   Riegner cable message about, **3**: 174-175
   Riga "large" ghetto, **3**: 176
   Rovno, **3**: 185-186
   Rumbula, **3**: 187
   Simferopol, **4**: 9
   Skarżysko-Kamienna, **4**: 10
   Starachowice, **4**: 35
   Tarnów, **4**: 53
   Ternopol, **4**: 55, 56
   timing of, **3**: 136, **4**: 99
   Ukraine, **4**: 85-86
   using Zyklon B, **2**: 39
   Vilna, **4**: 102, 103
   Vitebsk, **4**: 106
   See also Camp procedures for prisoners
   See also Corpses, Nazi efforts to conceal
   See also Death marches
   See also Gas chambers
   See also Gas vans
Master Plan, **2**: 42, 43
Master race
   Himmler's concept of, **2**: 90
   Nazi concept of, **1**: 186
   Rosenberg's concept of, **3**: 184
Mauthausen, **3**: 45-51
Mayer, Saly, **3**: 51-52
Measure for the Elimination of Jews from the German Economy, **1**: 26
Medical experiments, **3**: 52-61

   at Dachau, **1**: 146
   at Ravensbrück, **3**: 156
   using Natzweiler gas chamber, **3**: 80
   victim testimony of, **4**: 82
   See also Nazi doctors
Mein Kampf (Hitler), **2**: 94, **3**: *61*-62
Memorials
   for Anielewicz, Mordecai, **1**: 24
   Babi Yar, **1**: 55-56
   ceremonies of remembrance at, **3**: 74, 187
   created by Yad Vashem, **3**: 76, 77
   Dvinsk, **1**: 175
   for Hirsch, Otto, **2**: 92
   Natzweiler-Struthof crematorium, **3**: 80
   Prague, **1**: 99
   Riga garden, **3**: 177
   Soviet, at Rumbula, **3**: 187
   Tower of Faces, **3**: *75*
   U.S. Holocaust Memorial Council, **4**: 137
   Westerbork camp, **4**: 136
   See also Monuments
   See also Museums
Mengele, Josef, **3**: *62*-63
   death of, **3**: 99
   racial experiments by, **3**: 58-59
   survivor's memory of, **1**: 40
Messerschmitt Aircraft Company, **3**: 79
Meyer-Hetling, Konrad, **2**: 41, 42
Minsk, **1**: 72-73, **3**: 63-66, **4**: 22
Mischlinge, **3**: 66-68
   with black fathers, **2**: 188-189
   gypsies considered to be, **2**: 82, 84
   legal definition of, **3**: 28
   Nazi discussions about, **4**: 112-113
   survivors in Germany, **2**: 59
Mixed blood, persons of. *See* Mischlinge
Mixed marriages
   Berlin survivors in, **1**: 87
   categories of Mischlinge in, **3**: 66
   Catholic support for, **1**: 120
   German laws against, **2**: 52
   Germans in, **3**: 67
   Hitler's intervention on behalf of Jews in, **3**: 67
   Jewish survivors in occupied Austria, **1**: 53-54
   job dismissal of both partners in Austria, **1**: 50
   Lösener, Bernard, rescuing Jews in, **3**: 29
   Minsk ghetto incarceration of Aryans in, **3**: 64
   Nazi conferences about, **4**: 112-113
   Nazi denial of matrimony loans to those in, **1**: 25
   See also Mischlinge
Moeser, Hans Karl, **1**: 171
Mogilev-Podolski, **3**: 68-69
Monowitz. *See* Auschwitz
Monsky, Henry, **1**: 15
Monuments
   Baum Gruppe, **1**: *62*
   Bełżec, **1**: 77

INDEX

Drancy (French transit camp), **1:** 174
Kielce, **2:** 153
mass-murder sites in Lithuania, **3:** 18
Treblinka cemetery, **4:** 69
Warsaw Transfer Point (Umschlagplatz), **4:** 61-62
See also Memorials
See also Museums
Moravia. *See* Bohemia and Moravia, Protectorate of
Moreshet, **3:** 69
Morgenthau, Henry, Jr., **1:** 18, **3:** 69-71
Motives
American beliefs about Nazis' motives, **1:** 20
Nazi doctors, **3:** 58
Poles who aided Jews, **1:** 1, 3
those who deny the Holocaust, **2:** 102-104
Movies about Nazis, **3:** 13, 76
Müller, Heinrich, **3:** 71-73
Munich, **2:** 135
Munich Agreement, **2:** 70, 110
Murders by Nazis. *See* Executions by Nazis; Extermination camps; Mass murders by Nazis; Medical experiments
Muselmann, **3:** 73
Museums, **3:** 74
Anne Frank house, **2:** 31-*32*
Ghetto Fighters', **4:** 155
Jewish Museum of Prague, **1:** 99
Majdanek, **3:** 45
United States Holocaust Memorial Museum, **3:** 74-75
Yad Vashem Historical Museum, **3:** 76, 77
Mushkin, Eliyahu, **3:** 78-79
Muslims, influence on Nazis, **1:** 57
Mussolini, Benito, **2:** 1, *3*
photographs of, **2:** *118*
reactions to antisemitism, **2:** 119-120
relationship with Hitler, **2:** 123

N

Nathan, Tikva, **4:** 50
National Socialism and antisemitism, **1:** 33
National Socialist Party. *See* Nazi Party
Natzweiler-Struthof, **3:** 79-80
Nazi actions on holidays
Christmas Eve, **4:** 43
Day of Atonement, pogroms, **4:** 99
Passover, arrests of Judenrat officials, **4:** 52
Passover, liquidation of Warsaw ghetto, **4:** 127, 131
Rosh Hashanah and Day of Atonement aktions, **4:** 117
Yom Kippur, Aktion, **4:** 103
Nazi deceptions
about deportations, **4:** 125
about existence of extermination camps, **1:** 193-194
about purpose of concentration camps, **4:** 28
camp "showers." *See* Gas chambers

cover-ups about war crimes, **1:** 4-6, **2:** 158-159
decorations around camp "showers," **2:** 38
of deportees, **4:** 17
disguised gas vans, **2:** 37
of émigrés, **2:** 148
"examination room" for prisoners, **4:** 1
fabricated causes of death for prisoners, **2:** 61
ghetto currency, **4:** 57
"infirmary" for the sick, **4:** 67
letters to relatives of dead Jews, **4:** 18
"model ghetto" at Thereseinstadt, **1:** 181, **4:** 57-58, 59-60
murder of crematorium laborers, 50
murder of Jews who volunteered to be sterilized, **3:** 67
not adding odor to Zyklon B, **4:** 157
promise of jobs for unemployed Jews, **3:** 88, 89
propaganda films about Jews in Third Reich, **4:** 60
receiving ransom and killing hostages, **3:** 37
rumors about Jews being murderers, **3:** 37
staged attack on German soldiers, **4:** 103
use of special language. *See* Sprachregelung
See also Camp procedures
See also Liquidation of camps
Nazi-Deutsch. *See* Sprachregelung
Nazi doctors
at Bergen-Belsen, **1:** 82
Clauberg, Carl, **1:** 123-124, **3:** 59-60
at Dachau, **1:** 146
in the Euthanasia Program, **1:** 186-189
Eysele, Hans, **4:** 82
Mengele, Josef, **1:** 40, **3:** 58-59, *62-63*, 99
Ritter, Robert **2:** 82
See also Medical experiments
Nazi euphemisms
"asocial elements," **1:** 126
"disinfected" persons, **1:** 189
"Final Solution," **4:** 27
"Harvest Festival" (Erntefest), **1:** 8, 184-186
"quarantine," **1:** 42
"sauna," **1:** 42
"total removal," **2:** 43
See also Nazi deceptions
Nazification, **2:** 50-51
Nazi foreign policy, **3:** 61
Nazi Four-Year Plan
Hitler's memo on, **2:** 53
and I. G. Farben, **2:** 116
Nazi ideology
about the "Jewish question," **2:** 8, **3:** 94, 49, 61, 184
difference from fascism, **2:** 4
Rosenberg's writings about, **3:** 184
Nazi newspapers, **4:** 38, *39*
Nazi nurses, **1:** 186-189

Nazi officials
Auerswald, Heinz, **1:** 39
Biebow, Hans, **1:** *92-93*
Bormann, Martin, **1:** *100*-101
in charge of German police departments, **3:** 162
Endre, László, **1:** 183-*184*
Goebbels, Joseph, **1:** 84, **2:** *66-67*, **4:** 27
Kaltenbrunner, Ernest, **2:** 144-145
Korherr, Richard, **2:** 162
Lohse, Hinrich, **3:** 28
Lösener, Bernard, **3:** 28-29
Müller, Heinrich, **3:** 71-73
Novak, Franz, **3:** *95*
Rauff, Walther, **3:** 154
Rohm, Ernest, **2:** 105
Rosenberg, Alfred, **2:** 86, **3:** 148, **3:** 182-*184*
Seyss-Inquart, Arthur, **4:** 7-*8*
Stangl, Franz, **4:** *34*-35
Stricher, Julius, **4:** *37-38*
Stuckart, Wilhelm, **4:** 41-42
See also Frank, Hans
See also War criminals
Nazi Party, **3:** 80-83
anti-Jewish objectives, **1:** 24
Foreign Organization, **4:** 106
importance of Dachau to, **1:** 144
and the "Jewish Question," **2:** 49, **3:** 184
Mischlinge belonging to, **3:** 67-68
Program of the National-Socialist (Nazi) German Worker's Party, **4:** 171-173
rise to power, **2:** 50-55, 94
similar groups in other countries, **3:** 152
Nazi rationales
attacks on Berlin Jews, **1:** 84
conducting medical experiments about wounds, **3:** 56
deporting Czech Jews to Poland, **1:** 99
detentions of political prisoners, **1:** 126
"Final Solution," **3:** 147-148
Kristallnacht, **1:** 26, **2:** 171-172
massacre at Babi Yar, **1:** 54
mass murder of Belorussian Jews, **1:** 72
murder of Berlin Jews, **1:** 63
murder of Czech prisoners, **3:** 48
murder of 300 Lutsk Jews, **3:** 33
murder of Vilna Jews, **4:** 103
removing Hitler's opponents, **2:** 105
See also "Final Solution"
Nazi resistance fighters in Allied territories, **3:** 148
Nazis
attitudes toward Zionism, **2:** 52, **4:** 140
categories of, **1:** 156
decision-making under Hitler, **2:** 33, 95-97
Declaration of the Boycott by the Nazi Party Leadership **4:** 173-177
image in film and fiction, **3:** 13
pagan roots, **4:** 30
postwar arrests of, **1:** 155
power gained from antisemitism, **1:** 33

203

INDEX

return to public office after the war, **4:** 70
stages in persecution of Jews, **4:** 75-76
their ideal woman, **2:** 99
who followed orders, **4:** 73, 81
Nazis and Nazi Collaborators (Punishment) Law, **2:** 135
Nazi symbols, **4:** 29-30
    black shirts, **2:** *122*
    German flag, **3:** 96
    swastikas, **2:** *93*, **3:** 184
    uniforms, **4:** 30, 32, 87
Nazi terminology
    "collective responsibility" of prisoners, **3:** 173
    Sprachregelung, **4:** 27-28
    See also Nazi euphemisms
Nazi war criminals. *See* War criminals
Nazi youth, photograph of Hitler with, **2:** *93*
Nebe, Arthur, **3:** 84
Neo-Fascist groups, **2:** 103
Neo-Nazi groups, **2:** 103, **3:** 82-83
    See also Denial of the Holocaust
Netherlands, **3:** *85-91*
    Bogaard, Johannes, **1:** 96-97
    Catholics, **1:** 121
    deportation of Jews from, **1:** 164
    Jewish badge, **1:** 59, 61
    Jewish Brigade Group activities, **2:** 128
    position at Evian Conference, **1:** 190
    Protestants, **1:** 122
    Seyss-Inquart, Arthur, **4:** *7-8*
    treatment of Mischlinge in, **3:** 66-67
    underground groups, **1:** 96-97
    Westerbork, **3:** 88, **4:** 135-137, 89, 90
Neuengamme, **3:** 91-92
Newspapers
    Lithuanian Communist, **4:** 153
    reports on the Holocaust, **1:** 20-21
    underground Jewish, **2:** 170, **4:** 122, 123
    See also Reports to the outside world
New Zealand's position at Evian Conference, **1:** 190
Nice (France), **4:** 151
"Night of the Broken Glass." *See* Kristallnacht
Night (Wiesel), **1:** 14, **4:** 138
Nisko and Lublin Plan, **3:** 92-95
    See also Madagascar Plan
Nobel Peace Prize winner Elie Wiesel, **4:** *137-*138
Non-Aryans, definition of, **1:** 24-25
Non-Jews who aided Jews
    execution by Nazis, **1:** 2
    in Italy, **2:** 122
    in the Netherlands, **3:** 90
    in Poland, **1:** 1-2, **4:** 7, 128
    See also Righteous Among the Nations
Nordhausen, death march from, **1:** 152
Norway, deportation of Jews from, **1:** 164
Novak, Franz, **3:** *95*
Nowak, Franz. *See* Novak, Franz
Nowicki, Klemak, **3:** 166
NSDAP. *See* Nazi Party

Nuremberg
    Nazi Party meeting at, **3:** *81*
    reason for holding trials at, **4:** 72
Nuremberg Laws, **1:** 25, **3:** 96-97
    application to Gypsies, **2:** 82
Nuremberg Military Tribunals. *See* Trials of war criminals
Nuremberg Trial, **4:** 71-74
    different types of, **4:** 70-71
    judges, **2:** *117*
    Otto Ohlendorf's testimony, **3:** *101*
    questions about legitimacy of, **1:** 136-137, **2:** 102, **3:** 184
    See also International Military Tribunal (IMT)

O

Oberg, Carl Albrecht, **3:** 97-98
Oberschlesische Hydriewerke (German company), **1:** 42
Occupied territories. *See* German-occupied territories
Office of Special Investigations, **3:** 98-100
Ohlendorf, Otto, **3:** 100-*101*
Olympic games in Berlin, **2:** 53
Oneg Shabbat, **3:** 180
"One-Two-Three" (Szenes), **4:** 51
Open ghettos, **3:** 26
Operational Squads, **3:** 101-108
    difficulties in carrying out mass murders, **2:** 12
    in Poland, **3:** 129, 130-131
    relationship to Reich Security Main Office (RSHA), **3:** 163
    relationship to SD, **4:** 5
    in the Ukraine, **4:** 84
    Volksdeutsche units, **4:** 107-108
    See also Special Commando
Operation "Barbarossa," **3:** 103, **4:** 21-22
Operation "Erntefest." *See* Erntefest ("Harvest Festival")
Operation 1005. *See* Aktion 1005
Operation Reinhard. *See* Aktion Reinhard
Oradour-sur-Glane, **3:** 108
Orchestras
    prisoners, **1:** *45*, **2:** *125*
    Warsaw ghetto, **4:** 122
Order Banning the Emigration of Jews from the Reich **4:** 188-189
Organisation Schmelt, **3:** 108-110
Orthodox youth organization, **4:** 150
OSI. *See* Office of Special Investigations
Osijek, Jews in, **1:** 141
Oświęcim *See* Auschwitz
Owens, Jesse, **3:** *150*
    See also Black people

P

Palestine
    American Jewish Conference and, **1:** 16
    British army regiment from, **2:** 127-129
    British limits on immigration to, **1:** 17
    creation of Jewish state in, **1:** 10-11

Eichmann's views about, **1:** 179
illegal immigration to (Aliya Bet), **1:** 9-13
Jewish parachutists from, **3:** *170*, **4:** 14, *51-52*
policy towards Jewish refugees, **3:** 160
postwar emigration by Jews to, **1:** 168, 169
prisoners of war from, **3:** 144
Paris, **3:** 111-113
    deportations from, **2:** 22
    Jews in, **2:** 24-25
    police, **2:** 35-36
Parnes, Joseph, **2:** 125, **3:** 37
Partisan leaders
    Atlas, Yeheskel, **1:** *38*
    Glazman, Josef, **2:** 63-65, *64*
Partisans, **3:** 113-119
    Belorussian, **2:** 74
    French, **3:** 157
    in Lithuania, **2:** 165
    in Poland, **4:** 152
    relationships with Jewish resistance groups, **3:** 64-65
    in the Soviet Union, **4:** 24
    in the Ukraine, **3:** 186, **4:** 85
    See also Jewish partisans
    See also Soviet partisans
Part Jews. *See* Mischlinge
Patches. *See* Badges
Pechersky, Aleksandr, **3:** 119-120
Periodic Table, The (Il Sistema Periodico) (Levi), **3:** 8
Phenol injections, Nazi use of, **1:** 82, **2:** 157, **3:** 156
Płasów, **3:** 120-122
Plotnicka, Frumka, 122-123
Poems of the Holocaust
    "A Cartload of Shoes," **3:** 10
    "Babii Yar," **1:** 56
    Ballad of Mauthausen, **3:** 51
    "Holocaust 1944," **4:** 46
    "In Auschwitz-Birkenau," **1:** 40-41
    "Night," **4:** 138
    "One-Two-Three," **4:** 51
    "Shema," **3:** 7
    "Terezín," **4:** 59
    "To Caesarea," **4:** 150
    "Waiting," **4:** 33
Pogroms
    Antwerp, **1:** 66
    Austria, **1:** 52
    Belorussian, **1:** 69
    Berlin, **1:** 84
    definition of, **1:** 31
    Lithuania, **3:** 16, 17
    postwar Kielce, **2:** 153, **3:** 141
    Ukraine, **3:** 33, **4:** 84, 85
    by Ukrainians in Lvov, **3:** 37
    See also Kristallnacht
Pohl, Oswald, **3:** 123
Poland, **3:** 121-141
    aid to Jews in, **1:** 1-3
    antisemitism in, **1:** 31
    Białystok, **1:** 71, **2:** 74, 75-76, 88-92
    Catholics, **1:** 121

INDEX

death marches, **1:** 149
deportations of Jews from Germany to, **1:** 161
effect of German occupation, **2:** 9-10
extermination camps, **1:** 192-194, **2:** 65-66
Generalplan Ost for, **2:** 41-43
German subdivisions of, **3:** *125*
Gypsies, **2:** 86
Jewish badge, **1:** 58
Jewish resistance groups, **2:** 131-132, **3:** 122-123
Jewish youth movements, **4:** 147
Kielce, **2:** 151-152
Kolbe, Maximilian, **2:** 156-158
Lvov, **2:** 124-126, **3:** 36-40
Nazi destruction of Polish culture, **2:** 40-41
Nazi plan for elimination of Jews in, **1:** 6-9
rescue of Jews in, **2:** 166-167
role of Wilhelm Koppe, **2:** 159
Tarnów, **4:** 52-53
trials of war criminals by, **4:** 81-83
underground groups, **3:** 114
Volksdeutsche, **4:** 107
Zamość, **4:** 151-152
See also Generalgouvernement
See also Kraków
See also Lublin
See also Warsaw
Poles
attitudes towards Jews, **3:** 135
Nazi deportations of, **1:** 162
Nazi treatment of, **2:** 15, **3:** 47, 43
response to the "Final Solution," **3:** 138
Police
auxiliary, **1:** 149, **4:** 84, 85, 87-88, 124
French, **2:** 35-36
German, **3:** 161-163
Hungarian, **2:** 83, *112*
Latvian, **3:** 3
Lithuanian, **3:** 17
Swiss, **2:** 79
Vienna, **3:** 50
See also Gestapo
See also Jewish ghetto police
Polish government
anti-Jewish policies, **3:** 128
anti-Jewish policies in Belorussia, **1:** 69
in-exile, **3:** 125-126, 128
Polish Jewish refugees, **3:** *159*-160
Polish prisoners
intellectuals, **3:** 47
Jewish, **1:** 132
at Mauthausen, **3:** 48
at Płasów, **3:** 121
status of, **1:** 131
Polish prisoners of war, **3:** 143-144
Polish underground groups, **3:** 128, **4:** 119
See also Zegota (the Polish Council for Aid to Jews)
Polish women, Nazi medical experiments on, **3:** 56-57
Political antisemitism, **1:** 32-33

Political organizations. *See* Jewish organizations; Underground groups; Youth movements
Political prisoners
Bereza-Kartuska, **2:** 5
Buchenwald, **1:** 104, 106
Communists, **1:** 126
Dachau, **1:** 144
detention of, **1:** 125-126
extermination at Auschwitz, **1:** 46
French communists, **2:** 80
in Italy, **2:** 120, 121
Kistarcsa, **2:** 154-155
Leon Feiner, **2:** 4-5
mass murders of, **1:** 147
Mauthausen, **3:** 46
medical experiments on, **3:** 56
murdered by Soviets in Lvov, **3:** 37
relative proportion in camps, **1:** 126
Spanish Civil War, **1:** 130, **2:** 80, **3:** 47, 48
See also Kommissarbefehl (Commissar Order)
Politics and racism, **3:** 151-153
Ponary, **3:** 141-*142*
See also Vilna, **4:** 105
Poniatowa, liquidation of, **1:** 184-186
Pope Pius XI, **1:** 119
Pope Pius XII, **1:** 78, 120
Portugal, Aristides de Sousa Mendes' role, **4:** 19-*20*
Portugal's policy towards Jewish refugees, **3:** 160
Postal services in ghettos, **3:** 135
Postwar
aid to survivors, **3:** 165
antisemitism, **1:** 33-34
Belgium, **1:** 68
Christian churches, **1:** 122
controversy over role of the Judenrat, **2:** 143
denazification efforts, **1:** 154-157
France, **2:** 25
I. G. Farben, **2:** 117
literary responses to the Holocaust, **3:** 12-13
Lublin, **3:** 33
Netherlands, **3:** 90-91
Prague, **1:** 99
prisoners' adjustment to freedom, **1:** 133-134
racism, **3:** 153
Soviet Union, **4:** 25
See also Displaced persons
See also Trials of war criminals, **2:** 135
Potsdam Agreement, **1:** 154-155
Prague, **1:** 98-99, 112
Pregnancy experiments by Nazis, **3:** 58, **4:** 30, 60, 151
Prejudice against Gypsies, **2:** 81
Prejudice against Jews. *See* Antisemitism; Racism
Preventative arrests, **2:** 82
Prisoners
about to be executed, **1:** *133*
after liberation, **1:** 133, **4:** 48-49

badges worn by, **1:** 61
barracks at Dachau, **1:** *146*
barracks at Theresienstadt, **4:** *58*
barracks in Majdanek, **3:** *45*
at Buchenwald, **1:** *105, 106*
categorization by SS, **1:** 131
"collective responsibility" of, **3:** 173
convicts, **1:** 81-82, **2:** 77
daily life, **1:** 43-44, 130-131
"the dentists," **4:** 17
disabled, **2:** 77
diseases and epidemics among, **1:** 147
drafted for the German army, **3:** 156
Gypsies, **2:** *82, 85*
in Italian concentration camps, **2:** 120
Latvian, **3:** 3
medical experiments on, **1:** 44, **3:** 52-61
in the Muselmann stage, **3:** 73
orchestras, **1:** *45*, **2:** *125*
photographs of, **1:** *145*, **4:** *2*
psychological effects of the camps on, **1:** 134, **4:** 47-48
registration of, **3:** 46
role of criminals, **3:** 45, 48, 121
roll call, **1:** 43
Selektion, **2:** 38
sick, **1:** 81, 146-147
striped jacket, **2:** *147*
types of, **1:** 126, 128, 131-132, 144
unregistered, **1:** 43
See also Camp conditions
See also Camp procedures
See also Death marches
See also Escapes and escape attempts
See also Forced labor
See also Jewish prisoners
See also Kapos
See also Political prisoners
See also Prisoners of war
See also Prisoners' tasks
See also Resistance by prisoners
Prisoners of war, **3:** 142-146
definition of, **3:** 142
forced labor, **2:** 13
Jews classified as German POWs, **2:** 110
Nazi medical experiments on, **3:** 59
Nazi violation of rights of, **2:** 158
at Płasów, **3:** 121
See also Soviet prisoners of war
Prisoners' tasks, **1:** 130-131
in the armaments industry, **1:** 128-129, **3:** 48
construction, **2:** 76, 77
at Dachau, **1:** 145-146
digging canals, **3:** 91
disposing of corpses, **1:** 4
picking up belongings of victims, **1:** 42
quarrying granite, **3:** 79
Sachsenhausen brickyard, **4:** 1
serving camp guards, **4:** 16
skilled and professional labor, **4:** 63, 65-66, 68
at Westerbork (transit camp), **4:** 136
working in the crematoria, **1:** 43

205

INDEX

Prisons
    Łódź ghetto, **3:** 21
    Pawiak (Warsaw), **4:** 115
Professions, Nazi laws banning Jews from, **1:** 24-25, 26, 35
Program of the National-Socialist (Nazi) German Workers' Party, **4:** 171-73
Propaganda
    antisemitic poster, **2:** *20*
    effect on news reporting, **1:** 20
    film by Nazis about Jews, **4:** 60
    Goebbels' role, **2:** 66-67
    Nazis felt was unfair, **1:** 102
    torching of Nazi anti-Communist exhibit, **1:** 63
    transmitted by Hitler Youth, **2:** 99
    See also Sprachregelung
"Protective custody" of enemies of the Reich, **2:** 62
    used as category for prisoners, **3:** 46
Protective documents for Jews, **1:** 110, **3:** 35, **4:** 108
    Schutz-Pass, **4:** *109*
Protectorate of Bohemia and Moravia. *See* Bohemia and Moravia
Protestant churches and Nazism, **1:** 119, 121-122
    Le Chambon-sur-Lignon, **3:** 5-6
Protocols of the Elders of Zion, **1:** 30, **3:** 146
Prussian Gestapo, **2:** 60-61
Psychology of survivors. *See* Holocaust survivors: psychology of
Public employment, Nazi ban of Jews from, **1:** 35
Public humiliation of Jews
    hair and beard cutting by Nazis, **3:** *31*, **4:** *13*, *129*
    by Lithuanians, **3:** 17
    in Lublin, **3:** 30
Purtzmann, Hans-Adolf, **3:** 148

Q

Quakers, **1:** 13-14, **3:** 167
Queen Elizabeth, **1:** 66-67

R

Rabbis, rescue of, **3:** 164
Racial experiments by Nazis, **3:** 58-59
Racial ideas about Gypsies, **2:** 82
Racial ideas about Jews, **1:** 32
Racial laws in Italy, **2:** 120
Racial purity standards of Nazis
    and homosexuality, **2:** 104
    and medical experiments, **3:** 53-54
    penalty for violating, **2:** 15
    pregnancy experiments and euthanasia, **3:** 151
    requirement for SS officers, **4:** 29
    See also Mischlinge
Racism, **3:** 149-153
    German perception of, **3:** 164
    See also Black people
Rademacher, Franz, **3:** 41
Radom District, **2:** 77
    camps in, **3:** 43, **4:** 10

Ranasinghe, Anne, **4:** 46
Ransom payments to Nazis
    "Blood for Goods," **1:** 181, **2:** 148, **4:** 142
    Europa Plan, **3:** 52
    for hostages in Lvov, **3:** 37
    See also Fines on Jewish communities
Rasch, Emil Otto, **3:** 153-154
Ration cards, **4:** 115
Rauff, Walther, **3:** 154
Ravensbrück, **3:** 154-156
Rayman, Marcel, **3:** 156-157
Reagan, Ronald, **4:** 137
Reawakening, The (La Tregna) (Levi), **3:** 7
Redcliffe, Sir John (pseudonym), **1:** 30
"Red Friday," **1:** 88
Refugees, **3:** 157-161
    from Austria, **1:** 52
    in Budapest, **1:** 108
    children in Great Britain, **2:** *72*
    from Croatia, **1:** 140
    in Denmark, **1:** 157-158
    Dutch assistance to, **3:** 85-86
    Evian Conference, **1:** 189-192
    German Jewish children, **3:** *167*
    from Germany, **2:** 9
    in Great Britain, **2:** 71-73
    helped by the Quakers, **1:** 13-14
    in Hungary, **2:** 36
    Hungary's acceptance of Polish, **2:** 111
    Judenrat aid to, **2:** 140
    in Lithuania, **1:** 184
    in Lvov, **3:** 37
    in the Netherlands, **3:** 88
    in occupied France, **2:** 21
    in Poland, **2:** 157
    from Poland to Soviet Union, **3:** 129-130
    rabbis, **3:** 164
    in Rome, **1:** 78
    in the Soviet Union, **4:** 21
    United States' responses, **4:** 92, 96
    See also Rescue of European Jews
    See also Rescue of Jewish children
Refugee ships, **3:** 160
    Hikawa Maru, **3:** *159*
    Manhattan, **3:** *167*
    St. Louis, **4:** 36-37
Regulation for the Elimination of the Jews from the Economic Life of Germany, **4:** 183-184
Regulation for the Establishment of the Jundenräte, **4:**184
Reich Association of Jews in Germany, **1:** 26, 37-38, 114
Reich Citizenship Law, **1:** 25, 26, **3:** 96
Reich Committee of Jewish Youth Organizations, **4:** 146
Reich Concordat, **1:** 119
Reichenau, death marches from, **1:** 153
Reichenau, Walter von, **3:** 163-164
Reich ghetto in Minsk, **3:** 65
Reich Representation of German Jews, **2:** 51-52, 55, 56
    in Berlin, **1:** 84

Reich Security Main Office (RSHA), **3:** 161-163
    effect on Gestapo, **2:** 62
    role in Generalplan Ost, **2:** 41, 42-43
    Wisliceny, Dieter, **4:** 141-142
Reichstag, **3:** 82
Relief and Rescue Committee of Budapest, **2:** 148-149
Religious antisemitism, **1:** 28
Reparations. *See* Financial reparations
Reports about the Holocaust in American newspapers, **1:** 20-21
Reports to the outside world
    Auschwitz Protocols, **4:** 14
    from the Bund, **2:** 5
    from Central Union of German Citizens of Jewish Faith, **1:** 113
    about Kristallnacht, **2:** 174
    from occupied Poland, **1:** 2-3, **3:** 123
    from United Partisan Organization (FPO), **4:** 89
    U.S. State Department suppression of, **4:** 92
    via World Jewish Congress, **4:** 144
    from Warsaw, **3:** 181
    words used to describe Holocaust, **2:** 100
    See also Riegner cable
Rescue, Nazi experiments on, **3:** 54-56
Rescue Committee of United States Orthodox Rabbis, **3:** 164-166
Rescue of European Jews
    American Jewish Conference and, **1:** 16
    in Belgium, **1:** 67-68
    by Benoît, Father Marie, **1:** 78-79
    Bergson Group plan for, **1:** 19
    by Bogaard, Johannes, in Netherlands, **1:** 96-97
    in Budapest, **4:** 108-111
    by Choms, Władysława, **1:** 118-119
    by Deffaught, Jean, **1:** 153-154
    in Denmark, **1:** 157-161
    as a form of resistance to Nazis, **3:** 171
    in France, **2:** 23
    by Grüninger, Paul, **2:** 79
    Horthy, Miklós, and his role in, **2:** 106
    from Hungary, **4:** 114
    in Hungary, **1:** 181, **2:** 36
    by Italians and the Italian government, **2:** 122, 123
    by Italians in Yugoslavia, **1:** 140
    from Italy, **4:** 114
    by Jewish Brigade Group, **2:** 128
    Judenräte efforts to, "rescue by labor," **2:** 142
    by Kasztner, Rezső, **2:** 148-149
    by Kolbe, Maxmilian, **2:** 156-158
    by Kowalski, Wladyslaw, **2:** 166-167
    Morgenthau, Henry, Jr., and his impact on, **3:** 69-71
    by Palestine Jews, **2:** 137
    by partisans, **1:** 38
    in Poland, **2:** 5
    by Ringelblum, Emanuel, **3:** 182
    by the Romanian government, **1:** 77

Slovakia, **1:** 181
by SS official, **1:** 87
by Sugihara, Sempo, **4:** *44*-45
by Swiss diplomat in Hungary, **3:** 34-36
Switzerland, **3:** 51-52
by a town in southern France, **3:** 5-6
United States' role, **4:** 94
U.S. State Department role, **4:** 92
See also Joint Distribution Committee (JDC)
See also Righteous Among the Nations, **3:** 177-180
See also War Refugee Board, **4:** 96
Rescue of Jewish children, **3:** 166-170
Choms, Władysława, **1:** 118-119
Cohn, Marianne and, **1:** *124*
Deffaught, Jean and, **1:** 153-154
Getter, Matylda and, **2:** 63
by Jewish youth movements, **4:** 151
Sendler, Irena and, **4:** 6-7
Research about survivors of the Holocaust, **4:** 46-47, 49-50
Research by Nazis, **3:** 52-61
See also Nazi doctors
Resistance by prisoners, **1:** 131, 133
Auschwitz Fighting Group, **1:** 47
Buchenwald, **1:** 106-107
Chełmno, **1:** 117
Dora-Mittelbau, **1:** 171
Robota, Roza, **3:** 182-*183*
Skarżysko-Kamienna, **4:** 10
Sobibór, **4:** 19
theft of weapons by forced-laborers, **1:** 111
Treblinka, **4:** 68-69
See also Escapes and escape attempts
See also Uprisings
Resistance to Nazis
by Jews, **3:** 170-174, **4:** 59
Summons to resistance in the Vilna Ghetto, **4:** 193-195
See also Jewish resistance groups
See also Partisans
See also Underground groups
Revisionists, **2:** 101-104
Riegner cable, **3:** 174-175
Riga, **3:** 2-3, 175-177
Righteous Among the Nations, **3:** 177-180
Adamowicz, Irena, **2:** 165, **3:** 179-180
Bogaard, Johannes, **1:** 96-97
Choms, Władysława, **1:** 118-119
Deffaught, Jean, **1:** 153-154
Grüninger, Paul, **2:** *79*
from Le Chambon-sur-Lignon, **3:** 6
Lutz, Carl, **3:** 34-36, *35*
Matylda, Getter, **2:** 63
Schindler, Oskar, **4:** 2-4, *3*
Sendler, Irena, **4:** *6*-7
Sousa Mendes, Aristides de, **4:** 19-*20*
Sugihara, Sempo, **4:** *44*-45
Wallenberg, Raoul, **4:** 108-111, *110*
Righteous Among the Nations Avenue, **3:** 77
Ringelblum, Emanuel, **3:** *180*-182
Riots. *See* Uprisings

Ritter, Robert, **2:** 82
Robota, Roza, **3:** 182-*183*
Rohm, Ernst, **2:** 105
Roman Catholicism. *See* Catholic Church
Romani. *See* Gypsies
Romania
antisemitism in, **1:** 31
deportation of Jews from, **1:** 165
Gypsies, **2:** 86
Jewish badge, **1:** 60
racist political movements in, **3:** 152
refusal to surrender Jews to Nazis, **1:** 77
Volksdeutsche, **4:** 107
Romanians at Mogilev-Podolski, **3:** 68, 69
Rome
deportation of Jews from, **1:** 165
rescue of Jews in, **1:** 78
Roosevelt, Eleanor, **2:** 30-31
Roosevelt, Franklin D.
and B'nai B'rith, **1:** 15
denazification efforts by, **1:** 154
effect of American antisemitism on, **4:** 94
founding of the War Refugee Board, **4:** 114
Jewish advisors, **1:** 17-18, **3:** 69-*71*
reaction to Kristallnacht, **2:** 174
role in Evian Conference, **1:** 189-190
Rosenberg, Alfred, **3:** 182-*184*
influence of *Protocols of the Elders of Zion* on, **3:** 148
policy on Gypsies, **2:** 86
Rovno, **3:** 184-186
Równe. *See* Rovno
RSHA. *See* Reich Security Main Office (RSHA)
Rudashevski, Yitskhok, **4:** 102, 105
Rudninkai Forest, **3:** 187
Rumbula, **3:** 187
Rumkowski, Mordechai Chaim
and the chronicles of the Łódź Ghetto, **3:** 25
role in Łódź Judenrat, **3:** 20, 22
Russia. *See* Soviet Union

S

SA
photographs of, **1:** *102*
relationship with SS, **4:** 29
Sabotage of German installations, **2:** 7-13, **4:** 89
Nazi anti-Communist exhibit in Berlin, **1:** 63
Sachsenhausen, **4:** 1-2
See also Gross-Rosen
Samosc, **4:** 151-152
Sarajevo, **1:** 139, 141
Sartre, Jean-Paul, **1:** 29-30
Schmelt, Albrecht, **3:** 108-110
Schools
in the ghettos, **3:** 134, **4:** 59, 122
Jewish retraining courses for emigrants, **4:** 98, 100
Nazi laws prohibiting Jews from, **1:** 25

Netherlands, exclusion of Jews from, **3:** 88
Schutz-Pass, **4:** *109*
Schutzstaffel. *See* SS
SD, **4:** 4-6
Latvians in, **3:** 3
relationship to Reich Security Main Office (RSHA), **3:** 161, 162, 163
role in deportations, **1:** 161
See also Operational Squads
Secret State police. *See* Gestapo
Security Police (Sipo)
relationship to Reich Security Main Office (RSHA), **3:** 161, 162
relationship with SS, **4:** 30
in Warsaw, **4:** 115
See also Central Office for Jewish Emigration
See also Operational Squads
Security Service of the SS. *See* SD
Seizures of Jewish possessions
"A Cartload of Shoes" (Sutzkever), **3:** 10
Aktion M ("Operation Furniture"), **3:** 88
during Aktion Reinhard, **1:** 8
at Auschwitz, **1:** 48, 49
in Belgium, **1:** 65
to benefit the Volksdeutsche, **4:** 107
at Chełmno, **1:** 116
by Croatians, **1:** 139
of dead prisoners, **4:** 66
effect on classification of Mischlinge, **3:** 67
for funding camp entertainment, **4:** 136
German disputes over disposal, **3:** 139
by Institute for the Investigation of the Jewish Question, **3:** 184
Jewish "tidying-up detachment" at Łódź, **3:** 24
kibbutzim in Kherson, **2:** 151
in Kovno, **2:** 164
Nazi laws permitting, **1:** 26
Pohl, Oswald, and his role in, **3:** 123
in Poland, **3:** 132
storage camps, **1:** 172
from wealthy Austrian families, **1:** 50
where the gold and jewelry went, **3:** 99-100
See also Aryanization
Seizures of Jews by Nazis. *See* Anti-Jewish measures; Deportations; Emigration of Jews; Forced labor
Selektion at the camps, **1:** 42
Sendler, Irena, **4:** *6*-7
Serbian minority in Croatia, **1:** 138
Seventh-Day Adventists, **2:** 108
Sexual relations
homosexuality in the Third Reich, **2:** 104-105
Nazi laws restricting, **3:** 96
Nazi views about, **2:** 90, 104
Seyss-Inquart, Arthur, **4:** 7-*8*
letter to Martin Bormann regarding the "Jewish question," **4:** 191-193

INDEX

Shanghai, Jewish refugees in, **3:** 159, 164
She'erit ha-Peletah. *See* Displaced persons; Refugees
Shelters for Jews
    Confessing Church, **1:** 121
    in convents and with families, **1:** 118
    "International" ghetto, **1:** 110, **3:** 36, **4:** 110
"Shema" (Primo Levi), **3:** 7
Ships. *See* Deportation ships; Refugee ships
Sho'ah. *See* Holocaust
Shostakovich, Dmitri, **1:** 56
Sicherheitsdienst. *See* SD
Silesia, **1:** 97
    Organisation Schmelt, **3:** 108-110
Simferopol, **4:** 9
Simon Wiesenthal Center for Holocaust Studies, **3:** 75-76, **4:** 139
Skarzyski-Kamienna, **4:** 9-11
Slave labor. *See* Forced labor
Slovakia, **4:** 11-14
    annexation of Polish areas, **3:** 127-128
    Catholics, **1:** 121
    deportations of Jews from, **1:** 164, **4:** 142
    Gypsies, **2:** 86
    map of, **4:** *11*
    national uprising, **3:** 171, **4:** 13-14
    partisans, **3:** 119
Slovakian military, Jews in, **4:** 13
Slovenia, **1:** 59
Smuggling in Warsaw ghetto, **4:** 121-122, 123
Sobibór, **1:** 7, **4:** 15
    uprising led by Aleksandr Pechersky, **3:** 119-120
Social class and racism in Germany, **3:** 152
Social Democratic Party prisoners, **1:** 126
Social welfare in Polish ghettos, **3:** 134
Society of Friends, **1:** 13-14, **3:** 167
Soldier-literature, **3:** 12
"Some Thoughts on the Treatment of Alien Populations in the East" (Himmler), **3:** 40
Sonderkommando. *See* Special Commando
Sonderkommando 1005. *See* Aktion 1005
Songs about the Holocaust, **3:** 51
Soup kitchens
    for children, **3:** 135
    Warsaw ghetto, **4:** 118
Sousa Mendes, Aristides de, **4:** 19-*20*
Sovietization, **4:** 21
Soviet military, **4:** 23
    Jews in, **4:** 24-25
Soviet occupation
    Białystok, **1:** 88
    eastern Poland, **3:** 125-125
    Hungary, **2:** 113
    Latvia, **3:** 1-2
    Lithuania, **3:** 15-17
    Lutsk, **3:** 33
    Lvov, **3:** 37
    Vilna, **4:** 101
    Western Belorussia, **1:** 69-70
Soviet partisans, **4:** 86
    acceptance of Jews as members, **3:** 115

Ziman, Henrik, **4:** 152-153
Soviet prisoners of war, **3:** 145-146
    at Auschwitz, **1:** 45, 48
    in concentration camps, **1:** 128
    death marches for, **1:** 149
    Jewish, **3:** 144
    mass shootings of, **1:** 147
    at Mauthausen, **3:** 48
    murder of, at Babi Yar, **1:** 55
    murder of, at Sachsenhausen, **4:** 1
    murder of, by German army, **3:** 163-164
    at Neuengamme, **3:** 91
    Waffen-SS camp for, **3:** 43
    who served the Nazis, **1:** 73
Soviet Union, **4:** 20-25
    annexation of Polish areas, **3:** 127-128
    antisemitism in, **1:** 30, 31-32, 33
    commissars, **2:** 158-159, **3:** 59, 104
    danger perceived by Nazis from, **3:** 164
    documents of the Holocaust in, **3:** 99
    Gypsies, **2:** 86
    Hitler's plan to resettle parts of, **2:** 42
    impact of Babi Yar massacre, **1:** 56
    impact of *Protocols of the Elders of Zion*, **3:** 147
    Jewish badge, **1:** 58
    map of, **4:** *22*
    Nazi murder of Jews and Soviet officials in, **2:** 89
    Nazi treatment of Russians, **2:** 15
    policy about antisemitism, **3:** 152
    Polish Jewish refugees in, **3:** 160
    postwar Jewish settlement of Riga, **3:** 177
    treatment of Hungarian Jews, **2:** 110
    treatment of Jews in Eastern Belorussia, **1:** 72
    Volksdeutsche, **4:** 107
    See also Belorussia
    See also Estonia
    See also German invasion of the Soviet Union
    See also Latvia
    See also Lithuania
    See also Ukraine
Soviet zone denazification efforts, **1:** 154
Spain's policy towards Jewish refugees, **3:** 160
Spanish Civil War, effect on Axis powers, **2:** 119
Special Commando, **4:** 25-26
Special Commando 4a, **1:** 54
Special Commando Bothmann, **1:** 101, 114
Special Commando Kulmhof, **1:** 114-115, 117
Special Commando Lange, **1:** 114
Special Commando prisoners, **1:** 133
Special courts of Poland, **4:** 82-83
Speer, Albert
    concerns about SS Economic-Administrative Main Office, **1:** 176-177
    role at Natzweiler-Struthof, **3:** 79
Spiritual resistance to Nazis, **3:** 171-172

Sporrenberg, Jacob, **4:** 26-27
Sprachregelung, **4:** 27-28
    Gestapo use of, **2:** 62
    See also Nazi deception
    See also Nazi euphemisms
SS, **4:** 28-31
    Central Office for Jewish Emigration
    control of political prisoners, **1:** 126
    Death's-Head Units
    dog battalion, **1:** 45
    Ethnic Germans' Welfare Office (VoMi), **4:** 106
    Fountain of Life experiment, **3:** 151, **4:** 30
    Latvian Legion, **3:** 3
    objectives for concentration camps, **1:** 127-128
    powers relating to "Jewish question," **1:** 26
    structure from 1942 to 1944-1945, **1:** 128
    Ukrainian division, **4:** 84, 87
    See also Economic-Administrative Main Office
    See also SD
    See also Special Commando
SS companies
    German Armament Works, **2:** 124
    German Earth and Stone Works, Ltd., **2:** 76, **3:** 79, 91
    See also German weapons factories, **3:** 103
SS men
    at Bełżec, **1:** 73
    Italian unit, **2:** *122*
    massacre of French village, **3:** 108
    numbers of, in camps and on death marches, **1:** 152
    reactions to killing people, **1:** 45, **2:** 37, **3:** 107, **4:** 90, 173
SS officers, **4:** 29
    Bach-Zelewski, Erich von dem, **1:** 56-57
    Barbie, Klaus, **1:** *61*-62
    Bothmann, Hans, **1:** 101, 114
    Best, Werner, **1:** 87-88
    Blobel, Paul, **1:** 94-95
    in charge of Operational Squads, **3:** 104
    Clauberg, Carl, **1:** 123-124, **3:** 59-60
    Dannecker, Theodor, **1:** 147-148, **3:** 111
    Dirlewanger, Oskar, **1:** 166
    Eicke, Theodor, **1:** 181-183
    Globocnik, Odilo, **2:** 65-66
    Höss, Rudolf, **1:** 45-46, **2:** *107*-108, **3:** 13, **4:** 156
    Jager, Karl, **2:** 124
    Jeckeln, Friedrich, **2:** *126*-127, **3:** 3
    Koch, Karl Otto, **2:** 155-*156*
    Kramer, Josef, **1:** 82, **2:** 171
    Krüger, Friedrich Wilhelm, **2:** *174*-175
    Krumey, Hermann, **2:** 175
    Liebehenschel, Arthur, **3:** *8*

208

INDEX

Mengele, Josef, **1:** 40, **3:** 58-59, *62-63*, 99
Nebe, Arthur, **3:** 84
Oberg, Carl Albrecht, **3:** 97-98
Ohlendorf, Otto, **3:** 100-*101*
Pohl, Oswald, **3:** 123
Purtzmann, Hans-Adolf, **3:** 148
Rasch, Emil Otto, **3:** 153-154
Sporrenberg, Jacob, **4:** 26-27
Stahlecker, Franz Walter, **4:** 34
Stroop, Jürgen, **4:** 38-42, *40*
at the Wannsee Conference, **4:** 111
Wirth, Christian, **4:** 139-140
Wisliceny, Dieter, **4:** 141-142
Wolff, Karl, **4:** 142-143
See also Camp staff
See also Eichmann, Adolf
See also Heydrich, Reinhard
See also Himmler, Heinrich
See also Nazi officials
See also War criminals
St. Louis (ship), **4:** 36-37
Stahlecker, Franz Walter, **4:** 34
Stalin, Joseph
denazification efforts by, **1:** 154
purge of Red Army, **2:** 88
Stangl, Franz, **4:** *34*-35
Starachowice, **4:** 35-36
State Department. *See* United States Department of State
Statute of limitations in Germany, **4:** 76-78
Sterilization. *See* Forced sterilization by Nazis
Stockman, Noah, **1:** 111
Stores, Nazi seizures of Jews'. *See* Aryanization
Stricher, Julius, **4:** 37-*38*
Stroop, Jürgen, **4:** 38-42, *40*
Stuckart, Wilhelm, **4:** 41-42
Stutthof, **4:** 42-44
death marches from, **1:** 151-153
Styria, **1:** 52
Subsequent Nurenberg Proceedings, **4:** 75-76
Sudetenland labor camps, **3:** 109, 110
Sugihara, Sempo, **4:** *44*-45
Suicides
after introduction of Jewish badges, **1:** 60-61
in the face of deportations from Berlin, **1:** 86-87
by Judenrat leaders, **3:** 185, **4:** 123
at Mogilev-Podolski, **3:** 68
rates in Austria, **1:** 50
Survival, Nazi experiments on, **3:** 54-56
Survival in Auschwitz: The Nazi Assault on Humanity (Levi), **3:** 7
Survivors. *See* Holocaust survivors; Victims and survivors
Survivors' syndrome, **4:** 47
Sutzkever, Abraham, **3:** 10
Swastika, **2:** *93*, **3:** 184
Sweden's policy towards Jewish refugees, **3:** 160, **4:** 108-111, 161
Switzerland

Federation of Swiss Jewish Communities (SIG), **3:** 51
and funds for refugees, **2:** 138
Jewish refugees to, **2:** *79*
policy towards Jewish refugees, **3:** 160, 161
Protestants, **1:** 122
Saly Mayer's role, **3:** 51-52
Synagogues, destruction of
Bohemia and Moravia, **1:** 97
Dvinsk, **1:** 174
Graz, **1:** 50, 52
Klagenfurt, **1:** 52
during Kristallnacht, **2:** *172*, 173
Łódź, **3:** 20
Paris, **3:** 111
Riga, **3:** 175-176
Tarnów, **4:** 52
Warsaw, **4:** 132
Systematic extermination of Jews. *See* "Final Solution"
Szenes, Hannah, **4:** 51-*52*, 150

T

T4 institutions, **1:** 188-189
T4 Operation. *See* Euthanasia Program
Tarnopol. *See* Ternopol
Tarnów, **4:** 52-53
Tarviso, **2:** 128
Tatooing of prisoners, **1:** *42*
Tenenbaum, Mordechai, **4:** 53-55
in Białystok, **1:** 90
opinion of Adam Czerniaków, **1:** 143
photograph of, **4:** *54*
role in Grodno, **2:** 74
Terezín. *See* Theresienstadt
"Terezín" (Hachenburg), **4:** 59
Terminology, Nazi. *See* Sprachregelung
Ternopol, **4:** 55-56
Terror. *See* Violence as a Nazi tool
Tesch and Stabenow Company, **4:** 74
development of Zyklon B gas, **4:** 157
Theresienstadt, **4:** 56
children in, *60*
Denmark's efforts on behalf of prisoners at, **1:** 160
family camp at Birkenau, **1:** 46
Nazi use as model ghetto, **1:** 181, **4:** 57-58, 59-60
youth movements, **4:** 149-150
They Fought Back (Suhl), **3:** 120
"To Caesarea" (Szenes), **4:** 150
Totalitarianism roots in war, **2:** 1-2
Trade unions, Nazis and, **1:** 126
Trains. *See* Deportation trains
Transfer Office, Warsaw ghetto, **4:** 121
Transfer Point (Umschlagplatz), **4:** 61-62
Transit camps
Drancy, **1:** 172-174
Kistarcsa, **2:** 154-155
Mogilev-Podolski, **3:** 68
Nisko, **3:** 94
for Poles from Warsaw, **4:** 116
Theresienstadt, **1:** 181
Westerbork, **4:** 135-137

Transports. *See* Deportations; Deportation ships; Deportation trains
Transylvania, **2:** 111
Trawniki, **4:** 62-63
liquidation of, **1:** 184-186
Treaty of Versailles, effect on World War II, **2:** 70
Treblinka, **1:** 7, **4:** 63-69
Trials of war criminals, **4:** 69-84
Auschwitz staff, **1:** 48
Barbie, Klaus, **1:** *61*-62
Bełżec staff, **1:** 77
Bergen-Belsen staff, **1:** 82
Buchenwald staff, **1:** 107
Chełmno staff, **1:** 117-118
Dachau staff, **1:** 147
disparities among sentences, **1:** 156
Dora-Mittelbau staff, **1:** 171
Eichmann, Adolf, **1:** 181, **3:** 13
for genocide, **2:** 44-45
by Hungarian courts, **1:** 34
Jewish ghetto police, **2:** 135
Koppe, Wilhelm, **2:** 159
Lithuanian collaborators, **3:** 19
Majdanek staff, **3:** 44
medical experimenters, **3:** 60
in the Netherlands, **3:** 90-91
officers of German companies, **2:** 116
Operational Squad leaders, **3:** 107
Simon Wiesenthal Center role in, **3:** 75
Skarżysko-Kamienna staff, **4:** 10-11
Sobibór staff, **4:** 19
SS members, **4:** 31
Treblinka staff, **4:** 69
Ukrainian guards, **3:** 120
U.S. Office of Special Investigations role, **3:** 98
Vichy officials, **2:** 19
Truman, Harry S.
and Displaced Persons' Act of 1948, **1:** 168
opinion about rebuilding Germany, **3:** 71
Tuberculosis experiments by Nazis, **3:** 58
Turkey's policy about Jewish refugees, **3:** 160
Typhus experiments by Nazis, **3:** 58

U

Ukraine, **4:** 84-87
forced labor, **2:** 124
Gypsies, **2:** 86
Hitler's plan to resettle, **2:** 42
Kamenets-Podolski, **2:** 145-146
Kharkov, **2:** 149-150
Kherson, **2:** 150-152
Lutsk, **3:** 33-34
Lvov, **2:** 124-126, **3:** 36-40
map of, **4:** *85*
Mogilev-Podolski, **3:** 68-69
partisans, **3:** 117
Rovno, **3:** 184-186
Simferopol, **4:** 9
Ternopol, **4:** 55-56

209

INDEX

Volksdeutsche, **4:** 107
Ukrainian Military Police, **4:** 87-88
    camp guards, **1:** 73, **3:** 122, **4:** 62
    role in liquidating Lvov ghetto, **3:** 39
Ukrainians, treatment by Nazis, **2:** 40
Underground Army, the (Grosman), **2:** 76
Underground groups
    Belgium, **1:** 66
    Białystok, **1:** 89-91
    Denmark, **1:** 159-160
    effect of forced labor on, **2:** 14
    Germany, **1:** 122, 155
    Lithuania, **2:** 63-65, **3:** 15-16
    Paris, **3:** 111, 112
    Poland, **1:** 2, **3:** 126, 128, 135
    Polish Home Army (Armia Krajowa), **1:** 1, 2, **3:** 114, **4:** 88-89, 117
    types of resistance by, **3:** 114
    Warsaw, **4:** 116
    See also French Resistance
    See also Jewish resistance groups
    See also Partisans
    See also Resistance by prisoners
Uniforms, Nazi, **4:** 30, 32, 87
United Kingdom. *See* Great Britain
United Nations, **1:** 167
United Nations Genocide Convention, **2:** 44
United Partisan Organization (FPO), **4:** 88-90, 104, 105
United States, **4:** 93-97
    antisemitism in, **1:** 28
    attitudes of Americans towards the Holocaust, **3:** 14
    efforts to rescue Jewish children, **3:** 166, 167
    Harrison Commission on displaced persons, **1:** 168
    Hungary's declaration of war on, **2:** 111
    immigration laws, **1:** 18, **4:** 92, 170
    immigration laws concerning Nazis, **3:** 98-99
    immigration of children, **3:** 166-169
    immigration of displaced persons, **1:** *169*-170
    impact of *Protocols of the Elders of Zion*, **3:** 147
    Jewish American literature, **3:** 11-12
    military tribunals, **4:** 75
    Neo-Nazi groups, **3:** 82
    policy towards Jewish refugees, **3:** 160-161
    position at Evian Conference, **1:** 192
    protests against Nazi Germany by Jews, **3:** 165, **4:** *141*, 143
    racism in, **3:** 151, 152
    reaction to Kristallnacht, **2:** 174
    support of British war effort, **2:** 68
    Wise, Stephen Samuel, **4:** 140-*141*
United States Army aid to Holocaust survivors, **4:** 90-92
United States Committee for the Care of European Children (USCOM), **3:** 167
United States Department of Justice Office of Special Investigations, **3:** 98-100

United States Department of State, **3:** 70, **4:** 92-93
United States Department of the Treasury, **3:** 70
United States Holocaust Memorial Museum, **3:** 74-75
United States War Department, **4:** 114
Uprisings
    Białystok ghetto, **1:** 71, 91
    Jewish youth movements, **4:** 149
    Kielce, **2:** 153
    Lutsk labor camp, **3:** 34
    Lvov ghetto, **3:** 39
    Paris, **3:** 112-113
    by prisoners, **1:** 194, **3:** 173-174
    by prisoners, at Janówska, **2:** 126
    by prisoners, Auschwitz Special Commando, **1:** 47
    by prisoners, Himmler's fear of, **1:** 185
    Sobibór, **3:** 119-120, **4:** 19
    Treblinka, **4:** 68-69
    Vilna, **4:** 90, 105
    Warsaw ghetto, **4:** 129-133, 154
    Warsaw Polish, **4:** 116, 133-134
    Westerbork, **4:** 135
    See also Escapes and escape attempts
U.S. State Department. *See* United States Department of State
USSR. *See* Soviet Union
Ustaša movement in Croatia, **1:** 138, 139

V

Vallat, Xavier, **4:** 97
Vatican
    Hitler's plan to occupy, **2:** 120
    policy on Nazi Germany, **1:** 119, 120
    See also Catholic church
Vernichtungslager. *See* Extermination camps
Vichy France
    Jewish badge, **1:** 59
    Nazi deportations of Jews into, **1:** 162
Vichy government, **2:** 18-19
    Darquier, Louis, **1:** 148
    Jewish Law (Statut des Juifs), **2:** 135-136
    Jewish policy, **2:** 22
    Laval, Pierre, **3:** 4-5
    Vallat, Xavier, **4:** 97
Victims and survivors
    of all concentration camps, **1:** 130
    of all extermination camps, **1:** 194
    Auschwitz, **1:** 44, 48
    Belgian Jews, **1:** 64
    Bełżec, **1:** 76, 77
    Bergen-Belsen, **1:** 82
    Berlin, **1:** 87
    Białystok, **1:** 71, 91
    Bohemia and Moravia, **1:** 99
    Buchenwald, **1:** 107
    Dachau, **1:** 147
    determining the facts about, **1:** 6
    Dvinsk, **1:** 175
    of euthanasia, **1:** 188-189
    France, **2:** 25

    Gross-Rosen, **2:** 78-79
    Hungary, **2:** 113
    Italy, **2:** 123
    Jews in Croatia, **1:** 141
    Jews in Germany, **2:** 59
    Kharkov, **2:** 150
    Kovno, **2:** 166
    Kraków, **2:** 170-171
    in Latvia, **3:** 2, 4
    Lithuanian Jews, **3:** 18
    Łódź, **3:** 24
    Lublin, **3:** 32
    Lutsk, **3:** 34
    Lvov, **3:** 39
    Mauthausen, **3:** 50-51
    Minsk, **3:** 65
    Mogilev-Podolski, **3:** 69
    of Nazi medical experiments, **3:** 53
    Paris, **3:** 112
    Płasów, **3:** 121-122
    Poland, **3:** 140
    Ravensbrück, **3:** 156
    Riga, **3:** 177
    Rovno, **3:** 186
    Slovakia, **4:** 14
    Starachowice, **4:** 35-36
    Stutthof, **4:** 42
    Tarnów, **4:** 53
    Thereseinstadt, **4:** 61
    Ukraine, **4:** 86
    Vienna, **4:** 100-101
    Vilna, **4:** 104, 105
    Vitebsk, **4:** 106
    Warsaw, **4:** 115, 127-128
    Warsaw Polish uprising, **4:** 134
    See also Deportations
    See also Mass murders by Nazis
Victim testimony, effect of, **3:** 12-13
Vienna, **4:** 98-101
    anti-Jewish measures, **1:** 50, 53-54
    antisemitism in, **1:** 31
    Central Office for Jewish Emigration, **1:** 112
    deportations of Jews from, **1:** 162
    influence on Hitler, **2:** 93
Vilna, **3:** 16, **4:** 101-105
    Diary entry of Jewish youth in, **4:** 199
    See also United Partisan Organization (FPO)
Violence as a Nazi tool, **3:** 127
    See also Anti-Jewish measures
    See also Anti-Polish measures
    See also Mass murders by Nazis
    See also Pogroms
Vitebsk, **4:** 105-106
Volksdeutsche, **4:** 106-108
    and Nazi deportations of Jews, **1:** 162
Volksdeutsche Mittelstelle. *See* Volksdeutsche
Volksliste, **3:** 126, **4:** 107
Volkswagen Company, **3:** 92
VoMi (Ethnic Germans' Welfare Office), **4:** 106
Voting rights, Nazi laws against Jews', **1:** 25

INDEX

W

Waffen-SS, **4:** 30, 32, *133*
Wagner, Richard, **1:** 30
"Waiting" (Levi), **4:** 33
Waldheim, Kurt, **3:** 99
Wallenberg, Raoul, **4:** 108-111, *110*
Walther weapons factory, **3:** 91
Wannsee Conference, **2:** 12, **3:** 137, **4:** 113-115
War
    and government control of individuals, **2:** 1-2
    See also World War I
    See also World War II
War crimes, offenses defined as, **1:** 134-135, **2:** 45, **4:** 72, 74
War criminals
    bringing them to trial, **3:** 75
    difficulties of extraditing, **4:** 82
    in Germany, disability payments to, **4:** 80
    "major" and "minor," **4:** 69-70
    numbers sentenced by Allies, **4:** 76
    responsibility for actions, **4:** 73, 81
    tried at Nuremberg, **4:** 71-72
    tried in Poland, **4:** 83
    wanted poster for Josef Mengele, **3:** *63*
    Wiesenthal, Simon and his hunt for, **4:** 138-*139*
    See also Crimes against humanity
    See also Trials of war criminals
War Refugee Board, **4:** 96, 113-115
    Bergson Group influence, **1:** 19
    and Wallenberg, Raoul, **4:** 108
Warsaw, **4:** 115-129
    death march from, **1:** 149-150
    Jewish badge, **1:** 58
    Jewish resistance groups, **2:** 129-130
    Transfer Point (Umschlagplatz), **4:** 61-62
Warsaw ghetto uprising, **4:** 129-133
    Anielewicz, Mordecai, **1:** 23-24
    Blum, Abraham, **1:** 95-96
    Zuckerman, Yitzhak, **4:** 154
Warsaw Polish uprising, **4:** 116, 133-134
Warthegau region, **1:** 116-117, 164
    See also Łódź
War wounds, Nazi experiments on, **3:** 56-57
Wehrmacht. *See* German military
Weimar Republic, **1:** 84, **2:** 49-50
Welfare efforts in Polish ghettos, **3:** 134
    See also Judenräte
Werwolf bands, **3:** 148
Westerbork, **3:** 88, **4:** 135-137, 89, 90
Western Belorussia, **1:** 69-71
Western Europe
    antisemitism in, **1:** 28-29
    partisan activity by Jews, **3:** 115
    resistance to Jewish badge, **1:** 59, 61
    resistance to racism, **3:** 152
West German trials of war criminals, **4:** 79-81
West Germany, denazification by, **1:** 156-157
Wetzel, Erhard, **2:** 41
White Paper of 1939, **1:** 17
Wiesel, Elie, **4:** *137*-138
    survivor stories, **3:** 14
Wiesenthal, Simon, **4:** 138-*139*
    See also Simon Wiesenthal Center
Wilczyńska, Stefania, **2:** 160, 161
Wirth, Christian, **4:** 139-140
Wise, Stephen S., **4:** 140-*141*
    and the Riegner cable, **3:** 174
Wisliceny, Dieter, **4:** 141-142
Wittenberg, Yitzhak, **4:** 88, 89-90
Wolff, Karl, **4:** 142-143
Women
    medical experiments on, **3:** 56-57, 60
    Nazi ideal of, **2:** 99
    partisans, **3:** *118*
    pregnancy experiments by Nazis on, **3:** 58, **4:** 30, 60, 151
    war criminals, **4:** 74
    See also Jewish women
Women camp guards
    Bergen-Belsen, **1:** 82
    Ravensbrück, **3:** 153
Women prisoners, **1:** *49*
    at Auschwitz, **1:** 41
    barracks at Theresienstadt, **4:** *58*
    death marches, **1:** 151-153
    forced labor, **2:** *14*, **3:** *155*, **4:** 16-17, 78
    in France, **2:** *80*
Women's camps, **1:** 131-132
    Bergen-Belsen, **1:** 82
    Birkenau, **1:** 41, **3:** 183
    Majdanek, **3:** 43, 44
    Ravensbrück, **3:** 155, 156
    Silesia and Sudetenland labor camps, **3:** 110
Work. *See* Jobs
Workers. *See* Forced labor; Labor camps
"Working Group" in Slovakia, **4:** 12-13, 142
Work permits. *See* Certificates of employment for Jews
World Jewish Congress, **4:** 143-144
    Federation of Swiss Jewish Communities (SIG) and, **3:** 51
World War I
    effect on fascism, **2:** 1
    effect on Germany, **2:** 49
    effect on Nazi Party, **3:** 82
    effect on U.S. policy, **4:** 93
    Hitler's views about, **3:** 61
    impact on World War II, **2:** 70
World War II
    British role in, **2:** 67-69
    effect on Nazis' anti-Jewish measures, **2:** 56-57
    effect on Poland, **3:** 129-133
    effect on the British Empire, **2:** 69
    Gestapo during, **2:** 62
    impetus for finishing "Final Solution" during, **2:** 12
    Jewish refugees, **3:** 159-161
    SS activities, **4:** 30-31
    as a "war of aggression," **4:** 72
    See also Allies
    See also Axis Powers
WVHA. *See* Economic-Administrative Main Office

Y

Yad Vashem, **3:** 76-77
    See also Righteous Among the Nations
Yalta Statement, **1:** 154
Yelin, Haim, **4:** 144-145
Yellow badge. *See* Jewish badge
Yellow fever experiments by Nazis, **3:** 58
Yellow Schein, **4:** 103
Yevtushenko, Yevgeni, **1:** 56
Yiddish literature of the Holocaust. *See* Literature of the Holocaust
Youth groups in Germany (Hitler Youth), **2:** 97-99
Youth movements, **4:** 145-151
    conferences of He-Haluts groups, **4:** 149
    in Denmark, **1:** 159
    See also Fighting Organization of Pioneer Jewish Youth
    See also Zionist youth movements
Yugoslavia, **1:** 95
    death march in, **1:** 150
    Gypsies, **2:** 85
    invasion of, **2:** 111
    partisans, **3:** 119
    rescue of Croatian Jews by Italians in, **1:** 140
    Volksdeutsche, **4:** 107-108
    See also Croatia

Z

Zagłebie, **3:** 137
Zagreb, **1:** 139, 141
Zegota (the Polish Council for Aid to Jews), **1:** 118, **3:** 138
    creation of, **4:** 128
    Irena Sendler's role, **4:** 6-7
    in Kraków, **2:** 170
Zentralstelle für Jüdische Auswanderung. *See* Central Office for Jewish Emigration
Ziman, Henrik, **4:** 152-153
Zionism
    and antisemitism, **1:** 33
    Central Union of German Citizens of Jewish Faith and, **1:** 113
    Communist attitudes toward, **4:** 152-153
    definition of, **1:** 10
    Nazi attitudes toward, **2:** 52, **4:** 140
    poem for, **4:** 150
Zionist groups, **1:** 9-11
    Bergson Group, **1:** 19
    in Germany, **2:** 49
    in Italy, **2:** 118, 120
    Jewish Brigade Group, **2:** 125-127
    Joint Rescue Committee, **2:** 137
    in Kovno and Vilna, **3:** 186
    relationships with Communist underground groups, **2:** 74, 165
    youth movements, **4:** *146*, 148

INDEX

Zionists
    and B'nai B'rith, **1:** 15
    friction with Jewish communities, **1:** 159
    and Jewish Fighting Organization (ŻOB), **2:** 131
    Kasztner, Rezső, **2:** 148-149
    Wise, Stephen Samuel, **4:** 140-*141*
    in the Warsaw ghetto, **2:** 130
Zionist youth movements
    arrests of members in Croatia, **1:** 139
    in Brussels and Antwerp, **1:** 67-68
    first ones, **4:** 148
    See also Ha-Shomer ha-Tsa'ir
ŻOB. *See* Jewish Fighting Organization (ŻOB)
Zuckerman, Yitzhak, **4:** 153-155
Żydowska Organizacja Bojowa. *See* Jewish Military Union (ZZW)
Zyklon B, **2:** 39, **4:** 155-157
Zyklon B Trial, **4:** 74
ZZW (Jewish Military Union), **1:** 2, **2:** 131